D1756832

Gallica
Volume 34

UNSETTLING MONTAIGNE

Gallica

ISSN 1749–091X

General Editor: Sarah Kay

Gallica aims to provide a forum for the best current work in medieval and Renaissance French studies. Literary studies are particularly welcome and preference is given to works written in English, although publication in French is not excluded.

Proposals or queries should be sent in the first instance to the editor, or to the publisher, at the addresses given below; all submissions receive prompt and informed consideration.

Professor Sarah Kay, Department of French, New York University, 13–19 University Place, 6th floor, New York, NY 10003, USA

The Editorial Director, Gallica, Boydell & Brewer Ltd., PO Box 9, Woodbridge, Suffolk IP12 3DF, UK

*Previously published volumes in this series
are listed at the end of this book.*

UNSETTLING MONTAIGNE

POETICS, ETHICS AND AFFECT
IN THE *ESSAIS* AND OTHER WRITINGS

ELIZABETH GUILD

D. S. BREWER

© Elizabeth Guild 2014

All Rights Reserved. Except as permitted under current legislation
no part of this work may be photocopied, stored in a retrieval system,
published, performed in public, adapted, broadcast,
transmitted, recorded or reproduced in any form or by any means,
without the prior permission of the copyright owner

The right of Elizabeth Guild to be identified as
the author of this work has been asserted in accordance with
sections 77 and 78 of the Copyright, Designs and Patents Act 1988

First published 2014
D. S. Brewer, Cambridge

ISBN 978-1-84384-371-9

D. S. Brewer is an imprint of Boydell & Brewer Ltd
PO Box 9, Woodbridge, Suffolk IP12 3DF, UK
and of Boydell & Brewer Inc.
668 Mt Hope Avenue, Rochester, NY 14620-2731, USA
website: www.boydellandbrewer.com

A catalogue record for this book is available
from the British Library

The publisher has no responsibility for the continued existence or accuracy of
URLs for external or third-party internet websites referred to in this book,
and does not guarantee that any content on such websites is,
or will remain, accurate or appropriate

This publication is printed on acid-free paper

CONTENTS

ACKNOWLEDGEMENTS

This book owes much to the invigorating and generous colleagues with whom I have had the great pleasure of interacting. At the University of Cambridge I have gained hugely from working with such outstanding early modernists as Philip Ford, Gillian Jondorf and Neil Kenny, and with colleagues, past and present, who are interested in psychoanalysis. I am also grateful to all the wonderful students I have taught over the years who have kept renewing my interest in Montaigne. In Robinson College the intellectual and practical support and warmth of colleagues, notably Deborah Thom and Mary Stewart, have been invaluable. Many of those with whom I have trained and worked in the field of psychoanalysis have creatively challenged and extended my thinking, and I have learned a great deal from them. I should particularly like to thank Chris Oakley, for enlivening and bracing support, and Sarah Greaves, for understanding. Great thanks also to Hilary Thomas, for extraordinary friendship and hospitality. My two greatest debts are to Simon Gaunt, for intellectual stimulation, matchless friendship and play, and to Gyles Glover, who knows better than anyone what it has taken.

I am very grateful to Robinson College for granting me the study leave that made it possible to embark on this book. I should also like to thank Sarah Kay as series editor, enabling as ever, and Boydell & Brewer's reader, from whose comments this book greatly benefited. A last word of thanks goes to Simon Gaunt and Neil Kenny for very thoughtful comments on early drafts.

Cambridge and Udaipur,
July 2013

AUTHOR'S NOTE

All references to Montaigne's *Essais,* unless otherwise stated, are to the Villey-Saulnier edition (Paris, 2004), and all translations of Montaigne, unless otherwise stated, are my own. Much of the argument of this book works with my interpretation of Montaigne's language, and therefore my own translations seem to me to best convey that understanding. In the bibliography I have listed two published English translations of Montaigne, for readers who wish to explore further my quotations from the text.

Occasionally the letters (A), (B) and (C) occur in quotations from the *Essais.* These letters indicate three different editions of the text: (A) the text of 1580; (B) the text of 1588; and (C) that of 1592, on which Montaigne was working at the time of his death. (B) and/or (C) therefore indicate Montaigne's additions or changes to the text of an earlier edition.

ABBREVIATIONS OF JOURNAL TITLES

BHR   *Bibliothèque d'humanisme et Renaissance*
BSAM   *Bulletin de la société des amis de Montaigne*
MLN   *Modern Language Notes*
PMLA   *Publications of the Modern Language Association of America*
RHLF   *Revue d'histoire littéraire de la France*

CHRONOLOGY

1572–73   Fourth War of Religion; ends with the Edict of Boulogne
1574   Death of Charles IX, accession of Henri III
1575–76   Fifth War of Religion; ends with the Treaty of Monsieur (also known as the Edict of Beaulieu), conceding more to the Huguenots than previously. From now on, if not already, Montaigne refers to the wars as civil, not religious, wars
1576   The extremist national Catholic *Ligue* (League) forms, uniting existing local factions, partly in response to the Treaty of Monsieur. The Treaty is later rejected by the Blois Estates General i.e. legislative assembly
1576–77   Henri III becomes leader of the *Ligue*. Sixth War of Religion, ending with the Treaty of Bergerac, which reverses the decisions of the Treaty of Monsieur
1578   Montaigne first suffers from kidney stones
1579–80   Seventh War of Religion; ends with the Treaty of Fleix, reiterating the terms of the Treaty of Bergerac
1580   First two books of the *Essais* published in Bordeaux. Between 1580 and 1588 there are five editions, evidence of their appeal
          June: start of Montaigne's journey through Germany and Switzerland to northern Italy
1580–81   November–April: Montaigne in Rome. On his entry to the city, customs officials take all his books for inspection, including his *Essais*
1581   March: Papal censors return his *Essais* to Montaigne
          May–June: Montaigne in Bains della Villa
          August: returns to Bains della Villa
          September: Bains della Villa, the arrival of the summons requiring Montaigne to return home to take up office as Mayor of Bordeaux
          November: Montaigne arrives home
1583–84   Montaigne is re-elected as Mayor for a second term, despite his reluctance to hold the office. Bordeaux remains loyal to Henri III, although Roman Catholic extremists unsettle the city. Huguenot forces are close by
1584–   The prospect that Henri de Navarre, baptized a Roman Catholic, but raised a Huguenot, will succeed Henri III, who is childless, increases Roman Catholic extremism and political infighting. Montaigne is already involved in diplomacy between Huguenot Navarre and Roman Catholic France, and will continue to be; and while he remains loyal to Henri III, he is also able to represent Henri de Navarre
1585   Plague in Bordeaux, killing almost half the population
1585–89   Eighth War of Religion
1586   Montaigne retires to his estate. As a moderate, he is harried by extremists on both sides, but maintains an open door. He and his family have to leave their home and travel for six months when the plague

	spreads from Castillon, a besieged Huguenot city some 10km from his estate
1587	Montaigne writes the third book of *Essais*, and adds to the first and second books
1588	Paris, publication of a three-book edition of the *Essais*. Montaigne travels to Paris for the publication and also for reasons of public office: his Roman Catholic–Huguenot diplomacy continues. While there he meets Marie de Gournay, who will become his *fille d'alliance* (adoptive daughter) and his first editor
	Popular uprising in Paris, backing Guise and the *Ligue* against the king, who is forced to retreat to Chartres; the Guise family assumes increasing power in France and royal authority recedes. Henri has the two most influential Guises killed, in response to which the *Ligue* acts as if it were a revolutionary body, with popular support
1589	Henri III is assassinated, and is succeeded by Henri de Navarre, who becomes Henri IV; the succession is intolerable for Roman Catholic extremists
1589–90	Paris, still pro-*Ligue*, is under siege by Henri IV, initially at Henri III's instigation
1589–98	Ninth War of Religion
1589–	Montaigne continues to revise his *Essais*, working in the margins of the 1588 edition. This comes to be known as the *exemplaire de Bordeaux,* the Bordeaux Copy
1592	13 September, still revising, Montaigne dies
1593	Henri IV re-converts to Roman Catholicism, as a means to uniting France
1594	Henri IV enters Paris and then is crowned in Chartres
1595	Marie de Gournay publishes the first posthumous edition of the *Essais*, incorporating Montaigne's revisions
	Henri IV receives papal absolution
1596	The *Ligue* is disbanded
1598	April: the Edict of Nantes marks the end of the wars. It grants considerable rights to Huguenots, and freedom of conscience to individuals. It will be revoked in 1685

Introduction

'Je suis affamé de me faire connoistre … mais je crains mortellement d'estre pris en eschange par ceux à qui il arrive de connoistre mon nom' (I am hunger-starved to make myself known … but I am mortally afraid of being mistaken by those who come to know my name).[1] These words capture something of the complexity, demands and cost of Montaigne's desire to make himself known. The metaphor of appetite conveys the specific intensity of this desire; it simultaneously engages and unsettles the reader, signalling the kind of attention required by this communication. But desire rapidly gives way to fear: terrified recognition of desire's cost, given the vulnerability of words to misinterpretation and misappropriation; and already between these two clauses there is in fact a corrective: 'ou pour dire mieux, je n'ay faim de rien' (or, to put it better, I hunger for nothing). No hunger; no desire, only fear? Yet Montaigne goes on writing about himself. Perhaps this lack of hunger does not mean no desire; rather, a lack of lack: a surge of anxiety related to this urgent and consuming desire to make himself known without knowing what readers will make of him.

How are we to understand this acute instance of the revisions which are characteristic of his self-exploration? How to square Montaigne's mortal fear with his commitment to not having the last word, and how does the desire to communicate survive such fear? This sentence speaks of the interplay of personal and cultural anxieties at the time of writing, and invites us to wonder what kind of writing encourages readers towards open, unpossessive interpretations, and of what kind of culture might such interactions form part?

This is just one example of the kinds of questions that are the subject of this book; they have to do with thinking, self-knowledge and their communication, with the complexities of intersubjectivity, and with related stylistic and semantic devices. This analysis of Montaigne's *Essais* and other writing follows on from others' studies of his sceptical thinking, his ethical preoccupations and his use of figuration, and explores the poetics, ethics and psychic economy of such thinking, in the expression of which figuration has a distinctive and creative function.

---

[1] 'Sur des vers de Virgile' ('On some verses of Virgil') (III, 5), pp. 846–7. All references, unless otherwise stated, are to the Villey-Saulnier edition of Montaigne's *Essais* (Paris, 2004). All translations are my own, unless otherwise stated. 'Hunger-starved' is among the entries for 'affamé' in Cotgrave, *Dictionarie of the French and English Tongues* (London, 1611).

The poetics and psychic economy of Montaigne's tolerant, sceptical, uncertain thinking are laced with anxiety: unsettled experience, unsettling for the reader. Tranquillity was a good for some of the classical thinkers loved by Montaigne. In particular, Pyrrhonist suspension of judgement should bring *ataraxia*, tranquillity, and, according to Montaigne, freedom from such passions as fear and greed which fuel our illusions of knowledge and a possessive relationship with our ideas and opinions. But when ideas, understanding and desires are acutely tested, the ideals of resisting false certainties, of allowing differing opinions, of keeping one's thinking moving, frequently produce not tranquillity but a more provisional containment of anxiety. My focus is on Montaigne's capacity to sustain open and disillusioned thinking without arriving at tranquillity, and on ways in which his writing carries the reader through disquiet towards the forms of thoughtfulness required to sustain a culture of what we call tolerance. This goes somewhat against the sociocultural and psychic odds of the time of writing, a protracted period of civil and religious wars, in which intolerance and the breakdown of ethical relations were acted out, and in this lies some of his writing's enduring significance for readers.[2]

Tolerance (not merely toleration, a more narrowly legal form of recognition) would not have been the chosen term at the time of writing – far from it; at that time the issue, instead, would have been freedom of conscience. Freedom of conscience has the additional value of being associated with the developing problematic of the private, inner life of the individual, on which Montaigne reflects acutely; however, in what follows I shall tend to work with tolerance because of its specific further significance for questions relating to the psychic economy of doubt and suspension of judgement, as states which it is not easy to bear – tolerate. For what is it really like to live without the consolation of answers, exploring the limits of what is thinkable? How do you maintain such doubt and openness, particularly in a time of violence and schism? Why is tolerance difficult?

Doubtful thinking is often both charged with, and constrained by, fear, loss, fear of loss and anxiety, which is an under-examined aspect of Montaigne's texts. Indeed, while other studies of Montaigne's scepticism have focused on its philosophical significance, its place in intellectual history, or its semiotics, the psychic economy of such thinking for both writer and reader has been much less explored.[3] Such unsettling conditions as loss and anxiety may tend to precipitate rigid thinking and a desire for premature resolution, in recoil from doubt and uncertainty; so what we encounter in Montaigne's writing is all the more signifi-

---

[2]   For classic studies of Montaigne and his significance, see Friedrich, *Montaigne*, trans. Porter (Berkeley, 1991) and Sayce, *The Essays of Montaigne* (London, 1972).

[3]   See, for instance, Brahami, *Le Scepticisme de Montaigne* (Paris, 1997), Maclean, *Montaigne philosophe* (Paris, 1996), Popkin, *The History of Scepticism from Erasmus to Spinoza* (Berkeley, 1979), Giocanti, *Penser l'irrésolution* (Paris, 2001), Demonet, *A Plaisir: sémiotique et scepticisme chez Montaigne* (Orléans, 2002) and Sellevold, *'J'ayme ces mots –': Expressions linguistiques de doute chez Montaigne* (Paris, 2004).

cant, for what tested and unsettled Montaigne leaves its trace in his writing, but is transformed so that, while it remains unsettling, it can engage our enjoyment. This is writing designed to move the reader beyond anxious certainties, beyond oppositions such as us and them, self and other, right and wrong, your truth system or mine.

My first chapter sets out the questions, conceptual framework and methods of this book, and also situates Montaigne's writing in its context of civil and religious war. Each chapter thereafter explores a specific site of unsettling thinking in the text, moving through questions of knowledge, love and ethics. The place of the other in relation to the self as, variously, a site of knowledge, love, ethical responsibility, loss, anxiety, or haunting, is a recurring focus; so too is the place of the reader in relation to the text.

Detailed semantic and rhetorical analysis is used to reveal the complexities of Montaigne's communication of his thinking. While stylistic or semantic features such as repetition, hesitation, concession, ambiguity, paradox, dislocation or even opacity play their part in the representation of unsettled and unsettling thinking in Montaigne's writing, my readings prioritize the work of figuration. Cave has already argued the significance of antiperistasis, functioning as a figure of thought, for sixteenth-century French Pyrrhonist writing.[4] What I propose is that in Montaigne's sceptical writing the functions and force of figuration extend beyond the heuristic effects of this specific figure of thought. In so doing, I am working with models of figuration which have moved beyond those of rhetoric, as in Montaigne's time, while still working closely with the concepts of figures of speech and thought then current.[5] Figuration – a linguistic 'turn' or 'turning' according to some classical theorists – generates specific textual space and structures in which the connection between things 'can be expressed in a language that takes account of the possibility of their being otherwise'.[6] The kinds of structure and space for thinking that figuration affords are crucial: in Montaigne's writing metaphor is particularly significant, but in relation to tolerance and anxiety, figures such as irony (in classical rhetoric, a figure of thought) and the structure of anamorphosis, which like forms of figuration generates specific space in the text, and for some theorists is a structure which is particularly salient at the time, also deserve further analysis. Together with the structural cognitive force of figuration, Montaigne's highly charged vocabularies and motifs – for instance, those that figure desire as hunger, or internalization as

4 Cave, *Pré-histoires: textes troublés au seuil de la modernité* (Geneva, 1999), p. 39.
5 Particularly since the early twentieth century, there has been a burgeoning of interest in figuration across such different discourses as philosophy, psychology, psychoanalysis, linguistics and anthropology, too vast to list fully here. To name but a few of the most influential: Richards, *The Philosophy of Rhetoric* (Oxford, 1936, 1971), Black, *Models and Metaphors* (Ithaca, 1962), Derrida, 'La Mythologie blanche', in *Rhétorique et philosophie, Poétique* 5 (Paris, 1971), Ricoeur, *La Métaphore vive* (Paris, 1975), and Ortony (ed.), *Metaphor and Thought* (Cambridge, 1979).
6 White, 'Introduction: Tropology, Discourse, and the Modes of Human Consciousness', in *Tropics of Discourse* (Baltimore and London, 1985), p. 2.

Eucharist

incorporation – are also very significant, not least in terms of how they situate his thinking in relation to its sociocultural context.

Montaigne wrote during decades of war. A major linguistic symptom of this strife was debates over signification and symbolization, over the relationship between signs and what they signified. Roman Catholics and Reformers of all hues fought over more than one doctrine, but Eucharistic conflict over the nature of the sacramental sign and what it signified was paramount. Not only a site of fundamental theological and semiotic disagreements, the Eucharist was critical in sociocultural and political terms: traditionally for Roman Catholics the symbol of social unity, now, for Reformers, in the form of the Lord's Supper, symbolic site of their identity.[7] Whether the nature of 'this … body' in the Eucharist was believed to be a site of transubstantiation, or plain metonymy; the consumption of bread and wine representing the invisible transcendent reality of Christ's body and blood, or theophagy, hence 'cannibalism'; sacrifice or mere commemoration; and the nature of the individual's relationship with 'this … body', were matters of belief as well as interpretation, worth dying or killing for – threatening the symbolic social and political body. Whether complex theological or doctrinal publications or vituperative Eucharistic tracts, whether irenic, moderate or extremist in tone, texts proliferating during the decades during which Montaigne wrote confirm that theological strife turned around linguistic questions. Even though Montaigne largely avoided reference to the details of the religious debates, so widespread and influential were such debates and their terms that his use of seemingly conventional tropes such as the social body and the body politic, and digestive tropes relating to desire and knowledge, seems indissociable from these overdetermined and profoundly contested meanings. Psychic ingestion, as it figures in his writing (as it often does), and cultural anxiety to do with the nature of the Eucharist, are related issues and, in a context of much discursive polarization, Montaigne's usage is a site for relative interpretive independence. Such figurative vocabulary as the hunger for knowledge, for the other, and other variations on fantasized cannibalism, need to be situated in this context of embattled interpretive difference. These are risky figures which test the reader's desire to keep interpretations open; also, they perhaps reveal something of the changing thinking and subjectivity that were emerging through such conflicts.

Montaigne's figuration enables a vital coupling of idea and affect which, together with the emotional and psychic complexities of his thinking and the relationship between the individual subject and the world he inhabited, still need further analysis. Therefore I shall draw on psychoanalytic theory and other modern theory that engages with psychoanalytic questions and perspectives, coupled with relevant philosophical discourses and rhetorical and linguistic theories, and on historical analysis.

---

[7]   On this tradition, see Rubin, *Corpus Christi* (Cambridge, 1991), and for the symbolic and political significance of the Eucharist in the sixteenth-century conflicts, see Elwood, *The Body Broken* (Oxford, 1999).

There are of course chapters in the *Essais* on matters such as sadness, fear, cruelty and cowardice, but Montaigne's curiosity about the relationship between affect, fantasy, thought, judgement and behaviour pulses all through his writing, as do reflections on the interrelatedness of private and public identities, identity and identification, and of the psychic and the social. Moreover, in his exploration of the meaning of what it is to be human he was drawn to such questions as: why do we fail, why do our losses haunt us, why do we desire not knowledge but ignorance, why do we deceive ourselves, why are we unjust, or cruel, why do we destroy what is good? All are questions which have greater urgency in the context of violent conflict. In this, the text has a capacity to articulate dangerous and painful ideas as well as exciting ones; but at times it resists or fails its own designs.

This is equally the terrain of psychoanalysis. Also, bearing in the mind the time of writing, psychoanalytic theories help us to think about subjectivities and groups which are bound to rigid, self-destructive as well as deadly identities or identifications, which their avowed beliefs are not sufficient to explain. The psychoanalytic theories on which I draw offer fruitful ways of understanding the relationships between knowledge and desire, between idea and affect in both the production and reception of the text, and also the relations between the psychic and the social, especially when they are troubled, destructive, inert, perverse, opaque or intractable.

There are discourses neither of the unconscious nor of (what we call) anxiety in Montaigne's text; nor is there yet a substantivization of the pronominal 'moi', the self.[8] But even readers wary of a psychoanalytic approach might agree that anxiety, as a phenomenon or form of affect, is evident in the writing, and that Montaigne's reflections lead to understanding of himself as in some ways divided and unknowable. Certain psychoanalytic approaches to early modern texts have been vulnerable to accusations of universalism or ahistoricism, of irrelevance or insensitivity to pre-modern subjectivities, sharing these perceived flaws with other modern theories. Here, however much store I set by psychoanalytic theories as one element in textual analysis, I draw on them only insofar as they resonate with aspects of the text and can be used in conjunction with historical analysis and attentiveness to the discourses and heuristic strategies available at the time of writing. This works in the spirit of Cave's notion of 'pre-history', or Moriarty's rigorous attention to historical and cultural specificity.[9]

These observations on the productivity of psychoanalytic thinking for the interpretation of Montaigne's writing bear further development, in two directions. First, a point about intersubjectivity and internalization. Consider Cave's comment that: 'there is no clear borderline between what is "inside" and what is "outside" in the *Essais*. The linking thread that is the first-person-singular

---

[8]   See Cave, *Pré-histoires,* pp. 111–27.
[9]   See for instance his *Early Modern French Thought* (Oxford, 2003) or *Fallen Nature, Fallen Selves* (Oxford, 2006).

subject connects them together.'[10] Psychoanalytic understanding of the formation of the thinking and writing subject, the *interrelatedness* of 'singular' subject
and other, which may also be understood in terms of identification or relations
between subjects and objects, can bring valuable precision and logic to one's
readings. In his representation of his reflections and inquiries Montaigne recognizes the porousness, and potentially unstable relation, of 'inside' and 'outside'
and what this implies about his intersubjective construction as a subject. Where
this remains intuitive, or where his understanding reaches a limit, Lacanian
theory can aid our analysis. Also, if we read Montaigne's writing as in some
way symptomatic of emergent secularization and also of a culture in which the
internal was increasingly valued, with consequences not only for the individual
'self' but also for the collective 'selves' that constituted the community, this is
a method of analysis which helps us think about the mechanisms and processes
involved.

The second point also relates to the time of writing, in terms of the cata-
clysmic events to which all were subject, the consequences of which would
reverberate throughout the next century. The kinds of understanding Montaigne
offers in the course of the *Essais* of the causes and effects of dogmatism and
polarization evident in the civil and religious wars, and the role of fear, hate
and anxiety in the production of a culture in which the most destructive effects
of excessive certitude and dualism take irresistible hold, seem to me to resonate
with a much later comment which approaches the relationship between 'inside'
and 'outside' and the problem of tyranny. Rose, echoing Freud, observes: 'it is
because we are creatures of the unconscious that we try to exert false authority
over ourselves';[11] that is, our semblance of 'self-control' is a way of denying
whatever our unconscious transmits to us that challenges the coherent, orderly
versions of ourselves to which we are attached. In order to resist tyranny
'outside', we need disillusioned understanding of it 'inside', and of how the
two are related. If we accept that rigid or autocratic thinking or behaviour may
usefully be understood as a response to what we do not understand, control
or fear, 'inside', this may help us to counter authoritarian behaviour, thinking
and discourse, and their silencing of internal as well as external difference or
conflict. To focus on how the unconscious operates socially and politically as
well as 'inside' the individual subject, and to understand it as a transindividual
phenomenon, supplements such analyses of tyranny as that of Montaigne's
beloved friend, La Boétie, which focused on the voluntary dimension of subjugation and self-subjugation.

I tend to draw on Lacanian and post-Lacanian theories, primarily because of
the specific light they shed on the intersubjective formation of the subject, and
on anxiety, and because they enable acute analysis of the relationship between

---

10   Cave, *How to Read Montaigne* (London, 2007), p. 96.
11   Rose, *The Last Resistance* (London, 2007), p. 23.

the psychic and the social.[12] Jacqueline Rose's psychoanalytic understanding of political and public questions, particularly in *The Last Resistance*, also informs my readings. But I shall also draw on other recent theories, particularly the work of those whose reflections on ethics engage critically with psychoanalysis, such as Butler's. Derrida's writing on friendship is particularly fruitful in relation to that of Montaigne, and his emphasis on themes of sacrifice and secrecy in ethics, as well as the part that figuration plays in one of his discussions of ethics, all resonate productively with Montaigne's writing.[13] The gift for me of all these thinkers, when engaging with a writer such as Montaigne, with his extraordinary capacity to think across a range of questions, dimensions and what are now distinct discourses and disciplines, is their creative connecting of what might otherwise remain unacknowledged or unconnected.

What follows are new readings of topics in the *Essais* and other texts by Montaigne such as: how the subject capable of doubtful thinking is formed; what can be known by the cannibal, a figure on the limits of what may be thought human, who is uncannily akin to Montaigne's beloved ideal, La Boétie, who haunts Montaigne's writing; why love is devouring; hospitability as a principle of what it means to live well; the complexities of the desires to which Montaigne confesses; how anxiety makes its presence felt in his writing; the connections between physical and psychic pain and sceptical thinking; the vulnerabilities and limits of Montaigne's thinking; and the particular significance of writing in relation to questions such as these.

To shape my explorations of the complexities of such epistemological, existential and ethical issues, the desires bound up with them, and how figuration functions to convey them, each of my chapters considers selected figures and motifs in a chapter or a cluster of chapters in the *Essais*, and in other related texts by Montaigne, such as his *Journal de voyage* or his letters. Questions of psychic ingestion, and related figuration, run through all the chapters.

My inquiry starts in 1562, which began with the Council of Trent reconvening for its final session, which was to produce, not least, an affirmation of the doctrine of Real Presence. The year 1562 also began in France with an Edict of Toleration; but by March the First War of Religion had broken out. It was the year of publication of Henri Estienne's Latin translation of Sextus Empiricus's *Hypotyposes*, the most significant text for sixteenth-century French Pyrrhonist sceptics like Montaigne; and in November, in Rouen, Montaigne encountered three (supposed) cannibals, as recorded in his famous chapter. The readings of

---

[12] I shall draw on many of Jacques Lacan's seminars, but those to which I shall return most often are *Le Séminaire livre VIII: Le Transfert* (Paris, 1991), *Le Séminaire livre IV: La Relation d'objet* (Paris, 1994), *Le Séminaire livre VII: L'Ethique de la psychanalyse* (Paris, 1994), and *Le Séminaire livre X: L'Angoisse* (Paris, 2004).

[13] The texts in question are *Politiques de l'amitié* (Paris, 1994), *Donner la mort*, in *L'Ethique du don* (Paris, 1992), and '"Il faut bien manger" ou le calcul du sujet', in *Points de suspension: entretiens* (Paris, 1992), pp. 226–302.

the cannibal I propose – both literal and figurative, the one who eats what is same – argue the inseparability of these events in France. The cannibal forms the focus of a discussion of problems of knowledge and interpretation which call for a sceptical response, expressing an unpossessive desire for knowledge.

Chapter 3, on the desire for what is good and what it means to live well, begins by exploring the problematics of moderation, that classical virtue, which, belying its ancient credentials here, proves neither productive of good living nor much of a buffer against destructive extremes. Moderation thus in question, I turn to the value of love and sacrifice (by this time a fraught concept), which return us to the cannibal, along with Montaigne's metaphorical hunger and the metonymy of eating well, as a figure for living well and supplement to moderation's limits.

Montaigne's metaphorical hunger also figures in chapter 4, which analyses the vulnerabilities and anxieties relating to the communication of self-knowledge and desire. Then, as Montaigne's sceptical tendencies are a recurring focus, chapter 5 explores the question: what is required for extreme doubt to be productive and livable, and, therefore, how is such a thinker formed? Embodiment is so important an aspect of Montaigne's thinking about being human that my analysis of these processes gives corporeal metaphors particular significance. Montaigne's metaphors of shaking and tickling convey aspects of his understanding of processes of internalization, or psychic ingestion of knowledge and experience, and are also performative aspects of his writing: surprise, unsettlement and unpredictability are both values and stylistic devices, ways of engaging with the reader so as to encourage her towards this kind of thinking and writing (or shit – Montaigne's word).

Montaigne pursues his ideas to their limits and conveys a capacity to enjoy doubt and uncertainty. However, it is important to recognize his anxiety's effects on his thinking and his sense of his place in the world. In the next, darker chapter the topos of place connects themes of physical and psychic pain and personal and cultural loss, enabling exploration of the anxious impact of all of these on Montaigne's thinking and self-knowledge.

My concluding chapter (chapter 7) returns to ethical questions relating to writing and to a practice of interpretation which both responds to, and enacts, the importance of doubt and suspension of judgement. It develops ideas already touched on earlier, particularly to do with the problematics of sacrifice and an ethics of vulnerability, and Montaigne's scepticism and disillusionment. The different strands of the analysis converge here in a discussion of the sustaining, even therapeutic, role of writing for Montaigne and of the imagined relationship between his writing and its readers. Montaigne's writing – not only what he writes about but also the ways in which he writes – moves us to imagine and think of a potentially different future, without certainties, and beyond meanings he can anticipate.

Some scepticism is dispassionate, but not all. There is much in his text that requires a sceptical capacity to keep questions open even at the cost of disquiet and anxiety, not least the writer's anxiety about the risk of being misinterpreted:

vulnerability and anxiety are the cost, even condition, of the commitment to such openness.

Anxiety also has implications for tolerance. A culture of tolerance – not that of the time of writing – requires the capacity to accept that differing versions of what is right and true may coexist. This, far from being easy liberalism, or achieved tranquillity, may be psychically difficult to bear. Such is the doubt and openness to interpretation that, in Montaigne's words, shakes itself, or the doubting attitude that reaches the limits of what is thinkable.

1

The Possibility of Their Being Otherwise

Je ne hay point les fantasies contraires aux miennes[1]

Consider this short passage from an early chapter in the first book of the *Essais*:

> Feu mon pere, homme, pour n'estre aydé que de l'experience et du naturel, d'un jugement bien net, m'a dict autrefois qu'il avoit desiré mettre en train qu'il y eust és villes certain lieu designé, auquel ceux qui auroient besoin de quelque chose, se peussent rendre et faire enregistrer leur affaire à un officier estably pour cet effect, comme: Je cherche à vendre des perles, je cherche des perles à vendre. Tel veut compagnie pour aller à Paris; tel s'enquiert d'un serviteur ... qui cecy, qui cela, chacun selon son besoing. Et semble que ce moyen de nous entr'advertir apporteroit non legiere commodité au commerce publique: car à tous coups il y a des conditions qui s'entrecherchent, et, pour ne s'entr'entendre, laissent les hommes en extreme necessité. (p. 223)

> (My late father, a man of very clear judgement for one who had only experience and natural talent to draw on, once told me that he had wanted to arrange for there to be a designated place in our towns where those who needed something could go to register their requirements with an officer appointed for this purpose. For instance: I want to sell some pearls, I want to buy some pearls. Someone wants company for the journey to Paris; someone is looking for a servant ... one man this, another that, each according to his need. And it seems that this way of keeping each other informed would be no small benefit to public commerce: for there are always people whose needs match, but who, for lack of finding each other, are left in extreme want.)

So begins 'D'un defaut de nos polices' (I, 35), on a lack in the constitution of our community. Montaigne remembers his dead father with love and respect, for he knew his own mind. His father's vision opens as an economy of perfect symmetry, in which supply and demand, lack and answering need correspond. Not a blueprint for business; rather, a response to the problem of want: unless there is a symbolic place in which diverging needs can be communicated and converge, there will be 'extreme necessité', extreme want.

But already his report of his father's vision hints at its limits; the list of needs quickly veers away from its initial symmetry. Moreover, can an economy

---

[1] 'I really do not hate opinions contrary to my own' (p. 785).

of need simply substitute for one based in desire and all the ways in which desire complicates need? Montaigne's focus rapidly moves from the need-based mutuality of this vision to the operations of desire without regard for need, mutuality and egalitarian community. What ensues? Absence of satisfaction, failure to realize possibilities, and acute societal failure. Montaigne's thoughts turn to two scholars, both of whom died of starvation: 'j'entens, avec une grande honte de nostre siecle, qu'à nostre veue deux tres-excellens personnages en sçavoir sont morts en estat de n'avoir pas leur soul à manger: Lilius Grego-rius Giraldus en Italie, et Sebastianus Castalio en Allemagne' (I hear, to our century's great shame, that before our very eyes, two exceptionally learned men have died for lack of food: Lilius Gregorius Giraldus in Italy and Sebastianus Castalio in Germany) (p. 223).

The current economy neglects needs, and its exchange values seem also to fail. Moreover, it inhibits an alternative principle, that of hospitability, which is closer to an economy of the gift. If only we had known, Montaigne continues, they could have been saved. In even the most corrupted of cultures there would still be one person who would gladly give what was his to rescue the vulnerable:

> et croy qu'il y a mil'hommes qui les eussent appellez avec tres-advantageuses conditions, ou secourus où ils estoient, s'ils l'eussent sçeu. Le monde n'est pas si generalement corrompu, que je ne sçache tel homme qui souhaiteroit de bien grande affection que les moyens que les siens luy ont mis en main, se peussent employer ... à mettre à l'abry de la necessité les personnages rares et remarquables en quelque espece de valeur, que le mal'heur combat quelquefois jusques à l'extremité.

> (I believe that there are very many men who would have sent for them with a very generous offer, or helped them where they were, had they only known. The world is not so utterly corrupted that there is not someone who not would wholeheartedly wish to use what he has inherited to protect from want those who are rare and remarkable in some way, whom misfortune sometimes assails terribly.)

Montaigne's second example, the death through poverty and starvation of Se-bastian Castellio, is particularly significant and poignant, as is the inclusion of that indirect comment on the time of writing, on the world being 'corrompu', corrupted: a time of civil and religious wars, in which moderate voices tended to be drowned out or coopted by more polarized positions, and Roman Catholics and Huguenots battled to destroy the intolerable wrong represented by the 'An-tichrist', the other side. These wars, lasting several decades, acted out a crisis of refusal to allow a balance between others' beliefs, needs, desires and place, and one's own.

Castellio, a Reformer, argued in the name of freedom of conscience; his moderation made him as critical of extremist Reformers as of Roman Catholics, and tolerant of a range of non-extremist positions. A simple example: Castellio uses the metaphor of 'maladie', sickness, to describe the state of France on the verge of war in 1562, whereas a contemporary text attributed to La Boétie, pro

personal a public context

concord ('one faith, one law, one king') and against toleration, uses the intransigent dualist metaphor of 'mal', evil or harm as well as disease. Early in the text within a sentence he tacitly redefines diversity, an accurate term, as duality: 'tout le mal est la diversité de religion ... un même peuple ... divisé en deux parts' (the evil is entirely caused by religious diversity ... a single people ... split in two).[2]

The inclusion of Castellio, whose belief so differed from Montaigne's own, as an example of rare integrity, conveys Montaigne's identification with those who preferred freedom of conscience to forced identity of, and by, belief, or even argued that freedom of conscience is what guarantees peace and order.

Montaigne avoided religious debate and its moral dualism; but while we would call his stance tolerant, he uses 'tolerance' only once, meaning patience or the capacity to endure, his tolerance being, rather, integral to his thinking.[3] To describe the confused reality of the lived experience of the wars, he preferred, along with 'confusion', figuration such as the diseased or dismembered 'body politic', or, as here, a term such as 'corrupted': *altogether* broken (from Latin, *cor + rumpere*), a more apt adjective than those used by other contemporaries, who reduce a complex situation to polarities – thus it is the 'other' who is 'vermin' or 'barbaric'. Even when, by 1562, all hope of interconfessional reconciliation was exhausted, Castellio continued to write, to his own detriment, on the need for (in our terms) toleration, preferring the politically and theologically complex coexistence of two churches to loss of freedom of conscience.[4] His death by privation symbolizes the prevailing refusal of such views.

These issues situate my interpretation of Montaigne's writing. We need to be alert to its context: not only that of civil and religious war, 'brother' against 'brother' (to use a recurrent topos of the period), which put in question cherished philosophical, ethical and political ideals, but also of personal loss, the death of his father and of his dearest friend, Etienne de la Boétie, and of the threat to personal ideals such as hospitability. And with the polarizations and constraining alignments that are part of war and its discourses, the need to allow uncertainty and suspension of judgement (without loss of responsibility) is intensified.

The passage from 'D'un defaut' suggests Montaigne's attentiveness to vulnerability. The movement of his thoughts from an economy of need-based exchange to the desire to give to the other conveys the significance of hospitability, both culturally and intellectually, and, with it, non-sectarian, humane preoccupations. That failure to so act is a matter of deep shame makes this ethics clear. Conversely, that disregard for the needs of the other is *the* instance

---

[2]   La Boétie, *Mémoire touchant l'edit de janvier 1562*, in Gontarbert and Prassoloff (eds), *De la servitude volontaire ou Contr'un* (Paris, 1993), pp. 268–303 (p. 268).

[3]   In sixteenth-century religious and political discourse toleration is only a reluctant means to preserving the key principle of concord: one faith, one law, one king.

[4]   See Castellio, *Conseil à la France désolée*, ed. Valkhoff (Geneva, 1967). On Castellio, see Guggisberg, *Sebastian Castellio 1515–1563,* trans. Gordon (Aldershot, 2003).

of failure suggests an ethics grounded in a concern for the relatedness of individuals and in recognition of the other's vulnerability. Moreover, the example of Castellio's death is an aspect of Montaigne's writing that is central to my interpretation: its capacity to contain differing, even conflicting positions, to allow testing and unsettling ideas, or ambivalence, and, with them, anxiety.

At a time when moderation was difficult to preserve, and toleration a product of political expediency rather than the driving principle,[5] Montaigne's taste for generous inconclusiveness is the more striking. One of the processes by which his writing sustains tolerance and encourages plural interpretations is its exceptionally creative use of figuration: its ideational and affective force is, I think, even greater than others have argued.[6] To recognize in figuration a rhetorical structure that may be a form of semantic tolerance is also to recognize its significance for sceptical thinking. Montaigne's preference for Pyrrhonist scepticism, a model of which had become available with the 1562 Latin translation of Sextus Empiricus's *Hypotyposes*, over other classical philosophies can be understood as a corollary of the ethical importance of what we call tolerance. In turn, the function of figuration – whether a structure or specific motifs – in Montaigne's writing is symptomatic of these conceptual and ethical contexts: it allows the articulation of the kinds of epistemologically unsettling ideas and perspectives that such open thinking keeps in play, and opens the reader to engage with them.

Tolerance is also sustained by the associative mobility of his articulation of his ideas. After the passage already cited, Montaigne returns to recollections of his father, shifting into seeming self-reproach for failing to follow his father's admirable practice of having the daily events of life on his estate recorded, a 'papier journal ... jour par jour les memoires de l'histoire de sa maison' (a journal ... recording the daily stuff of his family's history) (p. 224). He lacks both the enjoyment and the memories that such a record might have offered. The chapter ends: 'me trouve un sot d'y avoir failly' (what a fool I am to have failed to do this) (p. 224). But his reflections open with the admission that he could not have: 'cet ordre, que je sçay loüer, mais nullement ensuivre' (this orderly habit, which I can praise but cannot follow). Montaigne allows not only others' conflicting positions but also internal difference, such as the coexisting desire to emulate his father and acceptance of its impossibility.

The father is loved and lost: both an impossible ideal and a necessary perspective on what was currently missing. His good practice is unrepeatable; but Montaigne's equanimity, mark of his differentiation from his father, of identification at best being not identical, matters more. His desires and ideals are reproduced here as food for thought, in the – *new* – form of the *essai*, a very different kind of 'papier journal', for unknown readers, who may or may not enjoy or under-

    [5] As with the 1576 Peace of Monsieur, which allowed Huguenots limited freedom of worship.
    [6] See Clark, *The Web of Metaphor* (Lexington, Ky., 1978) and 'Seneca's Letters as a Source of Some of Montaigne's Imagery', *BHR* 30/1 (1968), pp. 249–66. For wider discussion, see Rigolot, *L'Erreur de la Renaissance* (Paris, 2002).

stand them. This is the very condition of hospitability: the capacity to be open
to the unknown, to be like and unlike, to desire to be like the other and to accept
that one is not. Hence the capaciousness that enables the gift of hospitality – a
possibility by which Montaigne set wider cultural store: it was unimaginable to
him that many people, despite contemporary conflicts, would not wish to act this
way. Although this ethics has a cultural and psychic hinterland in Montaigne's
ego-ideal as a gentleman, this passage suggests that it was also closely bound
to the heightened sense of fragility that comes with the loss of a loved one, and
intensified by the experience of the hostilities of war.

'A rearrangement of the field of knowability'

Metaphor and other forms of figuration have been the subject of too many works
of rhetoric, philosophy, aesthetics and linguistics to mention them individually
here. I shall simply gather some of the theories most significant for the place of
figuration, particularly metaphor, in Montaigne's writing.

We find a complex linguistic topography. Theories of figuration as the trans-
ference or transport of meaning hug the original meaning of metaphor from
metapherein (Gk), 'transfer, carry over', from *meta-* 'over, across' + *pherein*,
'to carry, bear'; trope (as some figures were categorized) means turning (Gk
trepe-), and topos, motif, meaning place (Gk *topos*).[7] Since Aristotle and other
classical philosophers, rhetoricians and grammarians, via structural linguists
such as Jakobson, to Lacan and others with psychoanalytic interests in the
work and play of language, metaphor has been theorized as both creative and
deviant, a form of turning and a form of substitution. Accordingly its use grows
out of lack (of a 'proper' term), is covertly aggressive (taking the place of a
'proper' term), or in it a term is 'improper', out-of-place. All of this is suffused
with anxiety, as the proliferating justifications for, and regulation of, its use
seem to attest, including emphases on the need to seamlessly incorporate the
figure into the textual 'body'. That anxiety hovers over its use is also clear in
the strand of theory which, more explicitly than substitution theories, conceptualizes the space in which meaning is produced, and casts metaphor, along
with other tropes, as a turn, therefore a turning as if away, or deviation (from
the 'proper' term); or in the idea of erring, which for Augustine exemplifies
the erring and exile of all human language. It might seem a simple matter to
dissolve this anxiety: if it is no longer presupposed, or sacrosanct, that there is
a clear distinction between 'proper' and 'improper' or figural usage, then a clear
line between the two need not be so policed. But this also means renouncing the
identification between 'proper' usage and transparency and reliable adequation
between a word or phrase and their referent. The linguistic and philosophical

---

[7]   For an invigorating analysis, see Parker, 'The Metaphorical Plot', in *Literary Fat
Ladies* (London, 1987), pp. 36–53.

arguments which have painstakingly moved theory away from a founding belief in a distinction between the proper and the figural need not be elaborated here. Instead, let me invoke Montaigne's metaphor for his thinking and writing: 'mon stile et mon esprit vont vagabondant de mesmes' (my style and my mind go wandering together) (p. 994): this is the condition of both, without it being a wandering away from an originary or determinant proper path.

If we rethink the time and space of the production of linguistic meaning implied by substitution, we reach another range of theories which are more significant for Montaigne's practice.[8] Theories such as Black's and Ricoeur's identify the creative space produced by the presence of metaphor in relation to the more linear operation of the sentence, metaphor's power to suspend (and thus enhance) prosaic descriptive reference; others', its capacity to give 'room' for the creative production of meaning, or delay the movement towards meaning. All emphasize the importance of the play of language, in which the reader joins, co-creating meaning. Lastly, for now, I shall mention two further writers for whom the power of figuration is not only stylistically enhancing but conceptually paramount, Hayden White and Leo Bersani. For White, figuration turns not only away from but, more creatively, towards another potentially equally valid notion: 'both a movement *from* one notion of the way things are related *to* another notion, and a connection between things so that they can be expressed in a language that takes account of the possibility of their being expressed otherwise'.[9] Both, and otherwise: hold these in mind while considering the next proposition, which lends figuration even greater conceptual power. Here Bersani comments on the operation of similitude in Godard's *Passion*; he emphasizes the terms' continuing difference as well as identity: 'the experimental initiation of a connection, or a correspondence ... the beginning of a rearrangement of the field of knowability'.[10] For Lacan also, metaphor's reconfigurative conceptual and affective potential is great; what matters for Montaigne's practice is that, although Lacan's theory draws on Jakobson's model (metaphor: substitution, metonymy: displacement), which also echoes Freud, he argues that the prior condition of metaphoric substitution is always metonymic displacement. Here, too, is a theory not of fusion or identification between the terms but of metaphor's capacity to contain both difference and likeness as one of its key conceptual contributions. What we also have is theorization in terms of the affective *and* cognitive force of metaphor.

This both/and-ness can be traced back to Aristotle, despite his recurring to such concepts as deviation or substitution; thus these later theories are not anachronistic in relation to Montaigne's text. In Aristotle's *Rhetoric* we find: 'it

---

[8]   Already once theorists such as Richards, Black and Ricoeur replace the substitution model of classical rhetoric with the concepts of the tension or interaction between its terms, metaphor's semantic and ideational power is greatly expanded.

[9]   White, *Tropics of Discourse*, p. 2.

[10]   Bersani, 'The Will to Know', in *Is the Rectum a Grave?* (Chicago, 2010), pp. 154–67 (p. 166).

coherence imaginary, alienating

is metaphor above all that gives perspicuity, pleasure and *a foreign air, and it cannot be learned from anyone else*' (my italics). He goes on: 'we must make use of metaphors ... that are appropriate ... by observing due proportion'; metaphor works with 'the similarity in things that are apart', and has the strategic potential to 'mislead at the same time as pleasing' – misleading being the potential to redirect the reader's understanding or making of meaning, which seems close to Bersani and Lacan's notions of rearrangement and reconfiguration.[11] Aristotle's comments recognize the ambiguity of metaphor's working, its both/and-ness, its capacity to tolerate difference; and whilst attentive to propriety, he locates it in the relationship *between the terms*. All of this, particularly the attentiveness to the relationship between, allowing likeness and difference together, requiring the reader's participation in rearranging or reconfiguring, illuminates Montaigne's writing practices. Indeed, it could make figuration a paradigm of Montaigne's project, for often it is the relationships between things, in all their complexity, mobility and ambiguity (which also reminds us of the structural force of figuration), that fascinate him.

Figuration is a key element of Montaigne's style. His comments on this tend to emphasize the elements that most distinctively energize his words' potential to address and engage their readers: poetics and ethics combined. I shall return to questions of address shortly, but shall focus first on aspects of Montaigne's writing that seem most his own, including figuration, and their function, beginning with what he claims is most alien to his style: 'il n'est rien si contraire à mon stile qu'une narration estendue' (there is nothing so contrary to my style as extended narration) (p. 106). This, from the end of 'De la force de l'imagination', has a double focus. Firstly, wariness of the illusions of coherence sustained by narrative prose, coherence being imaginary and alienating, a self-deception diverting us from recognizing the more contingent and incoherent nature of our being. Secondly, his preference for effects that work against this illusion, interrupting the drive of syntax towards meaning; unorthodox effects, which resist or trouble interpretation, and so engage the reader as to unsettle her reading or sense-making habits. His language is 'trop serré, desordonné, couppé, particulier' (too dense, disorderly, abrupt, individual) (p. 252), his writing 'trop espais en figures' (too 'thick' in its use of figures) (p. 875). In both these remarks, the adverb 'trop' corresponds to the reader's doubts about how to read these features of the text; and whether the effect is compaction, dislocation or opacity, all call upon her to pause, allow uncertainty, and let words and ideas play.

To develop this point, which should also be situated in relation to the conditions in which Montaigne wrote, for they bear on the ways in which his writing engages us, consider the fuller context of the second remark:

> quand j'escris, je me passe bien de la compaignie et souvenance des livres, de peur qu'ils n'interrompent ma forme ... Pour ce mien dessein, il me vient

[11] Aristotle, trans. Freese, *The Art of Rhetoric* (Cambridge, Mass. and London, 1926), III, ii, 9; III, xi, 5–6.

aussi à propos d'escrire chez moy ... Je l'eusse faict meilleur ailleurs, mais l'ouvrage eust esté moins mien; et sa fin principale et perfection, c'est d'estre exactement mien ... Quand on m'a dit ou que moy-mesme me suis dict: Tu es trop espais en figures ... Voilà un discours ignorant. Voilà un discours paradoxe. En voilà un trop fol. Tu te joues souvent; on estimera que tu dies à droit, ce que tu dis à feinte ... me represente-je pas vivement? suffit! J'ay faict ce que j'ay voulu: tout le monde me reconnoit en mon livre, et mon livre en moy. (pp. 874–5)

(when I am writing I happily do without the company and recollection of my books, lest they interfere with my style ... It suits my project best if I write at home ... I might have done it better elsewhere, but it would have been less my own; and its principal aim and perfection is to be precisely my own ... When I have been told, or have told myself: 'Your writing is too 'thick' in its use of figures ... This is an ignorant argument, and this paradoxical, and this one here is too mad. You are often playful; people will think you are serious when you are not really ...' am I not representing myself to the life? Isn't that enough! I have done what I wanted: everyone recognizes me in my book, and my book in me.)

His aim is that his writing be 'exactement mien', exactly his own, just like him. So: paradox, mobility, energy, plurality of perspective, and deceptive simplicity, readily exposed as such by analysis of the complex multiplication and repetition of first-person subject and object pronouns, possessive adjectives and that last disjunctive pronoun in the passage. They indicate the refractory nature of the syntax of self-representation, pulling against the proclaimed ideal. Far from persuading of the achievability of an ideal correspondence between writer and writing, this passage worries away at the difficulty of the project, from point of departure, in anxiety, to outcome. If readers, unknown and unpredictable in their response, even Montaigne himself as a reader, are to recognize him in his text, it will be precisely, or so it seems, through his writing's so-called excesses, lack, deviation and unsettling effects. So what engages the imagined reader are his writing's quiddities, its not meeting expectations: a paradox in itself given that *essais* are a new form and therefore already invited recalibration of reading habits. That which fails to meet expectations seems, according the movement of his thoughts, that which represents him; for despite disappointment, or frustration, or bafflement, he reports or imagines lively engagement along the way towards his readers learning how to understand the movement of his thinking and what his writing seeks to convey.

The first imagined criticism relates to figuration: 'trop espais', not necessarily too many, but too dense or forceful. The figurative adjective matters as much as the idea of excess, which may stem from irrelevant expectations. If a 'thick' text deviates, is it from the illusion that meaning is a product of clear linear language; moreover, that to arrive at meaning is the aim? Instead, the function of figuration is to invite the reader to enjoy and explore the process by which meanings are produced, particularly in terms of the process by which self-understanding emerges, as the following examples illustrate.

Les autres sentent la douceur d'un contentement et de la prosperité; je la sens ainsi qu'eux, mais ce n'est pas en passant et glissant. Si la faut il estudier, savourer et ruminer ... Ils jouyssent les autres plaisirs comme ils font celluy du sommeil, sans les cognoistre. A celle fin que le dormir mesme ne m'eschapat ainsi stupidement, j'ay autrefois trouvé bon qu'on me le troublat pour que je l'entrevisse. Je consulte d'un contentement avec moy, je ne l'escume pas; je le sonde. (p. 1112)

(Others feel the sweetness of contentment and prosperity; as do I, but not in passing, or fleetingly. For we must study it, savour it and ruminate on it ... They enjoy the other pleasures as they would, sleep, without knowing them. So that sleep itself doesn't escape me in this stupid way, at one time I chose to have mine disturbed, so as to be able to glimpse it. I reflect on my contentment, I do not skim over it, I sound it.)

'Savourer' is glossed by 'estudier' and 'ruminer', but complicates the notion of reflection by implying that it should include lingering pleasure akin to that of particularly tasty food, and by reminding that reflection is an aspect of the process of absorbing and integrating experience, and the ideas to which it gives rise, into oneself. Coming after 'estudier', it both displaces and substitutes for 'savoir', which its first syllable matches; coming before 'ruminer', it alerts us to pondering also being 'chewing over'. 'Escumer', to skim (which amplifies the earlier 'en passant et glissant') as a seabird might the surface of the waves, implants the contrasting idea of depth, which then becomes explicit with 'sonder', to sound the depths, and so to deeply integrate and understand one's experience, pleasant or not. These metaphors animate the representation of personal pleasures and their analysis; the idea of savouring (food), an experience which is both general and highly personal, helps to convey the intimately individual experience and experiment – having himself woken up so as to not sleep through the experience of sleep; and in turn, the sleep-experiment takes on figurative resonance as an analogy for all that one is not awake to, and to which others, by troubling one's inertia, can open one's mind, as can forms of expression such as figures which are out of the sleepy ordinary.

Metaphor also acts powerfully in Montaigne's representation of his self-exploration as a site of ambiguity, a form of tolerance of unresolved difference, and index of this 'doubleness'.[12] 'Je n'ay veu monstre et miracle au monde plus expres que moy-mesme. On s'apprivoise à toute estrangeté par l'usage et le temps; mais plus je me hante et me connois, plus ma difformité m'estonne, moins je m'entens en moy' (I have seen nothing more monstrous or miraculous in the world than myself. Time and use accustom us to everything strange; but the more I haunt myself and know myself, the more my deformity astonishes me, and the less I understand myself) (p. 1029). The two sentences are full of figuration, partly designed to throw the reader, emphasizing the strangeness with

---

[12] 'Nous sommes, je ne sçay comment, doubles en nous mesmes' (we are, I know not how, double within ourselves) (p. 619).

refl^ on self — haunting

which Montaigne's thinking grapples, as will the reader's. Metaphor's capacity to hold together different meanings and affective resonance has the performative power to convey the doubleness that the reader wants to engage with; it acts as a specific form of address to the reader's thinking, intuition and emotion.

Leaving behind the hyperbolic extremes of the monstrous and miraculous, Montaigne's thoughts turn to the notion of the unknowable difference or otherness within the subject, a paradoxically constitutive deformation exceeding all other extremes. Nothing external is so strange that it cannot come to be accepted; but the project of self-understanding leads to the recognition that the untameable strangeness that inhabits the subject will always unsettle and remind that the subject exceeds full understanding. The more one knows, the less one understands – except insofar as this itself suggests a transformed understanding.

The desire for self-understanding is not therefore futile; but the reflexive verb, 'se hanter', to haunt oneself, conveys the ambivalent and anxious nature of the process. The etymology of 'hanter' is disputed: Old French *hanter* (to inhabit, frequent, resort to) and Old Norse *heimta* (to bring home, fetch, lead home, pull, claim) and *haimithôn* (to shelter) compete with vulgar Latin *ambitare* (to go to and fro, hither and thither), from *ambitus* (a roundabout journey).[13] If we prefer the latter, we foreground restless return. If the former, the appealingness of being at home or returning home is shadowed by the more troubling desire: to *pull* (home) – so away from what? or claim – taking home is aggressive possession. Add to these the unease encountered in the process of self-exploration: far from the recognition that is associated in fantasy with returning or being at home, what emerges is an absence of at-homeness, an awareness of the strange unknowableness of the self, more akin to the *unheimlich* than the *heimlich*, an uncanny, traumatic encounter (as with the kinds of things we might call monsters). Moreover, there are insistent associations with death, or the undead – for that which haunts is that which will not rest in peace but returns to inhabit the living.

That Montaigne's reflection on himself, a creative desire, is expressed as a metaphorical haunting opens the cognitive process out into its more complex affective, intuitive and unconscious dimension: self-understanding involves encounters with aspects of the self that are so forgotten as to no longer animate it, or which elude understanding, and also with a desire to know fully – to bring home, or to claim – which should be resisted. Metaphor provides a structure in which these disturbing connotations can hover, available to those who want to hold together the troubling with the creative, and to suspend the push to resolve meanings into a clear conclusion, without these differing connotations having so unsettling an effect in the sentence as to alienate the reader.

To give metaphor such epistemological and psychological force in the process of self-analysis and its interpretation is, partly, to extend Cave's observation

---

[13] See Baldinger, *Dictionnaire étymologique de l'ancien français* (Quebec and Tübingen, 1997–2000), pp. 144–6.

about the specific power of antiperistasis for Pyrrhonist texts. 'Elle désigne une sorte de thérapie par contraires qui consiste à faire passer l'esprit par une phase de trouble épistémologique, pour qu'il retrouve ensuite l'ataraxie' (it designates a sort of allopathic therapy which consists of obliging the mind to undergo a phase of epistemological disturbance so that it may subsequently reach a state of ataraxia).[14] In doing so, I am also underlining the sceptical tendencies of Montaigne's thinking and the writing it requires, and suggesting the capacity of figures such as metaphor to work in a way similar to antiperistasis. Thus, to be symptomatic in Montaigne's text of his doubt and of his desire that readers suspend judgement. However, where my reading of their operation differs from what Cave notes as the desired outcome is that, while I am suggesting that metaphors, by containing difference, have the capacity to make plurality, ambiguity and uncertainty tolerable, I am not suggesting that they necessarily produce tranquillity. They contain difference, are a site of tolerance, but the continuing uncertainty or opacity which they allow sustains less tranquillity than the precarious suspension of excessive 'trouble' (to echo Cave's word).

Montaigne's writing embarks in anxiety (see the passage on p. 1 above) and out of loss (the death of loved ones, the failures of intellectual, political and ethical ideals), and eschews conclusion; it is on the side of tolerance, a vanishing possibility at the time; and, without its ideal reader, La Boétie (already dead), it must address its explorations of the question 'who am I?' to unknown, diverse readers who potentially will not understand, and whose response to the accompanying question, 'who am I to you?' remains unpredictable. Riskily so, but this is the ethical condition of his writing which, in keeping with the principle of tolerance, must assume that its readers will differ from its writer. Montaigne's desire to write grew out of the experience of overwhelming incoherence: 'm'enfante tant de chimeres et monstres fantasques ... sans ordre et sans propos' (give birth to so many chimeras and fantastic monsters ... without order or purpose) (p. 33). Whatever consolation writing may have brought, it generates the terrible anticipation – 'je crains *mortellement*' (I am *mortally* afraid) (p. 847, my italics) – of readers who will take him for other than he is. This is a project driven and inhabited by anxiety: 'l'angoisse est corrélative du moment où le sujet est suspendu entre un temps où il ne sait plus où il est, vers un temps où il va être quelque chose où il ne pourra plus jamais se retrouver' (anxiety is the correlative of the moment in which the subject is suspended between no longer knowing who he is and the time when he will become something else, in which he will never find his former self again).[15] Anxiety and vulnerability are the irreducible condition of its ethics; and figuration, notably metaphor, is

---

[14] Cave, *Pré-histoires*, I, p. 39, translated as 'Imagining Scepticism in the Sixteenth Century', in Kenny and Williams (eds), *Retrospectives: Essays in Literature, Poetics and Cultural History* (London, 2009), pp. 109–29 (p. 120). Originally a term in the natural sciences rather than rhetoric, Cave's point is that antiperistasis takes on the function of metaphor and acts as a figure of thought in Estienne's Preface to the *Hypotyposes*.

[15] Lacan, *Le Séminaire IV*, p. 226.

a key linguistic, epistemological and psychological resource and structure for containing anxiety so as to enable suspension of judgement, and for encouraging a more generalized desire in readers to think 'otherwise' and tolerate uncertainty and 'le branle et les secousses diverses du doute' (the shocks and jolts of doubt) (p. 644). Montaigne's zetetic, his metaphorical 'vagabondage' captures this: the freedom to rove, wander, keep moving without a fixed destination in mind, which also involves the uncertainty of being adrift from origin and end, homeless. His writing must be such as to arouse and sustain the reader's desire to go along with this.

'Il n'est point d'hostilité excellente comme la chrestienne'

As the wars continued over the decades, Montaigne contested that their governing rationale was religious, calling them, instead, civil wars. He frequently commented on the mixed motives of those involved, on the rarity of zeal while political and self-interest masqueraded as it, and on zealotry feeding hatred, cruelty and primitive violence. He also largely avoided explicit reference to events and discussion of detail of cause or policy, while maintaining a political philosophy that preferred conservation of the status quo to the incalculable consequences of aggressive change. In a thinker who, in most respects, was more radical than his contemporaries, this conservatism may seem surprising. Over the years, Montaigne's ideas on the need for the pluralism required by freedom of conscience and as a guarantee of peace, working for rather than against unity, did fluctuate: we might say, two conflicting priorities. However, his arguments against the justification of war as a means to change or unity were constant; they conjoined ancient Greek political thought and Christian belief.

> Platon de mesme ne consent pas qu'on face violence au repos de son pays pour le guerir ... J'estois Platonicien de ce costé là, avant que je sçeusse qu'il y eust de Platon au monde ... Je doute souvent si, entre tant de gens qui se meslent de telle besoigne, nul s'est rencontré d'entendement si imbecile, à qui on aye en bon escient persuadé qu'il alloit vers la reformation par la derniere des difformations ... L'ambition, l'avarice, la cruauté, la vengeance n'ont point assez de propre et naturelle impetuosité; amorchons les et les attisons par le glorieux titre de justice et devotion. (p. 1043)

> (Plato likewise does not consent to violent disruption of his country's peace even to cure it ... I was a Platonist in this sense before I knew Plato existed ... I often doubt whether, among the very many people who are caught up in such matters, a single one has been found who is so feebleminded as to have been genuinely convinced that the worst of deformations was really bringing him reformation ... Ambition, avarice, cruelty, vengeance lack sufficient impetuosity of their own; let us add a spark and fan their flames by giving them the glorious title of justice and piety.)

soul body divided

Hatred, greed, primitive vengefulness, cruelty – Montaigne's most hated vice – drove the worst of this conflict under the guise of belief and justice, ruthlessly displacing conscience and claiming, whether in delusion or cynicism, to act for God. To which sources of violence we might also add the anxiety that toleration and its requirement not to act can bring. Despite the horror of these wars which lasted intermittently throughout the years he was writing, and their direct impact on him and his family, Montaigne strove to remain sufficiently free to inquire, think and write as he wished, and to allow himself doubt, uncertainty, possibility, all marks of both intellectual and ethical tolerance, at a time when moderation yielded to false certitudes and taking of sides.

Although there are measured exceptions that argue for forms of moderation,[16] a marked feature of many of the texts these wars produced, and symptomatic of the violence and hate fuelling their language, is their dualist stance: the other is the enemy, to be destroyed in print or on the field of battle. Religious extremism and all manner of mixed motives and interests drove the wars, but in their midst, religious experience was more confused: many families, like Montaigne's, contained members of both confessions: brother or sister could be other; and there were differences, both negotiable and insurmountable, *within* each of the churches. These multiple fractures are what resonate in Montaigne's figuration of the desolate social and political body: not only is it infected (a common recurrent metaphor), but also it is dismembered and dislocated: 'ces desmambremens de la France et divisions où nous sommes tombez' (these divisions into which we have plunged, which tear France limb from limb) (p. 993). Dismemberment is the social body's descent into violent antagonism and self-destruction, both rhetorical and physical; the dishonouring of it, its integrity no longer guaranteed, as it had been for Roman Catholics, by its analogy with the spiritual body of the Christian community; its disintegration therefore, under Reformed ascription of (for Montaigne) excessive authority to individual subjects, no longer united in the ideal of the social body governed by divinely sanctioned institutions; the rejection by Reformers of the symbol at the heart of the social and spiritual body, the Eucharist ('corpus Christi'); and the disintegration of that sacrament in Calvinist doctrine, which put in question the immanence in it of Christ's presence. A disastrous list of divisions; but unless divisions, plural, were acknowledged, the further catastrophe of binary thinking would take hold, and unless those divisions were accepted, as Montaigne did, as involving all, they were also catastrophically cast as the other's doing.

In striking contrast, the Huguenot D'Aubigné offers: 'ce vieil corps tout infecte, plein de la discratie' (this aged, utterly infected, dyscrasic body).

---

[16] These include, to name but two, among Reformers, texts by Castellio such as the *Conseil à la France désolée* (1562), and among Roman Catholic moderates, texts by Pasquier, notably his *Exhortation aux Princes et Seigneurs du conseil privé du Roy* (n.p., 1561). It is worth noting that Pasquier also later wrote polemic against the Jesuits, *Le Cathéchisme des Jésuites* (Paris, 1602), that is, could be openly and strongly critical of fellow Roman Catholics.

'Discratie' originally means dissension, then, in medical terms, an imbalance of the four humours, but is not adrift from its Greek origin, *diskratis*, meaning not so much division as 'governed by *two* heads'. A binary structure, but governed by a fantasized unitary identity – that model of 'concord' that now eluded the French. In the early 1560s, increasingly, even moderates such as the Chancellor Michel de l'Hôpital reiterated that political unity required the existence of only one church. Those who could envision the peaceful coexistence of two or more churches dwindled – although it was still possible to think that unity could take this form. Whilst in living memory there had been only 'one true faith' in France, the emphasis on unitary identity in confessional texts may well be a fetishistic back-formation, driven by the anxiety that its loss would result in a void rather than a livable coexistence of more than 'one true' faith. For centuries of course, since the Early Church, there had been debates and at times major controversies within the one church, not least over the meaning of the presence of Christ in the sacrament, rather than consistent unity.[17] The loss dreaded, of a perfectly unified one, is a loss of a fantasy. The split into two is the figure of deadlock, or of triumph and loss, indeed triumph through loss, enacting the fantasy of return to there only being one. Being one had come to be thinkable only in terms of a single, self-same identity, rather than one being a form of unity which could contain difference, conforming to an ethics and understanding deriving from tolerance of loss and of its accompanying anxiety and vulnerability. It is just such an openness to difference – freedom of conscience as well as free inquiry – that informs Montaigne's thinking and ethics.

This structural logic is well illustrated by the *Mémoire touchant l'édit de janvier 1562* attributed to La Boétie; this edict, also known as the Edict of Toleration, may have been one of the catalysts for war. The *Mémoire*'s author anticipated war, and rejected toleration as a solution to confessional conflict. His text might seem prescient or realistic; for a decade already there had been increasing unrest, physical and verbal violence, identitarian conflict, anxiety over the loss of traditional givens, and in 1561 the Colloque de Poissy had failed to find reconciliation. Perhaps; but that is not to say that his analysis of the situation is sufficient or just. *De la servitude volontaire*, La Boétie's earlier essay, exploring why subjects relinquish their defining freedom, the potential to act politically, had been an inspiration to Montaigne.[18] The thinking in the later text is more constrained, perhaps because of the unprecedented religious schism of the time of writing; also, whilst the earlier was abstract, and focused neither on religion nor on the masses, in the later text, contemporary reality, religious conflict and the masses form the driving problem.[19] Moreover, while the *Discours* invokes a classical ideal of fraternal community as the antithesis of a regime of subjugation to the tyrant, the *Mémoire* struggles to understand

---

[17] See Macy, *The Banquet's Wisdom* (Mahwah, NJ, 1992).

[18] The two texts are published together in *De la servitude volontaire ou Contr'un*.

[19] For discussion of the *Mémoire*, see Smith, *Montaigne and Religious Freedom* (Geneva, 1991); in Smith's view, La Boétie favours oligarchy.

the existential reality of social antagonisms other than by recourse to a model of the social field as requiring identity of vision. Identity or atomization: earlier, the possibility, still, of civilization – the sublimation of murderous impulses into brotherly love, to revert to Freud's argument in *Civilization and its Discontents*; later, its collapse.

According to the author, the 'vraie semence de tous les malheurs du monde' (truly the seed from which all the world's unhappiness springs) (p. 294) is reformed religion, its dissent from acceptance of the doctrines and practices of the Roman Catholic church. He rejects toleration on both political and theological grounds.[20] He accepts the need to reform many of a corrupted church's 'cérémonies et observations' (rituals and practices) (p. 286)), and argues that reforms to practice and governance would be enough to resolve the conflict. But while he diagnoses (implicitly curable) 'maladie' (illness) (p. 271) within the Roman Catholic church, on the side of reform he identifies 'mal' (evil, harm, ill): its source, uneducated Reformers. For a text which claims to be conciliatory, its version of Reformers is extremist, polarized into its theologians ('les chefs de leur religion' (the heads of their church) (p. 286)) and the mass of followers, the 'peuple' (people); as if, between the two, no educated people or people of conscience existed or had influence. He insists on the inability of those he calls the 'peuple', or the 'populaire' (populace), to understand the issues, and denies their good faith; they act out of ignorance, delusion or perversion; their 'conscience' is no more than 'la persuasion de leur esprit et leurs fantaisies' (merely their own ideas and imaginings) (p. 268) and they are 'monstrueux' (monstrous) (p. 269), that is, denatured. This 'peuple' reads like a version of Plato's populace of Athens in decline, whose damaging desires must yield to the authority of the statesman.[21] It connotes an aggressive mass; a *bloc* rather than a group bonded in social relations and religious concerns. To revert again to the argument of *Civilization and its Discontents* as it develops complexity: the willingness of the 'peuple' to die and kill for their faith, their personal love of God, as would the corresponding Roman Catholic 'peuple', exposes the narcissistic, anti-social aggressivity that love, brotherly or other, was – all along.[22] The coexistence of confessional differences, so recently thought still possible, is dismissed; the predicted outcome is 'calamités' (calamity) (p. 277). Rather than posit French society as a state of antagonism in which differences were not only

---

[20] 'Nulle dissension n'est si grande ni si dangereuse que celle qui vient pour la religion: elle sépare les citoyens, les voisins, les amis, les parents, les frères, le père et les enfants, le mari et la femme; elle rompt les alliances, les parentés, les mariages, les droits inviolables de la nature, et pénètre jusqu'au fond des coeurs pour extirper les amitiés et enraciner des haines irréconciliables' (Religious dissent is the gravest, most dangerous form of dissent. It divides citizens, neighbours, friends, relatives, brothers, fathers and children, husbands and wives; it destroys unions, kinship, marriages, inviolable natural rights, and affects what is held most dear, undoing friendships and planting irreconcilable hatred) (p. 276).

[21] See Plato, *Gorgias*, *Laws* and *Republic* for examples of this strand in his thinking.

[22] See Bersani, 'Introduction' to Freud, *Civilization and its Discontents* (Harmondsworth, 2002); also published as 'Can Sex Make Us Happy?', *Raritan* 21/4 (Spring, 2002), pp. 15–30.

tolerable but legitimate (freedom of conscience), even inevitable, and a healthy collective which was neither idealized brotherly love nor its opposite extreme, here the other is taken to be nothing but the enemy whose belief is false and inadmissible. The rhetoric of the other as Antichrist and source of 'le mal', evil, supplants that of our 'maladie', illness and confusion.

The author concedes the need to reform corrupt practices, and emphasizes their reformability, arguing that this would renew the old church enough for Reformers to return. However, he downplays the most intractable differences between the 'ancienne' (ancient) and 'nouvelle' (new) doctrines and consequent practices, such as the nature of the Eucharist and the question of apostolic succession (to which in other polemic the term 'nouvelletez' (new things) refers, and are therefore latent here in the use of 'nouvelle'), and he forecloses discussion by making the issue one of ignorance versus (implicitly) wisdom and therefore legitimate authority. The people lack the capacity – authority – to think or judge: 'le peuple n'a pas moyen de juger, étant dépourvu de ce qui donne ou confirme le bon jugement, les lettres, les discours, l'expérience' (incapable of judgement, having neither the education, arguments nor experience required for good judgement) (p. 271). That most were uneducated is undeniable, but not that this caused irremediably perverse choices in matters of belief and political ideology (unless it presupposes that they could not but be victims of demagogy); moreover, 'experience' is categorized as a lack, when arguably, aligned with custom, habit and so forth, it offers an alternative to education as a grounds for socially conservative judgement.

If such representations of doctrinal tension seem a puzzling underestimate of already stubborn differences, particularly over the Eucharist, the cause is not just this version of the people. What seems to determine these arguments is attachment to the idea of the inviolable one and only; this drives the calculus – and drives it aground. A single people has split into two; only a few pages later the split is imagined as irreparable fracture: 'une extrême désolation et les pièces éparses d'une république démembrée' (utter desolation, the scattered parts of a dismembered republic) (p. 273). The presiding metaphor of the body politic dramatizes, even informs, this catastrophic vision. In the terms of this kind of argument, differences, split, schism, disintegration in the end are all the same; all are not one. All – or nothing. If a people must be single and therefore by definition one and the same ('un même peuple' (a single people) (p. 268)), then the coexistence of differences seems inconceivable: calamity of disaggregation, or nightmare of polarized opposition. The insistent use of 'le peuple' calcifies the representation into binary terms, and the analysis of the relationship between the old and new church, identified with 'le peuple', is foreclosed. Analysis of the position of the Reformers, in their plurality, as a necessary supplement, or as the return of the repressed might be productive; as might analysis led by the principle of even limited toleration. But here difference is conceived as destruction; if the doctrines of the old church are true, then the new must be false; and the coexistence of the two, toleration, is not allowed by this calculus. If not one, then incalculable fraction; toleration is an incomputable 'entre-deux' (between the two) leading to 'manifeste ruine' (clear ruin) (p. 274) rather than to a different form of one. But what kind of state requires that all be the same?

The earlier *Discours* had explored, precisely, the structural ambiguities of the relations between subjects and ruler in regimes which require all subjects to be the same, victims of unjust power; but the structure is not that of all helplessly submitting to one. All are implicated in their position as victims, in voluntary servitude. La Boétie's response to his conundrum, why would anyone give up his natural freedom, turned on the intrication of what he calls nature and custom. Custom, which habituates the subject to loss of freedom, acts against nature, but is nonetheless experienced 'as if' it, too, is nature; moreover, our relationship with that primary nature may also be 'as if', a lost state only imagined from within the enclave of custom – and less powerful than it:

> la nature de l'homme est bien d'estre franc et de le vouloir estre; mais aussi sa nature est telle que naturellement il tient le pli que la nourriture lui donne. Disons donc ainsi, qu'à l'homme toutes choses lui sont comme naturelles, à quoy il se nourrit et accoustume; mais cela seulement lui est naïf, à quoy sa nature simple et non altérée l'appelle ... si faut-il confesser qu'elle [la nature] a en nous moins de pouvoir que la coustume, pource que le naturel pour bon qu'il soit se perd s'il n'est entretenu, et la nourriture nous fait tousjours de sa façon. (pp. 102, 96–7)

> (Man's nature is, surely, to be free and to want to be; but his nature is also such that he naturally assumes the traits that his culture feeds him. So let us put it this way: everything he has absorbed and is accustomed to, seems natural to man, but only those things that stem from his own first and unadulterated nature are truly his by nature ... we must admit that nature has less power over us than custom, because no matter how good what is ours by nature may be, it fades unless we sustain it, whereas culture always makes of us what it will.)

Without attentiveness to the historical and social imaginary, without this structure of intrication, which allows analysis of the complexity of intersubjectivity, social interrelation, and the complexities of the formation of individual and collective desire and fantasy, why subjects remain subjected seems inexplicable. Without it, analysis of the contemporary conflict is blocked by either binary polarization or catastrophic thinking.

Decades later, reflecting on the state of France and other questions of difference and tension, Montaigne would echo the thinking of the *Discours*, and whilst sharing the disillusionment of the *Mémoire*, would resist its logic. His understanding of custom's operation, its being mistaken for nature, its constraining power, exemplifies his thinking about falsely distinct terms and problematic, conceptually violent, dualism. Here are just a few examples:

> c'est à la coustume de donner forme à nostre vie, telle qu'il lui plaist; elle peut tout en cela: c'est le breuvage de Circé, qui diversifie nostre nature comme bon luy semble ... Nous apelons contre nature ce qui advient contre la coustume ... Les loix de la conscience, que nous disons naistre de nature, naissent

> de la coustume ... c'est la coustume qui nous faict impossible ce qui ne l'est
> pas. (pp. 1080, 713, 115 and 225)

> (It is for custom to shape our lives, just as it pleases; it can do whatever it
> wants; it is Circe's brew, changing our nature as it wills ... What we call
> against nature is in fact against custom ... The laws of conscience, which we
> say stem from nature, stem from custom ... it is custom that makes impossible
> for us things which are not in themselves impossible.)

Despite his otherwise tolerant ethos, Montaigne did not speak for religious toleration; but his stance is not that of the *Mémoire*. It is governed by a desire
for peace after devastating wars had already taken hold and contamination by
illegitimate personal and political interests of the original religious 'justifications' for them was clear, as were the brutalizing and self-perpetuating effects
of violence. Where the *Mémoire*'s version of unity should be understood as
imaginary, Montaigne's, in the face of the perversity of the wars, is an appeal to
the Law, for the restoration of a secure Symbolic order – the foundation required
for freedom of conscience and toleration.

The lack of discussion of contemporary confessional differences may reflect
both Montaigne's awareness of the more confused and shifting motives for
continuing war and also the important freedom to choose silence. Montaigne's
position was shaped by respect for the principle of the Law and a commitment
to his own freedom of conscience and thought; and about who else's conscience
could he know with sufficient certainty to judge? His critique of Reformers
focuses on their *excess*: excessive authority and certitude in matters which fell
beyond human reason, and in which certitude is symptomatic of 'incertitude
extreme' (extreme uncertainty) (p. 541), and, we might add, anxiety. His position shows, in tandem with acceptance of the limits of human reason, a preference for sceptical thinking, which requires a tolerant attitude and upholds a
principle of intellectual hospitality, both of which rest on a capacity to bear the
anxiety of irresolution and of the encounter with difference, without which open
inquiry into the complexities of the lived experience of disorder, ambivalence
and disintegration would be radically curtailed. Conversely, Montaigne's use of
sceptical inquiry implicitly reminds of where it belongs: not coopted for confessional purposes (as tended to happen), but as free thinking, 'molle' (p. 503),
mild, because free of fear of both others' views and remaining in doubt.

Moderate discourse continued to be produced throughout the wars, by writers
of all doctrinal tendencies, whether for genuine theological reasons or for prag-
matic and prudential ones, but one way or another, written for peace and forms
of solution to the conflict. But alongside it the rhetoric of violence and hate grew,
inciting in its turn more violence and hate. In 'De la praesumption' and 'De la
vanité' we find interesting examples of Montaigne's free-thinking relationship
with extremist writing or writers. In the former chapter, Theodore de Bèze, poet,
divisive participant at the Colloque de Poissy, subsequently Calvin's successor
and writer of vicious anti-Catholic satire, such as the *Satyres chrestiennes de la
cuisine papale*, is included in a list of those Montaigne considers good poets,

as is Michel de l'Hôpital, Chancellor and, for a long period, moderate Roman Catholic; Montaigne's literary preferences are inclusively non-sectarian. Nor, unlike other Roman Catholic writers, does he here invoke Bèze's youthful erotic poetry to discredit his theology. In the other chapter, Bèze is not named, but the enigma Montaigne considers, the inconsistency and dissociation evident in human behaviour, exemplified by a writer's divergent output, is thought to refer to him: 'j'ay veu en ma jeunesse un gallant homme presenter d'une main au peuple des vers excellens et en beauté et en desbordement, et de l'autre main en mesme instant la plus quereleuse reformation theologienne de quoy le monde se soit desjeuné il y a long temps' (in my youth I have seen a gentleman with one hand offer verses of outstanding beauty and licentiousness to the public, while at the same time, with the other, he offers the world the most contentious work of reformed theology it has consumed for a long time) (p. 989). The coexistence of conflicting impulses is not rationalized; he accepts these contradictions as endemic: 'les hommes vont ainsin' (this is just how men are).

'Manger son pere'?

Much fine analysis of the discourses symptomatic of these wars has been published,[23] as have accounts of the wars' influence on Montaigne.[24] Recent Reformation historiography questions earlier overarching interpretative models and emphasizes less the intransigent polarization of the situation which after 1561 rapidly locked into protracted wars than its 'state of indecision' and 'confused living experience'.[25] Nonetheless, these studies confirm that moderate discourses tended to be coopted for prevailing extremist purposes, and that attempts at conciliation were often driven as much by fear of a supposed shared enemy as by a desire for unity.

What matters for my reading is the nature of this polarizing and destabilized discursive context for Montaigne's writing, and the anxieties that such tendencies represented, which Montaigne recognized in his understanding of the 'confusion' – disorienting loss or lack of clear sociocultural, religious identity – and state of ethical ambiguity, in which the traditional grounds of mutual trust no longer held.[26]

---

[23] Among it, Crouzet, *Les Guerriers de Dieu*, 2 vols (Paris, 1990), and El Kenz, *Les Bûchers du Roi* (Paris, 1997).

[24] Studies include Nakam, *Les Essais de Montaigne, miroir et procès de leur temps* (Paris, 2001) and Quint, *Montaigne and the Quality of Mercy* (Princeton, 1998).

[25] See Racaut and Ryrie, 'Introduction: Between Coercion and Persuasion' and Greengrass, 'Conclusion: Moderate Voices, Mixed Messages', in Racaut and Ryrie (eds), *Moderate Voices in the European Reformation* (Aldershot, 2005), pp. 1–12 (p. 2) and pp. 196–211 (p. 198). Stimulating analyses of the theological and ideological complexities of the Reformation are also to be found in Grell and Scribner (eds), *Tolerance and Intolerance in the European Reformation* (Cambridge, 1996) and Wanegffelen, *Ni Rome ni Genève* (Paris, 1997).

[26] See the opening of 'De la conscience' (II, 5).

While vituperative polemic sharpened conflict, the intensification and dura-
tion of the wars indicate the failure of civic rhetoric, a key skill in the formation
of many of the political leaders; thus, the loss of a humanist ideal for Montaigne's generation, as well as a disastrous loss of humane options. The wars'
words frame significant aspects of Montaigne's use of figuration. His use of
metaphors such as the social and political body is one instance of the way in
which figures in his writing have a double function. Not only do they sustain
the affective intensity of significant thinking about the relationship between the
individual and the collective; they also reverberate between his text and others',
acknowledging the discursive context of his writing ('*nos* guerres civiles' (*our*
civil wars)), implicitly engaging with others' texts, and at the same time inviting
readers to recognize the difference between those texts and his thinking. This is
an instance of the power of figuration *per se*: to allow the possibility of thinking
'otherwise'. Take the figurative body politic: where in polemical texts the cause
of the body's illness or destruction is the other, in Montaigne's *Essais* it is the
site of suffering which we, 'nous', all undergo. Where others' are discourses
of hate, Montaigne's use of shared vocabulary acknowledges these discourses
but opens the terms out towards other possible perspectives or interpretations,
guided by a principle of tolerance: 'je ne hay point les fantasies contraires aux
miennes' (I really do not hate opinions contrary to my own) (p. 785).

In the course of the *Essais* he refers directly to the Eucharistic debates only
once, and there, his emphasis is on interpretative difficulties and differences,
and the inadequacies of communication:

> la plus part des occasions des troubles du monde sont Grammairiennes. Nos
> procez ne naissent que du debat de l'interpretation des loix; et la plus part des
> guerres, de cette impuissance de n'avoir sçeu clairement exprimer les conven-
> tions et traictez d'accord des princes. Combien de querelles et combien im-
> portantes a produit au monde le doubte du sens de cette syllabe, Hoc. (p. 527)

> (The troubles of the world are mostly occasioned by disputed grammar. Our
> lawsuits stem only from debate about the interpretation of the laws; and most
> wars, from our inability to express clearly the conventions and accords of
> princes. How many, very important disputes have been produced by doubt
> over the meaning of that syllable, 'hoc'.)

These debates generated some of the most violent and corrosive writing of the
period. For Roman Catholics the symbol of the Eucharist was central to their
community's social and political unity as well as their spiritual wholeness; for
Reformers, the Lord's Supper likewise, but incompatibly, symbolized their
holiness and social identity.[27] Theologians debated its sacramental value, the
dominant Reformers' distinction between the 'temporal sign' and 'transcendent signified' radically at odds with their complex, mysterious inseparability

---

[27] See Elwood, *The Body Broken*, pp. 163–72.

in Roman Catholic doctrine.[28] Conflicts in the understanding of symbolization, signs and signifieds extended beyond theological debate, reverberating through secular debates about the referential function of language, and are unleashed in the wider social instability that preceded the wars, between those who identified with, or sought their identity in, one or other of the sacramental positions, all perhaps equally subject to the anxiety attendant on the loss of stable meaning.

While each accuses the other of being the Antichrist, execrable, polluted and polluting, and while some of the narratives, myths and rhetoric driven by fear and hate are common to polemics on both sides – notably the figuration of the disease, toxicity and barbarity of the other – there is one lexical field that is almost entirely exclusive to Reformers' attacks on the Real Presence in the Eucharist, whereby Roman Catholics are cannibals, 'Anthropophages' (anthropophagists), 'Theophages' (god-eaters), 'Theologastres' (god-gobblers), even 'Polyphages diffamées' (vilely excessive eaters).[29] Extremists also often sexualized their attacks on Roman Catholics, for instance: 'cette puante et abominable Sodome Sorbonnique, et Sorbonne Sodomique' (that stinking, abominable Sorbonnical Sodom, that sodomous Sorbonne).[30] The figure of the cannibal, whose 'unnatural', excessive appetite for human flesh was often associated with perverse sexual appetite, combines and dramatizes the fears and hostilities about which these writers were not thinking, but rather, were histrionically intensifying. The taboo is of desire for what is same – also the recoil evident in that invocation of Sodom. The prohibition connotes acts or desires that are supposedly against nature, desires and acts than which nothing worse can be imagined. Its logic is evacuated from the satirists' use of it: the blindspot in this figuration is that it is mustered by those who, precisely, desire the same (and the exclusion or death of the other). Moreover the figuration is used as if it is a fixed and monovalent denotation: x stands for y. No possibility of plural interpretations here.

For Montaigne, however, figuration is a resource for the play of connotations and interpretation, for inviting readings which would prevail beyond predetermined substitutions, and which he himself might not predict. He was not,

[28] Elwood, *The Body Broken*, p. 166.

[29] Bèze, *Satyres Chrestiennes de la cuisine papale*, ed. Chamay (Geneva, 2005), Satyre II, line 443. Also calqued on the cannibalism imputed to Roman Catholics in the Eucharistic debates is the language used at times of the killing of Reformers: thus the assassin of the Huguenot leader Coligny is: 'un meurtrier Sathan, glouton de sang humain' (a murderous Satan, glutton for human blood) (see Pineaux, 'Poésie de cour et poésie de combat', *Bulletin de la Société du Protestantisme Français* (jan.–mars 1972), pp. 32–54 (p. 52)). The exception to this interconfessional rhetoric of the cannibal other is the existence of attacks in these terms by Calvinists on Lutherans, whose doctrine on the Eucharist was perceived as too close to Roman Catholic transubstantiation (hence condemnation as 'cannibals'), and as a threat to the unity of Reformed identity.

[30] Mainardo, *Anatomie de la messe et du missel* (Lyon, 1562), p. 540. This text, translated into French by Calvin's secretary, was written in the context of division among exiled Italian Reformers, as an authoritative statement of Calvinist doctrine. For further searching discussion of this discursive context, see the work of Lestringant, for instance, *Une Sainte Horreur ou, Le Voyage en eucharistie: XVIe–XVIIIe siècle* (Paris, 1996).

of course, producing satire; and although evidently Roman Catholic, did not actively identify himself with a side or cause. Thus the function of figuration in his writing and those of the polemicists is not directly comparable, important and symptomatic though the difference in their practice is. The issue for my interpretation is that in this overdetermined discursive environment, as well as in the context of less vituperative but no less fundamental conflicts between theologians over the meaning of the Eucharist, Montaigne's focus on cannibals both figurative and existent, and his use of related figuration such as that of appetite for knowledge or for other people, resonates with the discourses whose rigidity, polarization, hate and fear his own thinking avoids or challenges. In polemics, that the 'other' is barbaric is both paradigmatic and a specific symptom of the situation of civil war and doctrinal schism: for the first time on this scale, the enemy is not external, is both other and yet intolerably same, to be called by the name traditionally given to those beyond one's own race whose existence threatened – or shored up – one's 'civilized' identity as a human.[31]

The barbarian or savage who is also cannibal is *the* figure of anxious horror. But the cannibal of Montaigne's famous chapter is not barbaric, and also exposes how much greater is 'our own' barbarism. He is nonetheless a cannibal: this ambiguity acts to maximize the unsettling interpretative openness and challenge to habits of thought of this – ambiguously – figurative and existent other. Montaigne's unbarbaric cannibal unsettles the discourse of barbarism used so aggressively at the time. This is a particularly significant example of the risks taken by his writing, in its respect for complexity. His very use of the term 'cannibale' also seems to invite interpretative freedoms: it was not yet in common usage and seems to have been less identified with anthropophagy than with savagery;[32] thus his reflections, which travel from savagery to man-eating, among other significances, seem designed to extend and amplify existing meanings and allow new possibilities. Other contemporary versions of the thought experiment figured by his cannibal culture, one without the inequities, cruelties, illusions and unfreedoms of sixteenth-century France, tended to require that an idealized people and culture be altogether new, for instance: 'si d'avanture il naissoit aujourd'huy quelques gens *tous neufs* ni accoustumés à la subjection' (should a *new* people be born now, free from the experience of subjection).[33] These cannibals also unsettle the discourse of 'pure origin' with which the savage was associated, asking the reader to reflect on the meaning of the desire for such a possibility. They represent both ideals and atavistic horror, and are that which usually challenges what is accepted as human rather than a version of a culture in which the difficult freedom that makes us truly human exists.

---

[31] Crouzet's magisterial work on the wars of religion and their discourse, with its compelling focus on the anxieties inherent in their violence, acknowledges the significance of the use of this vocabulary but does not connect the functions of barbarism and cannibalism in the discourse. See Crouzet, *Les Guerriers de Dieu*, vol. 2, pp. 147–83.

[32] Thanks to John O'Brien for this angle.

[33] La Boétie, *De la servitude volontaire*, p. 94 (my italics).

In their unsettling range of significances they are a different kind of experiment, as required by contemporary conditions, so intolerant that difference, even freedom of conscience, would be sacrificed to maintaining as the 'one and only' true religion that of either Roman Catholics or Reformers. To resist this, eschewing antitheses and dualism, exploration of ideals and their absence needed to be structured in terms of their intrication, not a foreclosed either/or, same/other, good/evil, ideal/dystopia.

Cannibals are significant enough to warrant a whole chapter in the *Essais*, and anthropophagic practices also feature elsewhere in the text; one instance, in particular, exemplifies the openness of Montaigne's thinking. I have already touched on his awareness of the power of custom and habituation, and the processes of identification and internalization through which they operate. For him, custom works against open-mindedness and, more perniciously, fuels the tendency to reject what falls beyond it, making the unknown or not-yet known the unthinkable. One aspect of Montaigne's questioning of prejudice is the inclusion of examples of cultural difference, one of the most dramatically challenging for readers being what other cultures do with their dead. The example of eating one's father, elaborated on twice, is an extreme instance of difference which should be understood, reframed, a challenge to the reader's open-mindedness. In the 'Apologie' he walks the reader through his argument, as if anticipating squeamish resistance:

> il n'est rien en somme si extreme qui ne se trouve receu par l'usage de quelque nation. Il est croyable qu'il y a des loix naturelles, comme il se voit és autres creatures; mais en nous elles sont perdues, cette belle raison humaine s'ingerant par tout de maistriser et commander, brouillant et confondant le visage des choses selon sa vanité et inconstance … Les subjects ont divers lustres et diverses considerations: c'est de là que s'engendre principalement la diversité d'opinions. Une nation regarde un subject par un visage, et s'arreste à celuy là; l'autre, par un autre. Il n'est rien si horrible à imaginer que de manger son pere. Les peuples qui avoyent anciennement cette coustume, la prenoyent toutesfois pour tesmoignage de pieté et de bonne affection, cerchant par là à donner à leurs progeniteurs la plus digne et honorable sepulture, logeant en eux mesmes et comme en leurs moelles les corps de leurs peres et leurs reliques, les vivifiant aucunement et regenerant par la transmutation en leur chair vive au moyen de la digestion et du nourrissement. Il est aysé à considerer quelle cruauté et abomination c'eust esté, à des hommes abreuvez et imbus de cette superstition, de jetter la despouille des parens à la corruption de la terre et nourriture des bestes et des vers. (pp. 580–1)

(In short, there is nothing so extreme that it is not accepted usage in some nation. Let us believe that there are natural laws, as are evident among other creatures, now lost to us: our fine human reason intervenes in everything, claiming mastery, taking command, muddling and confusing the face of things in accordance with its own illusions and inconsistency … We consider things in various lights and from various viewpoints, which is principally why we form such diverse opinions. One nation looks at one side of a thing, stopping there; another, at another. We can imagine nothing more horrible than eating our fathers. But for those whose custom this was in ancient times, it was a testament to their piety and true affection, an attempt to give their progenitors the most worthy and honourable sepulture; lodging in themselves, as if in their own marrow, the bodies of their fathers, their remains, giving them a form of life, regenerating them by transmuting them into their living flesh, by digesting them and being nourished by them. We can easily understand how cruel and abominable it would have been to men who were sustained by this superstition to abandon the mortal remains of their parents to the corruption of the earth, there to become food for beasts and worms.)

A similar point is made in 'De la coustume et de ne changer aisément une loy receüe', where Montaigne invokes the practice to dramatize an observation about confusing cultural difference with supposedly unnatural, therefore inadmissible practice. The reader is not asked to embrace an alien practice, but to understand its significance and allow it, while acknowledging that, therefore, her own cultural practices might seem equally repulsive and indefensible, or superstitious, to others. Montaigne's examples have both a conceptual, rhetorical function, and imaginative and affective force. The desire for knowledge (hunger or appetite for it) needs to be able to deal with (digest) such extreme, and nourishing, challenges to conceptual and psychological habit.

The cannibals most significant to my interpretation are those of 'Des cannibales' and also, figuratively, the cannibal who is Montaigne himself, in 'De l'amitié', and also in 'Sur des vers de Virgile'. Love is figured as the hunger for the other, a desire to know his innermost being and truth – his 'entrails'. In the later chapter, the desire for self-knowledge and to communicate it is figured as overwhelming hunger: so we might say, the desire to reach the other, here the reader, calls for a vocabulary which excludes neither the body nor a primitive and unsettling resonance. Hunger supplements and complicates the wish to know, be known, or put into words, identifying mind, speech and desire with embodied being, working not with the reader's cognition so much as recognition, imagination, intuition and affect.

Neither of these forms of figuration were new; on the contrary, Montaigne's choices draw on existing discursive conventions. Some of them were commonplace, such as metaphors of taste, or nourishment. Take the figuration of the text as a body (or even as an author's embodied child): the associations between reading as an aspect of the desire for knowledge, and a recognition of the embodiment of readers and writers, are traceable here. But the text is also a source of metaphorical nourishment, and the form of inspiration sparked by others' writing that we call intertextuality was called, rather, 'innutrition'. As others before me have observed, the figuration of practices of reading and writing as a form of textual cannibalism is calqued on the nourishing body.[34] Perhaps the most familiar French occurrence for modern readers is in Du Bellay's treatise on

---

[34] For instance, Cave, *The Cornucopian Text* (Oxford, 1979), ch. 2 passim.

the vernacular, at a time when its credentials rather than Latin as the language of French culture, law and learning still needed to be established.

> Si les Romains (dira quelqu'un) n'ont vaqué à ce labour de Traduction, par quelz moyens donques ont ilz peu ainsi enrichir leur langue, voyre jusques à l'esgaller quasi à la Grecque? Immitant les meilleurs Aucteurs Grecz, se transformant en eux, les devorant, et après les avoir bien digerez, les convertissant en sang et nourriture, se proposant chacun selon son Naturel, et l'Argument qu'il vouloit elire, le meilleur Aucteur, dont ilz observoint diligemment toutes les plus rares, et exquises vertuz, et icelles comme Grephes ... entoint, et apliquoint à leur langue.[35]

> (Someone will ask, if the Romans had not paid serious attention to the work of translation, how else could they have so enriched their language that it came to equal Greek? Imitating the best Greek authors, transforming themselves into them, devouring them and then, having digested them well, converting them into flesh and blood, each would choose the best author for his own natural talents and the themes he wanted to promote, would carefully note that author's most valuable and exquisite qualities and strengths and, using them like grafts ... would transplant them into his own language.)

This figuration was readily accepted and used by readers, although they wrangled with other aspects of Du Bellay's text; this suggests how acculturated it had become, and perhaps, how abstracted it was from its origins in material 'reality'.[36] By the end of the sentence in which the metaphors of devouring and digestion occur, they have already metamorphosed into the analogy of a graft: good husbandry, increased yield and quality, nature improved by human skill, rather than primitive violence, which also suggests how dislocated the figuration was, how exclusively 'figurative'. But neither figure here really illuminates the complexities of the process of reading and how it informs one's subsequent writing or, we might say, relationship with one's own language, or, in Montaigne's case, the relationship with himself and the self-understanding that emerges through writing.

That we unreflectively go on using the metaphors of 'devouring' or 'gobbling' a book reminds us that the edible text – still – has intuitive resonance and purchase, more than the metaphor of grafting. That words and what they convey 'nourish' us seems an unproblematic proposition: even though, in a sense, they do not. Also unproblematic, although a more dilute figure, is the textual body – as in the 'body' of someone's creative work. The figuration of reading and writing as devouring and digesting the body captures the aggressivity of the process by which anything other becomes one's own and the anxiety involved in processes which trouble a sense of separate or distinct identity: trouble, by

---

[35] Du Bellay, *La Deffence et illustration de la langue françoyse* (Paris, 1948), pp. 42–3.
[36] The digestion metaphor pre-exists Du Bellay. Seneca's letters to Lucilius are one of Montaigne's intertexts; see Clark, 'Seneca's Letters', pp. 254–6.

unconsciously reminding of the origins of that identity in the (identified-with) other, and the lifelong porousness of the relations between self and other. In the chapters that follow here I suggest that it is resonances such as these that play in the function of this kind of figuration in Montaigne's writing. This figuration always operates in relation to conceptualizations of the relationship between bodies, minds and emotion, and the interrelations of individuals and others. Its continuity – or attenuation – at times disguise radically different underlying models. While our neurological understanding of processes of cognition, of affective response and of interaction seems increasingly precise, these are still processes about which we lack knowledge and in which we go on failing (even despite knowledge).

We also unreflectively use the figuration of eating, appetite and nourishment in the discourses of love and desire: for instance, 'good enough to eat', 'peachy', 'consumed by desire'. If we then add, 'mother's milk', life-giving food and love, we need Bion's question: 'the milk, we may assume with a degree of conviction we cannot feel about love, is received and dealt with by the alimentary canal; what receives and deals with the love?'[37] In the lover's discourse, this figurative vocabulary is joined by that of death and dying: love kills, you're killing me, killing me softly, 'dressed to kill and look who's dying' … one could go on – and on.[38] This figuration, which at its most serious in twelfth- and thirteenth-century texts sustains a model of sacrificial love, is pervasive in sixteenth-century love lyric in France, continues throughout the seventeenth century, notably in Racine's tragedies, in which passion as a fire or flame destroys or always threatens to, and we keep encountering it, not only in torch songs such as the one just quoted, but in the most ordinary, or prosaic language. These are figures of great longevity and mobility, belonging not only to discourses of the darkest seriousness, with their original themes of the sacrifice required by desire, but also to those which are playful and light. The lover's discourse of dying for or of love is not (mis)read as meaning that everyone affected *really* died for, or of, it. This is to be able to 'tell the difference', to not make category errors; but we should also allow that sometimes, without it being pathological or perverse, love really does kill, and that while usually broken hearts mend, people really do die of them.

On the other hand, whatever their fantasies, unless they are perverse, lovers tend not literally to eat their beloved. When Montaigne writes of his hunger for his beloved friend La Boétie, he neither conveys perverse desire, nor is he anxious that his metaphor is vulnerable to this misreading. It conveys the intensity and vital necessity of the relationship, and plays its part in the reader's intuition of the nature of his loss when his friend died. However, his vocabulary is both potent and risky. For in France, at the time of writing, when interpretation of the Eucharistic ingestion of divine flesh and blood was so prevailing a

---

[37] Bion, *Learning from Experience* (London, 1962), p. 33.
[38] The last is from Bryan Ferry, 'Dance Away'.

source of deadly conflict, and so powerful a cause of a hate- and anxiety-fuelled invective, use of figuration even tangentially related to spiritual nourishment, such as that of the articulation of desire in terms of a longing for (emotional) nourishment, became problematic and constrained. The violence of the conflict was sustained by polemic characterizing the Roman Catholic sacrament as a cannibalistic feast, even orgy, culminating in the sacrilege of the digested sacraments ending up as discarded waste in the latrine. While some of these invectives have a certain linguistic brio, they also demonstrate the linguistic crux of the conflict: if the theory of transubstantiation is rejected, and the relationship between the distinct elements of the Eucharistic narrative (bread/body, wine/blood) is therefore understood as being no more than one of (Augustinian) resemblance, whether analogy or metonymy, then those who persist instead in belief in transubstantiation, from bread into body, wine into blood, must be condemned: their miraculous metamorphosis exposed as error by relentless reduction in this polemic not just to alternative, restricted figuration, but to a literalized narrative.

An instance of the anxious restriction that also occurred is, arguably, the disappearance, except in attenuated form, of the long tradition of 'eaten heart' narratives which we associate particularly with the Occitan poet Guillem de Cabestanh and the romance *Le Castelain de Couci*,[39] while the vocabulary of love killing, or love requiring the sacrifice of life or of everything in life but love, continued to circulate in love lyric and also prose. The eaten heart did not return until the seventeenth century, and then, only in the very circumscribed and chaste form of Counter-Reformation exemplary narrative.[40] Although sacrifice also became a contentious theme, in the light of conflicts between Roman Catholics for whom the sacrament of the Eucharist was a sacrifice and Reformers for whom the Lord's Supper was a ritual of commemoration, it does not disappear altogether from secular writing, or writing that is secular with a spiritual trajectory.

The *Heptaméron*, a collection of stories and their discussion, by Marguerite de Navarre, who was deeply involved in earlier sixteenth-century Roman Catholic reform, and which Montaigne had read, is an interesting case in point.[41] The seventy-two stories told by the text's protagonists include some versions of earlier narratives, such as the mid-thirteenth-century romance *La Chastelaine de Vergy*; but if they revisit aspects of courtly love, they distance themselves

---

[39] On this tradition see Doueihi's fascinating but contentious study, *A Perverse History of the Human Heart* (Cambridge, Mass., 1997); on the theme as one of transgression, see Jeay, 'Consuming Passions: Variations on the Eaten Heart Theme', in Roberts (ed.), *Violence Against Women in Medieval Texts* (Gainsville, Fla., 1998), pp. 75–96; and as it touches on the theme of the gift of the self, see Allen, 'La Mélancolie du biographe', *Neophilologus* 85 (2001), pp. 25–41.

[40] See in Camus's *Spectacles d'horreur*, ed. Cremona (Rennes, 2010), 'Le Coeur mangé' (pp. 39–43).

[41] He refers to the text three times in the *Essais*: in 'Des prieres' (p. 324), 'De la cruauté' (p. 430) and 'Sur des vers de Virgile' (p. 896).

from its ethos, and redirect the narratives to suit contemporary preoccupations. A number of stories explore themes of sacrificial desire and also the relationship between love and secrecy. In earlier romance, secrecy might have been treated as a requirement of the ethics of love.[42] In the *Heptaméron*, however, it is usually severed from ethics, featuring instead as a symptom of the hypocrisies that beset relations between the genders and, rather than protecting the pure gift of love from the contamination of exchange (by putting it into linguistic circulation), it serves as an aspect of all manner of inventive dissemblances serving conscienceless and self-gratifying desire. Secrecy is suspect, required by secular honour to preserve a semblance of feminine chastity, reduced to pragmatism, or to the role of plot device (and there is no shortage of secrets being kept or broken for this purpose).

The theme of sacrificial desire also occurs in the *Heptaméron*, but as the need to sacrifice (human) desires and love God: thus if sacrifice has a place, it is identified with divine love. In stories in which love kills these are not sacrificial deaths; they may even be dismissed in the discussion that follows as waste or stupidity. Whilst aspects of the ethics of human love are explored, the text's emphasis is on that love as a chastening distraction or threat to subjects, and on the need to discover, through this or that vicissitude, the value instead of love of the divine.

In its versions of eaten heart narratives – only one story and in the course of one discussion – there remain few traces of the earlier themes of sacrificial desire. The story presents a diluted displacement, and in the anecdote in a discussion, a heart is eaten and enjoyed knowingly, within a narrative of revenge minus love; the passion that fuels it is tribal hatred (Guelphs versus Ghibellines), and the actions of the avenger so exceed the rather strict logic of the eaten heart tradition as to seem unhinged rather than rooted in any tradition. Here brutalized excess combines with a lack of compelling narrative logic to indicate so strong a resistance to the tradition as to seem to want to destroy it by grossing it and the listener out. From fascination to repulsion.[43]

The thirty-second story, a narrative of revenge and redemption, retains a stronger narrative logic but dilutes the tradition. An outraged nobleman kills his wife's lover, places his skeleton in her wardrobe for her to contemplate daily, and has a vessel made of his skull from which she must drink nightly. The guest to whom the husband recounts the events is so moved by the silent, shaven-headed wife's penitential bearing that he urges the husband to reconsider; after all, he still needs an heir. The husband finally relents, pardons his wife, and the story ends with the words: 'et en eut depuis beaucoup de beaulz enfans' (and has since had many fine children) (p. 245). Elements of the eaten heart tradition are traceable here: agonizing, protracted, visual punishment replaces unwitting cannibalistic incorporation of the dead beloved, and drinking knowingly from

---

[42] See Gaunt, *Love and Death in Medieval French and Occitan Courtly Literature* (Oxford, 2006), ch. 3.

[43] See Marguerite de Navarre, *L'Heptaméron*, ed. François (Paris, 1967), pp. 331–2.

his skull displaces unknowingly eating the heart. Gory enough, still a narrative of transgressive passion and revenge. But diverted, diluted: where the original narratives allowed the surviving woman to remain true to her love and her (eaten) beloved, allowing her to kill herself declaring him her heart's desire – the best thing she had ever eaten – here, she lives on, fulfilling her husband's desire, to secure his property for the future. The brief discussion is preoccupied with sin, emphasizing the weakness of women, debating the proportionality of the punishment, and the question of feminine shame and dishonour. One of the female participants invokes Mary Magdalene.

On the one hand, excess; on the other, redirection or turning away; otherwise, exclusion. The articulation of desire and sacrifice via such narrative motifs and such figuration seems to have become too problematic for use by sixteenth-century writers acutely aware of the linguistic conflicts of the Eucharistic debates and also of the dangers of misinterpretation and misappropriation. For most, it no longer offered a safe means of exploring troubling desires and ideas. However, as we shall now see, in Montaigne's writing figurative hunger and other related vocabulary complexify the representation of epistemological, psychological and affective desires, and, along with other corporeal metaphors, are a particularly effective means of articulating unsettling ideas, as well as supporting suspension of judgement.

Each chapter here explores different aspects of Montaigne's desire for knowledge, self-knowledge and to make himself known, and also, what he resisted knowing, and the anxieties shaping that resistance. Throughout what follows, the structural significance of forms of figuration, ranging from expansive metaphors to figures so dislocating as to have anamorphic effects, remains constant, as does a focus on what is psychically difficult to bear and understand: ambivalence, anxiety, pain and loss, as well as uncertainty. Figuration's work in the text is also to make these states tolerable, and even to transform them into potentially creative or enjoyable thinking, as my first example, the cannibal, will demonstrate.

2

'Je ne vois le tout de rien': The Cannibal and the Place of Knowledge

Rouen 1562

Trois d'entre eux, ignorans combien coutera un jour à leur repos et à leur bon heur la connoissance des corruptions de deçà, et que de ce commerce naistra leur ruyne, comme je presuppose qu'elle soit desjà avancée, bien miserables de s'estre laissez piper au desir de la nouvelleté, et avoir quitté la douceur de leur ciel pour venir voir le nostre, furent à Rouan, du temps que le feu Roy Charles neufiesme y estoit. Le Roy parla à eux long temps; on leur fit voir nostre façon, nostre pompe, la forme d'une belle ville. Apres cela quelqu'un en demanda leur advis, et voulut sçavoir d'eux ce qu'ils y avoient trouvé de plus admirable: ils respondirent trois choses, d'où j'ay perdu la troisiesme, et en suis bien marry; mais j'en ay encore deux en memoire. Ils dirent qu'ils trouvoient en premier lieu fort estrange que tant de grands hommes, portans barbe, forts et armez, qui estoient autour du Roy (il est vray-semblable que ils parloient des Suisses de sa garde), se soubsmissent à obeyr à un enfant, et qu'on ne choisissoit plus tost quelqu'un d'entr'eux pour commander; secondement (ils ont une façon de leur langage telle, qu'ils nomment les hommes moitié les uns des autres) qu'ils avoyent aperçeu qu'il y avoit parmy nous des hommes pleins et gorgez de toutes sortes de commoditez, et que leurs moitiez estoient mendians à leurs portes, décharnez de faim et de pauvreté; et trouvoient estrange comme ces moitiez icy necessiteuses pouvoient souffrir une telle injustice, qu'ils ne prinsent les autres à la gorge, ou missent le feu à leurs maisons. Je parlay à l'un d'eux fort long temps; mais j'avois un truchement qui me suyvoit si mal, et qui estoit si empesché à recevoir mes imaginations par sa bestise, que je n'en peus tirer guiere de plaisir. (pp. 213–14)

(Three of them, unaware how much their knowledge of the corruptions on this side of the ocean will cost their tranquillity and happiness, even that their exchanges with us will cause their ruin, which is already by now well advanced, I suppose – how wretched to have let themselves be tricked by the desire for novelty and to have left their gentle land to come to see ours – three of them were in Rouen during the late King Charles IX's visit. The king spoke to them for a long time; they were shown our ways, our ceremonies, what makes a fine city. Someone asked them what they thought, and wanted to know what they had found most wondrous. They said three things, the third of which I have forgotten, much to my dismay; but I do still remember two. Firstly they said that they found it very strange that so many grown men, bearded, strong and armed, grouped around the king (they were probably talking about his Swiss guard), should submit to the orders of a child rather than choosing one of their own to command them. Secondly (in their language it is their habit to call men each other's halves), that they had noticed that among us there were men who had their fill and more of all kinds of good things, and that their other halves were beggars at their doors, so poor and hungry that they were skin and bone. They found it strange that these halves who were so in need tolerated such an injustice and did not take the others by the throat or set fire to their houses. I spoke with one of them for a very long time, but my interpreter followed me so poorly, and was so incompetent that he could not grasp my ideas, so I did not enjoy it much.)

Late in 1562 three aboriginal Brazilians who were visiting Rouen were invited to speak about what most struck them in their experience of France. They focused on three things, but Montaigne, who was present along with the king, Charles IX, and court, could apparently only remember two of them.[1] He had some further conversation with them, but his interpreter's incompetence frustrated the exchange.

Now to flesh out this rather spare account. The encounter, cited here, is represented towards the end of 'Des cannibales'. In March that year over three decades of civil and religious wars in France began, with the massacre of Huguenot worshippers at Vassy. Rouen was one of the first cities to come under Huguenot control, in April, and was only restored to Roman Catholic control in October after weeks of siege.[2] The child king's presence in the city in November was a piece of political theatre dramatizing the return to legitimate governance, as underscored by the king's participation in the All Saints' Day Mass, reaffirming the divine sanction of the monarchy.[3] His courtiers invited the Brazilian – cannibal – visitors to comment on what they found most wondrous in France; they chose to comment on power structures, inequity and injustice they had witnessed: firstly, that a child was in command of men; secondly, the injustice of the chasm between the rich and the abjectly poor. Montaigne recorded neither their last comment nor the king's reaction. What has interested many readers of this chapter is Montaigne's use of the perspective of the cannibal 'other' to reflect on his own culture.[4] There has been some focus on the Rouen encounter,

[1] On reasons for his presence there, see Hoffmann, *Montaigne's Career* (Oxford, 1998), ch. 6.

[2] Reformers took control of the city on 15 April 1562; Roman Catholics recovered control after a month's siege, in October. For the history of Rouen during the civil and religious wars, see Benedict, *Rouen During the Wars of Religion* (Cambridge, 1981).

[3] On this dimension of the visit, see Hoffmann, 'Anatomy of the Mass: Montaigne's "Cannibals"', *PMLA* 117/2 (March 2002), pp. 207–21.

[4] For examples of the range of studies see: Duval, 'Lessons of the New World', in *Montaigne: Essays in Reading*, Yale French Studies 64 (1983), pp. 95–112, Ginzburg, 'Montaigne, i cannibali e le grotte', in *Il Filo e le trace* (Milan, 2006), pp. 52–77, Pot, *L'Inquiétante Etrangeté* (Paris, 1993), and Tournon, *Montaigne: la glose et l'essai* (Lyon, 1983).

gap (3rd answer)   *self-other destabilized*

not least on the cannibal as a means to uttering unpalatable 'truths' about the state of things in civilized France, but the passage has been rather neglected.[5]

The fuller implications of what is missing in Montaigne's representation, beyond his seeming to fail to remember the cannibals' third insight, have also been overlooked. The reading I shall develop here suggests that what is missing is as significant an aspect of Montaigne's work with this symbolic other, the cannibal, as the critique of France that his presence enables. It is part of the destabilization of the conventional self-other structure which his chapter allows, and which becomes most significant in this closing phase of his inquiry into who and what the cannibals are for us.

Our attention is drawn to there being something missing, and as it comes last, as well-trained readers we perhaps anticipate that it would be most significant. The absence draws the reader's attention, curiosity and speculation, as well as triggering and testing habitual interpretative responses to both what is represented and what makes its presence felt – through absence. But there are three other missing elements also, less insistent but still important, which are both distinct and convergent. Namely, explicit contextualization of the presence in Rouen of the king, the cannibals and Montaigne; aspects of the temporality of what is represented; and Montaigne's enjoyment.

more gap

This encounter with cannibals is a switchpoint in Montaigne's representation, for it locates in a precise place and time what had hitherto been a primarily symbolic figure. Until this point they – Tamoio or Tupinamba – are nameless and unlocatable, described, rather, as inhabiting an 'autre monde' (other world), a 'païs infini' (boundless country) (p. 203). This historicization of the cannibal tests the functions of the figure; but the representation of a historical event is, equally, an exploration of the temporality of understanding and also of the – creative – effects of the frustration of the desire for full knowledge.

There remains much to understand about the relation between the time and place of the encounter and the rest of Montaigne's chapter. Lestringant's exploration of the event is fascinating, but the temporality of the representation is not his focus.[6] Hoffmann has also focused on the event; however, where he discerns in the chapter 'an arc from myth to eyewitness' of 'undeniable beauty', I find a more complex structure, with the tension not of an arc but of coexisting connections and dislocations across different planes.[7] The displacement of the cannibals to a specific, contingent place and time (Rouen 1562) with great economy complicates the array of potential meanings of the cannibal other, who initially, stripped of the specific historical details of other representations such as Thevet's and Léry's, with which Montaigne was familiar, had shared some of the symbolic significance (Hoffmann's 'myth') of the savage, as a locus

---

[5]   To name but one study, Hoffmann, 'Anatomy of the Mass'.

[6]   Rouen acts as the threshold to Lestringant's *Le Cannibale* (Paris, 1994), the site of others' encounters with the 'savage' as well as Montaigne's.

[7]   See Hoffmann, 'Anatomy of the Mass', p. 207.

ethnographical fantasy of immed. pres.

of pure or full truth.[8] Thus this displacement asks the reader to reflect on the function for her of supposedly universally significant symbols – a matter of urgent importance at the time of writing. Moreover, it unsettles what Derrida identifies as a feature of ethnographical writing: 'une téléologie et une eschatologie; rêve d'une présence pleine et immédiate fermant l'histoire, transparance et indivision d'une parousie, suppression de la contradiction et de la différence' (a teleology and an eschatology; the dream of a full and immediate presence closing history, the transparence and indivision of a parousia, the suppression of contradiction and difference).[9] Historicized, the erstwhile symbolic cannibal is a means of problematizing the reader's desire for the full knowledge associated both with supposed symbolic universalism and with the turning to a supposed site of origins or pure truth. Here we shall be left to find a way to enjoy more partial and contingent understanding.

There was no origin, singular, of the outbreak of war in 1562: instead, a long prehistory and several debated catalysts. Whilst Montaigne's representation seems to isolate the Rouen encounter from its political and historical origins and causes, the problematic of origins is written through it. *Symbolically*, like the savage, the cannibal already could function as a representation of a point of natural origin ('une nayfveté si pure et simple ... si peu d'artifice et de soudeure humaine' (a naturalness so pure and simple ... so little artifice and human solder) (p. 206)), from which civilization or culture had grown (away), or of a desire for lost origins; and Montaigne draws on this earlier in his chapter.[10] There, textual versions already displaced the 'original', and here, the question of origins returns, problematized. For Montaigne's representation rested on a cluster of hybrid textual sources, ranging from Herodotus to a nameless contemporary who had travelled to Brazil with Villegaignon and seen its indigenous society with his own eyes: sources ranging so far and vaguely over time and place that the cannibal seems an ahistorical other, with symbolic significance largely freed from explicit historical, geographical or cultural determinants. The Rouen encounter is in tension with this. But already, even Montaigne's 'faithful' eyewitness was no guarantee of a true or pure account, for his experience was

[8]   Many thanks to Neil Kenny for this observation about the absence of detail. The accounts in question are Thevet, *Les Singularités de la France antarctique* (Paris, 1982), and Léry, *Histoire d'un voyage faict en la terre du Bresil*, ed. Lestringant (Paris, 1994).

[9]   Derrida, *De la grammatologie* (Paris, 1967), p. 168; also cited in Lestringant, *Le Cannibale*, p. 297.

[10]   For an instance of the preoccupation with the cannibals as a form of origin, and thus with the question of their origins, see Léry, *Histoire d'un voyage*, p. 419. In his view, they are the descendants of Ham. In the *Essais*, however, it might be more pertinent to note the contrast between the atemporal cannibals and other (New World) others, the Aztecs and Incas. In 'Des coches' ('On coaches') they are explicitly identified with 'un monde enfant' (p. 909), the origins of human historical chronology. In some psychoanalytic discussions of the formation of the individual subject the equivalent is 'cannibalism' as originary oral desire. For this kind of reading, see 'Destins du cannibalisme', special number of the *Nouvelle Revue de Psychanalyse* 6 (1972), notably Green, 'Cannibalisme: réalité ou fantasme agi?', pp. 27–52.

framed by the desires driving Villegaignon's expedition to Brazil in the 1550s: to found a French colony, free from religious conflict, and by its failure: with the return of religious conflicts, the colony's end.

On the page, the textual versions (both classical and contemporary, both purportedly authentic and unquestionably not) of the cannibals who materialize in Rouen precede them; and historically, this is not the first recorded appearance of Brazilian 'savages' in the city. There had been an earlier encounter in Rouen between the King of France, then Henri II, Charles's father, and the savage other. This 1550 encounter is particularly relevant because: 'to obviate the scarcity of real savages available, sailors of various South American expeditions had been used to impersonate them, i.e. to dress, behave and speak in a manner thought to befit savages'.[11] So the original historical presence in Rouen was already fraudulent, and this historical counterfeit has the potential to perturb the symbolic function of the cannibal as a representation of origin, for apparently, here, a substitute for the original would do.[12]

Montaigne's encounter is followed by comments on what is lost in translation and then by the famous ironic last words of the chapter, which further unsettle the accumulated readings of the significance of encounters with cannibals, as well as throwing open even more widely the question of the function of the other for the construction of the self. 'Tout cela ne va pas trop mal: mais quoy, ils ne portent point de haut de chausses' (that's all well and good: but so what? They don't wear breeches) (p. 214). I shall return to the effects of these last words in the final section of my analysis; for now, let's note that the unsettling shifts, plural, of perspective at the end of Montaigne's reflections on, and via, cannibals, which had been built upon a perspectival structure, destabilize the structure and reinforce the critique of the fixed and inequitable uses of the 'barbaric' other by the self, as already thematized: namely, to other the other, seen only as alien and lesser; that which is not like oneself. So, far from a source of truth, the other is typically used to support self-deception. From start – with its choice of cannibals for its 'ideal' other – to finish, the chapter is unsettling and on the side of ambiguities and ambivalence; if it looked at the outset as if

---

[11] 'Il y en avoit bien cinquante naturelz souvages, freschement aportez du pays ... le surplus de la compagnie, ayant frequenté le pays, parloit autant bien le langage, et exprimoit si nayvement les gestes et façons de faire des sauvages, comme silz fussent natifz du mesmes pays' (there were fifty or more real savages, who had just arrived from their country ... the remainder of the group had been there and spoke the language and reproduced the savages' gestures and ways as well as if they had been natives themselves). From *C'est la deduction du sumptueux ordre plaisantz spectacles et magnifiques theatres dresses*, in McGowan (ed.), *L'Entrée de Henri II à Rouen 1550* (Amsterdam, 1970), n.p. See Blanchard, 'Of Cannibalism and Autobiography', *MLN* 93 (1978), pp. 654–76 (p. 670), drawing on Chinard, *L'Exotisme américain dans la littérature française au XVIème siècle* (Paris, 1911), p. 106. Lestringant mentions the event in 1550 (*Le Cannibale*, p. 25) but does not comment on the authenticity of the savages; he refers the reader to Massa, 'Le Monde luso-brésilien dans la joyeuse entrée de Rouen', in *Les Fêtes de la Renaissance*, vol. 3 (Paris, 1975), pp. 105–16.

[12] As was also the case with the identification of Virgil's Francus as the originator of the Franks.

its explorations of the other might produce a clearer sense of the identity of the self, the last words, as we shall see, veer away from this, and place the emphasis elsewhere.

Even so apparently defined a signifier as a specific time, 'du temps que le feu Roy ... y estoit' (during the late king's visit) (p. 213) may prove a decoy; it draws our attention while distracting us from what it is not: not a date, not the time of writing (which cannot be clearly determined). It is perhaps as unlocatable as the deictic position of the earlier parts of the chapter, and also unlocatable in relation to the when and where of Montaigne's becoming curious about existent and/or figurative cannibals and their value in his exploration of questions important to him. Nor does the date as given here reveal its fuller significance for Montaigne as a thinker and writer.[13]

Montaigne's contemporaries would probably have recognized the event and recalled its timing; they also would have associated the year with an important intellectual event: the first publication of the Latin translation of Sextus Empiricus's *Hypotyposes* (*Outlines of Pyrrhonism*) by Henri Estienne (a Huguenot); that is, one of the texts which made Pyrrhonist sceptical thought available to those readers in France interested in this kind of thinking – notably Montaigne.[14] Although there had already been interest earlier in sixteenth-century France in Academic scepticism, as in Cicero's *Academica*,[15] the publication of the translation of the *Hypotyposes* was crucial to the development of Pyrrhonist scepticism. Coincidence? Perhaps, but we may well find evidence of a sceptical turn in Montaigne's reflections on cannibals; for now, let us reserve judgement – as his representation seems to require. For it emphasizes the contingent, unfolding meaning of past events as reinscribed in the present, and with this, reflections on the temporality of our understanding. The encounter is preceded by proleptic reflections on what will have happened to the cannibals between 1562 and the time of writing, signalling this. The temporal perspective initially takes the form of future tenses, 'coutera' (will cost) 'naistra' (will cause), followed by a hypothetical subjunctive future perfect tense, 'comme je presuppose qu'elle soit desjà avancée' (which will already by now be well advanced, I suppose): that which will doubtless have happened. The play between Montaigne's knowledge (now also the reader's) and the cannibals' lack of it informs our interpretation, and insists on the importance of the deferred meaning of what is represented.

The responsibility of the interpreter and the scope of interpretation are themes written through the representation. Montaigne's own interpreter failed him,

---

[13] An interesting point of contrast which illustrates the complexity of the use of this date here is Sebastian Castellio's *Conseil à la France désolée*. It was published in 1562, and treats two of the year's events – the January Edict of Toleration and the Vassy Massacre – as two of the three key causes for the war. So, 1562 is the time of both its events and its writing. Written and published so immediately, its analysis of both causes and remedies are equally that of its moment.

[14] The key discussion of the significance of the *Hypotyposes* for my reading of the *Essais* is in Cave, *Pré-histoires*, ch. 1, pp. 23–50.

[15] See Schmitt, *Cicero Scepticus* (The Hague, 1972).

depriving him of pleasure; so the reader seems called upon to be a better interpreter of what is both present and absent, and to translate a frustrated encounter
into a more potentially meaningful one – without falling into the trap of seeking
full meaning. What becomes most generative in Montaigne's account, along
with what is missing, are the ways in which uncertainties and ambiguities play
through it, along with its unsettling of its two dominant structuring forces. On
the one hand, in terms of rhetorical patterning, the triplet: three cannibals/visi-
tors, the courtiers' three paeans to France, three comments – but only two of the
three comments travel the distance. And on the other, the binary: crude opposition, 'us' and 'them'. This section of the chapter on cannibals prolongs and
intensifies the work of the chapter as a whole, which is to disturb the illusion
that such opposition holds, to expose its logic in all its vulnerability and ideological coercion, and to insist on the unbridgeable difference between what might
be possible were the world new and all that is possible in a world deformed by
existing tradition.

> Et certes toutes ces descriptions de police, feintes par art, se trouvent ridicules
> et ineptes à mettre en practique … Telle peinture de police seroit de mise en
> un nouveau monde, mais nous prenons les hommes obligez desjà et formez
> à certaines coustumes … Par quelque moyen que nous ayons loy de les re-
> dresser et renger de nouveau, nous ne pouvons guiere les tordre de leur ply
> accoustumé que nous ne rompons tout. (p. 957)

> (certainly all these descriptions of polities are artifices which would be ridicu-
> lous and inept in practice … A polity such as this might work in a new world,
> but we take men who are already duty-bound and formed by certain customs
> … Whatever means we have the right to use to reform and re-establish them,
> we can't forcibly straighten out their acquired kinks without breaking every-
> thing.)

Questions of knowledge and ignorance, blindness and insight, the desire for
meaning and the importance of meaning's deferral, together with the responsibilities of the interpreter, which are presented more abstractly in other chapters, are given a specific urgency here. Montaigne's chapter uses the historical
encounter as a way of staging questions of the ethics and politics of interpretation and address, of the possible range of relations with the other, whether for
instance cannibal, or religious dissenter.[16] The cannibals' observations resonate
uncannily with themes inescapably associated with La Boétie's *De la servitude
volontaire* – who, let's not forget, Montaigne represents himself in 'De l'amitié'
as hungering for. Just one year later, La Boétie died. In the years between 1562
and the time of writing (thought to be some seventeen years later) private loss

---

[16] For analysis of issues of ethical responsibilities, violence and the limits of knowledge
and self-knowledge which resonates with the questions investigated by Montaigne and folds
together philosophical, ethical, political and psychoanalytical perspectives see Butler, *Giving
an Account of Oneself* (New York, 2005).

and trauma joined public traumas. Montaigne failed – albeit for sound reasons – to keep his promise to his beloved friend, to publish his work.[17] By the time of writing the view ascribed to the cannibal in 1562 will have become unutterable except in the form of this (possibly fictitious) anticipation, presented as if it did not yet mean what it would go on to mean; and yet for readers, after 1579, who cannot unknow what they already know, it means all that and more, for it invites reflection simultaneously on what might have been different had the consequences been anticipated earlier and on why they had not been thinkable.

In the intervening years, between event and representation, Charles IX had died, two years after another massacre, that of St Bartholomew's Day in 1572, which resulted, according to one Huguenot contemporary, in 100,000 deaths. Whether or not he, as king, was directly responsible for it remains perhaps unknowable, but at the time, his association with it seemed irrefutable.[18] The massacre prompted others, such as that of Huguenots in Rouen a month later, mostly of have-nots: 'envyron de trois a quatre cens huguenotz ... pauvres et de bas estage les autres se sauverent par fuittes par argent et par amys' (between three and four hundred poor, low-born Huguenots, the others saved by flight, by paying for their freedom, or by friends' protection).[19] Thus the child of 1562, the fitness and injustice of whose rule is questioned by the cannibals, for readers in 1579 or later already had a history of association with polarisations and injustices so intractable as to have led to decades of war as well as outbursts of traumatic collective violence.

The aboriginal Brazilians in Rouen may or may not have been cannibals. But because Montaigne's account is placed at the end of his chapter on (unidentified) cannibals, and they are identified as 'trois d'entre eux' (three of them) (p. 213) they are inseparable from the symbolic significance of the cannibal. And by their presence in France they also figure the cannibal other who is in our midst, which potentially disturbs the notion of coherent self-sameness.[20] Earlier, while

---

[17] Namely, to forestall its being drawn on by Huguenots arguing the case for tyrannicide. See the next chapter for further discussion.

[18] Roman Catholics set the toll much lower, unsurprisingly; historians still debate the number of dead. An accurate count is not what mattered at the time; what mattered, rather, was that it represented for many Huguenots and also for those among the more moderate Roman Catholics, incalculable loss and 'wrong'. On the massacres, see Diefendorf, *Beneath the Cross* (Oxford, 1991), Crouzet, *La Nuit de la Saint-Barthélemy* (Paris, 1994), Kingdon, *Myths about the St. Bartholomew's Day Massacres 1572–76* (Cambridge, Mass., 1988), Arlette, *La Saint-Barthélemy* (Paris, 2007), and Benedict, 'The Saint Bartholomew's Massacres in the Provinces', *The Historical Journal* 21 (1978), pp. 205–25.

[19] Handwritten marginalia on a copy of a *Brief Discours sur la mort de la Royne de Navarre*, cited in Weiss, 'Un témoin de la Saint-Barthélemy', *Bulletin de la Société de l'Histoire du Protestantisme Français* (1901), pp. 445–8 (p. 445).

[20] This may be read as an instance of the combining of the three functions or 'levels' ascribed by Todorov in 'L'Etre et l'autre: Montaigne', *Montaigne: Essays in Reading*, *Yale French Studies* 64 (1983), pp. 113–44, to representations of the relationship between self and other: '1. the relation between *us* and others: the manner in which a community perceives those who do not belong to it; 2. the relation between *I* and the other (*autrui*):

his narrative is preoccupied with cannibal culture, Montaigne makes explicit the already implicit function of this other people: by displacing his perspective, locating it in a literal and symbolic elsewhere, he could take his critical distance from events at home. Now the strategy is reversed: the cannibal has left home and become the displaced commentator on what to him was other, as if to underline the function of displacement and what it alone allows us to see, while simultaneously bringing the questions, who and where the 'cannibal' is, closer to home.

All these meanings are possible for Montaigne's cannibals. Whilst traditionally the cannibal tended to share the savage's positive associations with uncorrupted natural origins, he was never as idealizable, and increasingly was thought of as inhabiting the extreme edge of what is culturally accepted as (still) human, if not rejected outright. Indeed, in sixteenth-century France, the cannibal other had become the site of that which is unassimilable and must therefore be excluded or destroyed.[21]

So this plurality of meaning is a mark of a certain absence of anxiety in Montaigne's thinking about the extraordinary array of themes he gathers via this figure: unlike those contemporaries who anathematized the cannibal, he produces different positions, in which the unassimilability of the other is potentially (although not wholly) respected and non-traumatic. This may possibly be read as an example of the achieved and tranquil suspension of judgement of a sceptical thinker whose thought is hospitable to ideas that others rule out; but this interpretation still needs to be tested.

Absolute difference?

Before exploring further the distinctive significance or potential for Montaigne of the cannibal, it is worth gathering together the cultural meanings of this extreme figure: meanings which Montaigne inherited and which his chapter went on to shape.

The literature on the cannibal and anthropophagy, in anthropology, history, cultural studies, to a lesser extent psychoanalysis, not to mention 'horror' stories, is vast, and their significance for inhabitants of the civilized West, still debated.[22] Here I shall include only the issues most relevant to Montaigne's

---

the very existence of beings other than myself; and 3. the other *in* the self: multiplicity and heterogeneity internal to the subject' (p. 113). For refinement of his account of the third 'level', see Kristeva, *Etrangers à nous-mêmes* (Paris, 1988). Instances of the third 'level' abound in the *Essais*: for example, comments on our 'variation et contradiction' (variations and contradictions) (p. 335), 'diversité et division infinie' (diversity and infinite division) (p. 563) and our 'rapiessement et bigarrure' (patchwork and motley) (p. 675).

    21 See Blanchard, 'Of Cannibalism', p. 663.

    22 For those interested in anthropological discourse it makes sense to begin with Arens, *The Man-Eating Myth* (New York, 1979) and follow the debates which it accelerated. An excellent, concise summary of issues in a range of discourses is to be found in Hulme's

interests, and particularly the symbolic functions, which are more relevant here than the cannibalism associated with famine or starvation due to siege.[23]

For some, historically, cannibalism is associated with the theme of vengeance; for others, the cannibal is a figure of horror and absolute difference, a key marker for 'us' of all that 'we' – humans – are not. This version represents what is beyond our knowledge or our categories of understanding, although whether this is because our recoil from horror is such as to disable our capacity to think about the phenomenon or because it objectively challenges available conceptualizations is not always clear in the texts. In *Marvellous Possessions* Greenblatt conveys the 'horror' version of cannibalism: 'a native practice that does not fall in the category of familiar European vices, a practice that is not part of the European repertory of moral disasters such as extreme cruelty or lust or blasphemy ... an unmitigated horror marking an absolute difference'.[24]

This 'absolute' difference seems to be what Blanchard, with reference to the original Greeks' *barbaron* (barbarian), calls 'difference outside the context of analogy' (p. 663), that is, not thinkable in terms of likeness or unlikeness, the customary structures and logic with which meanings were made. To be more precise: this figurative 'cannibal' is a symbolization of what we dread knowing, or, more paradoxically, being unable to know, as we cling to our capacity to 'make sense'; or of what is excessive in our 'civilized' selves. He may also be a figure of what we dread being like, or wanting to be like – another kind of paradoxical, unwanted knowledge. These more paradoxical dimensions are even more marked if the cannibal is a site of ambivalence, of both horror and fascinated recognition.[25] The pre-modern literary tradition of the 'eaten heart', eroticized anthropophagy, is worth noting, as obliquely significant for Montaigne's writing. This is a dimension curiously marginalized by studies to date,[26] and which I touched on earlier as an indication of the culturally and psychically interconnected nature of different instances of figuration relating to appetite, different forms of desire, and both literal and figurative incorporation.

'Introduction' to *Cannibalism and the Colonial World*, eds Barker, Hulme and Iversen (Cambridge, 1998), 'The cannibal scene' (pp. 1–38); and for a similarly punctual and useful summary in psychoanalytic literature, see 'Destins du cannibalisme', special number of the *Nouvelle Revue de Psychanalyse* 6 (1972). For further literary and cultural analysis of cannibalism as metaphor, see, for instance, Kilgour, *From Communion to Cannibalism* (Princeton, 1990), and Doueihi, *A Perverse History of the Human Heart*.

[23] See, for instance, Léry, *Histoire memorable de la ville de Sancerre* (Fribourg, 1975).

[24] Greenblatt, *Marvellous Possessions* (Oxford, 1991), pp. 131–2.

[25] In this respect, the cannibal could be called a phobic object: for interesting discussion of such 'points of alienation and identification, scenes of fear and desire' of which he suggests the cannibal is one, see Bhabha, 'The Other Question', in *The Location of Culture* (London, 1994), pp. 94–120 (p. 104).

[26] Although there is a chapter related to this literary tradition in *Le Cannibale*, Lestringant does not connect the themes of this tradition, nor their mutations in earlier sixteenth-century French writing, with either the function of the cannibal or the powerful network of related figuration in writing such as Montaigne's. In *Une Sainte Horreur*, such literary cannibalistic 'vengeance amoureuse' (amorous vengeance) is only accorded a footnote (p. 62, n. 1).

Cbl = 0 (in fill)

The term that recurs across many investigations into the cannibal is the
'other'. As with so many other others, there comes recognition that the other
represents something disavowed, alarming, repellent … in ourselves. In continuing debates over the significance of the other, antinomies are frequent, as are
attempts to unsettle them, to argue that supposed 'absolute difference' rests on
prior, denied, 'kinship' (both literal and figurative) or likeness, or a resonance of
recognition. For instance, in the sixteenth century, Reformers attacked Roman
Catholic theophagy as being a cannibal feast, a perception which travelled with
Léry to Brazil where he lived among cannibals and folded his disgust for the
Eucharist into what he thought he recognized in the cannibals' rituals. Or taking
a rather banal psychoanalytic turn, we recognize that disgust may partner desire,
or that cannibal devouring confronts us with our own (dissembled) rapacious-
ness.

Such different instances and sites sit clearly with the issues explored by
Montaigne. So too do two other issues which seem to pull in different directions,
but do converge. Firstly, the recourse to the savage other's world, idealized as a
lost origin in nature, appears quite often in the early modern period, conveying,
in a turbulent time, what may be interpreted as a sense of the loss of social
wholeness. Whilst this replaces one myth with another, what matters is that it
was symptomatic of cultural dislocation and uncertainties, of profound anxieties, yet still seemed to hold out for the possibility of wholeness. Secondly, set
against this, the cannibal functions as an extreme figure, a site of and for sceptical thinking, challenging the limits of understanding and possibility, inviting
suspension of judgement. The two stances converge because both are responses
to problems of knowledge, to loss and uncertainty; what is interesting in Montaigne's chapter, as we shall see, is that they can coexist.

'Escrire chez moy, en pays sauvage'

The already idealizable savage could have served the purposes of Montaigne's
argument very well. So why did he prefer the more ambiguous cannibal to the
'savage' or 'barbarian' who turned out to be even less so than Montaigne's
fellow Frenchmen? 'Nous les pouvons donq bien appeler barbares, eu esgard
aux regles de la raison, mais non pas eu esgard à nous, qui les surpassons en
toute sorte de barbarie' (we may well call them barbarians, in terms of the rules
of reason, but not in terms of ourselves: we surpass them in every kind of barbarity) (p. 210). Why choose to use a term not yet much used and work with
this extreme, risking resistance, rejection and the potentially distracting drama
of all its 'anthropological' details? The savage would have been much simpler
to work with.

Home, 'chez moy', was already 'sauvage'. What was savage at home, where
Montaigne wrote, is somewhat simpler than the savagery which is so closely
associated with what is barbaric in 'Des cannibales'; there, Montaigne dwelled on

hospitability (in time of civil war)

how overdetermined and misleading the usage of both adjectives had become.[27] Here, along with the adjective's positive connotation of wild nature and its pure fruitfulness,[28] it ironically echoes Aristotle's identification of the barbarian with those who live on the edge of community, as if self-sufficient.[29] For Montaigne was not barbaric, nor, he was aware, was his self-sufficiency anything other than an illusion or an intermittent possibility. But it reflects the inhospitability ('ou personne ne m'ayde ny me releve' (where no one helps or corrects me) (p. 875)) of the place in which he wanted to write. However, Montaigne the thinker and gentleman, 'moy qui suis si hospitalier' (I who am so hospitable) (p. 1048), valued being hospitable; moreover, 'Des cannibales' is a good instance of how hospitable his thinking was to what was other. His intellectual ethos met its reflection in the cannibal culture of hospitability. While hospitability was historically a factor in the demise of Latin American aboriginals, for it made them vulnerable to European exploitation and disease, Montaigne's intellectual hospitability remained a source of strength.[30] Indeed, as my next chapter will explore in greater detail, hospitability, welcoming in the other and giving to eat to the other, 'eating well', was a form of ethical ideal for him.

This helps answer the question, why savage; but not, why cannibal? A clearer answer, also about hospitability, is found in contemporary context. Hospitability in a time of civil and religious war is suspended or, if not, may involve risk of dispossession: who would welcome in a stranger who might prove an enemy, intent on taking possession of one's home? The place of the cannibal resonates with this, in terms which have squarely to do with the time of writing.

With the Reformation, the 'place' of the cannibal is particularly relevant because European Christianity faced attack from within, not least in the Eucharistic controversies, rather than its 'enemies' being external. Among other religions, Islam and Judaism were traditionally the most reviled or exploited others. One strand of Christian polemic against Judaism already had long associated it with cannibalism as an index of the horror it represented.[31] Attacks on Judaism did not abate in the sixteenth century in France; nor were they replaced by the conflicts internal to Christianity; they continued alongside them or were

[27] On this section of the chapter, albeit with more emphasis on the significance of 'barbare', see Todorov, 'L'Etre et l'autre'.

[28] This is also valued in 'Des cannibales': 'ils sont sauvages, de mesmes que nous appellons sauvages les fruicts que nature, de soy et de son progrez ordinaire, a produicts' (they are wild in the way that fruit which nature has produced herself, unaided, is wild) (p. 205). The larger point made here is that what *really* deserved to be called savage was the way in which civilized peoples had contaminated nature: 'là où, à la verité, ce sont ceux que nous avons alterez par nostre artifice et detournez de l'ordre commun, que nous devrions appeller plustost sauvages' (when really it is those we have changed through our artifices and led astray from the common order that we should call wild).

[29] *Politics*, 1253a, 28–9, cited in Greenblatt, *Marvellous Possessions*, p. 68.

[30] For Montaigne's comments on European betrayals of the indigenous South American peoples, see 'Des coches'.

[31] For further insight into the long history of such attacks, see Schäfer, *Judeophobia* (Cambridge, Mass., 1997) and for contextual discussion, see Rubin, *Corpus Christi.*

cb ∂ = Jew = RC

displaced and consumed by them. The cannibal and the Jew merged as figures of horror; we find particularly clear instances of this in Léry's *Histoire d'un voyage faict en la terre du Bresil*. The external 'horror' was displaced onto an other site of horror, so as to figure the horror inside; in the most virulent polemic, the Jew was the cannibal was the Roman Catholic. Montaigne allows no such resonance or rigid antinomy into his representation of the many significances of the cannibal, as well as recognizing what we call anti-Semitism: witness, for instance, his account of the expulsion of Jews from Castille (see pp. 249–51).

For others, particularly among Reformers, cannibalism was riveted to the Eucharist, as theophagy: this was a site of horror and acute anxiety.[32] The use of the cannibal marked divisions between Roman Catholics and Reformers above all in terms of meaning of the Eucharist: was it transubstantiation, a sacred mystery; 'cannibal' feasting on the body of Christ; or analogy or Augustinian affinity?[33] Rather than containing extreme ambiguity, here the cannibal indexes extreme polarization. He is captured to uphold an opposition, the intractability of which was intensified by the other (the Antichrist) being internal to Christianity. Lestringant identifies the cannibal as an essential element in 'une configuration imaginaire d'une extrême cohérence' (an extremely coherent imaginary configuration), even key to a 'herméneutique' (hermeneutics) – an array of figures relating to ingestion, incorporation, digestion and so forth, which could not but have resonated with, or returned a reader or listener to, the agonizing Eucharistic debates.[34]

So the cannibal is a risky figure; given how foreclosing and rigidly binary the meanings of the cannibal had become in doctrinally driven debates, and what intense anxieties and hate the figure served to convey, how could the cannibal's semantic significance be released? Could he be used to generate thoughtful openness to difficult ideas rather than the paralysis of thought or excessive certainties symptomatic of anxiety? Such are the stakes of 'Des cannibales', which conveys a desire to restore further potentialities to the cannibal.[35]

[32] There may be a case, therefore, for it being interpreted as having to do with the Real. Greenblatt, for instance argues that the Host was the Real, materialized; there is mileage in this interpretation, but perhaps more so in thinking about the meaning of the Eucharist as a whole, including believers' desire for communion, as a version of the Real – to its opponents. See Greenblatt, 'Remnants of the Sacred in Early Modern England', in Grazia, Quilligan and Stallybrass (eds), *Subject and Object in Renaissance Culture* (Cambridge, 1996), pp. 337–45.

[33] For the different positions among Reformers (Luther, Calvin, Zwingli, among others), see Macy, *The Banquet's Wisdom*.

[34] See Lestringant, *Une Sainte Horreur*, ch. 1 (p. 4) and 'Catholiques et cannibales', in Margolin and Sauzet (eds), *Pratiques et discours alimentaires à la Renaissance* (Paris, 1982), pp. 233–46 (p. 234). See also *Le Cannibale*, in particular chapters 6 and 7. Among examples of the studies which develop Lestringant's work are Persels, 'Cooking with the Pope', *Mediaevalia* 22 (1999), pp. 29–53, and Hoffmann, 'Anatomy of the Mass'.

[35] In tandem with this, it also seems important not to follow too closely those readings of the chapter that lay most emphasis on its religious dimension (such as Hoffmann's) or take too markedly a religious turn at moments, such as Tournon in his comment on the third, missing observation: 'S'agirait-il d'autre chose que de la religion?' (what else would it be but

We might call this an extreme conceptual *essai* (test or experiment) on Montaigne's part of the power of figurative language, as well as of his readers' capacity to be open to thinking about what the cannibal could symbolize beyond his congealed meaning in religious controversy, while not forgetting that. This reading is appropriate because the chapter also draws indirectly on another, related, tradition of symbolism, also contested by the time of writing. Namely, the concept of community as the more than simply social 'body': at the time, still, 'the body social, the body politic and the body of Christ' were interdependent concepts.[36] This social 'body', derived from the sacred 'body' of the church, was a 'body' which symbolized an 'integrated whole of no longer alienated social parts'.[37] However, this conceptualization was being challenged. For Reformers such as Calvin the social 'body' was not sacred, and their beliefs produced a version of the individual with more potential autonomy and authority than that of the individual conceived as a member – limb, organ, cell – of the Roman Catholic social body.[38]

Montaigne's chapter explores the cultural, political and ethical economy of cannibal society; not as a social 'body', true, but such is the emphasis on the symbolic significance of the body in this society that different connotations of the body such as the social 'body' hover, particularly for readers whose currency this is. His reflections on this other culture, then, may be indirectly interested in the possibility of different articulations of the social body – without this being too tightly attached to its meanings in France.

Lastly, we might think of the cannibal in terms of rhetorical and linguistic theory, with sources spanning from Aristotle, via debates current at the time of writing, to more recent theorists such as Peirce.[39] The figure of the cannibal exemplifies one source of power of metaphor for Aristotle; it 'gives perspicuity, pleasure and a foreign air'.[40] The foreign, strange or other element, here both the use of figure and the figure used, was designed to be illuminating in the text. As for contemporary debates, arguments about the nature of signs and symbols, and the relationship between signs and referents, were wider than the interpretation of the Eucharist. This controversy was the critical site of what was being debated, but not all that was debated; the doctrinal crisis was also

---

religion?), *La Glose et l'essai* (Lyon, 1983), p. 219. Rather, what matters is to respect the play of possibilities in the chapter; this, broadly, is rather more akin to Lestringant's interpretation of the cannibal.

[36] Diefendorf, *Beneath the Cross*, p. 48.

[37] Elwood, *The Body Broken*, p. 20; see Elwood also for further valuable discussion of this aspect of the context for Montaigne's chapter.

[38] For further information, see Monter, *Calvin's Geneva* (New York, 1967) and Mentzer and Spicer (eds), *Society and Culture in the Huguenot World* (Cambridge, 2002). For a compelling study of how this conflict played out in an urban environment, see Davis, 'The Sacred and the Body Social in Sixteenth-Century Lyon', *Past and Present* 90 (1980), pp. 40–70.

[39] I am drawing on Elwood for this perspective.

[40] Aristotle, *Rhetoric*, III, ii, 9 (pp. 354–5).

symptomatic of wider issues of interpretation, as different theories of reference and symbolism developed between Roman Catholic thinkers and Reformers, although also at times the differences were non-sectarian.

Peirce's thinking helps situate a rhetorical analysis within the sociocultural dimensions of sign-systems:

> [a] symbol [is] a culturally specific device that organizes perceptions and facilitates conceptualization ... rooted in a particular historical and cultural environment ... symbols elicit human responses, create social worlds, and regulate communal life ... [a symbol's] meaning is fundamentally dependent on historical individuals whose ways of knowing are governed by the networks of social and symbolic relations that constitute their world ... [not] fixed norms insulated from the exigency of historical transformations ... susceptible to change ... and capable of facilitating new conceptualizations and practices.[41]

This underlines how overdetermined the use of the cannibal was; also how high were the stakes in Montaigne's use of him as a means of critical analysis of things at home as well as an opportunity to indulge his curiosity about things far away – which proved not, after all, so very distant.

So, what does the cannibal mean in Montaigne's text? He has a more than double function; he has literal and figurative value, and also, he is both offered for interpretation and invited to offer his own interpretations (or so it seems). We should keep this more-than-doubleness in mind throughout the chapter.

Desire and interpretation

For Montaigne cannibals had a textual prehistory; his approach begins via others' accounts.[42] First ancient, then contemporary accounts, unnamed (including Herodotus, Tacitus, Plutarch, Thevet and Léry), all raising important questions for him here about the nature of testimony and of representation, discursive mediation and the problematic of 'the whole truth'. Along with textual witnesses, Montaigne had his own, exemplary witness, who apparently altered nothing in his account: 'j'ay eu long temps avec moy un homme qui avoit demeuré dix ou douze ans en cet austre monde qui a esté descouvert en nostre siècle' (a man who worked for me for a long time, who had spent ten or twelve years in that other world which has been discovered this century) (p. 203). This man's nature, 'simple et grossier' (simple, uncultured) (p. 205), lent his words more weight than the traditional textual authorities. For erudition, rhetorical skill, an elevated sense of one's own worth and investment in the representation

---

[41] Elwood, *The Body Broken*, p. 7.

[42] Certeau's reading of the chapter, not least of this aspect, is compelling and inflects my interpretation. See 'Montaigne's "Of Cannibals"', in *Heterologies*, trans. Massumi (Minneapolis, 1986), pp. 67–79.

cbls : ns dissimila
envy
property
desire

of events all incline, according to Montaigne, towards misrepresentation: 'ils ne vous represent jamais les choses pures, ils les inclinent et masquent selon le visage qu'ils leur ont veu ... Ou il faut un homme tres-fidelle, ou si simple qu'il n'ait pas dequoy bastir et donner de la vray-semblance' (they never show you the things themselves, they bend and disguise them as they saw them ... Either you need a very truthful man, or one so simple that he is incapable of building things up and giving them plausibility) (p. 205).

Like all the chapter's themes, those of representation and truth come and go: first explicitly addressed, only then to keep fading. Reading the chapter it is difficult to know at any point whose perspective prevails; the deixis is strikingly indeterminate. At the outset Montaigne ascribes one particular detail to witnesses, plural: 'à ce que m'ont dit mes tesmoings, il est rare d'y voir un homme malade' (according to my witnesses, you rarely see a sick man) (p. 207): but who? Thereafter, reference to a witness or witnesses vanishes, allowing the illusion of first-hand, unmediated experience. Vanishing or forgetting then returns explicitly in the representation of the Rouen encounter, when Montaigne draws attention to his forgetting, and will be discussed in more detail shortly. Whether this indeterminacy is an example of recycling one's reading as a form of figurative cannibalism or, rather, is a deliberate destabilization of the identity of 'self' in anticipation of that of the self–other relation remains to be seen. For now, it is enough to wonder why, when so alert to the problematics of the true account, does Montaigne seem to break his own rules?

The features of the innocent cannibal society most significant for my reading are its lack of dissimulation and envy and its corollary, the possessive accumulation of private property. Also, an apparent absence of desire: 'ils sont encore en cet heureux point, de ne desirer qu'au tant que leur necessitez naturelles leur ordonnent: tout ce qui est au delà, est superflu pour eux ... ils n'ont faute d'aucune chose necessaire, ny faute encore de cette grande partie, de sçavoir jouyr de leur condition et s'en contenter' (they are still in that happy state in which their desire matches their natural needs: anything exceeding this, they consider superfluous ... they lack nothing they need, nor do they lack that great thing, the knowledge of how to enjoy their condition and be content with it) (p. 210).[43]

This, then, is 'perfection' (p. 207): a condition not of lack (and therefore of desire), but of only need. We might say this makes them other than human – not Montaigne's aim. His representation actually lets desire in: 'ne desirer qu'au tant que': but this would be desire which is commensurate with, and identical but secondary to, need, rather than desire as we in a post-Freudian (and capitalist) world understand it. So perhaps this is about us more than them: reminding us that we cannot conceive of a human condition without desire, as

---

[43] This description is echoed in the 'Apologie', where Montaigne emphasizes the tranquillity, serenity and health of this people; they are free from passion, toil, difficulty and from such issues as beset France at the time, for they have neither king, law or religion (see p. 491).

the use of negation suggests. What they did not suffer from were such ills as lies, betrayal, deceit, envy: in the sixteenth century categorized as sins, or passions, but Montaigne's representation avoids this, and therefore so can we.[44] To think, instead, of these elements as aspects of fear and desire is not too free a translation, especially given his use of the term shortly after in that summing up of what makes them so different. But by using 'desirer', to desire, while pointing up the difference, Montaigne both connects and differentiates between us and them rather than, as was conventional, distinction being emphasized.

He presents us with a version of what had been lost (without our knowing it); and given the power of the ills – the 'corruptions' (corruptions) (p. 213), 'barbarie' (barbarity) (p. 212) and 'loix … abastardies' (corrupted laws) (p. 206) that stem from desire – he has emphasized the fragility of the cannibal's world. When they come to France this becomes entirely clear. Montaigne's representation emphasizes what they will lose: tranquillity, happiness, innocence, indeed, if we give the word 'ruin' serious weight, all that matters: 'trois d'entre eux, ignorans combien coutera un jour à leur repos et à leur bonheur la connoissance des corruptions de deçà, et que de commerce naistra leur ruyne, comme je presuppose qu'elle soit desjà avancée, bien miserable de s'estre laissez piper au desir de la nouvelleté' (p. 213, see translation p. 40 above).

This proleptic sentence plays between knowledge and its absence, and links desire and knowledge: not that it is the desire *for* knowledge that corrupts (Montaigne's chapter avoids (so explicit) a theological turn), but the desire for change. Desire is a way of thinking about or imagining the future, not in itself problematic. But it becomes so here: the knowledge that things can be different, which comes from seeing how others live, maps onto troubling desire, when acquired knowledge opens up a sense of lack. The missing term in Montaigne's reflection is 'possess'. Neither the desire for knowledge nor the desire for what others are or have, *per se*, are troubling, until the particular form of want, namely, the desire to possess knowledge, or possess what others have, or are, takes hold. This enters a world which operates in terms of what is yours and what is mine, divided accordingly.

However, here the visitors are represented as being not quite so vulnerable to the 'corruptions' of this new world as the text seems to dread.[45] As yet they have neither the Europeans' desires nor their accompanying anxiety. But by prefacing their presence with that disjunction between what he would later know but they still did not, Montaigne makes three points. Firstly, this prompts the reader to think about what other later knowledge she too should also bring to

---

[44] Indeed there is notably scant use of the noun 'peché' (sin) in the *Essais* as a whole: only twenty-nine occurrences.

[45] In many ways this was well founded. What might not yet have been known other than hypothetically in 1562 would already, by the time of writing, over seventeen years later and with more reports available as to the ways in which the presence of Europeans was harmful to indigenous peoples, have been empirical knowledge. This is another instance of the kind of knowledge that needs to be read back into this representation of how things were in 1562.

her interpretation of what will follow. Secondly, freedom from anxiety may have enabled the cannibals to see and say what they did – unlike their French contemporaries. Thirdly, an oblique point about the cost of knowledge: 'ruyne', ruin, and anxiety. Knowledge is not a free gift, and whatever freedom or power it offers, its cost is excessive.

At this point, despite Montaigne's anxious foreknowledge, they neither like nor want what they see; paradoxically, at this point what they were vulnerable to was their vision and words being forgotten – by Montaigne himself. Despite fears for their vulnerability and loss (through the development of desire), and in the clear knowledge of the power of appropriative, acquisitive *and* sectarian desire in France, the cannibals thus seem to figure the (slight) possibility of release from such desires – figuring the possibility of the future in France to be imagined differently. But no such Utopian moment is allowed, in two different ways. Firstly, we know this is 1562 and what happened that year; moreover, that at the time of writing the wars still dragged on. Secondly, as we shall see, because of Montaigne's forgetting. Paradise was always already lost, and forgetting is symptomatic of the difficulty of our relationship with knowledge which we do not want, but which we cannot unknow; forgetting is a particular kind of remembering.

What also emerges here is that although cannibals had been represented as lacking desire except insofar as it matched need they nonetheless reveal a recognizable form of desire, by responding to the question about what they thought of France. The text pulls in two different directions: even if the translation of their words into French was not perfectly faithful, their words suggest that how they 'saw' France was true to the values of their own desireless culture. But that they responded, and that they interpreted what they had seen, suggests a liminal form of desire. Even if their interpretation was couched in terms of what they found strange, or very strange, suggesting both that they wanted to keep their distance and that they were not passing judgement, they do interpret, and interpretation is not a desire-free process. And in keeping their distance, they also preserve their own ways of seeing: such as, for instance, the use of the word 'moitié', to which Montaigne particularly draws attention with the following parenthesis: '(ils ont une façon de leur langage telle, qu'ils nomment les hommes moitié les uns des autres)' (in their language it is their habit to call men each other's halves) (p. 214).

They respond, engage and bear witness: this third term is not used, despite the rather emphatic reflections on testimony earlier in the chapter. There the emphasis was on oral and written representations, from antiquity to Montaigne's time, of new worlds and their inhabitants, cannibal or not. Now the situation is reversed. And with this, two problems of testimony are flagged, only the second of which had been acknowledged earlier. Questions of validity had focused on witnesses and their language, neglecting the potential frailties and failings of the listener or reader. And how to evaluate accounts which are unassimilable to the listener's or reader's knowledge, understanding and experience? This is an instance of a wider epistemological issue, the many dimensions of which Montaigne explores repeatedly in the *Essais*, leaning towards a sceptical suspension of judgement in the face of what is on, or beyond, the limits of our available conceptual systems. But how to allow the anxieties and doubt aroused by encounters with unrecognizable perspectives and phenomena – such as cannibals – and settle for limited understanding, in an overriding desire for tranquillity? How to be sceptical without the gain of peace of mind? To put it more sharply still: is this representation a test for Pyrrhonist scepticism, given that the cannibal's potential to disturb seems to put the desire for tranquillity into tension with the desire to go on exploring meaning?

The cannibals are represented as finding what they have seen 'fort estrange'. They acknowledge otherness without seeming to judge it, as if unknowingly akin to sceptics, reminding the reader to neither exclude nor too quickly assimilate ideas that are alien – engineering a (fully intended) paradox. Even if one perspective (cannibal, other) is offered in preference to an other (French, one's own), and even if it may only be by recourse to that preferred, distanced perspective that blindness to one's own condition can be cured, what leads is the preference for seeing things in one's own terms, which is still a form of not understanding – unless something less than distance can be taken, unless a third position, a point of convergence, can emerge. And this is where what initially looked like (partial) blindness turns out to be insight. But for it to emerge, we have to move beyond what seemed to be a couple (cannibal, French) and intro-duce a third, fourth or even fifth term. Montaigne, who had set up the paradox, has been a third term all along – identified fully with neither one nor the other; the reader, called upon to interpret the paradox, is the fourth. However, to extend our understanding of the idea we are now being asked to reflect on, we shall need a fifth term: La Boétie.

So, to move beyond resistance to the foreign perspective: what were the cannibals supposed to have said? They were asked what they found 'de plus admirable' (p. 213), most remarkable, wondrous; in fact they were expected to ventriloquize the courtiers' paean to France – our ways, our ceremonies, our urban planning … The currency of their reply translates marvellous wonder into doubt and strangeness. They wondered why soldiers took orders from a child, and why they did not prefer a form of meritocracy – elect who you think best – to such a state. Under cover of their being 'only' barbaric cannibals, this could be said in the presence of that child, without it being seditious, and Montaigne's representation could escape censure, although their view translates easily out of cannibalese into radical French. The text's safety from censure confirms the blindness Montaigne identifies with the French. For not only did the cannibals question the child's power; they proposed that elective republic replace it, as if unaware of the still prevailing belief in the divine sanction of monarchy. Let's not forget that Montaigne, on his travels in Italy, expressed his desire to be in Venice as hunger;[46] and that he commented elsewhere in the

---

[46] 'La faim extrême de voir cette ville' (his extreme hunger to see that city), *Journal de Voyage* (Paris, 1983), p. 165. All references hereafter are to this edition.

Essais that had La Boétie had the choice, he would rather have been born in Venice than, as he was, in Sarlat, that is, have legitimately been a republican.[47]

The visitors' second observation needs more detailed interpretation, both in terms of what it says about the state of France at the time (and also about the impossibility of changing it), and in terms of the ideal human relations and an accompanying ideal of communication and interpretation it conveys. This turns around the term 'moitié' (half), which echoes the earlier description of the social and intersubjective relations of this people: 'ils s'entr'appellent generalement, ceux de mesme aage, freres' (they generally call those of the same age, brothers) (p. 210). Whilst it would produce a neatly radical version of Montaigne were this a community of symbolic brotherhood of undifferentiated equals, this is not the case; despite an absence of patriarchal family and property structures such as those in France, there were vestiges of patriarchy: 'et les vieillards sont peres à tous les autres' (and the old men are fathers to all the others) (p. 210). The retention of the lexis of familial identities, despite the structure's absence, makes this culture a less than radical alternative to what was familiar. However, the sentence leads with the idea of brothers and a horizontal rather than vertical structure, which makes it possible to relate this society to classical ideals of love and ethics (which Montaigne claims it prefigures).[48]

For it is akin to Aristotelian *philia* as discussed, primarily, in the *Nicomachean Ethics*, and in passing in the *Rhetoric*. Love for the other as for oneself: ideally, between those who are good and alike in virtue. *Philia* is a reciprocal relation, and implies symmetry between friends. One of its conditions is justice; authentic friendship with an unjust man is impossible. This lends us a conceptual framework for the coexistence in cannibal culture of the names 'brother' and 'half': idealized, symmetrical relationship is the foundation of this society. In the Rouen encounter, that 'half' is an ethical term is clear, for the topic is inequity and injustice:

> (ils nomment les hommes moitié les uns des autres) ... ils avoyent aperçeu qu'il y avoit parmy nous des hommes pleins et gorgez de toutes sortes de commoditez et que leur moitiez estoient mendians à leurs portes, décharnez de faim et de pauvreté; et trouvoient estrange comme ces moitiez icy neces-siteuses pouvoient souffrir une telle injustice, qu'ils ne prinsent les autres à la gorge, ou missent feu à leur maisons. (p. 214)

> (they call men each other's halves) ... they had noticed that among us there were men who had their fill and more of all kinds of good things, and that their other halves were beggars at their doors, so poor and hungry that they were skin and bone. They found it strange that these halves who were so in

---

[47] 'Et sçay ... que, s'il eut eu à choisir, il eut mieux estre nay à Venise qu'à Sarlac: et avec raison' (And I know that, if he had had the choice, he would rather have been born in Venice than in Sarlat – with reason) (p. 194).

[48] 'Surpasse ... la conception et le desir mesme de la philosophie' (surpass the very conception of philosophy and what it desires) (p. 206).

need tolerated such an injustice and did not take the others by the throat or set fire to their houses.)

In the cannibals' words, whilst the have-nots are identified as 'moitiez', the haves are not: they are 'autres', others; their otherness being that they are not recognizable within the cannibal ethics of *philia*.

How Montaigne and La Boétie were each other's 'halves' is for my next chapter. For now, what matters is that this comment, even more than the first, uncannily echoes a leading question of La Boétie's *De la servitude volontaire*: why do oppressed subjects not rise up against the tyrant? The tyrant who, in that text, also, was associated with metaphorical cannibalism. La Boétie's text had its own answers to its question; it was not, as here, left suspended – for the reader to reflect on, as would Aristotle's man worthy of *philia*. Montaigne could not posit this of all his readers; as a writer he risks (an ethical, affective and also epistemological risk) his words not being read as he might wish, and to allow that he might be misinterpreted.

To suggest that *De la servitude volontaire* was ghost-writing these comments is to bring into Montaigne's *Essais* a share of the text which he claimed he had to leave out, because of its political vulnerability by the time of writing, despite his having promised his dying friend to publish it.[49] One of his greatest ethical dilemmas, and not one that this passage redeems. However, to tease out the complex connections between the cannibal and La Boétie is important, unlikely though they seem.

Perhaps the death of his friend in 1563 had already transformed what might still have seemed thinkable to Montaigne in 1562. Even if by then he had not already lost hope in the future, the loss thereafter of La Boétie initiated a series of losses of what his friend represented: the chance to put, and publish, political questions which, by their very existence as questions, suggested it was still possible to imagine a different future; and the freedom to ask such questions openly without being judged disloyal. Such difficult observations, by the time of writing, well after 1562, need to be cast as belonging to the 'other'.

My analysis so far of what the cannibal represents has been an experiment in forgetting. It has focused on the cultural, political and ethical ideals that cannibal society symbolizes, and on the perspicuity of the questions about French society and polity possible from this perspective, quite forgetting the cannibals' key characteristic: their – apparently dehumanizing – taste for human flesh. Does this lapse delegitimize their questions? (Not, of course, their questions so much as the questions ascribed to them.) But why would Montaigne risk jeopardizing the questions?

Firstly, precisely, risk. The risk in the questions, in their excessive validity, at the time; it is to conceal what they reveal that they were supposedly (no more than) the questions of uncivilized, indeed questionably human, others. But why

---

[49] This will be discussed further in chapter 3.

does that appetite for human flesh necessarily symbolize their being question-ably human? Montaigne uses the just, wondering cannibal to explore what it means to be human. Moreover, he uses an extreme symbol combining ideal and horror, one that had been restrictively coopted by others, to test the power of symbols to open our thinking, despite or perhaps because of disturbing affect, to different ways of thinking about what it is to be human. This is not only a restoration of the cannibal's semantic potential beyond corrosive confessional polemic, but also a way of thinking unlike much traditional philosophy, not least in combining idea and affect, bound up with Montaigne's development of the *essai* form rather than adopting existing forms of prose discourse.[50] Moreover, it is thinking that sacrifices tranquillity without its loss being intolerable.

Montaigne's source texts noted the cannibals' appetite for human flesh. Wanting to eat flesh that is the same as one's own is typically a founding taboo; for European Christian culture this took a specific turn in sixteenth-century debates between Reformers and Roman Catholics over the meaning of eating the body that is Christ's. It became a further source of horror in France as knowledge or rumour spread of instances of cannibalism during the wars, in periods of siege or famine. Extreme polemic at the time of writing was anxiety- and hate-filled, symptomatic of a loss of thoughtfulness and of the capacity to think in terms other than those narrowly of one's own belief-system. Therefore, to invite readers to think differently precisely by using the cannibal, who had come to symbolize that about which *thought* as an ethical activity, engaging with different perspectives, had been jeopardized, was risky, counterbalanced only by the enjoyment generated by figurative language such as symbols and the play of interpretation they offer. So, rather than, say, 'he is a cannibal' having only one possible interpretation in the mind of the speaker, one which locked the identity of each term onto the other as if all potential for difference were obliterated, Montaigne's chapter tries to recover the plural possibilities of the figure, asking the reader to reflect on why it had come to mean what it had and whether that was just.

Montaigne approaches cannibal practices carefully, having first presented the ways in which their culture symbolized ideals that his civilization had lost. Their context is warfare, and this was not a desire to feed on human flesh but a symbolic practice: 'ce n'est pas, comme on pense, pour s'en nourrir, ainsi que faisoient anciennement les Scythes [a nod here to Herodotus, the original source]: c'est pour *representer* une extreme vengeance' (this is not, as is thought, for food, as in the case of the ancient Scythians: rather, it *represents* extreme revenge) (p. 209, my italics). Symbolic practices humanize them; and venge-

---

[50] 'Il y a peut-être des pensées plus pensantes que cette pensée qu'on appelle la philosophie' (there are perhaps forms of thought that are more thoughtful than the form of thought we call philosophy). Derrida, in Cahen, 'Entretien avec Jacques Derrida', *Digraphe* (1987), pp. 11–27 (p. 18).

we are our selves thro' ingestion of O

ance assimilates their practice to the honour code of European warrior culture.[51] Moreover, killing and eating are represented as being sacrificial. Montaigne also argues not only that they were like us, but even in their treatment of their enemies (before eating them), they were better.[52]

His representation of who ate whom is revealing of the nature of the self explored here. Much rests on the words of the song of a prisoner awaiting death and being eaten; but it already also turned around the emphasis on how non-possessive this culture was, and around what is suggested by ascribing to them the structure of relatedness symbolized by the word 'moitié', half.

> Qu'ils viennent hardiment trétous et s'assemblent pour disner de luy: car ils mangeront quant et quant leurs peres et leurs ayeux, qui ont servy d'aliment et de nourriture à son corps. Ces muscles, dit-il, cette cher et ces veines, ce sont les vostres, pauvres fols que vous estes; vous ne recognoissez pas que la substance des membres de vos ancestres s'y tient encore: savourez les bien, vous y trouverez le goust de vostre chair. (p. 212)

> (they should all boldly come and gather to dine off him: for in so doing they will be eating their fathers and ancestors, who had served as food and nour-ishment for his body. 'These muscles', he says, 'this flesh and these veins are your own, poor fools that you are; you don't realize that they still contain the very substance of your ancestors' limbs: savour them well, for in them you'll find the taste of your own flesh.)

So these idealized cannibals (source of full truth) actually have rather imper-fect memories and understanding. The 'truth' of the situation is spelled out by the one who was on the point of dying: what will be eaten is not simply, materi-ally, the same kind of flesh, but is constitutively the same, their flesh and blood. Across generations of cannibal consumption of the other, the boundary between what is self and what is other (flesh) has become permeable. Whether in Mont-aigne's terms elsewhere in the *Essais* (for instance in his reflections on familial bonds, education, language acquisition or social intercourse), or in terms more current now, not least in psychoanalytic thinking, the argument seems clear: understanding of the nature of the self rests on recognition of its constitution through its intimate relations with others. The ingestion of others' flesh symbol-izes the psychic ingestion of others; we are what others (now within us, a part of us) have made us. To not recognize this is to remain poor fools ('pauvres fols'). The consequence of this psychic cannibalism over generations and within each lifetime is that self and other are both distinct and indistinct. Understanding this may somewhat lessen our attachment to our prioritized, beloved selves:

---

[51] As has already been discussed elsewhere, by, among others, Quint, in *Montaigne and the Quality of Mercy*.

[52] This critique of French culture has been discussed so fully by others that there is no need to reiterate the detail here. See, for instance, Lestringant's various studies and Defaux, 'Un cannibale en haut de chausses', *MLN* 97/4 (1982), pp. 919–57.

whoever we think we are, it is a great deal more contingent on encounters with others and more other-inhabited than is unreflectively assumed. To give just two examples of this structure: that the counterfeit 'cannibal' as well as textual versions preceded the presence of the 'originals' in Rouen, and that Montaigne's mother tongue, 'la mienne maternelle' (my mother tongue) (p. 175) was not his mother's French, but Latin.

This is to interpret what is given narrative form here as an instance of what Moriarty has identified in texts by such writers as Montaigne, Descartes and Pascal as 'a disturbance or set of disturbances around notions of the self and identity rather than the emergence of fully fledged concepts ready to be inserted in a narrative of the emergence of selfhood or subjectivity in the early modern period'.[53] 'Disturbance' precedes 'emergence', and is registered as such by this being the insight of an intensely disturbing figure: a cannibal himself and also at that moment the imminent victim of cannibals. This disturbance will become all the more unsettling if we wonder why this sacrificial victim speaks in terms of the presence of the 'substance' of the other cannibals' ancestors in his body and blood, 'cette cher et ces veines' (this flesh and these veins). Substance is the term associated with Real Presence. Let's assume this is not a profane joke, or a gratuitous jibe at those who really agonized about what happened to the leftover 'flesh' either in the unconsumed Host or in the body of the communicant. But perhaps Montaigne allows himself to leave a coded trace for an attentive reader, the kind of thought that someone fully versed in the debate from a still faithfully Roman Catholic, but non-aligned and even somewhat secularizing perspective, might allow himself.

Moreover, this interrelatedness sits with Montaigne's recurring emphasis on becoming who one is, not least by representing that process in writing. Consider the relationship between his writing in this chapter and its sources, largely unacknowledged. It is fed by others' texts; Montaigne is a 'cannibalizing' reader, and we cannot tell where his ideas originated. Within himself? With others? Or through the absorption of others so fully that it was no longer possible to remember whose they were originally? This metaphor of reading as a process of ingestion, or to use the humanist concepts 'innutrition' and 'imitatio', spans a kind of ahistorical continuum of connotation, given its long history along with that of the text as a figurative body. But it also has more precise historical resonance, given its reactivation in such decisive sixteenth-century French texts as Rabelais's and in Du Bellay's *Deffence et illustration de la langue françoyse*; that is, in the generation and regeneration of French as a 'literary' language.[54]

To return to the other of the other, the cannibal's victim: he, akin to the commentators in Rouen, is given the privilege of knowing and telling the truth, as if it is only from the place of the other that the truth can be known. However, the text veers away from this as much as it keeps returning to it, and ambiva-

[53] See Moriarty, *Early Modern French Thought*, pp. 13–14, n. 18.
[54] See Cave, *The Cornucopian Text*, and Jeanneret, *Des Mets et des mots* (Paris, 1987) and *Perpetuum mobile* (Paris, 1997), chapters 6–11.

lence is written through the analysis, thus reproducing something of the difficulty of engaging with this place.

The resonances of this moment of insight for the time of writing, as well
as the chapter as a whole, with its use of this place to interrogate the state of
France, are clear. If the enemies' identities actually have much that is vital in
common with their own, without them knowing it, this unsettles the possibility
of locating an origin in clear and separate identity, and with that a 'natural'
order of reliably differentiated beings. It also indirectly challenges the rigid
hostility of us and them, right and wrong, faithful and heretic that had taken
hold in France. But what was the purchase of such a thought-experiment? Those
on each side saw themselves as the other's enemy or victim, their positions
rigidly conflicting; others as if their life depended on it. In such a situation,
for what the other knows to be heard he has to be displaced, located outside.
Thirdly, the victim's perspective introduces a form of history, with its emphasis
on intergenerational embodied and cultural realities, and on the impact of the
past on the present – which only is revealed when reinscribed in the present.
This temporality introduces a fundamental change into the 'historiless' world
of the cannibal;[55] however, what the victim, and what Montaigne's chapter as a
whole, leave suspended, is the question of the future. The victim intimates that
this is an issue of life and death, which nonetheless can be faced with equanimity and lucidity. However, as will shortly be seen, the ending of the chapter
seems to recoil from this, leaving the reader in a more problematic relationship
with the future and the possibility of change.

But again I seem to be forgetting that Montaigne was representing *cannibals*.
This is symptomatic of the way in which the actuality of the practice is muffled
in a representation which 'civilizes' it. Even if the victim spits at his captors, this
signifies his bravery. Even a closing apparent acknowledgement that these are
savages is less a return to conventional recoil than an intimation that they must
be savages lest we recognize our own savage selves. The conceptual legitimiza-
tion of their cannibalism is threefold: it is neither a form of nutrition nor raw
primitive appetite, it is sacrificial, and the victims desire their death: 'il ne s'en
void aucun qui n'ayme mieux estre tué et mangé, que de requerir seulement de
ne l'estre pas' (there is not one who would not rather be killed and eaten, than
merely ask not to be) (p. 210). If all desire it, and all are made up of each other,
then this cannibal economy is lifted away from horror, towards the possibility
of a different kind of cultural and relational calculus.

That every other is part of every self also lifts the idea of the 'moitié',
half, into something other than, literally, a half: selves dissolving into others
dissolving into selves over time make a half an incalculable fraction, emphasizing the symbolic significance of the half: an economy of symmetry, equality,
interchangeability. This produces a new basis for giving and taking, no longer

---

[55] For further discussion of temporality or its supposed absence and the functions of
ethnography in early modern texts, along with other key aspects such as orality, see Certeau,
L'Ecriture de l'histoire (Paris, 1975), pp. 213–88.

calculated in terms of taking possession. We might object that cooking someone and sharing his flesh with one's friends is the most literally intractable way of taking possession imaginable. However, Montaigne's representation glosses over this, presenting instead the hospitability and commonality of it, as well as the non-self-possessive basis for the practice: each recognizes that he is as likely as the next to be the eaten rather than the eater, and is already made up of those who had been eaten; subtract possessiveness of one's being, and concepts such as being taken over evaporate.

There is still more to say about the structure of 'moitiez', halves, in terms of communication and interpretation, beyond the Rouen encounter as well as in that context, not least when Montaigne's incompetent interpreter gets in the way. If the structure of relations was really parity and equity, of each seeming also to occupy the place of the other, as the cannibal economy suggests, communication and interpretation would also be on a very different basis; as Montaigne puts it in 'De l'experience': 'la parole est moitié à celuy qui parle, moitié à qui l'escoute' (speech belongs half to the speaker, half to the listener) (p. 1088). However, much more often he emphasizes what unbalances and obscures communication, the unreliability of interpretation and its having more to do with human failing and imperfection than this lovely ideal.

Here, too, that imperfect reality returns. The representation of the cannibals' temporality until this point was not that of Montaigne or his readers, contemporary or future. They existed in an idealized atemporal, ahistorical dimension: no desire, so no sense of the future, and, apparently, no memory of the past: until the victim reveals their genealogy to them, they inhabit an unchanging present. The inclusion of the Rouen encounter in 1562 puts this to the test of history and experience. The painful consequence is the loss of the ideals figured by the cannibal – or rather, a reminder that the ideals were already lost: firstly, to history. The year 1562 exemplifies the limits and instability of our understanding: from the Edict of Toleration (asking for trouble?) to war within three months. Who could have predicted it would start so soon, or last so long? And what could have been said, and heard, in 1562, was not what could have been said after 1572 or at the time of writing; also, the significance of all those present, not least the child with exorbitant power, had also changed. Knowing this, and encouraged by the proleptic framing of the encounter, we are invited to bring our knowledge of what had not yet happened to our reading. We could call this irony, or the insight that comes *après-coup*; it also reverberates with Montaigne's stance against political change on the grounds of unpredictable outcomes and, without that foreknowledge, insufficient justification to act. The cannibal others observe wrongs such as injustice and cruelty needing reform; and there was no shortage of reformers wanting change, whose theological ideals also might have led to a version of a more just polity and society.[56] But

---

[56] For analysis of this aspect of political thought, see Skinner, *The Foundations of Modern Political Thought: The Reformation* (Cambridge, 1978).

the changes that would ensue in France brought, rather, deepening injustice, cruelty and blindness, and the lessening of free speech and fair hearings.

History is not the only test: the ideal of a perfect balance between speaker and listener is also lost – by Montaigne's own forgetting. He makes himself an example of the precariousness of speech and interpretation, in a number of intricated ways. Unlike many other representations, the orality of the other's culture is not treated as a distinguishing vulnerability:[57] for from the moment that the other sets foot in France, the oral becomes, theoretically, the writable. Here, vulnerability and flaws are on the side of the culture of writing, Montaigne's.

Of course, perhaps what was said was precarious in the sense of being too incendiary to publish. Forgetting allows this possibility and invites reflection on what might have been said. Three comments by courtiers, three observations, by three observers: the play with the power of three, that rhetorical magic number, is unmissable, and is not lost with the loss of the third observation: 'j'ay perdu la troisiesme' (p. 213). The absence amplifies its power. The sequence appears cumulative; it works with the aesthetics of the tricolon structure, but also, seems to offer escalating insight into the ethical and political abuses of the time. The themes are injustice and inequity, and disproportion; this culture is adrift from 'natural' good order. The explicit observations need little interpretation; yet, in the second observation, there is a missing term, namely, cruelty. Cruelty so great that the observers wonder why its victims did not retaliate and destroy those who were so unjust – a comment suggesting that their exposure to 'civilized' ways has already corrupted their thinking, for it sits oddly with the views ascribed earlier to cannibals.

If the missing culmination were, 'why do they not kill them?', paraphrasing the other as mediated (or used) by Montaigne, we can trace the breaking of a non-existent commandment. 'Thou shalt not kill' is culturally foundational, and would offer a response to the others' puzzlement – but not to the underlying situation. There is no commandment: 'thou shalt not make the other suffer'. 'Thou shalt love thy neighbour as thyself' is not the same, despite its implied injunction against causing suffering, for it is cast in terms of the relation between Law and Love, not cruelty, and besides, what was happening in France at the time of writing dramatized the violability of this commandment, making appeal to its authority a less than winning move.[58]

Moreover, at this time, cruelty was not a sin, and did not fall within the array of socially destructive behaviours which confession traditionally was designed

---

[57] See, for instance, Lévi-Strauss, *Anthropologie structurale* (Paris, 1958) and *Tristes Tropiques* (Paris, 1955), and as debated and theorized, see Certeau, *L'Ecriture de l'histoire* and Derrida, *De la grammatologie*.

[58] For further, invigorating analysis, after Freud and Lacan, see Žižek, 'Love Thy Neighbour? No Thanks!', in *The Plague of Fantasies* (London, 1997), pp. 45–85, and for more on the relations between Law and Love, see, for instance, *The Puppet and the Dwarf* (Cambridge, Mass., 2003), pp. 92–121.

to mitigate.[59] If it was not culturally unsanctioned, then condemnation of it might have had to be voiced from beyond this culture's borders; that it falls to the supposed savage is another paradox for the reader to reflect on. But it has a specific turn: in cannibal culture, to kill a fellow human (and Montaigne only recorded killing that was part of their warfare) was not criminal; rather, it was sacrificial. In France, at the time of writing, and already in 1562, killing which may well have been criminal was sanctioned as if it were sacrificial, and judgements as to the nature of these acts, as happens in civil war, tended to depend on the not impartial perspective of whoever was judging.

So the other's observation is profoundly troubling: the injustice and cruelty, which Montaigne so hated, are palpable, and seem to convey a position close to his. But the concluding point (whatever it was) seems to prompt Montaigne to forget and to distance his position from the other's, without explicitly doing so. So the reader, in the absence of functioning commandments and law, must work this through, arriving, perhaps, at the following interpretation. Using the cumulative logic of the first two observations, and all that was woven into the second, the third (if it existed) might well have been, 'why do the suffering and subjugated not kill the king?' In countering this, the commandment 'thou shalt not kill', along with the 'missing' injunction 'thou shalt not make the other suffer', would have formal traction, but already in 1562 and all the more so by the time of writing some seventeen years later, such a question dangerously risked exposing the lack of authority of such injunctions. This forgetting, then, was perhaps more of a turning away from something so alarming that it could only be indicated by being made absent.

This interpretation presupposes that the cannibal had much to say: voice of an otherwise unutterable truth. This is tantamount to casting the cannibal as 'the one who knows'. This idea has been rhetorically leveraged by the use of threes, playing with the reader's expectations; but this may in fact be a lure. The presence of a memorable rhetorical structure coupled with a powerful fantasy seems legible, according to interpretative habit – an assumption which Montaigne's forgetting is designed to puncture. The presence of the one who knows, however compelling a fantasy it may be, must be recognized as just that, a fantasy: so, rather than locating and seeking knowledge in the other, what matters is to become disillusioned and arrive at the realization that the other does not in fact have the knowledge we lack and desire. Montaigne plays with the potential of the cannibal to function as a figure of the truth (as in the earlier part of the chapter) to put, now, instead, other truths, plural, into circulation and to encourage us to question our desire for there to be a locus of truth. It is not for nothing that it is the cannibal – the ideal/embodiment of horror – who figures

---

[59] See Bossy, 'The Social History of Confession in the Age of the Reformation', *Transactions of the Royal Historical Society*, 5th series, 25 (1975), pp. 21–38, Briggs, 'The Sins of the People', in *Communities of Belief* (Oxford, 1989), pp. 277–337, and Delumeau, *L'Aveu et le pardon* (Paris, 1990). On cruelty not being categorized as a sin, see Delumeau, *La Peur en Occident (XIVe–XVIIIe siècle)* (Paris, 1978), pp. 270–1.

here. This helps answer the question of Montaigne's use of the cannibal. His ambiguity anticipates this later undoing of the fantasy he figures.

Montaigne's staged forgetting perhaps calls for a different interpretation altogether. That is, as a textual turning point, at which the reader is asked to move beyond the fantasy of a locus of all knowledge, and, rather than turning to this other, to think for herself about her own partial, historically contingent understanding of the state of France at that time. Thus Montaigne's forgetting meets the cannibal's knowing, and the reader's different (also limited) perspective supplements the time and place of both the cannibal, as represented, and the time of writing and publication.

This interpretation gains weight in the light of the connection, already mentioned earlier, between the words in the cannibals' mouths and La Boétie's. There *is* a strong resonance between their perspective and his trenchant views on the ills of tyranny; not that Montaigne ever called the current monarchy by such a name, even via the cannibal. Even if connections strike the reader, it is equally important to allow the ways in which the cannibal is *not* La Boétie.

Let's think, instead, in terms of ambiguities and suspended judgement. Not only do the cannibals not name what they observe as tyranny, even if what they in consternation describe could be called 'servitude volontaire' (voluntary servitude) and thus could be heard as asking the same question as La Boétie's text. However, their questions are precisely located historically, unlike those of his essay, with its more abstract inquiry into this problem of political philosophy. The essay is theoretical, and transhistorical, and Montaigne recoiled from allowing the translation of this discourse into specifically historical terms. Moreover, although, as will be seen in the next chapter, there are ways in which we can draw a line between Montaigne, La Boétie and the cannibal in the *Essais*, we must not forget that for Montaigne there was no one like La Boétie. To respect this singularity, we have to differentiate carefully between cannibal words and his, while still hearing a resonance. Respect for singularity also preserves the otherness of the other: for all that we may hear something of La Boétie in the cannibals' words, each remains other.[60]

But what should we call that resonance? Not an echo, or a reminder; for the essay had not yet been published; nor a precursor, for Montaigne had already read it. However, with La Boétie's death only a year after the Rouen encounter, and the circulation of a pirated version of his text, *by the time of writing* the words begin to sound ghostly, or uncanny. The perturbation caused by the inclu-

---

[60] Derrida: 'quelque chose de cet appel de l'autre doit rester non réappropriable, non subjectivable, d'une certaine manière non identifiable ... pour rester *de l'autre* ... Ce devoir n'est pas seulement un impératif théorique' (Something of this call of the other must remain nonreappropriable, nonsubjectivable, and in a certain way nonidentifiable ... so as to remain *other* ... This obligation to protect the other's otherness is not merely a theoretical imperative). See '"Il faut bien manger" ou le calcul du sujet', pp. 290–1, trans. Connell and Ronell, '"Eating Well", or the Calculation of the Subject', in *Points ... Interviews 1974–1994* (Stanford, 1995), pp. 255–87 (p. 276). (My next chapter will work more extensively with some of the ideas which figure in this interview with Jean-Luc Nancy.)

sion of a precise event, quite some time and four key events after it (his friend's death, the pirated publication, the decision by Montaigne not to publish despite his promise to his dying friend, and the St Bartholomew's Day massacre), makes the question of the relationship between the historical and the wider significance of what was said difficult to determine.

Even if Montaigne's forgetting was only an instance of 'ordinary' forgetting, just one of the vulnerabilities of human communication, it brings the problem of the authority of testimony back into the text. In the course of a very sceptical passage in 'Des Boyteux' ('On the lame'), Montaigne comments: 'peu de gens faillent, notamment aux choses mal-aysées à persuader, d'affermer qu'ils l'ont veu, ou d'alleguer des tesmoins desquels l'authorité arreste nostre contradic-tion' (particularly when something is unlikely to be believed, few people fail to affirm that they themselves have seen it, or invoke witnesses whose authority stops us from contradicting) (p. 1027). That chapter emphasizes the misuse of (what passes for) eyewitnessing, and the comment conveys a sceptical mistrust of seeing being believing or being the grounds for others' believing, especially when used as a way of 'having the last word'. Montaigne, having already unset-tled the authority of different kinds of witnesses, now seems disarmingly honest, presenting himself as an unreliable witness. Or does he? Does his 'forgetting' not, rather, act as a way of problematizing the authority conventionally given to the witness? No loss for him; he could find his authority as the writer of this particular text in other ways.

His forgetting also sits with his comments about his interpreter. An incompe-tent, he says: 'j'avois un truchement qui me suyvoit si mal, et qui estoit si empe-sché à recevoir mes imaginations par sa bestise que je n'en peus tirer guiere de plaisir' (my interpreter followed me so poorly, and was so incompetent that he could not grasp my ideas, so I did not enjoy it much) (p. 214). So it was *he* who was deprived of pleasure; it was *he* who was not properly understood, not his interlocutors, who are not even mentioned. Self-interest joins forgetting – also a form of self-interest; and plays its part in undoing ideal communication and understanding. However, perhaps it is more than a petulant or self-interested moment: for here, Montaigne, unusually for him, reliant on a mediator, encoun-ters a troubling aspect of communication. Namely, that in all communication we are all vulnerable to the other's response; we have to recognize our vulner-ability to the other and to reflect on how this affects our capacity to inhabit the world together.[61]

This leaves the last words, with all their ironies. Irony, which plays on discordance, is a form of freedom as well as a way of negotiating between the different interpretations and understanding that emerge over time. But irony may also articulate loss: the forgetful Montaigne may be closer to the Montaigne who, in 1563, had lost the most important person in his life, remembered as he wrote about the 1562 encounter – using this 'remembered' encounter as a way

---

[61] For further analysis see chapter 4.

of bringing him back into the text (we still cannot know the extent to which the detail represented here is remembered experience or strategic fiction). The writing is tinged with melancholy, over a death as well as in the loss of hope for the future and in awareness of an ever-widening gap between ideals and lived reality.

The final turn to ironies may be a way of holding open interpretative freedoms; however, irony seems to be a practice and product of detachment, and to operate at the cost of affect. But this instance is not quite a move into dispassionate observation; the disproportion between all that has gone before and this rejoinder suggests that affect remains: some anxiety, some anger, some disillusionment. It invokes sceptical suspension of judgement, handing meaning over to the reader for interpretation, but something other than tranquillity or dispassion remains.

Not the last word

Questions of address and interpretation circulate throughout Montaigne's chapter, and do so, forcefully, in its last words. 'Tout cela ne va pas trop mal: mais quoy, ils ne portent point de haut de chausses' (that's all well and good; but so what? They don't wear breeches) (p. 214). Foreclosure, a dismissive tone: how can we not be suspicious? Not only the comment about breeches, but also the dismissive 'but so what?', which moves to avert our attention; already, 'that's all well and good' is inapt in relation to the representation of the cannibal ideal, and inept in relation to the account of Montaigne's encounter in Rouen which just preceded it. So the last words incite a scepticism in keeping with Montaigne's: these are not the last words, are they? To whom can they be ascribed, anyway? – the deixis here is as unlocatable as it had been earlier in the chapter. Is there not more to say? This is intensified by the use of 'haut de chausses': real fabric ones, to be sure, but also metaphorical breeches. This undecidably literal and metaphorical term offers a doubly open signifier for us to read as we think most just. And with the use of metaphor, which signifies without directly asserting its points of comparison, we need to find our own direction of interpretation (without making it the last word on the matter).

So, these trouserless savages: we could put the cannibal back in his primitive place and reassert our own smug superiority. Such would be the interpretation of an imagined reader unready, even after having read Montaigne's chapter, to rethink the cannibal other. It is not much of a step to associate this reader with all that Montaigne reiterates in the *Essais* about the paralysis and complacency in which habit traps us. This reader exemplifies the habit of drawing lines too tightly, of dualism and, with that, surreptitious (or even avowed) superiority and inferiority. Although not the desired reader, not too pernicious – were this stance not already too close to that which had become so destructive at the time of writing: only my (Roman Catholic/Reformer) way will do.

This reader may be quite closely related to various others: for instance, those who cannot come up with a better symbol for being civilized; those who over-value a certain form of civilization (their own); or again, those who cannot see that to go trouserless suggests self-sufficiency and lack of shame, a state of nature – were these judges so 'corrupted' by what passed for civilization as to not realize this?[62] More generously, Montaigne might accept the reader's wish to wear trousers: to cover his nakedness and his physical vulnerability. If that were all they did, all well and good; but let's not forget Montaigne's comments elsewhere about excessively large codpieces. Such clothing was associated not with perceived necessity so much as with dissimulation and the delusion of being (bigger and) better, being designed to supplement our lack. Breeches remind us of the recurring themes of deception and self-deception in the *Essais*, of the dissimulation from which the cannibals were free –not least because, as described (or imagined) by Montaigne, they were free from desire: theirs was a culture or economy of need. They apparently did not feel lack; and here breeches are symptomatic of, if nothing else, our lack.

If Montaigne's cannibals do not dissimulate, this has implications for their speech as well as their different dress: they, it seems, tell the truth, and their words require no interpretation – within their own culture. Even if this fantasy of transparent speech were possible anywhere, as soon as the cannibal has to communicate with those who speak other, fallen languages, translation is required and, with it, not only the risk of incompetence (to be deplored) but also a return to the gap (to be acknowledged) between language and its objects that was a recurring theme of sixteenth-century linguistic theory, along with theories of the imagination which went so far as to suggest that the 'gap' was distinctive of human thought. The gap was 'between being and mental representations of being … imagination … designates the usable capacity that mankind has for dissociating the image of the external world from its actual being'.[63] Not neces-sarily negative, in other words; but as debated, and with a negative prehistory, a site of anxiety, all the more so in tandem with doubts about speech being anything other than imperfect or deceptive.

On the other hand, without the gap between language and its objects, where would such powerful, creative and enjoyable devices as figures of speech and irony play? Montaigne's complex irony here acknowledges that while the cannibal might not suffer from this gap, it was the condition of the language of his own culture: not to be resisted, for it reminds of the creative potential of this imperfection as well as of its dependence on interpretation. Creative, in that the gap in which his irony plays is the gap between perception and actual being, between his 'civilized' contemporaries' self-deluding, imagined selves, and their vulnerable reality, rather than between them and us, the uncivilized and

---

[62] This is, after all, one of the connotations of the 'savage' in early modern culture, wrapped up as it was with a longing for the mythical lost wholeness of a state of nature, 'l'originele des hommes' (the original ways of humankind) (p. 225), a notion with which Montaigne was clearly familiar.

[63] Lyons, *Before Imagination* (Stanford, 2005), p. 55.

the civilized. Here the gap which is the locus of deception and self-deception is harnessed for disillusionment.

The ironic ending shakes the reader up: it is one of Montaigne's 'secousses' (jolts). In order to not only throw the reader, but to opt for a throwaway ending, the writer has not to be possessive of his idea or his perspective. So is this an instance of the affectless suspension of self-interest and judgement associated with the kind of scepticism disseminated by the 1562 publication of the *Hypotyposes*? It is not quite so affectless as it seems; nor is it necessarily an instance of the 'generous' irony that some associate with a liberal and sceptical turn of thought.[64] The future meaning of the text is implicitly transferred to the reader; this accepts that the text is vulnerable, and is equally a form of test of the reader, who must be anything but a poor interpreter. Her responsibility is to decide what her relation to the cannibal other is to be; and the writer's lot is to accept that whatever meanings emerge, some may exceed his own understanding.

There is a twist in the asymmetry or disproportion between the chapter's extensive reflections, all its food for thought, and this representation of a gesture of hasty exclusion of it all. It dramatizes the vulnerability of words which depend on interpretation, so it may be protective while being unpossessive. But perhaps the gesture, then, is equally to do with Montaigne being sceptical about his readers being up to the test?

---

[64] On further discussion see Rorty, *Contingency, Irony and Solidarity* (Cambridge, 1989).

3

Cannibal, Beloved: On Eating What is Good …

C'est dans la demande orale que s'est creusé la place de
… désir … La parole reste … le lieu de désir.[1]

The inhumanity and injustice observed by the cannibal visitors to France, where the affluent were indifferent to the starvation surrounding them, were incomprehensible to them from the perspective of their own culture. They are also the antithesis of the ideal relationship between Montaigne and La Boétie memorialized in 'De l'amitié'. In both cannibal culture and this ideal friendship-love, the other and the self are each other's 'moitié': 'nous estions à moitié de tout' (in all things we were halves) (p. 193), and in both chapters highly charged forms of hunger for the other are at the heart of the relationships described.

The metaphor of hunger seems to convey the essence of such idealized relationships – so long as it is predicated on perfect symmetry between the two eaters: 'd'une faim, d'une concurrence pareille' (with equal hunger and accord) (p. 189), and on each being each other's half. Other than in thus describing his relationship with La Boétie, let's remember, Montaigne had to explain the term: and with its absence goes a failure on the part of these 'hommes pleins' (men who had their fill) to give to eat to the other, both literally and figuratively. What it means, figuratively, to give to eat to the other, while at the same time being eaten by the other, or at least being willing to be, and why this was not possible except as an abstraction or a singular exception, are questions I shall explore now, extending the previous chapter's inquiries into subjectivity, sociality, knowledge and desire into analysis of the place of love and sacrifice in Montaigne's writing.

We have seen how Montaigne problematized the cannibal's place as a site of knowledge by the dislocation he introduces via the Rouen encounter and by the interpretative gap with which his chapter's closing irony works. This invites the reader to be more attentive to her own interpretative place and responsibilities and to what it means to be the one who is addressed.

Issues of address and responsibility link the cannibal and the questions now to be explored across the range of relationships represented by friendship-love and love lyric, in the form of twenty-nine sonnets by La Boétie which, between

---

[1] 'The place of desire is hollowed out by the oral demand. Speech remains the place of desire.' Lacan, *Le Séminaire VIII*, pp. 249 and 246.

1580 and 1588, were published as the twenty-ninth chapter of the first book of the *Essais*, but subsequently removed. 'De l'amitié' and 'Des cannibales' help us to understand questions of ethics and subjectivity which are fundamental to the *Essais* as a whole and staged urgently in these chapters. Although the first represents an exclusive relationship and the second concerns the whole social order, questions of the desire for knowledge and love and of what it means to live well run through both. For these seemingly different chapters both explore extreme questions to do with our wanting to be good and to have what is good, and how this fails. My focus here follows from the issues just explored; here the cannibal returns as a figure of love as much as a site of knowledge, and as a way of exploring tensions between the individual's good and the community's.

Between these two extreme chapters, in editions after 1592, along with the remaining dedicatory paragraph of chapter 29, is 'De la moderation' ('On moderation') (I, 30). Both it and La Boétie's sonnets which, while no longer presented, nonetheless make their presence obliquely felt, are significant for the flanking chapters. What have the traditional discourses touched on in 'De la moderation', which concerned themselves with living well – theology, philosophy and also, the more immediately practical expertise, medicine – to do with the issues they explore?

Between ideal friendship-love and the cannibal, traditionally a representation of horror and excess, but here a version of ethical and societal ideals, come love lyric and moderation, a prized classical philosophical virtue, an aspect of what might constitute living the life of a good person. If there is any moderation in the conventions of love lyric such as are found in his friend's poetry, we need to look to the moderating discipline of sonnet structure rather than to any strands in the lover's discourse of exorbitant passion and pain. Erotic love is set aside in 'De l'amitié': the excessive intensities and lack of durability of this 'volage' (fickle) state (p. 186), not least, demote it; and this love lyric was struck out in the Bordeaux copy, leaving in later editions merely a dedicatory paragraph and the direction to look 'ailleurs', elsewhere. Literally, the sonnets were then to be found in other editions of La Boétie's works.

My discussion has two sections: the first, longer section focuses on connections between chapters 28 and 31, and what the failures of moderation and rejection of love lyric suggest about Montaigne's testing, here, the limits of inherited discourses of subjectivity, love and ethics. My reading draws on two texts by Derrida, '"Il faut bien manger" ou le calcul du sujet' and *Donner la mort*, and on psychoanalytic thinking about the nature of desire and ethics.[2] Together they

---

[2] For very illuminating discussion of the interview between Derrida and Nancy, see Still, *Derrida and Hospitality: Theory and Practice* (Edinburgh, 2010), ch. 6. My use of the interview is less a critical consideration of its argument than a working through of the implications of its figuration for Montaigne's ethics of friendship, hospitality and tolerance. There is a commonality between the questions of hospitality in Derrida's writing that Still ponders and those explored here in Montaigne's, however different our emphases and scope – even a certain serendipitous hospitability between our two approaches.

help tease out the relations between sacrifice (a clamorous problem in 'De la moderation' as well as a quieter subtext of 'Des cannibales'), the nature of the subject, and how subjects can live well together respecting each other's other- ness. Derrida's metonymy of 'bien manger', eating well, comes to meet what is figured by Montaigne's cannibal and also by his own 'faim', hunger, for his friend.[3] The second section focuses on the thinking enabled by this figure of eating well. These themes need to be situated in the turbulence of the time of writing, when wars driven by confessionally divergent interpretations of what it meant to 'eat' the body and blood of Christ dramatized what it could mean to live and/or die well. To die a martyr for one's faith is not, after all, necessarily to die well, nor is the kind of living that might precede it: who can judge if this is true sacrifice or a self-deceiving simulacrum of it? Eating well supplements the ways such questions could be addressed in terms of the traditional discourses of living and dying well.

Failing to live well

In 'De l'amitié' erotic heterosexual passion is put down: it lacks constancy, and the traditional metaphors Montaigne chooses to deploy emphasize passion's destructiveness: not simply 'feu' (fire), but 'feu temeraire' (dangerous fire) and 'feu de fiebvre' (fevered fire) (p. 186). Although he insists that there is no com- parison between friendship-love and such passion, 'en comparaison jamais' (never to be compared) (p. 186)), the latter is nonetheless described in terms of what it lacks of, or how it exceeds, the former. Passion is bound not to last: as desire is for what one lacks it will evaporate if satisfied: 'ce n'est qu'un desir forcené après ce qui nous fuit ... suject(e) à sacieté' (it is just a frenzied desire for what escapes us ... subject to satiety) (p. 186). The quotation following, from *Orlando Furioso*, likening desire to the hunt, reminds us that Montaigne's reductive definition (it is just ...) is a prosaic reiteration of a poetic common- place, a reduction of a reduction. Thus, reflection on desire is articulated in such a way as to limit its resonance and to keep it in its place: to give all the more salience to friendship-love. I shall return to the other forms of relationship to which Montaigne contrasts this form of love, but for now, shall stay with erotic love and its expression in love lyric, a form to which Montaigne (as far as is known) did not turn his hand, unlike his friend.

Erotic passion has no further function in this chapter, but for a while was given a place in the sonnets in the following chapter, where La Boétie's verses were published. However, the value of this form of expression of erotic passion is pre-emptively delimited; for they are presented as a substitute: 'en eschange de cet ouvrage serieux, j'en substitueray un autre ... plus gaillard et enjoué' (in

---

[3] In addition, the connections between 'bien manger' and Montaigne's desire to be known need to be teased out; but that is for the next chapter.

↳ of love-lyric

exchange for this serious work, I shall substitute another … gayer, more playful)
(p. 195). They replace La Boétie's *De la servitude volontaire*, the writing which
brought Montaigne and him together in a relationship for which there could
be no substitute. There is more to say on this, but first let us give the dispar-
aged, then dismissed, sonnets, some attention. I shall focus on issues relating
to the expressed desire to write, the use of religious and political vocabulary to
convey the poet/lover's (apparent) total subjection to his beloved, and on the
only substitutive nature of the version of self-sacrifice delivered here. I shall
then explore how these fall aslant issues to do with the nature of the ethical
subject with which the *Essais* were concerned – which may suggest why the
sonnets came to be excluded from Montaigne's text.

The primary focus of my inquiry is not developments in love lyric at the
time; the rudiments of much larger and more complex interpretations of the
function of love lyric, as it grew out of the twelfth-century troubadour writing
in which courtly love has its origins, in the literary history of the early modern
ethical subject, must suffice here, just enough to situate my reading of this
small corpus.[4] The following themes are key: the representation of the lady as
sovereign, or divinity; the poet/lover's enjoyment of his subjection to her; and
his declarations of willingness to die for her and love – to give himself as a
sacrificial object. The blandness of the overfamiliar rhetoric of 'dying for love',
which seems readable as merely dramatic figuration for emotional pain and the
willingness to do anything to guarantee the desired ending, may camouflage
possible greater resonance, even seriousness.

But Montaigne's pre-emptive direction to readers is that this writing is not
serious, merely a substitute, and about what is only fickle. Not serious: its version
of 'servitude volontaire', willing self-subjection and even, here, its enjoyment
– 'J'ay espousé la douleur que je porte' (I am wedded to my suffering) (sonnet
24, line 4) – is not to be taken seriously, unlike La Boétie's essay on the theme.
How can one not take such a theme seriously, given its political and ethical
importance? Two forms of theory resonate particularly strongly with this writing
and help us explore its potential seriousness. Lacan's reading of the function of
the lady in the poet/lover's psychic economy in troubadour poetry, and thereafter in the discourse of courtly love and more broadly in discourses of love in
European culture, is particularly helpful, and Derrida's writing on gift, sacrifice
and ethical subjectivity further illuminates the issues. I shall draw primarily on
the former for now, focusing on the lady as Other, in terms of the structure of
the subject's desire.

Lacan's psychoanalytic writings keep returning to the subject's desire, but his
fourth seminar, *La Relation d'objet* and his seventh, *L'Ethique de la psychanalyse*, are those most pertinent to desire and sacrifice as articulated in love lyric,
and to the wider questions of desire, love, knowledge and writing in Mont-

---

    [4]   Among the range of studies, see Kay, *Subjectivity in Troubadour Poetry* (Cambridge,
1990), and Helgeson, *Harmonie divine et subjectivité poétique chez Maurice Scève* (Geneva,
2001).

desire is of & for the O

aigne's *Essais* which direct the second section of my discussion. The key aspect of Lacanian theory for my reading of these sonnets is its insistence that desire is of and for the Other: 'le désir de l'Autre', meaning both the Other's desire and desire for the Other. The doubleness encapsulated by the preposition 'de', of, which implies, as is explicit elsewhere in Lacan's writing, that desire to love the other is equally desire for the other's love, and that love of other and self converge, is important here; even more so is what is meant by the Other, and its implications for the structure of the relationship with the beloved in love lyric. She, if Other, encompasses 'la problématique de l'Autre, qui est bien cet Autre absolu, cet inconscient fermé, cette femme impénétrable, ou bien derrière celle-ci la figure de la mort, qui est le dernier Autre absolu' (the problem of the Other, which is indeed that absolute Other, the inaccessible unconscious, an inscrutable woman, or even, behind her, the figure of death, the ultimate, absolute Other).[5]

O = Ucs

In Lacan's thinking about the subject's psychic economy and about inter-subjective relations, the Other is not an other subject so much as the subject's unconscious, the dimension of his being seemingly beyond his conscious reach (except as, for instance, intimated in his dreams once they are put into words), as well as being the woman of love lyric and the 'figure of death' – which the rhetoric of love lyric seems to identify as one and the same. Love and death, fascination and recoil: love lyric may be read as a form of address to this Other, whose impenetrability is irresistible but equally a source of 'life-threatening' anxiety. By addressing the Other, the subject goes on entreating for an answer, both for there even to be an answer, and for the answer to the question: she/it seems inexplicably to want me to suffer, so what on earth does she/it want of me?

La Boétie's sonnets primarily address Amour, god of love, or an unnamed, frequently divinized, baneful beloved, and are about the poet/lover's total subjection to her and to love. This is expressed through the already conventional theme of painful devotion to Amour and to the desired woman and, despite her cruel rejections, a willingness to give his life to her for love and to give her his writing as a true witness to this.[6] These desires and the vocabulary articulating them would have been familiar to readers of early modern love lyric and, despite (sonnet 11) the poet/lover wishing to express his *own* pain, 'larmes … toutes miennes' (tears that are all my own) (line 2) rather than imitating masters of the tradition such as Petrarch, Catullus and Propertius and thereby limiting it (actually just another topos), these sonnets on the whole ventriloquize the conventions of the poetic representation of love, both its lexis and its structures. Love is a state of 'mal', pain, engendering only pleasures mixed with extreme suffering – as oxymorons such as 'venimeuse doulceur', poisonous sweetness

---

5   Lacan, *Le Séminaire IV*, p. 431.

6   On dying of and for love, and giving/losing his whole self to her or love, see sonnets 1, 2, 3, 12, 15, 21, 22, 24, 25, 26 and 27; on the devotional gift of his writing, or his writing as true witness to love, see in particular sonnets 7, 8, 11, 16, 17, 19, 20 and 28.

(sonnet 14, line 4), suggest. The object of desire is not only cruel but perverse: 'Elle n'est pas de ma peine assouvie:/ Elle s'en rit' (She is not assuaged by my pain:/ She laughs at it) (sonnet 25, lines 6–7). The totally subjugated poet/lover wants nothing more than to go on writing about this, to perpetuate his pain in verse and persuade her (and presumably the reader) of the sacrificial nature of his devotion: 'si veulx bien que je meure en t'aymant' (what I really want is to die loving you) (sonnet 15, line 13).

Despite voicing the desire to be authentic, indeed even as it does so, this writing goes on copying (not, of course, the first instance of this in love lyric). This reminds us that this discourse had become one of substitutability, in which one beloved could be celebrated or mourned or … in much the same terms as another. The force of the extreme rhetoric of love's power to give or take figurative life was diluted by repetition; and the theme of sacrifice demanded by love and willingly made, which was only ever a pseudo-sacrifice, might by now seem something of a travesty. Not 'serious'. However, given the diminishing returns of the theme, we might wonder why it retained such currency, as in these sonnets.

The poet/lover frequently expresses his willingness to devote himself and his writing to love and the beloved, and to accept the loss of self. So recurrent is the theme of writing that arguably the poet's desire to write emerges as stronger than that for the supposed object of his desire. It is in the context of the theme of writing about love and the beloved that the use of religious vocabulary is most striking: her 'sainct nom' (saintly name) (sonnet 7, line 8), her 'main divine' (divine hand) (sonnet 17, line 12), omnipotence, 'son oeil tout puissant' (her all-powerful look) (sonnet 18, line 13), possible miracles: 'Quels miracles en moy pensez vous qu'elle face' (imagine what miracles she might work through me) (sonnet 18, line 12). His writing is variously an altar, 'Je te donrois un autel' (I would give you an altar) (sonnet 17, line 11), an expression of devotion ('veoyez/ S'ainsi comme je fais, adorer je la dois?') (see how I owe her adoration) (sonnet 18, lines 10–11), or blasphemy (see sonnets 16 and 17).

Striking not because it persuades that the sacrifice of self and the devotional offering of words are 'real'; on the contrary, because these reproductions of the theme of sacrifice underscore its lack of authenticity or theological weight, despite the religious vocabulary deployed. For here the poet/lover's gift of himself is not 'free': rather, it is given in the hope of receiving something in return: love; less pain; an answer to the question implicit in so many of these sonnets: what do you/does she want of me? This last is particularly clear in sonnets 22 and 23, in which her perversity is figured by the contradiction between her eyes and her speech. Her effect is summed up in sonnet 23 as: 'Ores son oeil m'appelle, or sa bouche me chasse' (Now her eye summons me, while her mouth chases me away) (line 10). The split between look, or gaze, and speech, helps us to understand the representation of the relation to the beloved in the sonnets and also in the discourses of both sacrifice and of the gift of writing with which La Boétie worked.

There are two key lines of interpretation here. The first draws on Lacanian thinking, which has engaged particularly fruitfully with love lyric.[7] Drawing on this, let us cast the beloved as the Other, and focus on the narcissism of what the poet/lover 'sees': in her/the Other's gaze he sees what he wants to see, his own desire mirrored. But she refuses his desire, dismissing his narcissism. This needs to be read in conjunction with the figuration throughout the sonnets of this receiving/rejecting as a matter of life and death: Ovid's Narcissus drowned, but all *jouissance*, not just that which might be the outcome of narcissistic desire, will be destructive. *Jouissance* is not some lovely release to be simply wished for, but rather is terrifying beyond representation; moreover, it has to do with the subject's desire for his or her own destruction.[8] Her contrary gaze and speech palely figure this, in that she is represented as embodying what is both most desired and feared. But that she represents it, and that the poet's desire is to represent and go on representing it, indicates that it is not only sacrifice that is a simulacrum in this writing, but so too is *jouissance*. To it the poet prefers to remain firmly in the Symbolic and to write – even at the cost of muting the resonances of what it might mean to 'die' of or for love.

This line of interpretation, which connects themes of sacrifice, the expressed desire to lose himself for love (in which sacrifice and *jouissance* seem to converge), and the desire to write, suggests that only the last is not a simulacrum. My second but related argument, which also draws on Lacanian discussions of love lyric, is even more focused on the theme of sacrifice. To set it up, I can do no better than quote Gaunt:

> For Lacan ... the gaze is primarily the gaze of the Other ... the subject's desire instantiates an imaginary scenario in which he is construed as object, not as subject, in which his integrity and wholeness are guaranteed by the Other's gaze, just as sacrifice guarantees the Other's wholeness. The subject falls in love with his own *assujettissement* [subjection], and therefore paradoxically must sacrifice his subject position repeatedly in order to establish and then to retain it. (p. 32)

Gaunt's focus is troubadour poetry, in this instance that of Bernart de Ventadorn, but his analysis also applies acutely to this love lyric. There, the Other's/ her gaze addresses him ('m'appelle' (calls me) (sonnet 23, line 10)): that is, he recognizes himself in it (as he wants to be); it is also the guarantor of all his

---

[7] See Lacan, *Le Séminaire VII*, which articulates the connections between love and religion, and for development of these aspects of Lacan's ideas, see Žižek, *Enjoy Your Symptom!* (London, 1992) and *The Metastases of Enjoyment* (London, 1994), pp. 89–112. Also, for a particularly stimulating account within French studies, see Gaunt, *Love and Death*, especially chapters 1 and 2.

[8] Lacan's thinking builds on his rereading of Freud's 'Beyond the Pleasure Principle'. I shall return in due course to this symptom of the 'double', or perverse nature (in the ordinary sense), of the subject in the wider context of reflections in the *Essais* on pleasure and pain and what exceeds or troubles an ideal of moderation, for it bears on more than desire as expressed in love lyric.

hope, 'tout mon espoir' (sonnet 22, line 2). He embraces this state, even at the cost of his position as a subject; it is only by going on writing about this that he can keep on re-establishing himself as a subject. So much for the hapless poet/ lover. But there is still more to say about the theme of sacrifice, which plays so large a part in the process of writing and re-establishing himself as a subject.

The sonnets read as if they are designed to sustain the question, what does she want of me, and they frequently suggest that she wants his life. We need to turn this around, and think instead in terms of the willingness to offer one's life as what defines the individual as an ethical subject: for this is all one can truly give that is one's own.[9] Put like this, the sonnets go on staging the poet/ lover's need to keep re-establishing himself as a subject. But if that is the case, and in the context of this love lyric, in which or through which it is clear that no one is going to die, then the theme of sacrifice and the 'real' questions of ethical subjectivity that centre on it turn out to be reduced, coopted to the desire to write.

There is a further problem in the use of the theme of sacrifice here. Thematically, the desire to sacrifice is given priority; witness the opening lines of the first sonnet:

> Pardon, Amour, pardon; ô Seigneur! Je te vouë
> Le reste de mes ans, ma voix et mes escripts,
> Mes sanglots, mes soupirs, mes larmes et mes cris. (lines 1–3)

> (Pardon me, Love; oh Lord, to you I vow/ my remaining years, my voice and my writing/ my sobs, sighs, tears and cries.)

Presenting the desire to sacrifice to a divine figure seems to presuppose the existence of a fitting cause; it is used (and therefore already no longer properly sacrifice) as a means of representing the beloved/Other as if she/it is indeed without lack. But what if this covers over or distracts from the anxious possibility that she, or the Other, is not without lack? If the Other were not all she/it is imagined to be, then what she/it asked of the subject would be merely cruelly perverse rather than having the status of sacrifice, that is, the self-defining act which is what the subject desires. And if she is symbolizable, then she does lack. So the desire to write, and for writing to be a sacrificial gift, rests on an aporia which undermines the logic on which the discourse relies.

This analysis brings out ways in which these sonnets are problematic for a reader – Montaigne as well as his readers – whose concerns are 'serious'. Whilst serious issues can be identified, they take the form of diluted reproductions of existing versions, substitutes for a more powerfully engaged representation of the ethical dilemmas facing the subject who desires and desires recognition, and struggles to understand that which eludes him. Grounds enough, perhaps,

---

[9] This now touches on Derrida's writing about ethics and the subject, for instance in *Donner le temps* (Paris, 1991), *Donner la mort*, in *L'Ethique du don* and 'Il faut bien manger'. I shall explore this further shortly in relation to 'De l'amitié'.

for deciding to set these sonnets aside; all the more so if, as well as evaluating them in the terms of the discourse with which they work, we also return to their connection to *De la servitude volontaire*, and to the relationship between love lyric and love in the context of ethics as it concerns both the individual's *and* society's good, the theme of the last section of my discussion here.

The sonnets are announced as a substitute for La Boétie's essay, perhaps a distraction from its loss; but their representation of the shared theme of 'servitude volontaire' is no substitute for its serious exploration in the essay, as Montaigne's praise for it in 'De l'amitié' suggests. The complexities of self-subjugation are not to be toyed with as if independent of social, religious and political resonance, their vocabulary used as if it were exclusively figurative, as in the sonnets. Moreover, for Montaigne, the essay also seems to have more to do with love than do the sonnets that speak explicitly of it. For it was with reading it that his love for his friend originated: 'longue piece avant que je l'eusse veu ... me donna la premiere connoissance de son nom, acheminant ainsi cette amitié que nous avons nourrie' (long before I first saw him ... it acquainted me for the first time with his name, and thus began this friendship which we have nurtured) (p. 184).

Moreover, love as represented in the sonnets is not 'therapeutic'; there is no cure for the pain it brings. For all that the beloved, the 'dur tyran' (harsh tyrant) of sonnet 27, is reinscribed as the 'royne du coeur des hommes' (queen of men's hearts) in the last line of the final sonnet, there is no narrative motivation for this quasi-improvement; she is still predatory, ruthless and all-consuming, and the poet remains in pain: 'Ayant perdu tout l'aise que j'avois,/... cette playe' (having lost all ease I ever had ... wounded) (sonnet 28, lines 9 and 12). No *eudaimonia*, growth of understanding or insight; that is, a discourse of love that operates as if entirely independent of questions of love and ethics, such as, should one love, and how is love 'good', given the pain it may cause, and the disturbance to which it may subject one?

I shall return to the relationship between words, love and ethics in the context of what Montaigne's friendship with La Boétie represents about 'eating well', and explore further why, in relation both to La Boétie's essay and to Montaigne's writing, the sonnets were excluded, despite their earlier inclusion. But first, the meaning of 'De la moderation', which also comes between 'De l'amitié' and 'Des cannibales', needs some investigation.

Is rhubarb good for us?

Elsewhere in the *Essais*, for instance in 'De l'institution des enfans' ('On the education of children'), moderation is associated with freedom, equity, good judgement, physical and spiritual well-being; it is highly valued (a great Aristotelian virtue), and Montaigne squarely ascribes the wars to its lack.[10] However,

---

[10] See 'De la liberté de conscience' ('On freedom of conscience') (II, 19).

the chapter entitled 'De la moderation' is not, itself, moderate. It reflects on the limits and failures of authoritative discourses on the value of moderation or practices designed to moderate extremes. It ends with a long 1588 addition on religious sacrifice – of the kind which Christianity shunned; not that it had done away with a foundation in sacrifice, but it replaced it with symbolic ritual. But this is prefaced by the comment that *all* religions have encouraged rather than moderated extremes of human sacrifice: 'penser gratifier au Ciel et à la nature par nostre massacre et homicide, qui fut universellement embrassée en toutes religions' (to think that we please heaven and nature by acts of massacre and homicide, a belief shared universally by all religions) (p. 201). Notwithstanding that past tense, the resonance of this statement for Christians at the time seems unmistakable: not only because of confessional conflict over the meaning of the site of sacrifice that is Christ's body, or 'body', but also because martyr-dom, self-sacrifice during the ensuing wars, posed so many ethical issues while seeming self-evidently virtuous.

The chapter's closing reflections on what we want to think our acts mean and achieve are illuminated if we explore them in terms of desire and problems of knowledge and self-knowledge, which are already anticipated by its opening sentences. They require that the title's announced theme of moderation be understood in relation to human beings' tendency to spoil that which is good, through wanting (the good) too much, and through possessive desire: that is, our relationship with our objects is wrong and wrongs them. 'Comme si nous avions l'attouchement infect, nous corrompons par nostre maniement les choses qui d'elles mesmes sont belles et bonnes. Nous pouvons saisir la vertu de façon qu'elle en deviendra vicieuse, si nous l'embrassons d'un desir trop aspre et violant' (as if our touch were infectious, we corrupt things which are in themselves beautiful and good by handling them. Our grasp on virtue can make her vicious, if the desire fuelling our embrace is too harsh and violent) (p. 197).

Infection and corruption gesture towards both a medical analogy and a theological explanation; yet the chapter seems most concerned with problems caused by aspects of belief and theology's incapacity to explain or regulate behaviour; likewise, medicine's flawed cures. Here, medicine, as that use of 'infect' at the outset suggests, features both as the expert practice designed to restore health and as a source of analogy for philosophical practice aimed towards living well. But what really claims attention here are the opening words: 'comme si', 'as if'. The chapter offers a rapid survey of authoritative practical, philosophical and spiritual 'cures' for human 'misere' (wretchedness) (p. 200); but alongside the ideas of excess (and its contrary, lack, into which it reverses) which moderation might cure, it explores the problem of 'as if' behaviour. I am a martyr for my faith; I believe I am a martyr for my faith; I believe that I am justified in killing for my faith; I think this to be the full account of my choices and acts. But if I 'infect' all that touches me and that I touch, and if we accept that the locus of infection is the gap between what I think I know about this and about what I want and do, and what remains unknown to me (Lacan's inaccessible, inscrutable otherness within me) in what I want and do, then how can I, or we, tell the difference between genuine sacrifice and justification and what seems like it – (only) appears 'as if' genuine?

Montaigne's chapter explores a classical virtue, and includes medicine as both a practical art and an analogy for other discourses that attempt to moderate desire and belief; thus my reading takes its bearings from Nussbaum's discussion of Hellenistic ethics in *The Therapy of Desire*.[11] She explores the ways in which medical analogies work to 'underline ... the practical goal of ethics' (p. 59), in the pursuit of a good human life and greater understanding (knowledge through inquiry) of and (compassion) for the role in ethical living of passions such as love and sexuality, fear (of death), and anger. By focusing on Montaigne's interweaving of medical and philosophical perspectives, comparable to those traced by Nussbaum in the practices of, not least, Aristotle and Sextus Empiricus, I want to bring out the recalcitrance of desire and belief to sceptical 'cure', the implied arguments about the significance of the relationship between the 'expert' and the subject or 'patient', and therefore the need to turn elsewhere for alleviation.

'Philosophy makes itself the doctor of human lives' (Nussbaum, p. 484). Given Montaigne's negativity towards contemporary medical practice, it seems unlikely that medicine offered him a model, or even source of analogy, for other discourses with practical, socially, emotionally and ethically 'therapeutic' intentions.[12] On the contrary, it can be used as a means to identify limits or problems (as it was already, say, by Aristotle).[13] However, recourse to it as analogy *per se* works to underline the view that the measure of ethics, 'les sciences qui reglent les meurs des hommes' (the forms of knowledge which rule humankind) (p. 198), needs to be practical efficacy.

Montaigne begins with the idea of disease; we are infected spiritually and, in keeping with the dominant figure for society at the time, the social and political body is diseased; the use of the first-person plural subject encompasses society as a whole. Disease and figurative disease return explicitly towards the end of

---

[11] Nussbaum, *The Therapy of Desire* (Princeton, 1994). See also Viano, 'Lo Scetticismo antico et la medicina', in Giannantoni (ed.), *Lo Scetticismo antico* (Naples, 1981), pp. 563–658. With reference to Montaigne's discussions also, see O'Brien, 'Question(s) d'équilibre', in Peacock and Supple (eds), *Lire les 'Essais' de Montaigne* (Paris, 1998), pp. 107–22, and Brancher, 'Ny plus ne moins que la rubarbe qui pousse hors les mauvaises humeurs', in Demonet and Legros (cds), *L'Ecriture du scepticisme chez Montaigne* (Geneva, 2004), pp. 303–20.

[12] When at the end of 'De ne contrefaire le malade' ('On not pretending to be ill') (II, 25) Montaigne cites Seneca: 'si avons nous une tres-douce medecine que la philosophie: car des autres, on n'en sent le plaisir qu'apres la guerison, cette cy plait et guerit ensemble' (indeed we have a very sweet medicine in philosophy; for it pleases and cures us simultaneously, whereas we only feel the others' pleasure once cured) (p. 690), I do not think he is offering a simply generalizable metaphor: the opinion is given as Seneca's, not Montaigne's, without further evaluation, and Seneca's philosophy is neither all philosophy nor, necessarily, in Montaigne's judgement, a philosophy that would fit this description. But for further discussion of the value of cures which do not themselves hurt, see pp. 87–8 below.

[13] See Nussbaum, *The Therapy of Desire*, pp. 70 and 75.

the chapter, after focus on married love as a way of exploring sexual passion or appetite (it being legitimate in marriage, the foundation of social order), as that which is particularly resistant to moderation by philosophical or theological teaching about what is 'good health'. But it is not only the excesses of sexual appetite that threaten individual and social well-being. Here, as in Montaigne's other discussions of the value of moderation, the threat is also, more paradoxically, excessive attachment to what is thought to be *good*, be that virtue, justice or religious belief, as well as more evidently 'pseudo-goals', such as power, 'as if they had some sort of intrinsic value … [which] leads … to antagonisms and frenetic striving, to acts of cruelty, to the rupturing of ties that bind families, cities and the community of human beings' (Nussbaum, p. 501). This description of what Hellenistic philosophers identified and sought to cure might equally well be that of the *Essais*, with all their engagement with these Greek philosophers. Such 'pseudo-goals' were endemic in the continuing wars.[14] Montaigne's chapter gives the problems of excess particular urgency by mapping from more evident 'pseudo-goals' to the catastrophic antagonisms caused by dogmatic religious belief, thereby raising the question, how can justifiable good and 'pseudo-goals' be reliably differentiated in matters of belief and the behaviour it causes?

Two examples are given, Pausanius's mother, and the dictator Posthumius, both of whom ordered the death of their sons. The first does not identify the act or desire to which this was the response. In fact there is some sleight of hand in the presentation of both examples: in the first, had readers been reminded of the nature of Pausanius's 'crime', his mother's act might have seemed (to some) less starkly reprehensible, for he was guilty of betrayal of his people; and in the second, by pre-emptively qualifying Posthumius as 'the dictator', judgement is tilted against him, even before the disproportionate nature of his action has been confirmed as a savagely immoderate attachment to abstract virtue. Montaigne's presentation ensures that there is no doubt about his meaning. Both examples are instances of almost unspeakable 'rupturing of the ties that bind families': 'me met en peine de la baptiser' (I can scarcely bear to give it a name) (p. 197). How could a parent value something more than the life of their son? The underlying question posed by these non-Judaeo-Christian examples of 'immodération vers le bien' (immoderate desire for even what is good) (p. 197) links excess with problems to do with sacrifice: what human good could have such intrinsic value? The question is made more acute by the second example: what for Posthumius was a good, namely, rigid obedience to the rules of battle, is only a pseudo-good, worth a human life (only) in the judgement of a *dictator*, one who behaves as if his will and power were not, unlike other humans', limited. Thus self-delusion and dogmatism are also connected to such issues.

Whilst these examples are pagan and secular, the problem of relationships with what is (deemed) good, and the function of forms of sacrifice as acts which

---

[14] For historical analysis of mixed causes of the wars and their lengthy continuation, see for instance Carroll, *Noble Power during the French Wars of Religion* (Cambridge, 1998) and *Martyrs and Murderers* (Oxford, 2009).

are (deemed) true to the demands of the good, are inseparable from the Christian context of writing. Questions of religious belief and behaviour, and of the relationship between belief, knowledge and meaning, are already present in the chapter, initially (p. 197) via a citation from Paul's Epistle to the Romans: 'be not more wise than it behoveth, but be ye soberly wise' (12:3), then amplified by the addition of a reference to damage recently done to his religion, in the name of religion, by an unnamed French nobleman.

Montaigne condemns such excess as both 'estrange' (strange) and, more than once, 'sauvage' (savage) (p. 198): alienation from what is moderated and therefore necessary to good life, and also loss of those qualities needed for the individual to participate in community. Plato's *Gorgias* (484C–D) is drawn on at some length here, concluding that 'l'extremité de la philosophie ... nous esclave nostre naturelle franchise' (philosophy taken to extremes enslaves our natural freedom) (p. 198). Philosophy must be 'prinse' (taken) (p. 198) in moderation, or it will be damaging ('dommageable' (p. 198)). This use of a medical metaphor, which picks up on the figure of infection at the outset, is then developed more fully later, with more explicit articulation between medicine and philosophy, specifically scepticism's purgative methods and the concept of cure by contraries.

Montaigne's thoughts move on from alienating forms of virtue to sexual appetite via the observation that ethical discourses, be they philosophical or theological, affect everything in our lives: 'elles se meslent de tout' (get into everything) (p. 198). He focuses on the possibility of sensual enjoyment being moderated. Orthodoxies presented here, such as appeal to decorum, to the proper function of intercourse being procreation, and for husbands to be the keepers of their wives' virtue, lack purchase; and the asymmetry of the relationship is striking. Asymmetry, already in Aristotle's critique of the medical analogy for philosophy, which ascribes authority and agency to one participant (doctor/ethical expert/husband) and passivity to the other (patient/pupil/wife), undermines the curative power of ethical practice even if it may work in some medical treatment.[15] This chimes with Montaigne's versions elsewhere of productive, ethical relations (not least between his text and his readers), which thrive on more equal engagement. Here, however, the issue is not confronted, except insofar as all participants are, equally, infected; it is for the reader to tease out this theme, which is complicated by the fact that although the chapter opens by addressing an inclusive 'nous', the reader addressed in the section on marriage and sexual desire seems to be masculine. So, all are equally subject to disease; but not all are equally addressed.

Even if social, cultural and religious formation shapes desires of all kinds, this formation is not coterminous with them, particularly when it comes to sexuality. One of the problems the chapter works away at, with its vocabulary of excess, is *jouissance*: to guard against this (to invoke Freud) we need to enjoy

---

[15] See Nussbaum, *The Therapy of Desire*, pp. 70–5.

as little as possible. That excess, whether in the context of erotic desire or desire to be virtuous, is terrifying, is clear: 'elle m'estonne et *me met en peine de la baptiser*' (p. 197, my italics), which we might translate not just as 'it astonishes me and is almost unspeakable' but as 'almost unthinkable in Christian culture'. Not that Montaigne elaborates on why Christianity protects its adherents more effectively from excess than do other religions; on the contrary, towards the end of the chapter, all believers are cast as being equally prone to excessive acts *for* their religion.

The cure, analogous to Freud's 'enjoy as little as possible', is that quotation from Paul, 'be not more wise …' (p. 197); otherwise, the death drive takes hold, whether in the examples of the parents' appalling willingness for their child to be killed, in the destruction of the social fabric, or in perverse sexual behaviours, whether in love lyric or more generally practised.

Montaigne presents philosophy and theology as affecting our innermost being, getting in to everything: 'il n'est action si privée et secrete, qui se desrobbe de leur cognoissance et jurisdiction' (no action is so private and secret that it escapes their knowledge and jurisdiction) (p. 198). Yet the force of his reflections, examples and anecdotes countermands this assertion of our transparency to those who claim to know how to cure us: such are the limits of these discourses and practices that there must be aspects of our being which are beyond their, and our, knowledge. We might call this the unconscious, that which is beyond cognition; according to Nussbaum, Hellenistic philosophers recognized this already.[16] Here, there is something approaching this, obliquely, in what makes humans wretched: namely, the impurity, or mixedness, and incompleteness of our experience of, and relationship with, (good) objects: 'à peine est-il en son pouvoir, par sa condition naturelle, de gouter un seul plaisir entier et pur' (such is our nature that we can barely taste a single pleasure fully and purely) (p. 200). Moreover, we worsen our state by using our wisdom to attack what pleasure we do have, or, 'peigner et farder' (to disguise, even conceal) to ourselves what makes us suffer (p. 200). Thus the cost of alleviation is self-deception; we are divided from the world and we are internally divided. We are not transparent and capable of philosophically desirable moderation, because, as implied here and as is explicit in 'De l'utile et de l'honneste' ('On what is useful and honourable'), the coordinates of our desire are not so well ordered; we love both pain and pleasure: 'nostre estre est simenté de qualitez maladives … au milieu de la compassion, nous sentons au dedans je ne sçay quelle aigre-douce poincte de volupté à voir souffrir autruy; et les enfants le sentent' (diseased qualities cement our being … in moments of compassion deep down we feel an indefinable bittersweet prickle of enjoyment at seeing others suffer; even children feel it) (p. 790). No one, not Montaigne, not even Plato, is purely virtuous: 'je trouve que la meilleure bonté que j'aye, a de la teinture vicieuse. Et crains que Platon en sa plus verte vertu … il y eust senty quelque

16 See Nussbaum, *The Therapy of Desire*, p. 490.

ton gauche de mixtion humaine' (I find that my best goodness is tinged with vice. And I fear that Plato would have intuited some false note, some element of human imperfection in his liveliest virtue).[17]

The nature of our desire for virtue makes it vicious; 'De la moderation' does not explain this beyond recourse to the concept of excess being destructive, and the observation that human reason is not a guaranteed protection against it, but may even provoke it. Moreover, we are perverse and cruel, and the not-fully knowable locus of such ambiguity within us is 'indefinable' (p. 790). This aspect beyond our cognition is part of the set of problems of belief with which the chapter ends.

But en route, it turns towards scepticism, without naming it as such; instead, the focus is on medicine both as practice and as analogy for cures for mind and soul. 'Medecins spirituels et corporels' (spiritual and bodily physicians) (p. 200) converge in their requirement that cure take the form of acute physical *and* emotional or psychological suffering: 'veritable affliction ... aigreur poignante' (genuine afflictions ... stinging bitterness) (p. 200) according to the principle that 'le mal ... guerit le mal' (pain cures pain) (p. 200) – rather than that contraries cure. There is a touch of scepticism, loosely defined, in Montaigne's questioning and in the description of such practice through negation: 'ne trouvent aucune voye à la guerison ... que par' (find no way to a cure ... except by) (p. 200). It is also present more precisely in a reference to misguided practitioners believing that rhubarb must be unpleasant to be curative, and Montaigne's ironic comment that cure by contraries fails. That an effective counter-argument is, like rhubarb, purgative, is indissociable from Pyrrhonist scepticism, as transmitted to Mont-aigne by Sextus Empiricus, or from Montaigne's representation of it (in the 'Apologie'). Sextus's scepticism uses medical analogy in its arguments for its cure of the most serious disease from which a human suffers: to free him from disabling belief. But purgative drugs are not effective by inflicting pain; what matters is that 'aperient drugs do not merely eliminate the humours from the body, but also expel themselves along with the humours'.[18]

The counter-argument removes itself in the process of undoing the preceding argument. Montaigne criticizes the belief that cures must hurt to be effective; instead, that to cure pain, a gentle, painless approach is what works, needs open-minded consideration. Thus even if there were reasons, as Brancher argues, for Montaigne to be sceptical about the effectiveness of both medical and philosophical rhubarb, his doubt is not directed at the purgative method *per se* but at aspects of its practice.[19] His argument is with pain, and for its contrary, and he allows that for those who like rhubarb, well-cooked, and who

---

[17] 'Nous ne goustons rien de pur' (We taste nothing pure), pp. 674–5.

[18] Sextus Empiricus, *Outlines of Pyrrhonism* I.206, trans. Bury (Cambridge, Mass. and London, 1967), p. 123; see also II.188 (pp. 270–1) and in the *Adversus Mathematicos* (*Against the Logicians*), trans. Bury (Cambridge, Mass. and London, 1935), see II.480–1 (pp. 486–9).

[19] See Brancher, 'Ny plus ne moins que la rubarbe'.

do not find it strange ('qui accepteroit la rubarbe comme familiere' (who would accept rhubarb, being familiar with it) (p. 200)), it can be therapeutic. He also argues against a relationship in which the expert or authority uses his position to impose further pain on the one who suffers, in the name of cure. The principles of cure by contrary and also of non-dogmatism, which leaves the way open for further counter-arguments, is what matter, as does a desire to keep the arguments moving, 'enquesteuse, non resolutive' (inquiring, not concluding) (p. 1030). That the principles and practices of scepticism join a discussion of pain seems unsurprising: both the existence of pain and the difficulty of really understanding the specificity of another's pain test more assertive conceptual models.

It is to what is particularly difficult to comprehend, yet a matter of the most dogmatic belief, that the chapter then moves, in its closing passage on religious sacrifice as a universal problem. Although the anecdotes are located primarily in the newly discovered Americas, they are governed by the initial use of the first-person plural, the adverb 'universally' and the adjective 'all' (religions) (p. 201): examples addressing all readers for whom religious belief is meaningful, particularly readers at the time living through the 'massacre and homicide' of wars waged in the name of religion. An explicit connection is made between sacrifice and war: that the continuous need for 'gens sacrifiables' (people to sacrifice) fostered war: '*nourissoit* la guerre' (p. 201).

How does this bear on the contemporary wars? An answer was suggested some lines earlier, by the notion that such acts were thought to please heaven. The vocabulary is decisive; no martyrdom here, rather, the secular criminality of massacre and homicide. 'Penser', what we think, becomes, instead, how we delude ourselves. But false justification and self-justification are not all; what if it were not willingness to die for one's belief that led to war, but that war was fed by the desire to kill others or have others killed for that belief, others identified as the ones to be sacrificed; not a sacrificial purging of those who did not share one's belief so much as a travesty of sacrifice, example of the destructive nature of any belief that does not tolerate the existence of others?

The culture of human sacrifice both repels and fascinates in this writing; the excessive detail here is symptomatic, conveying the anxiety generated by an encounter with such horror. What implicates all, '*nostre* massacre et homicide', is too close to home to be represented, but is exiled, obliquely representable in a non-Christian 'ailleurs' (elsewhere). Close reading of the whole passage is beyond the scope of my discussion; what matters is the final anecdote of an encounter between native Mexicans and their conqueror, Cortez. A relationship in which the absence of symmetry between the participants counters moderation, indeed is the outcome of indifference to principles of moderation and symmetry – or worse: the preference for asymmetry on the part of the Conquistadors. And for 'having the last word', which Montaigne's use of the anecdote denies them, albeit temporarily.

> Je diray encore ce compte. Aucuns de ces peuples, ayant esté batuz par luy [Cortez], envoyerent le recognoistre et rechercher d'amitié; les messagers luy

desire / self-dec¹ / (H) drive

presenterent trois sortes de presens, en cette maniere: Seigneur, voylà cinq esclaves; si tu és un Dieu fier, qui te paisses de chair et de sang, mange les, et nous t'en amerrons d'avantage; si tu és un Dieu debonnaire, voylà de l'encens et des plumes; si tu es un homme, prens les oiseaux et les fruicts que voicy.

(p. 201)

(I want to tell you one more story. Some of these people, beaten by him, sent messengers to find out about him and seek his friendship. They offered him three kinds of gifts, thus: Lord, here are five slaves; if you are a fierce god who feeds on human flesh and blood, eat them, and we will bring you more. If you are a gentle god, here are feathers and incense; if you are human, accept these birds and these fruits.)

Contemporaries of Montaigne, not all yet familiar, as he was, through accounts such as Gomara's *Historia de Mexico* (1554) and Benzoni's *Historia del mondo novo* (1565), with the atrocities committed by the Conquistadors, would have gained some sense of them through his 'Des coches' (III, 6), and could have recognized the irony here. Human sacrifice was fundamental to some of the religions of the Latin American peoples, though not all; but Cortez was neither a God nor a gentle human, and exploited all that the conquered peoples gave him, without recognition of the cultural economy within which their gifts operated (as glimpsed in the anecdote), and indifferent to the pseudo-sacrifice of native life to his conquering Christian God.

This is an example not of human sacrifice as a problem *per se* but of the problem that arose once forms of pseudo-sacrifice were mistaken for, or used as if, genuine sacrifice. What was being done (as if) in the name of God, by Roman Catholics to Protestants and by Protestants to Roman Catholics, overshadowing what continued to be done by Christians to Jews and Muslims as well as to Latin American peoples, is perhaps what is most at stake here – as is theology's and philosophy's inability to moderate it. Indeed, dogmatic religious belief fuelled it. To have the last word; or to allow that one's argument is already making way for another. This alternative would only be livable if participants were equals not least in their respect for each other; only if each were the other's 'moitiez' (halves), which, the *Essais* suggest, is a singular ideal ('De l'amitié') or only found 'ailleurs', elsewhere ('Des cannibales').

A diet of rhubarb is preferable to human flesh. It does not feed war, and the appetite for rhubarb does not feed on itself (and thus feed war); rather, properly prepared, it restores a healthy appetite for something different. What we desire, value, take in, and why, and the ethics of it, are questions which glimmer in this chapter in its exploration of the difficulty of sustaining a (good) relationship with what we desire or what we deem good, and how we can judge what is required of us to maintain what is good. While our desires, particularly in their more intractable sexual form and in the form of belief, are sources of disease in and for us, they are joined and made more resistant to cure by self-deception and by what Freud called the death drive, our desire for pain and what is not, rationally, in our own good.

'La mort entre les dents'

Montaigne's cannibals in the next chapter, unlike their Inca neighbours or the Mexicans, were idealizable not least because their culture was free of the 'disease' of desire and because of their sense of justice and their ethics of each being each other's 'moitié', other half. This was alien to French culture at the time – with one, already past, exception, for Montaigne: his loving friendship with La Boétie: 'nous estions à moitié de tout' (we were halves in all things) (p. 193).[20] It is to 'De l'amitié' that I shall now turn, before extending the discussion towards the wider ethical implications of the other as 'other half' and of 'eating well' as a model for living well.

'De l'amitié' has already attracted much critical attention.[21] Rather than revisit the same ground, I shall focus on themes that emerge strongly when the chapter is read together with the three which follow it: its connections with themes of desire for the good and sacrifice, and the emotional and psychic economies of love that the chapter suggests, through its figuration. Figures are scant, making those metaphors there are, such as hunger and feeding, plenitude and void, more powerful: how do they relate to desire and language, as well as perhaps to the cannibal and to what it means to live well? In terms of psychic economy, there has been much interest in the writer's melancholy, and its role in the production of the *Essais*; along with melancholy, there has been some discussion of such issues as incorporation and identification.[22] Here I shall focus more on the fantasy sustained by melancholy, incorporation and sacrifice, and on *jouissance*, and how they all relate to Montaigne's desire to write. Anxiety, traceable in aspects of the chapter's figuration, will also be discussed, although fuller analysis of it together with other representations of the loss of La Boétie is mainly reserved for a later chapter with wider scope.[23] My interpretation starts

---

[20] Pot and Conley have both already touched briefly on 'moitiez' being the structure of both cannibal social relations and (perfect) friendship, and Conley has also noted the interest of reading the two chapters together. See Pot, *L'Inquiétante Etrangeté*, pp. 112–13, and Conley, 'The *Essays* and the New World', in Langer (ed.), *The Cambridge Companion to Montaigne* (Cambridge, 2005), pp. 74–95 (pp. 82–3). My reading takes a somewhat different direction.

[21] See, for instance, Merleau-Ponty, 'Lecture de Montaigne', in *Signes* (Paris, 1960), Regosin, *The Matter of my Book* (Berkeley and London, 1977), Starobinski, *Montaigne en mouvement* (Paris, 1982), Rigolot, *Les Métamorphoses de Montaigne* (Paris, 1988), and Langer, *Perfect Friendship* (Geneva, 1994), as well as articles too numerous to list.

[22] As well as Screech, *Montaigne and Melancholy* (London, 1983), see Murray, 'Translating Montaigne's Crypts', in Crewe (ed.), *Reconfiguring the Renaissance* (Lewisburg, 1992), pp. 121–49, Pot, *L'Inquiétante Etrangeté*, and Charpentier, 'Ecriture et travail du deuil dans les *Essais*', *RHLF* 5 (1988), pp. 823–38. Freud's 'Mourning and Melancholia' (1917), in *A History of the Psycho-Analytic Movement, Papers on Metapsychology and Other Works* (London, 1957), pp. 243–58, is the decisive psychoanalytic point of reference; Abraham and Torok, 'Introjecter – incorporer: deuil ou mélancholie', *Nouvelle Revue de Psychanalyse* 6 (1972), pp. 111–22 is also particularly interesting in relation to aspects of Montaigne's writing.

[23] See chapter 6.

figures of *void* *(absence of serv. vol.)* *fantasy*
SV

with the chapter's beginning, works through the ideas and ideals of symmetry and uniqueness and the impasses of substitution and exchange at which they arrive, and lastly explores the complexities onto which the chapter's figuration opens. It is in its figuration that ambiguities and dilemmas make their presence most felt, troubling its eulogy of ideal friendship-love.

'De l'amitié' opens with a visual image of a void, around a perfected painting, to be filled with the 'grotesques' of Montaigne's writing; the perfected centre is revealed as La Boétie's *De la servitude volontaire*. This bears on the role of fantasy in this chapter. Freud theorized fantasy as a visual scene, experienced as if imagined, a way of staging to oneself an otherwise unknowable unconscious desire. Characteristics are its fixity and its immobilizing effect on the subject, who may well have no consciously permissible wish to act on the desire thus glimpsed. Lacan's rewriting of Freud's theoretical beginnings develops away from the visual, preferring signifying structures, and underlines the double function of fantasy. Its double work is to enable the subject to sustain desire *and* to sustain himself at the level of his *elusive, enigmatic* desire (desire always being that of the Other): 'le fantasme est le soutien du désir, ce n'est pas l'objet qui est le soutien du désir. Le sujet se soutient comme désirant par rapport à un ensemble signifiant toujours plus complexe' (the phantasy is the support of desire; it is not the object that is the support. The subject sustains himself as desiring in relation to an ever more complex signifying structure).[24] But it is doubly double. For 'le réel supporte le fantasme, le fantasme protège le réel' (the fantasy is supported by the real, and the fantasy protects the real) (p. 41) *and* protects the subject from the real – it (here visual metaphor returns) screens it off. Kay, commenting on Žižek's take on Lacan's theory of fantasy, notes that it is 'shot through with the traumatic enjoyment' – associated with the real – 'which it helps to repress'.[25] If we accept (even provisionally for the sake of this argument) that the visual image with which the chapter opens is not only an unexceptional analogy for La Boétie's writing, but more, a form of fantasy, this may help us understand the relationship between the visual image, the written text (*De la servitude volontaire*), the man (La Boétie), Montaigne's loss of both man and text, and his relationship with his own writing, which here, with its analogy of filling the void surrounding the image, seems to incorporate that loss. To incorporate loss, in mourning more than tinged with melancholy, is to try to hold on to what no longer exists and must be given up. More precisely, to hold on to what the subject never had in the first place, an *ideal* other, the trauma of whose death, magnifying all the ordinary human pain of loss, was that it irrefutably revealed his lack – rather than lack or imperfection being all Montaigne's, as claimed here: 'je demeure court ... ma suffisance ne va pas si avant que d'oser entreprendre un tableau riche, poly et formé selon l'art' (I fall

---

[24] Lacan, *Le Séminaire livre XI* (Paris, 1973), p. 168. See also Evans, *An Introductory Dictionary of Lacanian Psychoanalysis* (London, 1996), pp. 59–61.

[25] Kay, *Žižek* (Cambridge, 2003), p. 163.

short … I lack the skill to dare to undertake a rich, polished painting, a work of art) (p. 183).

The visual image is rich, polished, artful, its composition already, as 'formé' underlines, fixed. Yet towards the end of the chapter, the unelaborated nature of the essay is emphasized, for it is described as a form of exercise, 'exercitation' (p. 194). A protective comment, but the difference between this and the visual image is significant. Perhaps rather than the essay being the object of the analogy, the scene is that of the deathbed, as commemorated by Montaigne in his letter to his father, given artful form? This traumatic scene is one of traumatic *jouissance*, but traumatic enjoyment is held at tolerable distance: the unsymbolizable real of death translated into the prestigious tradition of the written commemoration of the deathbed and of last words?

The opening image is located in a 'vuide', void; then, with the decision not to publish the essay the real void – already known to the writer, but not yet revealed to the reader, who is allowed the illusion that this perfected centre holds – turns out to be at the centre of the chapter, even perhaps of Montaigne's writing. The relationship between centre and surrounding has radically moved. A dilemma follows, stemming from the conflicting desires to fill the void and to preserve it as a void. The chapter opens with the perfected centre, moves towards its renunciation, as justified by Montaigne, but closes with that gesture towards the possibility of its replacement, filling the void with a form of substitute. What is symbolized by the movement from ideal to substitute, literally the replacement of the essay in political philosophy with love lyric, is worth exploring further, as are its significance for the representation of idealized love, and whether in an act of substitution, too much is sacrificed.[26] But perhaps, rather, what is offered is a keenly thoughtful engagement with the complexities of sacrifice?

For what is the significance of Montaigne's later act, the removal of what he had substituted for the unpublishable original? The shock of Montaigne's breaking his word to his friend that he would publish the essay, whatever the justification given in the chapter, has attracted more critical scrutiny than the later removal, understandably. As for the subtraction of the substitution, several hypotheses seem plausible. Was it recognition of the impossibility of any form of substitute for those multiple losses, through death, political and cultural vicissitude, as well as the loss of a version of himself as a man who would not betray his friend? Or had it to do with this particular form of substitute (love lyric)? Preference for (nothing but) his own writing as a suitable 'frame'? Recognition of the need to preserve a void, the 'contents' of which were unrepresentable? If the last, then what led to this change of mind and heart?

To begin to answer these questions, beyond Montaigne's own justification of his decision, we need to bring into focus two other beginnings and endings of

---

[26] If so, then not least in the statement in the dedication of the sonnets to Madame de Grammont that they are 'rien du mien' (nothing of my own) (p. 196): while this is literally true, it is also something of a denegation given the celebration in the previous chapter of the fusion of 'sien' (his) and 'mien' (mine).

the chapter on friendship-love. Not so much the void as a succession of texts, starting with La Boétie's essay, and what they have to do with love and living well, and also, what might be called the moment of the gift of texts with which it all began, that is, La Boétie's dying gift of his works to his friend: 'd'une si amoureuse recommandation, la mort entre les dents' (he entrusted so lovingly, with death in his mouth) (p. 184). To have death in one's mouth and in one's speech: how does the gift of death colour all that follows? Death *and* love, of course: Montaigne's words are clear.

While others, such as Rigolot, have explored the theme of loss in the chapter, I shall focus instead on the gift of death. The first step is to consider the succession of texts, and next, questions of identity and identification raised by phrases such as: 'ne nous reservant rien qui nous fut propre, ny qui fut ou sien ou mien' (neither of us held anything in reserve; nothing was either his or mine) (p. 189) as well as the metaphor of 'moitiez', halves. In both respects desire, fantasy and death prove to be entangled, and the desire to write seems the only escape from a deadly impasse for Montaigne, namely, that imaginary fusion which here represents ideal, incomparable friendship-love.

In representations of ideal friendship-love, our first texts and intertexts are Aristotle, the *Nicomachean Ethics*, Books VIII and IX, and the *Eudemian Ethics*, Book VII, echoed by Cicero, *Laelius de Amicitia*.[27] Plato meanwhile introduced other dimensions in the *Symposium*. Readings of Montaigne's reflections, particularly those interested in the political and ethical implications of friendship, tend to emphasize the Aristotelian and Ciceronian tradition, but some give more weight to Plato.[28] While all three classical writers shape the chapter and its questions, it is La Boétie's writing that calls for attention here. For it was most immediately with his *writing* that everything began. And it is with Montaigne's writing that it went on *not* ending, while writing was nonetheless the only exit. For all that language is, as Montaigne acknowledged, imperfect, to commit to it is to give up the illusion of the possibility of plenitude or perfection. These comments resonate with interpretations of 'De l'amitié', indeed of the *Essais* as a whole, in terms of melancholy resolving into mourning.

Let's put the sequence starkly: Montaigne 'fell in love' with La Boétie's writing 'avant que je l'eusse veu' (before I first saw him) (p. 184); Montaigne wrote (to his father) about La Boétie's exemplary death – in Starobinski's wry

---

[27] Aristotle, *Nicomachean Ethics*, trans. Rackham (Cambridge, Mass. and London, 1926) and *Eudemian Ethics*, trans. Rackham (Cambridge, Mass. and London, 1935); and Cicero, *Laelius de Amicitia*, trans. Falconer (Cambridge, Mass. and London, 1923).

[28] Rigolot makes a very interesting case for the place of Plato; see 'Montaigne et la "servitude volontaire"', in Zinguer (ed.), *Le Lecteur, l'auteur et l'écrivain: Montaigne 1492–1592–1992* (Paris, 1993), pp. 84–103. For a discussion of the philosophical and political theme of friendship, including Montaigne's writing, see Derrida, *Politiques de l'amitié*, and for an introduction to the question of the ethical and political place of friendship, see Scholar, *Montaigne and the Art of Free-thinking* (Oxford, 2010), ch. 6.

love for LB et lst for his writing

comment: 'il meurt comme un livre' (he dies by the book).[29] Montaigne's representation of his dying, a most intimately individual moment, worked with the
prestigious conventions of classical deathbed accounts and last words; [30] Montaigne did not publish the text with which the relationship began for others to
read, despite promising to; Montaigne then went on writing and finding substitutes for the not-to-be published text – and for his ideal love.

> Je fus autrefois touché d'un puissant desplaisir ... et encores plus juste que
> puissant: je m'y fusse perdu à l'avanture si je m'en fusse simplement fié à
> mes forces. Ayant besoing d'une vehemente diversion pour m'en distraire, je
> me fis, par art, amoureux, et par estude, à quoy l'aage m'aidoit. L'amour me
> soulagea et retira du mal qui m'estoit causé par l'amitié. (pp. 835–6)

> (I was once touched by powerful grief – a grief even more justified than it
> was powerful: it might very well have destroyed me, had I just trusted my
> own resources. But I needed a violent distraction to divert me from it, and so
> I made myself fall in love; art, effort and my youth all helped. Love consoled
> me and rescued me from the pain caused by friendship-love.)

Until Montaigne found substitutes for La Boétie (which he wrote about), the
sequence turns around *writing*. It begins with the text which led Montaigne
to 'fall in love',[31] a text whose political philosophy emphasized friendship as
(after Aristotle) an ethical ideal, impossible in the absence of the good man
and the good life, and whose absence was evidence of political ill; a Humanist topos maybe, but movingly expressed.[32] Then there is Montaigne's text on

---

[29] *Montaigne en mouvement*, p. 77. Blum's account is more precise and qualified. He
discusses the letter in terms of the three rhetorical models which framed, structured and
informed it, not least the tradition of the *ars moriendi*, the 'art of dying', and highlights the
aspects of it which do not, in fact, conform to such existing traditions. See Blum, 'De la *Lettre
sur la mort de La Boétie* aux *Essais*', *RHLF* 88/5 (1988), pp. 934–48.

[30] That he died like a book, that is, that his dying was exemplary, conforming to the
classical textual models of the deathbed, is disputed by Defaux, who argues that, in fact, the
abiding significance for Montaigne of his friend's dying was his failure to conform to the
ideal; see Defaux, 'Montaigne et l'expérience', in Demonet and Legros (eds), *L'Ecriture du
scepticisme chez Montaigne* (Geneva, 2004), pp. 289–302. I shall return to the moment on
which Defaux's argument turns shortly, without, however, following his interpretation.

[31] Compare Gournay's description (in her preface) of the impact on her of the *Essais*
which she read before meeting Montaigne: 'l'admiration dont ils me transsirent, lors qu'ils
me furent *fortuitement* mis en main' (the shock of wonder I felt when, by chance, they came
into my hands) (my italics). The echo of Montaigne's 'nostre premier rencontre, *qui fut par
hazard*' (our first meeting, by chance) (p. 188, my italics) is perhaps not accidental. In *Essais
de Michel Seigneur de Montaigne*, vol. 5 (The Hague, 1727), p. 143.

[32] In *De la servitude volontaire* the tyrant is unlovable and unloved, antithetical to
friendship, which the writer holds sacred. Friendship requires trust, integrity, equality,
absence of cruelty and a shared sense of justice (see p. 124).

This celebration of friendship has already been eloquently discussed by scholars
such as Starobinski (pp. 71–80), but it is still worth noting the implications of La Boétie's
insistence that a state of tyranny, thus the absence of a political economy, necessarily excludes

friendship, both heir to the classical philosophical tradition and insistent on its difference, on the exceptional nature of the relationship: 'les discours mesmes que l'antiquité nous a laissé sur ce subject, me semblent láches au pris du sentiment que j'en ay' (even the writings on it left to us by antiquity seem feeble to me compared with my feelings) (p. 192). Each was conscious of the tradition but each supplemented the already-written ideal, Montaigne especially. We next need to consider what Montaigne went on to do with La Boétie's text, with which it had all begun; and what this had to do with his own desire to write.

The chapter, which commemorates the relationship, begins with visual analogy rather than writing; but we should keep in mind Montaigne's use of visual analogies for his self-exploration through writing, his 'peinture' (painting) (p. 804). The visual analogy is an oblique approach to the other's writing, but perhaps also a lure: it sets up an identification between them, between their texts and desire to write, when perhaps their difference and separation are at stake.

Separation, however, is not achieved in this chapter, other than towards the end, thematically, with the representation of the loss of his friend. Rather, figuration works to allow incorporation and a deadly confusion of identification and identity to permeate the writing, and separation will only be enacted by recourse to a substitute – but not yet. For the gesture of substitution at the end of the chapter seems (given its later undoing) inadequate to its role and the void will have to be reinstated, before a real substitute can be given a place – around it, not filling it. Also, Montaigne will have to acknowledge fully his dedication to his own writing at the expense of his 'ideal'.

The perfect symmetry and non-fungible economy of the ideal are incommensurable with that of all other relationships such as marriage or family ties, which are asymmetrical (one having more than the other, be it power, status or rights), or have exchange value. Moreover, its incomparability to other relationships implies that it cannot, or should not, be translated into language, which is a system of lack and exchange, as demonstrated by sentences such as: 'cette cy [sc. 'conversation', that is, relationship] n'a point d'autre idée que d'elle mesme, et ne se peut rapporter qu'à soy' (this relationship has no other ideal than itself, and compares only to itself) (p. ·189). Irrespective of its theme of uniqueness, once this is translated into words and opened to interpretation, this quality is lost, strictly speaking. 'Si on me presse de dire pourquoy je l'aymois, je sens que cela ne se peut exprimer' (if you press me to say why I loved him, I feel that this cannot be expressed) (p. 188), paradoxically seems to preserve the incommunicability and sublimity of this love while simultaneously putting it into words; it can only communicate by being part of a system of exchange. This is one of the impasses of this chapter, symptomatic of irreconcilable desires, which may require that something be sacrificed for the sake of what matters most.

Can Montaigne's decision not to publish the essay be understood as a form

---

the possibility of friendship. Absence of friendship makes all enemies, *within* the state, when the field of the political, particularly in terms of sovereign power, would be constituted by the distinction between friends within its boundaries and the enemy outside them.

of sacrifice? Not an expedient response to the political vulnerabilities of the text at the time of writing, but the protection of the text despite this entailing the sacrifice of Montaigne's ego-ideal, of his being a good man, a perfect friend, who was 'true to his word'? Or might it, rather, be read in the light of the principles of perfect friendship-love as expressed here, and therefore stand as an act true to the priority of that unique relationship over any other form of obligation, political or social: 'l'unique et principale amitié descoust toutes autres obligations' (unique, principal friendship undoes all other obligations) (p. 191)? Is it to this ideal that Montaigne was willing to sacrifice an ideal version of himself?[33]

Perhaps sacrifice is too grand a concept for what is, rather, a cluster of irreconcilable desires: La Boétie's desire for Montaigne to be the one who published his work, and Montaigne's desire to be that one. Or Montaigne's desire to hold on to that text with all its personal significance, to not allow that it had meanings other than those it had for him alone; or to protect it from risk of misinterpretation (his avowed reason). Valid, perhaps, in the political turmoil of the time, but this seems to deny that other meanings would inevitably exist, separate from him. We need to think both directions of interpretation, sacrifice and desire, together: it may be an act thought to have the status of sacrifice, but that sacrifice is (in fact) a 'fantasy structure through which one seeks to affirm the existence and plenitude of the Other'.[34] Thus for Montaigne to be ready to allow a *substitute* for this unique friendship-love is not betrayal or lack of constancy; rather, acceptance that the sacrificial turn is a lure, that his relationship with La Boétie was one of lack (like any other): in short, to realize that all objects (of desire) are, despite the fantasy of their uniqueness, substitutes and substitutable even though, as subjects, they are irreducible.[35]

---

[33] On this as a problem in political philosophy, see Aristotle, *Eudemian Ethics*, and for discussion, see Derrida, *Politiques de l'amitié*: 'pas de démocratie sans respect de la singularité ou de l'alterité irréductible, mais pas de démocratie sans "communauté des amis" (*koína ta philōn*), sans calcul des majorités, sans sujets identifiables, représentables et égaux entre eux. Ces deux loix sont irréductibles l'une à l'autre. Tragiquement inconciliables et à jamais blessantes' (there is no democracy without respect for irreducible singularity and alterity, but there is no democracy without the 'community of friends' ... without the calculation of majorities, without identifiable, representable, equal subjects. These two laws are irreducible one to the other. Tragically irreconcilable and forever wounding), trans. Collins, *Politics of Friendship* (London, 1997), p. 40.

[34] Gaunt, *Love and Death*, p. 80.

[35] This reading could suggest that I understand Montaigne to have set aside his melancholy fidelity to who and what he has lost. Here I am choosing not to pursue others' discussions of the relationship between Montaigne, La Boétie and writing in terms of melancholy and/or mourning. However, if I were to stay with these terms, I might argue instead that melancholic incorporation is part of seeming to recover from the loss (mourning's work), while the lost object lives on, internally. This would be a reading which drew quite as much on Freud's later work, *The Ego and the Id*, as on *Mourning and Melancholia*, according to which Montaigne remained inconsolably loyal to what he had lost but nonetheless became capable of more disillusioned understanding of the nature of that loss.

If so, we arrive at another way of thinking about the first acknowledged substitute, La Boétie's sonnets, and their later removal. Perhaps their toying with love lyric's conventional themes of sacrifice, which seems to treat sacrifice as if it were genuine, rather than travesty or simulacrum, introduced a dimension that Montaigne did not wish his writing to contain. There are, of course, those who really do die of and for love; but not La Boétie. Or Montaigne, except the figurative dying that is loss of self, of existence as a subject: 'ce n'est que fumée … Depuis le jour que je le perdy' (it is nothing but smoke … since the day I lost him) (p. 193): what is moving is not only the force of negation, and the metaphor of smoke – solid substance destroyed – but the absence of a personal pronoun subject, only 'ce', it, grammatically the most minimal and inanimate pronominal subject.

Yet it was Montaigne, 'je', (I), who chose to inscribe himself at that moment as (no more than) 'ce'. Who continued to want to write, and through writing to recover a communicable subjectivity beyond 'ce'; to discover greater self-knowledge than that gained through the experience of love; and to be known by others rather than only to and by one, despite the anguishing risk of his words being misunderstood.[36] Thus his chief loyalty seems not to be to La Boétie, to an illusion of perfect fulfilment and fusion in love, but rather to writing, imperfection and the recovery of (life-saving) difference. 'L'amour est impuissant, quoiqu'il soit réciproque, parce qu'il ignore qu'il n'est que le désir d'être Un, ce qui nous conduit à l'impossible d'établir la relation d'eux' (love is impotent, though mutual, because it is not aware that it is the desire to be One, which leads us to the impossibility of establishing the relationship between 'them-two').[37] If the psychic economy of love is such that it unknowingly denies difference ('il ignore'), this means that it is unwittingly a desire for the same, so, narcissistic. Which is not to deny either the benefaction of love or the desolation of its loss; rather, to continue in the search for self-knowledge that love can enhance, all being well.

Does 'De l'amitié' support this view of love and desire as narcissistic in structure – using this adjective without moral judgement? The friends' lack of difference is emphasized: 'rien des lors ne nous fut si proche, que l'un à l'autre' (from then on, nothing was so close to us as each other) (p. 188); 'nos ames s'entretiennent' (our souls take care of each other) (p. 188), along with numbers of other reflexive verbs used to convey their relatedness; and the famous equivalence of 'la sienne' (his) and 'la mienne' (mine) (p. 189) records their reciprocal self-loss in each other. If difference were valued, the emphasis on reciprocal self-loss conveys the eradication of difference, and a desire for sameness, fusion as an ideal. And apart from Montaigne's description of La Boétie's potential as a writer as being currently incomparable whilst a match for ideal classical writers,

---

[36] See chapter 4.

[37] Here Lacan plays on the homophony of 'd'eux' and 'deux', between them, and (of) two; see Lacan, *Le Séminaire livre XX* (Paris, 1999), p. 12.

arguably his lack of specificity as to the nature of what each found in each other has to do with the proclaimed inexpressibility of what united them.

'D'une faim pareille'

However, the desire to keep nothing in reserve ('rien de reste' (p. 192)), to be fully known by, and to fully know, the other is conveyed in terms which, it is important to recognize, suggest residual disquiet. Analysis of the force of figuration in the chapter supports this reading.

It is in relation to 'parfaicte amitié' (perfect friendship) (p. 191) that the use of figuration has particular intensity, in three key, related ways. The use, among other reflexive verbs, of 'se nourrir' (to feed itself/oneself): 'nourir' is used, in passing, of other relationships, but the reflexive form is used exclusively of this; the use of 'faim' (p. 189); and of the phrase 'jusques au fin fond des entrailles' (in our deepest entrails) (p. 190). The last two both introduce questions about the place of the body and materiality in what is primarily *âmitié*, 'soul-friendship': 'nos ames ... se meslent et confondent l'une et l'autre, d'un mélange si universel, qu'elles s'effacent et ne retrouvent plus la couture qui les a jointes' (our souls ... mingle and melt into each other, so wholly that the seam between them dissolves, never to be found again) (p. 188). But through use of the figurative vocabulary of feeding, feeding each other, hunger, and the entrails, embodiment in some way insists along with the emphasis on soul and will, 'ma volonté ... sa volonté' (my will, his will) (p. 189). As it does, also, through its destruction, in the figure of 'fumée' (smoke) (p. 193), as all that is left of life after the death of the friend. This may be read, therefore, as a figurative network or economy which illuminates the psychic economy of this friendship-love. It articulates it in terms of the connection between food, hunger, desire and language. Moreover, it also resonates with the chapter's first metaphor relating to La Boétie, that of 'death in his mouth'. All the figuration of hunger, feeding and the inside of the body is prefigured and governed by 'dying words', the taste of death; not life-giving food or love but death in the mouth. This figuration intimates that the inexpressible process by which each became the other also incorporated death.

Two separable but convergent lines of interpretation follow from this. The first, to do with (the possibility of) death as the condition of this love, is more closely connected to the philosophical traditions which are written into these reflections: here I shall draw on Derrida's reading of this tradition, including Montaigne's chapter, in *Politiques de l'amitié*. Secondly, it is in the figuration that the ambiguities of desire and the aspects of the psychic economy which most test, or part company with, the philosophical ideals of friendship-love are most palpable; here Lacanian thinking about orality and desire can supplement the abstractions of the more philosophical approach. By putting these two lines of inquiry together, the nature of this specific friendship as a test of philosophical understanding will be clearer: the experience of it was perhaps not commensurate with its models in humanist as well as classical philosophical ideals, Christian as well as pagan, however much a match was desired.

Hunger and the taste of death have much to do with what enters and what goes out of the mouth. Food, the need and desire for 'food', nourishing words, and words which nourish desire; but before all these life-giving material and figurative things, we have the taste of death. So before the beginning of the narrative of this perfect friendship-love, its representation begins with death; not only because it is a work of mourning and commemoration, but because its writing conforms to the ideals in such exemplary classical texts as Aristotle's on friendship. Also, perhaps, as a work of mourning for those ideals?

The presence of death in this figure translates an ideal that Derrida's readings of Aristotle and Cicero bring out: that is, that the condition of *true* friendship is its beginning in full awareness of the possibility of death. This accompanies two other conditions: the first, the ideal of loving before being loved – as Montaigne loved La Boétie in his writing before they met.[38] The second, that to be loved in return will be something of a miracle, for it cannot be calculated in advance. This incalculability is suggested by Montaigne's underlining that he and La Boétie met only by chance (see p. 94). While La Boétie was loved without knowing it, his text gave Montaigne not only new knowledge in the sphere of political philosophy, about those matters which would go on being dear to him such as ethics, equity, justice – all essential if friendship is to flourish – but also new knowledge of what it means to love without yet knowing what perfect friendship might be. Without this willingness to love before being loved, without and despite the anticipation of death, what Derrida calls 'l'appréhension angoissée du deuil' (the anguished apprehension of mourning) (p. 31), the condition of true friendship-love is missing: 'l'acte endeuillé de l'aimer' (p. 31) (the grieved act of loving). However, as his reading also suggests, after Cicero, true friendship, while being founded on and incorporating death, may give unique hope for a future after death: perfect, exemplary friendship allows one to imagine 'un avenir qui passera la mort' (a future which will go beyond death), even go towards it: 'elle fait naître … un espoir qui d'avance illumine l'avenir … portant ainsi la renommée du nom par-delà la mort' (it gives rise to a hope that illuminates the future in advance, thereby transporting the name's renown beyond death) (p. 20). A friendship conceived as exemplary, and in the light of such classical ideals, would already be imagined to hold out this hope of life beyond death; such is Montaigne's testament here, that *even though* La Boétie is named only once in the chapter, early, pronouns thereafter replacing names as if the contingency of proper names were transcended, nonetheless the name still remains. A third classical ideal to which Derrida points (see pp. 204–6) is incorporated via Montaigne's use of the anecdote of Eudamidas's paradoxical bequest of personal and financial responsibility to his friends. Lest we puzzle over the value of the bequest, Montaigne prompts us: 'ses heritiers l'accepterent

[38] See Derrida, *Politiques de l'amitié*, pp. 25–6.

tension in model of symm. friendship

avec un singulier contentement' (his heirs accepted it with singular pleasure) (p. 191). They are a testament to true friendship: what is given by the friend to the friend is the 'contentement ... d'effectuer à son endroit ce qu'il désire le plus' (the pleasure ... of doing for him what he most desires) (p. 190).

The classical philosophical ideals seem clear; but here we reach less unambiguous ground, in terms of La Boétie's bequest to Montaigne and also in terms of the difficulty of thinking together a friendship which is perfect in being 'indivisible' (p. 191) and one which falls within a gift economy such as the testament confirms, in which the friend being given to gives more than the giver, but loving is greater than being loved. Both require a degree of difference rather than fusion and also a version of the ideal of symmetry which allows it to include such dissymmetry. That what they willed is described in identical terms, that their hunger for each other is described as being identical, equal, does not resolve this tension. Indeed, just here, one of Montaigne's later additions highlights this: '(A) c'est je ne sçay quelle quinte essence ... qui, ayant saisi toute ma volonté, l'amena se plonger et se perdre dans la sienne; (C) qui, ayant saisi toute sa volonté, l'amena se plonger et se perdre en la mienne' (it is an indefinable quintessence which, having seized my whole will, led it to plunge into his and lose itself in it; (C) and which, having seized his whole will, led it to plunge into mine and lost itself in it) (p. 189). That temporal disjunction in the writing troubles the illusion of perfect symmetry it is designed to convey.

But the fusion of souls, the indivisibility of two-become-one, always already exceeded the hope such friendship was held to offer; this is the knowledge that Montaigne conveys by founding his representation in the taste of death. But (again), this was also a recognition of the condition of possibility of such a friendship, if true to classical ideals. So we arrive either at aporia, or at a representation which, while attached to those ideals, contains something more: ambivalence, or even an acceptance of something irreconcilable in the demands and ideals of friendship? Or a test of abstract ideals by particular experience, when contingency moves our understanding beyond the philosophical knowledge of phenomena such as death? If this different form of understanding is born out of what is experienced as singular, it is not confined to or by singularity; on the contrary, its affective singularity needs to be thought in relation to philosophical abstraction, and abstraction needs to be rethought in light of it. If singularity were the highest value, it could only be honoured by not being expressed. The dilemma of this chapter is on the one hand the desire to be faithful to what was singular and exceptional about both this friendship-love and its anguishing loss, but on the other, the desire to articulate that singularity as transformative of existing knowledge and knowledge of love as they informed Montaigne's self-knowledge.[39] It is enough for now to open this dilemma out

---

[39] This resonates with what Nussbaum calls 'love's knowledge', an example of which, for her, is what Marcel can only 'know' by having lost Albertine, which is also an example of what literary texts may help us understand more fully than their counterparts in philosophy or psychology: see Nussbaum, *Love's Knowledge* (Oxford, 1990), ch. 11.

and restate it in a temporal, narrative form: from self-loss in the other (the becoming 'indivisible'), to loss of self with the loss of the other, as conveyed by the figure of there being only smoke, to recovery of a form of self, in the form of the desire to write.

What supplements philosophy can be traced in the chapter's figuration, with the help of some Lacanian ideas. This dimension is not beyond 'philosophy', as Montaigne's writing in this chapter makes clear, given its working together of classical ideals and ideas and something else besides. Rather, it needs a different form of analysis, in which thought and affect combine towards the communication and understanding of that which is beyond representation – death – but may be conveyed obliquely by figurative structures such as metaphor and anamorphosis.[40]

'Je voyois nonchalamment la mort, quand je la voyois universellement … par le menu, elle me pille. Les larmes d'un laquais … l'attouchement d'une main connue, la consolation commune me desconsole et m'attendrit' (when I saw death as an abstraction it caused me no disquiet … but particular instances ravage me. A servant's tears … the touch of a familiar hand, an everyday word of consolation desolates me and moves me to tears) (p. 837). Death not only moves him to tears, it 'ravages' him: 'death in his mouth' is the taste of death and, having it in one's mouth, death being in one's speech, and also death's bite, which will tear into, 'ravage', the survivor. Devour him? Leave nothing behind? There is only smoke: all is obscure; the world is all illusion; also, this is the obliteration of Montaigne's sense of being: the smoking ashes of the body are all that remain.

But, as I shall now tease out through further analysis of the network of figures, they convey more than the incorporation of death in melancholy mourning, as the friend's ashes becoming 'Montaigne' suggest. Figuration's work also relates to the destructive nature of the supposedly ideal fusion, 'indivisible'. It transmutes something violent, even deadly about this love of the other, which belies the idealization expressed by the concept of the fusion of souls.

Of course the need for food is not the same as the desire for love, or the desire to know. However, this protest on behalf of plain speaking does not help us understand why, then, a figurative vocabulary of hunger and eating should be used not only here, along with the very different vocabulary of being indivisible and of wills and souls being as one, but also pervasively in traditional discourses of love and the erotic.

'Se plonger et se perdre dans la sienne [sc. volonté] … se plonger et se perdre dans la mienne, d'une faim, d'une concurrence pareille' (p. 189). The adjective 'pareille', equal, seems to reinforce the idea of symmetry, even identity of the relation, in a total gift of self; the text continues: 'je dis perdre, à la vérité, ne nous reservant rien qui nous fut propre, ny qui fut ou sien ou mien' (I really mean lose, for neither of us held anything in reserve; nothing was either his

---

[40] For further discussion of this structure in Montaigne's writing, see chapter 6.

or mine). However, the function of the metaphor of hunger is double. Since it does not literally mean hunger for and therefore eating each other, it suggests an imaginary denial of the limits of the body, in keeping with an ideal of transcendence of separate identity. Yet it also is not fully free of what it denotes literally, so something of the body remains in the text. This doubleness is even more marked shortly after, in an entrails metaphor: 'nos ames ont charrié si uniement ensemble ... elles se sont ... de pareille affection descouvertes jusques au fin fond des entrailles l'une à l'autre ... je ... connoissoy la sienne comme la mienne' (our souls were yoked together in such unity ... with the same affection they revealed themselves to each other, right down to their deepest entrails ... I knew his soul as I knew my own) (pp. 189–90). Again, the vocabulary of souls, sameness, identity ('la sienne comme la mienne'); but in the midst of these abstractions, viscera: this reminder of corporeality is disjunctive, disturbing the fantasy of identity and union of souls, and, with its exposure of what is usually concealed 'inside' (until revealed by autopsy) implies that the desire to know the other has an unacknowledged violence.[41] To know and be known, to eviscerate and be eviscerated, to eat and be eaten ... As well as connecting this chapter's relational ideal and cannibal culture as imagined by Montaigne (along with the shared metaphor of 'moitiez'), these metaphors convey anxiety (as already perhaps does that figurative connection with the cannibal) and trouble the ideal of transcendence.

Perhaps Lacan can help us find the connection between hunger, desire, love and language, and the tension between two being one and the need to sustain one's difference. To eat, to get inside, to know and to desire or to love; to want to be loved, or desired, to be known, and to let oneself eat; this list is deliberately not symmetrical. While to love or desire may indeed be to want to be loved or desired, and the same might be said of knowing and being known, it is in eating, first literally and then figuratively, that the drama and asymmetry of desire, in its difference from love, is to be traced. For it is only by not letting oneself eat everything that desire can be sustained, as Lacan's distinction between demand and desire clarifies.[42]

'C'est dans la demande orale ['d'être nourri'] que s'est creusé la place de désir' (the place of desire is hollowed out by the oral demand) (p. 249): from the infant's cry of hunger, and that demand being met, develops a desire for other forms of nourishment: the food of love, the nourishing of thought and self-knowledge, the taste of and for words – speech, reading and writing.[43] The

---

[41] For a discussion of what he calls 'visceral knowledge', which touches very briefly on Montaigne, see Hillman, 'Visceral Knowledge', in Hillman and Mazzio (eds), *The Body in Parts* (New York and London, 1997), pp. 81–106.

[42] All quotations from Lacan in the rest of this section are from *Le Séminaire VIII*, unless otherwise stated.

[43] Just two examples from among those in the *Essais*: 'nul plaisir n'a goust pour moy sans communication' (unless I communicate it, pleasure has no taste for me) (p. 986), and: 'je me considere sans cesse, je me contrerolle, je me gouste' (I reflect on myself, monitor myself, and savour myself ceaselessly) (p. 657).

'cri de la faim' (cry of hunger) which communicates need and demand (for food) will become articulate, as the infant learns to speak: 'le désir maintient sa place dans la marge de la demande ... qui constitue son lieu' in which 'passe à s'articuler le creux qui s'esquisse déjà dès le cri de la faim' (desire maintains its place on the margins of demand, which is where it is constituted, and where its hollowed-out space which emerged with the cry of hunger comes to be articulated) (p. 249). It is by being articulated that desire comes into being: 'en le nommant, le sujet [le] crée' (by naming it, the subject creates it).[44] It's all in the mouth: hunger, speech, how we name and ask for what we want, how we keep desire alive, and death: 'entre les dents'. The ambivalence we find in Montaigne's figures may be understood in the light of the following passage, which underlines that desire can only survive if a margin of difference remains and the fantasy of being fully, perfectly 'fed' is renounced in favour of accepting that there is something beyond that first *fantasy* of fullness and perfection which we want to go on wanting. It is not just that desire and demand are not one and the same, and that we should 'go hungry' in order to ensure the preservation of desire. Also, within the circuit of desire our objects will always be substitutes for that fulfilling perfect other who never existed in the first place. Moreover, while in their narcissism love and desire may be the same ('le désir de l'homme, c'est le désir de l'Autre'/ 'aimer, c'est essentiellement, vouloir être aimé' (man's desire is the desire of the other/ to love is, essentially, to wish to be loved)) there is a fundamental difference.[45] In a way which is culturally consecrated, love entails a fantasy of fusion, an illusion of reciprocity; in this it is imaginary and deceptive, whereas desire exists in the Symbolic, and requires difference; the fantasy of fusion is the death of desire.

> Au premier conflit qui éclate dans la relation de nourrissage, dans la rencontre de la demande d'être nourri et de la demande de se laisser nourrir, il se manifeste que cette demande, un désir la déborde – qu'elle ne saurait être satisfaite sans que ce désir s'y éteigne – que c'est pour que ce désir qui déborde la demande ne s'éteigne pas, que le sujet qui a faim ... ne se laisse pas nourrir, et refuse en quelque sorte de disparaître comme désir du fait d'être satisfait comme demande – que l'extinction ou l'écrasement de la demande dans la satisfaction ne saurait se produire sans tuer le désir ... L'ambivalence première, propre à toute demande, est que, dans toute demande, il est également impliqué que le sujet ne veut pas qu'elle soit satisfaite. Le sujet vise en soi la sauvegarde du désir. (pp. 238–9)

(when the demand to be fed meets the demand to let oneself be fed, the first conflict erupts in the feeding relationship; it becomes clear that a desire overflows this demand which cannot be met without this desire being extinguished – it is so that this desire which overflows the demand not be extinguished that the subject who is hungry ... does not let himself be fed, and in a way refuses

[44] Lacan, *Le Séminaire livre II* (Paris, 1978), p. 266.
[45] Lacan, *Le Séminaire XI*, pp. 213, 228.

writing → love the prime commitment

to disappear as desire, which would result from the satisfaction of demand – to be rid of demand by its satisfaction cannot happen without killing desire … The first ambivalence in every demand is that every demand equally involves the subject not wanting it to be satisfied. The subject's aim is to safeguard desire.)

Language and a sense of separate identity take the place of the infant's not yet knowing the difference between its self and any other, its demand and desire and the other's; and it is in language that desire (and difference) are articulated: 'la parole reste le lieu de désir' (speech remains the place of desire) (p. 246). But never fully. Language goes on failing, for 'speech can never articulate the *whole* truth about desire',[46] and the subject also goes on failing in the sense of not achieving a full or fixed sense of identity. However, this failing is the condition of possibility of both desire and writing such as Montaigne's. If we accept (as I do) that Montaigne's most fundamental (though not unconflicted) commitment is to the Symbolic and to approaches to self-knowledge that take place through writing, then the imaginary fusion of love has to cede to the desire to write, and a sense of identity must be recovered (by writing) from the deadly confusion of identification with an ideal other as identity and sameness. Any similarity this may seem to have to the poet/lover's priority being the desire to write is fortuitous and misleading; here the stakes are much more serious. Arguably, then, the sonnets were excised to remove any distracting apparent similarity.

'To really love someone is to believe that by loving them you'll get to a truth about yourself. We love the one that [sic] harbours the response … to our question: "Who am I"?'[47] Perhaps the 'truth' of himself which Montaigne reached with the death of La Boétie, having experienced the reality of the abstract condition of 'true' love, was that his loyalty was less to love than to writing. The 'truth' or knowledge (of self) sought is not found in love, even the best, most philosophically sanctioned love, but is reached by passing through love to something beyond, and by doing without it.

This despite friendship-love being represented as having as its ideal an incomparable ethics ('cherchant l'un et l'autre, plus que toute autre chose, de s'entre-bienfaire' (each of them seeking, above all, the good of the other) (p. 190)). This verb, a *hapax*, conveys the uniqueness of symmetrical concern for the other's good. In practice this means: 'donnant ce contentement à son amy, d'effectuer en son endroict ce qu'il désire le plus' (giving his friend the pleasure of doing for him what he most wants to do). One first hint of what troubles the tradition of the relationship thus represented emerges in the line Derrida traces from Plotinus (via Heidegger) to Lacan, via Montaigne:

---

[46] Evans, *An Introductory Dictionary*, p. 36.
[47] Miller, 'On Love: We Love the One who Responds to our Question: "who am I?"', http://www.lacan.com/symptom/?page_id263.

Celui qui donne, c'est donc celui qui reçoit, nous dit 'De l'amitié'. Il ne donne ainsi qu'à la condition de ne pas avoir ce qu'il donne. La grande mais discrète tradition de ce 'donner ce qu'on n'a pas', qui de Plotin se lègue à Heidegger puis à Lacan (qui ne le lui rendent ou retournent jamais, bien sûr, et personne ainsi ne l'a), il faudrait y réinscrire Montaigne. (p. 204)

(The person who gives is therefore the one who receives, as we are told in 'On Friendship'. The former thus gives only on condition that he does not have what he gives. The great but discreet tradition of 'giving what one does not have' – which is bequeathed from Plotinus to Heidegger, then to Lacan (they do not return or give the gift back, of course; thus no one is in possession of it) – would now have to include Montaigne. (trans. Collins, p. 180))

The best giving is giving what you do not have; that is, giving what you lack to the other, knowing and assuming your incompleteness and dependence. The ideal of each benefiting the other seems, in its abstraction, a form of short-circuit, by which love of the good inhabits a dimension other than that of the vicissitudes of relatedness and the pain and anxiety of human lack – and mortality. It is not for nothing that Montaigne's example of Eudamidas offers the realization of the ideal only after the death of the friend: what is sought 'above all' is a sustaining but unrealizable fantasy for the living, whose reality is not of perfectly symmetrical union and through it a sustainable loss of lack. What *may* be articulated as an ideal in terms of ethics is, in terms of psychic economy, a fantasy.

The reality of loss of lack, as Montaigne's metaphors convey, is not blissful, but fraught with anxiety. Asymmetry, lack and difference are for the living, and the one left living, as Montaigne went on repeating, is left so bereft of subjectivity that the ideal of giving (in order for the other to give) must be jettisoned, for how can one give when one is no longer 'there' to give? Here, there is only smoke; in 'De la diversion', 'je m'y fusse perdu' (it might have destroyed me) (p. 836); and, in a passage cut from 'De la vanité': 'luy seul jouyssoit de ma vraye image et l'emporta' (he alone enjoyed my true image, and he has taken it with him) (p. 983, n. 4).

That passage continues: 'c'est pourquoy je me deschiffre, si curieusement' (this is why I decipher myself so attentively). Both the good and what Montaigne calls his 'truth' are identified with this friendship. What survives is the desire to go on *deciphering* himself (with its implication of meaning which is locked and enigmatic), so as to discover and leave something more than nothing of himself to others, perhaps even something of his 'truth' – part of which is the knowledge of the lack of full possession of himself. 'Je n'ay rien mien que moy, et si en est la possession en partie manque et empruntée' (I own nothing but myself, and my possession even of that is lacking and borrowed) (p. 968). This is a far cry from the version of 'mien', mine, presented in 'De l'amitié', where even if the cause of love remained unknowable, the insistence that each kept nothing in reserve but gave all to the other conveys the illusion that each had full knowledge of himself (see p. 101). The passage cut from 'De la vanité' underlines that Montaigne's truth as not fully knowable, but about which more remained to be known, is what went on mattering. 'Je me deschiffre', I decipher myself, I am deciphering, I go on deciphering; not, I have deciphered myself. The desire for potential knowledge takes the place of the illusion of knowledge in love; nonetheless without love this relationship with knowledge might not have emerged. For all the illusion of self-knowledge, there had to be a coexistent realization of something already being missing that only the other (in this case, initially, the other's writing) could supply. For this to have been recognizable, there must already have been an enigmatic sense of what that other would signify. So the self intuits that something fundamental about its being originates in the other. But what it has yet to learn is that this singular other and the otherness that is already part of his or her sense of self are not one and the same. Nor is the fusion of being (as if self and other were one and the same) an achievement of plenitude, two halves together forming a whole. The violence of the fantasy of full possession of the other and with it full self-dispossession at which the chapter's figuration hints, also conveys the anxiety caused by this fusion, which alerts the reader to the illusion of the other's desire being the mirror-image of Montaigne's own.

The clearest signal of this is in Montaigne's letter to his father in which he described La Boétie's dying. In a terrible moment, close to death, his beloved friend had asked: 'Mon frère, mon frère, me refusez-vous ... une place?' (my brother, my brother, do you refuse me a place?)[48] He had repeatedly already asked him to give him a place: 'il se print à me prier & reprier *avecques une extreme affection*, de luy donner une place' (he began to beseech me repeatedly, and with the greatest affection, to give him a place) (p. 1359, my italics). Montaigne represents himself as being bound to give not love but philosophy: 'il me contraignit de le convaincre par raison' (he forced me to convince him, by reason). I shall return to the haunting question of the 'place' and Montaigne's answer in chapter 6; here, what matters are its implications for the questions of address and responsibility to be explored shortly. Immediately what needs attention is Montaigne's recoil from the demand love placed him under. Put in question by love, he gave not love in return but reason; philosophy deflected the terror of the question of what the other wants of me, offering a vocabulary radically at odds with that of soul and wills being indivisible, each given fully to the other: 'puis qu'il respiroit et parloit, & qu'il avoit corps, il avoit par consequent son lieu' (since he was breathing and speaking and had a body, he did therefore have his place): not in me, or as one with me, but, it seems, returned firmly to his own place.

---

[48] Montaigne, 'Fragment d'une lettre que Monsieur de Conseiller de Montaigne escrit à Monseigneur de Montaigne son Père', in *Oeuvres complètes*, ed. Thibaudet and Rat (Paris, 1962), pp. 1347–60 (p. 1359). The phrase has already received some attention; see for instance Starobinski, Rigolot and Defaux, and Greenblatt, '1563: Anti-Dictator', in Hollier (ed.), *A New History of French Literature* (Cambridge, Mass., 1994), pp. 223–8.

It seems that the destitution of the loss of love and the loss of self-delusion to which it led were preconditions for the relationship with knowledge that would come to be articulated in the *Essais*. What I have in mind is Montaigne's attention to relatedness, and to the importance of an unpossessive relationship with objects of both desire and knowledge as the foundation of the ethics of intellectual analysis as well as being required for new kinds of thinking and understanding to be possible. Also, the attention to how inquiry goes on changing both the inquirer and whatever he or she inquires into: 'et le jugeant et le jugé estans en continuelle mutation et branle' (both the judge and the judged are constantly changing and moving) (p. 601), and in the acceptance of abiding uncertainty, full knowledge being only a horizon – or a mirage: 'il ne se peut establir rien de certain' (nothing certain can be established) (p. 601).

If love cedes to the desire for certain kinds of truth and understanding, but if without love and its loss this desire would not have found its place, this argues for reading 'De l'amitié' together with the three following chapters, as key chapters in Montaigne's exploration of problems of subjectivity, not least of its anguished vulnerabilities. Such exploration is the work of the *Essais* as a whole, which offer us insights into the emergent subjectivity that, from our historical perspective, will develop more clearly in the course of the seventeenth century. To take this point further, it is now time to develop the connections made here between desire, love, knowledge and ethics, between eating and 'eating well', Derrida's 'bien manger'.

Good enough to eat?

Loss informed the writing of these four chapters. La Boétie was dead, and with him certain ideals; the 'good' cannibals who had identified the state of France as one in which the conditions of the 'good life' no longer flourished had long since left France – and who knows if they survived the voyage home. By contact with Europeans their culture had lost its innocence, a destruction reiterated even more forcefully, later, in 'Des coches'. Certain forms of writing such as love lyric still having cultural value, or certain genres being even publishable, as in the case of La Boétie's political philosophy, was in doubt.[49] And despite Montaigne's swerve into reason in the face of his friend's dying call upon him, the loss of love and this death may relate to shifts in Montaigne's thinking and his loss of faith in the tradition of philosophy teaching us how to die. Rather, the encounter with death required that philosophical abstractions, having failed, be tested, increasingly, and with increasing scepticism. Philosophical discourse not only failed when tried by the singular experience of death, but also had failed, and went on failing, to hold open the possibility of non-violent resolution to

[49] 'Au milieu de la guerre, en un siècle sans foy/ ... est-ce pas grand'folie/ D'escrire de l'Amour' (In the thick of war, in a faithless age, is it not madness to write of love), Ronsard, *Les Amours Diverses* (1578), XXX (in Weber (ed.), *Les Amours* (Paris, 1963), p. 468.

religious conflict.[50] But such loss and failings also brought disillusionment – a potential good – and a set of ethical questions; Montaigne's thinking through of all of this may offer a glimpse into the forming of early modern subjectivity.

And, in Montaigne's writing, this brings questioning *per se*. The mode of the question, along with other grammatical forms such as modifiers, and syntactic strategies such as 'carefully calculated spaces, gaps, suspension of assent, shifts of direction',[51] and (my focus here) figuration and other rhetorical structures such as irony, which allow hesitation and make tolerable the uncertainty or anxiety the reader may feel in the face of ambiguities, of opaque or undetermined significations. The cannibal reminds us of this: both alien, a test of readers' understanding of what it is to be human, and remarkably close to the ideal friend – like that friend, a 'moitié', or in other Aristotelian terms, a *heteros autos* (other self);[52] both external 'other' and internal other self – the other in me of which I am not fully aware (and might not want to be).[53] Also an instance of the extreme hospitability of Montaigne's thinking: his capacity to entertain ideas and allow their play even when they arouse some anxiety.

The ethical questions which come together, spanning the singular relation (friendship-love), the political and the social, include those of address and responsibility, vulnerability, and the possibility of a relational ethics in an economy other than that of exchange, as articulated figuratively by Derrida:

> La question morale n'est donc pas, n'a jamais été: faut-il manger ou ne pas manger … mais puisqu'il *faut bien* manger de toute façon et que c'est bien, et que c'est bon … *comment* faut-il *bien manger*? Et qu'est-ce que cela implique? Qu'est-ce que manger? Comment régler cette métonymie de l'introjection? Et en quoi la formulation même de ces questions dans le langage donne-t-elle encore à manger? … La question infiniment métonymique au sujet du 'il faut bien manger' ne doit pas être nourrissante seulement pour moi, pour un moi, qui alors mangerait mal, elle doit être *partagée* … et non seulement dans la langue. 'Il faut bien manger' ne veut pas d'abord dire prendre et comprendre en soi, mais *apprendre* et *donner* à manger, apprendre-à-donner-à-manger-à-l'autre. On ne mange jamais tout seul, voilà la règle du 'il faut bien manger'. C'est une loi de l'hospitalité infinie. Et toutes les différences, les ruptures, les guerres (on peut même dire les guerres de religion) ont ce 'bien manger' pour enjeu. Aujourd'hui plus que jamais. (pp. 296–7)

> (The moral question is thus not, nor has ever been: should one eat or not, eat this and not that … but since *one must eat* in any case and since it is and tastes

---

[50] This point stands despite the persuasive evidence in Greengrass's invigorating study of surviving reliance among *parlementaires* on the power of philosophical eloquence to help heal France during the civil and religious wars: see Greengrass, *Governing Passions* (Oxford, 2007).

[51] Cave, *Montaigne*, p. 115; for more detailed linguistic analysis see Demonet, *A Plaisir* and Sellevold, *'J'ayme ces mots – '*.

[52] Aristotle, *Nicomachean Ethics* IX.9.10, pp. 562–4.

[53] A point also noted by Cave; see *Montaigne*, p. 91.

good to eat ... *how* for goodness sake should one *eat well*? And what does this imply? What is eating? How is this metonymy of introjection regulated? And in what respect does the formulation of these questions in language give us still more food for thought? ... The infinitely metonymical question on the subject of 'one must eat well' must be nourishing not only for me, for a 'self' which would thus eat badly; it must be *shared* ... and not only in language. 'One must eat well' does not mean above all taking in and grasping in itself, but *learning* and *giving* to eat, learning-to-give-the-other-to-eat. One never eats entirely on one's own: this constitutes the rule underlying the statement, 'One must eat well'. It is a rule offering infinite hospitality. And in all differences, ruptures, and wars (one might even say wars of religion), 'eating well' is at stake. Today more than ever. (p. 282))

Through the figuration of eating and eating well Derrida's 'infinitely metonymical' questions align key concerns of the chapters of the *Essais* just explored, to do with the cannibal, religious sacrifice, love or hate (or hate confused with love, as in the pseudo-sacrifices of the wars). As a bridge between Derrida's reflections and the discussion embedded in the *Essais*, I shall briefly return to an issue raised by friendship-love, namely how it relates to the political. It is presented as exceeding it, not answerable to it; also, grieving for the loss of love *seems* to isolate Montaigne, perhaps all those who mourn, from the life of the *polis*: 'depuis le jour que je le perdy ... je ne fay que trainer languissant' (since the day I lost him, I have only dragged through life listlessly) (p. 193).

In *Precarious Life* Judith Butler proposes that, rather than grief being 'privatizing', it may be precisely the experience of loss of the (loved) other that: 'furnishes a sense of political community of a complex order ... by bringing to the fore the relational ties that have implications for theorizing dependency and ethical responsibility'.[54] We are reminded of the form of community in which friendship flourishes, the antithesis of tyranny in La Boétie's essay. Butler suggests the texture of ethical, political and affective issues that should be woven together as part of what safeguards community against splitting into binaries and polarization, or worse, fundamentalism which furthers the existence of one position at the cost of an other, whether in the form of, for instance, us and them, included and excluded, Roman Catholic and Reformer, or Muslim and non-Muslim.

Let me translate this into the terms we find in 'De l'amitié'. Montaigne writes of being undone by the loss of La Boétie. His destitution resonates in the phrase, there is only smoke: this figure together with the loss of a personal, singular place of enunciation convey the vulnerability of grief, the absence of a sense of bounded self, porousness and insubstantiality. 'Ce n'est que fumée, ce n'est qu'une nuit obscure et ennuyeuse' (it is only smoke, only dark, dismal night): the darkness here is also the obscurity of the grave, the enigma of mourning, for what has been lost in the relationship may be as unknown as its cause ('cela

---

[54] Butler, *Precarious Life* (London, 2004), p. 22.

ne se peut exprimer' (it cannot be expressed) (p. 188)).[55] The loss of subjectivity expressed here conveys undecidably that self is lost quite as much as
the other, or that it is the other in the self that is lost. The metaphors of smoke
and enshrouding darkness, and, otherwise, inexpressibility, seem in tension with
the apparent calculability of the loss some lines later: 'j'estois desjà si fait et
accoustumé à estre deuxiesme par tout qu'il me semble n'estre plus qu'à demy'
(I was already so shaped by the habit of being one of two in everything that now
I feel scarcely half alive). One of two, one half: but these measures need also to
be read figuratively, for they grow out of the metaphor of the 'moitié', each the
other's other half. With it, the fantasy of plenitude, the perfect whole formed of
the two halves, the loss of which returned Montaigne to the reality – the brute
calculability – of being incomplete, the distress of which could only be assuaged
by addressing the lost other – having formerly been addressed by him: 'il n'est
action ou imagination où je ne le trouve à dire, comme si eut-il bien faict à
moy' (there is no action or thought in which I do not miss him, as he would
have missed me) (p. 193). This stages a constant repetition of the first encounter
with the Other's address, and is a paradox essential to our relation with language
as well as something essential to the ethical relationality with which Butler is
concerned, and with which Montaigne grappled, having lost the one he loved.

Here I connect Derrida, Lacan and Butler; in so doing I am suggesting the
connection, rather than the disjunction, between the concerns of psychoanalysis
(often misleadingly associated with what is 'privatizing') and the ethical and
the political. 'Dès qu'on parle, dès qu'on entre dans le milieu du langage, on
perd la singularité' (as soon as one speaks, as soon as one enters language,
one loses one's singularity):[56] by entering into the system of exchange that is
language, one loses a singularity that was imaginary, anyway – a fantasy of
uniqueness and being one-and-all that must be given up. Not only one's illusion
of singularity is lost, so too, here, is perfect friendship; because its purity and
freedom were guaranteed by its singularity and exclusivity, these qualities are
diminished also.

However, these ideals may veil what is also an excessive burden: what it
really means to hold the soul of the other. As already suggested by the metaphors examined earlier, this relationship may have been not without anxiety.
The question of this relationship's 'place', with which La Boétie had left Montaigne, grew out of what was already between them; it caused anxious recoil
but also speaks of an existent anxiety. Derrida continues, referring to *Fear and
Trembling*: 'La parole nous apaise, note Kierkegaard, parce qu'elle "traduit"
dans l'universel' (speech give us relief, Kierkegaard notes, for it 'translates' into
general terms): Montaigne's representation loses proper names and offers us,
instead, perfect friendship, puts into circulation what was said to be inexpressible, the perfection of which was conditional upon it not being in circulation,

---

[55] See Freud, 'Mourning and Melancholia', p. 245.
[56] Derrida, *Donner la mort*, p. 61.

but only being between two-become-one. But in so doing, necessary difference is recovered. Moreover, to represent its 'place', to put it into words for another addressee, is to return to the symbolic pact, the exchange which is the social tie, an intersubjective pact in which it is supposed that the singular is translatable into what is non-singular and recognizable.

With the representation of that which was held to be perfect, singular, unique, those qualities are sacrificed; the pure gift enters the economy of exchange, the 'parfaicte amitié' is brought into relation with other non-unique forms of love, at the moment of being described as incomparable. Also, it was never fully abstracted from other relations, or the call of politics and ethics; for friendship-love began with the words of *De la servitude volontaire*; Montaigne mourns La Boétie's civic and writing potential as well as his 'private' qualities; and it is to the words of his essay that Montaigne's writing returns towards the end of his chapter, having led the reader through his destitution and his going on imagining that the two halves formed a whole beyond which there was – nothing. This return to his words is to words no longer publishable in a culture of religious violence and hate, in which ethical relations, the ideal of which is friendship, seemed no longer possible; the social pact had broken down, the other was to be obliterated.[57]

When we recognize that Montaigne mourns the loss of the one who symbolized certain ideals in political philosophy and ethics, this places (not for the first time, but in a way which singularly moved Montaigne) friendship at the heart of the *polis*.[58] So to go on writing is also to honour this, in a commitment to symbolic exchange as the *locus* of whatever free thinking might still be possible about the good life lived in community with others. Both this and the truth about himself are located in speech, or in the case of Montaigne's writing, writing which mimics speech – 'tel sur le papier qu'à la bouche' (the same on paper as in the mouth) (p. 171), not so much because of an aesthetic impulse but because this emphasizes the significance of the addressee. Writing like speech 'qui vise, qui forme la vérité telle qu'elle s'établit dans la reconnaissance de l'un par l'autre' (aims at the truth, such as is established in the recognition of one subject by another),[59] in full recognition of the risk of being misread, as La Boétie's essay had been. 'La parole est moitié à celuy qui parle, moitié à celuy qui l'escoute' (speech belongs half to the speaker and half to the listener) (p. 1088); such perfectly balanced dialogue and recognition may have seemed possible for the two friends, those 'moitiez' – until Montaigne failed his friend's

[57] For discussion of the social pact in the *Essais*: 'nous ne sommes hommes, et ne nous tenons les uns aux autres que par la parole' (it is only our word that makes us human and binds us together) (p. 36), see for instance Nakam, *Les Essais de Montaigne* (Paris, 1984).

[58] In 'De la vanité' there is a faint echo of this kind of mourning in the commemoration of Pibrac and Foix de Candale, who both died in 1584; for Montaigne, these men of high integrity were out of place in the disintegrations of the time (see pp. 957–8). Thanks to Neil Kenny for this trace.

[59] Lacan, *Le Séminaire livre I* (Paris, 1975), p. 125.

call and death exposed the illusion. But in any other context this seems a lapse into false hopefulness, and it is important to engage with Montaigne's writing as offered in the awareness of recognition being against the odds.

Butler's work on the nature of address lends further precision to this analysis, as well as offering a way of thinking about Derrida's idea of ethical relations. Montaigne's chapter may be read as a working through of the problem of what Butler (engaging with Levinas and, despite Levinas' resistance to psychoanalytic thinking, converging on a Laplanchian analytic narrative of the coming-to-be of the subject) calls the 'ethical claim': 'we are first spoken to, addressed by an Other, before we assume language for ourselves. And we can conclude that it is only on condition that we are addressed that we are able to make use of language. It is in this sense that the Other is the condition of discourse' (pp. 138–9).

So an, or the, Other equated with language, prior to every 'self' – that loss of 'singularity', that heterogeneity that constitutes us: 'nous ne sommes jamais chez nous' (we are never at home) (p. 15). There is always something of ourselves that we do not know. We are always responding to an address rather than being the source of the 'first words': less 'I want this, not that' than 'who are you (to me)?' and the responding question, 'who I am to you?' In idealization this response-and-address-and-response … might take this following symmetrical form: 'il n'est action ni imagination où je ne le trouve à dire, comme si eut-il bien faict à moy' (there is no action or thought in which I do not miss him, as indeed he would have missed me) (p. 193).

If to respond is also to carry responsibility, this returns us to La Boétie's agonized question to Montaigne and his recoil into reasoning. But what the words just quoted remind us is that we go on, as discontinuous identities (as evident in Montaigne's emphasis on 'passage', on our mutating, on his change-ability, 'soit que je sois autre moy-mesme' (whether I am different myself) (p. 805)), being addressed and responding, always at risk of failing to hold that precarious balance between other and self (or – not the same – self and other).[60] Montaigne's writing thus becomes his response and his way of keeping the lost ethical relationality of friendship in mind as not entirely obliterated, as a form of possible future. It is equally a recognition of the need to keep addressing and

---

[60] While the unconscious is not part of Montaigne's conceptual lexis, his thinking about identity in terms of discontinuities seems to me to be open to, and even opened up by, psychoanalytic thinking, in a fundamental way here. To cite Jacqueline Rose: 'the unconscious constantly reveals the failure of identity. Because there is no continuity of psychic life, so there is no stability of identity … Nor does psychoanalysis see such "failure" as a special-case inability or an individual deviancy from the norm. "Failure" is not a moment to be regretted in the process of adaptation' (Rose, 'Femininity and its Discontents', in *Sexuality in the Field of Vision* (London, 1986), pp. 82–103 (pp. 90–1). What resonates with Montaigne's version of the subject, along with the acceptance of lack of stability (and therefore there being tensions between 'public' versions of the subject and 'private' desires and identifications), is that some resistance to adaptation is required of or for the subject: Montaigne seems to me to be more interested in non-adaptability, and in norms as difficulties.

being addressed by the Other as well as the other. He gives writing that is (an acknowledged illusion of being) like speech to unknown others (so, the Other), risking its being misunderstood; there is no last word, and philosophy, 'reason', is not 'the answer'. Instead, its limits are explored, and it is put in relation with everything else that makes, or undoes, the good life.

Or, in Derrida's figure, 'eating well'. The figurative turn here not only responds to Montaigne's resonant use of metaphors of eating and hunger in relation to love and the desire to know the other and to the desire to be known (see chapter 4), but also to the importance in his writing of themes of nutrition – what he likes (or not) to eat and drink, together with all manner of intellectual, spiritual, emotional nourishment, as well as his taste for putting this all into words. His writing is thus the metaphorical food he gives the reader; what remains to be teased out here is the ethical relation that is represented by his gift of words, his giving-the-other-to-eat.

> 'Il faut bien manger' ne veut pas d'abord dire prendre et comprendre en soi, mais *apprendre* et *donner* à manger, apprendre-à-donner-à-manger-à-l'autre. On ne mange jamais tout seul, voilà la règle du 'il faut bien manger'. C'est une loi de l'hospitalité infinie. (p. 297)

> ('One must eat well' does not mean above all taking in and grasping in itself, but *learning* and *giving* to eat, learning-to-give-the-other-to-eat. One never eats entirely on one's own: this constitutes the rule underlying the statement, 'One must eat well'. It is a rule offering infinite hospitality.)

Eating well and giving-the-other-to-eat are presented as imperatives; this relies on the non-possession of what is to be shared: not mine and thine, therefore, but ours, even when the others who constitute that plurality along with me are not known to me, do not love me, and may reject the food I want to give. This form of hospitability and responsibility for shared survival and for the possibility of good life, that is, this form of ethical relation, in which the subject truly assumes his or her responsibility as a subject (for the other) is, in Derrida's thought, excessive. It is a call on the subject exceeding its legal, political, social, codified obligations. For in being willing to give-the-other-to-eat is implied the willingness to let oneself be eaten: to give one's life for one who is not one's friend. Unlivable, this excessive call, this sacrifice; but what is at stake is not really going through with this so much as not giving up thinking about what it would really mean to be prepared to be eaten, if that were the food the other needed.

More livably, the precarious balance is in finding an answer to the question, how can one eat well at the same time as giving the other what is good to eat. Or to return to the terms of Butler's analysis, terms which also concern Derrida here, address and response: how can a relation between self and other be best sustained, so as to nurture one's responsibility towards the other, mindful that: 'quelque chose de cet appel de l'autre doit rester ... *de l'autre*, appel singulier à la réponse ou à la responsabilité' (something of this call of the other must remain ... *other*, a singular call to response or to responsibility) (pp. 290–1).

Each is thinking against violence; Derrida's use of the figure of eating allows into his writing a trace of the violent fantasy of wanting to 'eat the other up' (violent even when this stems from love rather than hate); this reminds us of the aggressivity and vulnerability which ethical relations need to contain. Butler addresses violence (more paradoxically) in terms of the 'violence' of the other's excessive, unwanted address which 'asked me to assume a responsibility ... the other who asks me not to let him die alone' (pp. 129–30). Butler engages with Levinas here in a radical articulation of what it means to be responsible, recognizing, as do (albeit each with different emphases in different and even conflicting discourses) Lacan (after Freud), Derrida *and* Montaigne, the destructiveness which drives human relations. She puts it in terms of the significance of the fear of death in founding ethical relations with the other, where the fear of death is 'my fear of my death', 'my fear that the other will kill me' and 'my fear of killing the other and that I want to kill the other'. This might also be cast in the figurative terms of eating/being eaten.

Montaigne's writing eschews abstract categories such as 'self' and 'other', thus enlivening, complicating and testing our thinking about the intersubjective relations being explored. We find echoes of these figurative terms in the social and political body dismembering itself. Destructiveness is also acknowledged in the recognition of the pleasure I/we take in the pain of the other (see above, p. 86). Even if I am capable of compassion (suffering with the other), in my response to the other's vulnerability something violent and hostile remains, which I enjoy. These different thinkers underline the vulnerability which needs to be recognized along with destructiveness. Vulnerability, not only fear of violence towards me but also my vulnerability to the violence I might inflict, a vulnerability all the more intense when the other is theorized as being a kind of double of the self – we are all 'autruy', other, to the other – as in these anonymized symmetricalizations in which 'self' and 'other' want the same, and when the other is not only over there but already a part of the self.

Arguably, the cannibal returns here: not only as a means for Montaigne to imagine a social pact in which eating the other is not taboo but honoured, or more symbolically in which Derrida's 'excessive' question is acknowledged and integrated, but also providing perspective on his own culture, so as to heighten the breakdown of a social pact. Montaigne pushes the terms: self and other are not distinct, but, he insists, via the (cannibal) victim, that, before taking a bite, what must be recognized is that self and other are one and the same. 'At home', the disintegration into killing the other went along with the failures of politics and ethics to moderate the destructive impulse fuelled by the fear that the other (Roman Catholic, Huguenot) wanted to take *my* (Huguenot, Roman Catholic) place as the one who holds the (one and only) truth, and propelled the desire to kill the other in order to not be killed. To act on this was apparently sanctioned by the religious belief that so to act was to act in the name of the good and truth (that 'massacre et homicide' of 'De la moderation').

The problem dramatized by the porous, heterogeneous cannibal is the absence of recognition that self and other were the same, insofar as each wanted the same, that is, to be identified as the one holding the one and only truth; rather than this being recognized as having the same desire, it was cast as irreducible difference, to be eradicated. The other's otherness was mistaken for what was intolerable, when what was, really, intolerable, was him wanting the same – identical desire. But before destroying, or taking even one bite, what the cannibal narrative reminds us is that it must be recognized that what is being destroyed is not other, in that each wants the same, and that for this to be tolerable, each needs to give up his sense of priority and his desire to possess this truth, and to translate what it means to want the same out of the impasse of imaginary rivalry and violence into a symbolic pact of tolerance. Not generous liberalism, but all the difficulty of enduring ((Lat.) *tolerare*, to bear, endure) the other who wants the same, which entails each finding an unpossessive relationship with what is wanted.

Towards the end of 'De la physionomie' ('On physionomy') there are two potentially life-threatening encounters with versions of the other. The first, in particular, indicates how Montaigne understands the relationship with the other who seems to want what is his. This other is his neighbour ('avois occasion de me fier de luy, comme de mon voisin' (I had reason to trust him as a neighbour) (p. 1060)); here the tenth commandment as well as the sixth is about to be disregarded: 'je n'ignorois pas ... combien ma maison pouvoit estre enviée' (I was not unaware ... how much my house might be envied). Montaigne's account is rather detailed: the neighbour gained entry to his house by the stratagem of claiming he had been attacked, was in fear of his life and needed Montaigne's protection. Montaigne welcomed him: 'je luy fis ouvrir, comme je fais à chacun' (I opened the door to him, as I do to everyone), but became alarmed as the man's soldiers kept on arriving, apparently also in danger. The focus of the account shifts here to Montaigne's way of dealing with what was happening, and why. In the face of extreme danger – the neighbour/enemy 'se veid maistre de son enterprise, et n'y restoit sur ce poinct que l'execution' (imagined himself master of his plan, and all that remained was for him to carry it out) (p. 1061) – his way was what he calls the most natural and simple, 'je me laissay aller au party le plus naturel et le plus simple' (I let myself take the most natural and simple course of action) (p. 1060). He invited the men in, as if what had initially seemed the case, that this was a man he could trust, remained so; thus he remained true to the principle of hospitability.[61] He also acknowledged that the situation was beyond him, and rested with 'la fortune' and 'le ciel', fortune and heaven. Why the neighbour/enemy did not execute his plan was beyond Montaigne's power and calculation, but he did not express his change of mind

---

[61] For a related set of reflections on the disarming effects of the openness I am associating with hospitability here, see the end of 'Que nostre desir s'accroit par la malaisance' ('That difficulty increases our desire'). There, the undefensive openness of the door to Montaigne's house, which seems to invite free entrance and exit, is represented as what protects it from violent attack, and becomes a figure for sceptical open-mindedness, free movement akin to free thinking.

face

in terms of what either fortune or heaven decreed: 'il a dict ... que mon visage et ma franchise luy avoient arraché la trahison' (he has said that my face and my open manner seized his treachery from him) (p. 1061). There was something about Montaigne's look and his bearing; not surprising, perhaps, in a narrative in a chapter on physiognomy. Yet the meaning of this instance is not evident, not only because of what had been asserted earlier with some certainty, namely, that: 'c'est une foible garantie que la mine' (the face guarantees very little) (p. 1059); also, because of what was unknowable or beyond calculation in this encounter: that which in behaviour or its consequences, according to Montaigne, does not belong to us: 'ne nous appartient' (p. 1061). We need to keep this theme of what is ours in mind; but first, the face.

That both Socrates's and La Boétie's ugly appearances, their 'mesavenance au premier regard' (lack of immediate attractiveness) (p. 1057) belied their inner qualities, in the latter's case his 'ame tres-belle' (very beautiful soul) (p. 1057), demonstrated to Montaigne the absence of fixed correspondence between 'outside' and 'inside'. Not a guaranteed opposition, the antithesis of the axiomatic correspondence between beauty and (inner) goodness, but rather, an unreliable relationship between the two.

How to read a face? Or a look? Can an open, hospitable face engender hospitability in the one to whom it turns? Whatever the impact of the face on the other, its incalculable and unreliable nature seems clear: anything but natural or simple. Not that Montaigne's face or look is Levinas's symbolic 'face'; the issue is, rather, the power of fragility in both kinds of face, which are different ways of asking the reader to think about intersubjective relations *in extremis*: we should not forget that Montaigne knew his life was at risk as well as his property. This neighbour is the antithesis of the cannibal, and of eating well. The incalculability of the face makes it too vulnerable to be relied on – and yet Montaigne did; in Levinas, the face is the fragility which instantiated and is exposed by the other's call upon the self, the archaic version of which is the hinterland of the commandment not to kill, and which must be recognized. Both resonate with Derrida's insistence that there is something excessive, which does not belong to us, in how we go beyond what is calculable in balancing between differing models of what is good, true, right ... and the different subjectivities that go along with this. Montaigne went on responding as if his neighbour/enemy were, rather than threatening his home and his life, calling upon his hospitality, which enshrined ideals of sociability and the good life; and in Montaigne's account it seems that it was his fidelity to his own overriding principle, the 'face' of hospitability, to which the neighbour/enemy responded. In this moment both the authority of the commandments not to kill and not to want what is not yours to possess and Montaigne's trust returned, suggesting (despite evidence to the contrary) that his face was readable, vouched for him, 'respondoit pour moy' (answered for him) (p. 1062), as did the principle of hospitability. This is, in other words, to give-to-others-to-eat.

Or in Montaigne's text, to hate no one: 'aussi ne hay-je personne' (moreover, I hate no one) (p. 1063). In the psychical conflicts which ethics seek to moderate, what is intractable is a collapse into imaginary opposition: either (love) or (hate). Montaigne is clear about the qualities and acts that he hates but these, and the affect that they draw, are separable from the person, even as he still holds them responsible. This is not a sentimental ideal; hating no one does not imply loving everyone. However, it is another way of representing the condition of the principle of hospitability, which is equally non-aggressivity towards the other, inviting the other in and not allowing a binary to take hold.

If this is the condition of ethics, it is equally the condition of sceptical thinking. Philosophical scepticism tests arguments and beliefs, but here the test was life-threatening; the result seems to be the restoration of a basis on which security and tranquillity might rest. But it is both provisional and specific. The chapter ends by returning to uncertainty, and the problem of acting for the good because passion, or primitive impulse, or a factor we do not recognize or control may contaminate our action. The problem is exacerbated if a situation is judged only in terms of opposites, which drives understanding towards an impasse.

Recalling his judicial role, Montaigne writes about the problem of judgement and sentencing: when what could be known as to what it would be to act well was tested, as in sentencing, Montaigne's preference was to not pass judgement: 'j'ay plustost manqué à la justice' (p. 1063). This echoes the desire expressed in 'Des boyteux' for the possibility of a judicial verdict of uncertainty: 'quelque forme d'arrest qui die: La court n'y entend rien' (some such form of sentence as: the court understands nothing in this case) (p. 1030). This declaration of lack of understanding is too assertive to be purely sceptical; but by asserting it, the urgency and intractability of the dilemma are conveyed. The specific tests to which the more abstract ethical models are put seem to lead Montaigne in two conflicting directions. On the one hand, when another's life is at stake, an insistence (which we can call sceptical) on the importance of not passing sentence, given the uncertainties of knowledge, motivation, consequence ... But on the other, faced with unjust threat to his own life, he presents as what matters, and what works, the imperative of acting according to an ideal which in reality is saturated with uncertainties and incalculability. So, acting against the odds, as if the principle were so significant as to call for such action, even though the uncertainties involved were guaranteed. In a sense, these directions converge: I welcome you, do not take what is mine, do not kill me; I will not kill you (even if justice requires). But what the examples bring out is the absence of symmetry, the imbalance of knowledge of self and other, and the need to refuse to engage as if relations were based on a self–other dichotomy.

So we find instances of ethical dilemmas explored by later thinkers in terms of figurative eating and of the impulses, conscious and unconscious, that 'Thou shalt not kill' seems designed to regulate. In the *Essais* they are both very close to home and far away; and the figure of the 'cannibal', whose very distance from Montaigne's home was a significant factor in the thinking for which he could be used, also needed to be brought closer to home, to give full resonance to what was being tested. With no guarantee that thinking about the figurative cannibal could be independent from Eucharistic conflict and all that went with it, as already discussed, the risk of overdetermined misreading was high. This suggests that the cannibal represents an imperative inquiry: into what happens when it is not recognized that ethics needs to contain the desire to kill the other who is both irreducibly other and yet already a part of the self.

What the figures of 'eating' and 'eating well' allow us to ponder in what may otherwise seem an excessively abstract ideal are layers of questions raised by the difficulty of thinking about ethical responsibility to others, particularly when their otherness makes 'me' recoil or want to fail to respect or find a way of really acknowledging that otherness (which threatens 'me'). They also help us think about the aggressivity and violence that ethical relations seek to contain, and, along with them, the vulnerability without recognition of which any model of ethical relations will tend to fail.

Montaigne encapsulated and allegorized all of that in his representation of France as witnessed by the cannibals in 1562; and all of that also suggests why psychoanalytic thinking can help our understanding of what fails and why. It conceptualizes eating the other as both love and hate, it proposes ways of understanding how we grow from the need to eat to much more complex desires, in all of which we depend on others or the Other, and it thinks in terms of the intersubjectivity that constitutes us and is the ground of ethics.

With all this in mind, let us now turn to further intricacies of intersubjectivity, as it bears on the relationship between desire and knowledge, and on the desire to speak of them.

4

Confessions: The Desire for Knowledge, the Passion for Ignorance

> Tout le mouvement du monde se resoult et rend à cet accouplage: c'est une matiere infuse par tout, c'est un centre.[1]

'Sur des vers de Virgile' courts danger: it speaks of what usually remained secret, unspoken, or might have been considered unspeakable. An ageing writer's thoughts turn to his erotic life, and through glimpses of his reading of mildly seductive Latin poetry opens up reflections on marriage, love and sex. Then, through discussion of the pleasures of literary texts and of his own writing practice, he explores the relation between body and mind, other aspects of love, and what he has learned through his experience of love and desire. This is re-membering, he says, as a cure, 'remede' (p. 842), for the mortification of the ageing body. But this is too bland a summary of the chapter, which is interested in exposing what is hidden, and why, and yet which also keeps on hiding things.[2] So, here is a less veiled version:

> Alexandre disoit qu'il se connoissoit principallement mortel par cette action et par le dormir: le sommeil suffoque et supprime les facultez de nostre ame; la besogne les absorbe et dissipe de mesme. Certes, c'est une marque non seulement de nostre corruption originelle, mais aussi de nostre vanité et de-formité. (p. 878)

> (Alexander used to say that it was this action and sleep that made him most aware of being mortal: sleep suffocates and supresses the faculties of our mind; fucking likewise absorbs and dissipates them. Truly it is a mark not only of our original corruption but also of our vain illusions and deformity.)

About sexuality and mortality, then, and what we come to know about our con-dition as humans through our sexual desires. Given Montaigne's allusion (in a chapter which largely does not take a religious perspective) to the Fall, it may be about problems not only of our erotic or sexual desire, but also of our desire for knowledge and our knowledge of our desire. Montaigne's chapter will test and expose something about the nature of desire enfolded with knowledge.

---

[1] 'All the world's movement resolves into, leads to, this coupling: this matter is infused through everything, it is the centre' (p. 857).
[2] This is also noted by Sellevold, '*J'ayme ces mots –*', p. 31.

Shortly after the passage just cited Montaigne clarifies the nature of our deformity: self-loathing and self-destructiveness. 'Quel monstrueux animal qui se fait horreur à soy mesme ... Nous ne sommes ingenieux qu'à nous mal-mener: c'est le vray gibbier de la force de nostre esprit, dangereux util en desreglement!' (what a monstrous animal, horrified by its own self ... our only ingenuity is in our mistreatment of ourselves: this is the true quarry of our minds in all their power; they are dangerous instruments when disordered!) (p. 879). The effects of these characteristics for the self and also as they affect others, together with the escape into self-deceptions that our condition tends to produce, are evident in the chapter. While Montaigne initially claims to want to remember pleasures past, these will not be separable from pain, confusion and disappointment.

The chapter's title gives nothing away about what will follow. It hints at the significance of texts, even though the main topic is the body and sexual desires. Many of Montaigne's chapter titles are oblique, but this one particularly so. For it is straightforwardly what the chapter is about – but only in part; and if it directs the reader's attention to texts, a question soon follows: what about Lucretius's verse, which is also discussed? Why not 'Sur des vers de Virgile et de Lucrèce'? It seems that the title has a missing half; or, to put it more scepti-cally, it draws our attention away from its missing half, as well as from whatever else it leaves out.

But no: to have left out what the reader will come to discover draws greater attention consequently to the fact that something was missing. Perhaps, then, it is a lure or a decoy: as will become clearer as Montaigne's chapter unfolds, lures are very much a part of the erotic play that it unashamedly reveals. The title exemplifies the power of leaving something hidden: not hiding Lucretius, specifically, so much as reminding of the power of hiding things: 'il est certaines ... choses qu'on cache pour les montrer' (there are some things we hide so as to reveal them) (p. 880), particularly when those things are prohibited, or are things about which one would particularly like to know. The chapter will, paradoxically, also go on to expose one of the powers of showing: namely, as a different way of still hiding what one does not wish to have found.

Let's allow that the title might act in all these ways, and more besides, and that perhaps the Virgil–Lucretius angle is itself a distraction from what may be the more important term, the preposition 'sur', about or on. What does it mean to write on or about? What does it mean to read, to interpret? What is the reader called upon to do, when thinking, speaking or writing about a text? About this particular text? These prove to be questions which run through the chapter. They are staged, even forced upon the reader, by the restless movement of the argument, which is almost structured by the 'mais', 'buts', that proliferate throughout, and which even at times have directive force, acting as if to say, 'no, that's not it, let's think again'.[3]

---

[3] Certeau notes a 'that's not it' dynamic in the development of the argument in 'Des

And what if the text in question has a very specific status: what if, like this chapter, it is presented as a confession?[4] If 'parler ouvertement' (to speak openly) (p. 890) is the intention, then why give this activity any other name, least of all so contentious a name at the time as 'confession'? It may be a metaphor, but is it not paradoxical to prefer a figure to those words, 'to speak openly' – unless we accept the peculiar potential of figuration to open up the reader's thinking? Many others have already creatively pursued the questions raised by such a term, exploring what Montaigne is confessing about.[5] However, it remains to keep the themes of the chapter in play with a set of other questions relating to what it means to want to confess, and with the role of the reader who 'hears' the confession.

So, in what follows, the chapter's exploration of textual representations of the erotic and of the pleasure of the text will not be primary; its presentation of erotic desire will be explored, but in its bearing on confession and the kind of (desire for) *knowledge* of the self that confession might lay bare. But, just as the title may suggest that what is left out matters as much as what is included, so too, I shall argue, does the reader who is not explicitly included in the chapter's versions of 'nous', us; not an interlocutor, not addressed, but rather only represented as if among the objects of Montaigne's reflections. What will such a reader find in the chapter? And what can someone who listens in hear? What if it is only by listening in – illicit eavesdropping, which Montaigne admits he was not above – that we can discover what we want to know? I shall explore the roles of both addressed and unaddressed reader, together with what emerges about what Montaigne can perhaps only hear by listening in to his own confession.

Who is listening is a very specific question in relation to confession, when this is a spiritual practice. Unlike some,[6] I read this 'confession' as both spiritual *and* secular; not in the least penitent, not inhibited by, or guiltily ashamed about, sexuality or the body as Christian culture so markedly had been, and more secular than spiritual, but yet, not separable from the spiritual practices of the

---

cannibales'. That Montaigne's ideas develop by being repeatedly unsettled is the common factor here; but in 'Des cannibales' he is distancing himself from 'increasingly authoritative discourses', and without such repeated recourse to the use of 'but'. See Certeau, 'Montaigne's "Of Cannibals"', p. 69.

4   The verb and noun are used eight times in the chapter.

5   See for instance Cottrell, *Sexuality/Textuality* (Columbus, 1981) and Kritzman, *The Rhetoric of Sexuality and the Literature of the French Renaissance* (Cambridge, 1991).

6   My emphasis is different from that of Cave, if only slightly, although his reading, linking this 'confession' with 'Du repentir', offers subtle precision: 'Montaigne calque sa confession laïque sur des pratiques religieuses analogues. Cette référence n'a aucune intention théologique; elle est au contraire métaphorique … Il serait imprudent, toutefois, d'en conclure que Montaigne se libère d'un seul coup de la lourde censure imposée par la religion chrétienne – sur le récit personnel' (Montaigne bases his secular confession on comparable religious practices, but uses 'confession' in no way theologically, but rather, metaphorically … Yet it would be rash to conclude that he altogether frees himself from Christianity's strict repression of the personal narrative). See *Pré-histoires*, pp. 126–7.

time. I am suggesting that it lifts off from spiritual confession, opening out into a new kind of practice. Even if we agree that the adverb 'religieusement', as in the phrase 'je me confesse religieusement' (I scrupulously confess) (p. 846), can be taken to mean 'scrupulously', it is not for nothing that this adverb was used; and, used in relation to the verb to confess it keeps a resonance of religion in play throughout the chapter, while also allowing a secular turn. It is perhaps only by keeping both spiritual and secular in play, or, by tracing out the ways in which this particular confession puts in question the habits and assumptions of spiritual practice, that all the resonances of the chapter can be heard.[7]

Put simply: if I set out to confess my sins, I speak according to the conventions of the practice of confession, and speak as if I know the nature of my sins, to someone who also knows their nature and weighs them accordingly. But – 'mais' – what if I do not in fact know the nature of my intentions and actions, which I do not call sins, am without conventions by which to speak of them, and what is more, am speaking to someone who turns out not to know their, or my, nature, either? Not a catastrophe; on the contrary. Perhaps what is being teased out by Montaigne's chapter is a process of discovery, about the desire to confess, to make oneself known, without any explicit wish for absolution. Only by embarking on this form of confession do I discover how to speak about myself to an other. In the process, both I and that other will have been transformed. Or not: no guarantee that I will fully recognize when the oily film of self-deception is still allowing me my precious illusions about who I am, as if I am who I want to be, or am indeed how I want to be known. No guarantee, but perhaps the possibility that in representing what I do not yet know of myself as well as what I think or want to know, the other may hear what it is I say, without my yet knowing it, (of) myself.

This sets great store by the listener or reader. But if the practice of confession is removed from its religious setting, with all the power and privilege it lends the listener, how do I know how what I say will be heard: is there any guarantee that I will not be misheard? A confession undertaken without desire for absolution, and which does not call the desires of which it speaks 'sins', may seem not only to have freed itself of the inhibiting desire for a conclusion, but also to absolve itself of shame and anxiety; and yet, as my analysis aims to show, Montaigne's chapter is traced through by anxieties, wraps itself around the profound anxiety of being misunderstood, and tussles with the question, what can be known of desire and spoken of to another?

This confession is not only a hybrid of the sacred and the secular but also tests philosophical forms of knowledge and self-knowledge; it drenches them in affect – not only anxiety but also more enjoyable affects; and, just as there is no desire for absolution, so there is no resolution. However, while this sounds like scepticism, the state of mind conveyed by the chapter is far from tranquil

---

[7]   What is proposed is, of course, in a kind of line with 'Du repentir', as reading of the implications of that chapter by Cave suggests, in 'Le Récit montaignien: un voyage sans repentir', in Samaras (ed.), *Montaigne: espace, voyage, écriture* (Paris, 1995), pp. 125–35.

(except insofar as it is not guilt-ridden): its restlessness, its dislocations, its 'buts' suggest otherwise, and require the reader to think beyond not only assertive systems of meaning but beyond scepticism, to read the intrication of ideas and affect here also as a way of testing scepticism, while at the same time they remain characteristic of a sceptical turn of mind.

This begins to sound rather like psychoanalysis – which is, of course, not confession. But it may be thought of as a mode of analysis which supplements forms of philosophical understanding which do not acknowledge their own affect. What follows here may be an analysis of Montaigne's words which is akin to a psychoanalytic listening; but only insofar as what is represented lends itself to this, and with respect for the specific subjectivity articulated here. The rationale for this approach is as a means to extend understanding of the difficulties Montaigne encounters in his attempts to arrive at a way of speaking openly, which is, or so this different phrase suggests, not the same as confessing, and of his anxieties about how his words will be heard. In this context it is worth noting that the time to speak openly ('il est à cette heure temps d'en parler ouvertement' (p. 890)) arrives only towards the chapter's close, and is immediately followed by a but, 'mais'.

This swerve away, as well as the deferring of speaking openly, seems consonant with how desire is spoken of in a psychoanalytic conversation – the ending of which will be reached, some say, when the analysand has come to be able to speak the truth of her desire, which will include a certain kind of knowledge of the endless failing of (psychic and sexual) identity – not failing as failure to achieve a norm, but rather a realization that (psychic and sexual) identity is never fully fixed.[8] It is this ongoing failure to arrive that is enacted by the movement of Montaigne's thinking in this chapter, and more generally by his preference for the essay form, as well as by his going on rewriting and rethinking, writing against a representation of himself as having a fixed or coherent identity.

I have already explored some of these questions of desire, knowledge of desire and the desire to know, and of the relation with the other, in his earlier chapters. Here I develop that analysis further, with three main focuses: firstly, signs of anxiety in Montaigne's confession, particularly in his use of the figure of hunger, and also in forms of excess and in the conjunction/disjunction 'but' which is so prevalent in the chapter: so, structures quite as much as themes. Secondly, who is addressed, and the limits and misrecognitions that this may entail – together with some residual freedoms. This develops into an analysis of the ways in which Montaigne's confession of his desires and what he knows of them turns out to be in some ways entangled in forms of misrecognition and to be a revelation of the passion for ignorance, a desire for the absence of knowledge; and yet, as the last section of my analysis suggests, within the chapter there remains the possibility of setting that passion for ignorance aside, allowing different sites of knowledge and desire – which could not have been

---

8   See Rose, *Sexuality in the Field of Vision*, pp. 90–1.

accommodated by a confession which did not transform and translate what, for a writer in Montaigne's day, it meant to confess. This site is the philosopher's body, as it speaks in an anecdote about Socrates towards the end of the chapter. Also required, as we shall see, is the reader's desire to recognize in the text elements of which it was not itself aware; for this, the initial anxieties about how the confession will be read need to be respected but, nonetheless, lifted.

'L'homme qui présume de son sçavoir, ne sçait pas encore que c'est que sçavoir; et ... l'homme, qui n'est rien, s'il pense estre quelque chose, se seduit soy mesmes et se trompe'[9]

Before going further, two presuppositions need further attention: sacred or/and secular confession? And what does 'passion for ignorance' mean? It seems alien to what we usually think about Montaigne, with his vigorous desire for knowledge and understanding and his unflagging challenging of forms of ignorance.

First, sacred or secular? To begin with another question: Augustine, or Plato – or both? Given the number of significant references to both Plato and Socrates in the chapter, and given its outspokenness about desire, which sits more comfortably with Plato's writing, particularly the *Symposium*, than with centuries of Christian shame-filled reticence, the chapter seems more secular, even 'pagan', in spirit, than Christian. Yet neither confession, at the time of writing, nor confession as a way of containing the disorders of sexuality and desire, nor again sexuality and desire as what are thought innermost and most revealing of what it is to be human – fallen, 'nostre corruption originelle' (our original corruption) (p. 878) – can be separated from Christian culture and practice and, particularly, Augustine and all the Christian thought that follows from him. To know myself, to have knowledge of myself, to have my own knowledge: that which is most hidden is equally that which is most 'me' and 'mine', and fundamental to the development of concepts of subjectivity. Only by examining this private self can I come to know myself; only by uttering something of it (in confession) do I come to acknowledge myself as a fallen human being. In this culture sexual desire is readily mapped onto greed of all kinds, and, with it, the desire to possess. Know this about yourself and you will know how you should live, resisting such drives and desires.

Yet, as Jameson reminds us, for Augustine: 'sexuality becomes the mode of explanation rather than the thing to be explained'.[10] This helps us read Montaigne's 'confession': neither sin, nor 'mode of explanation', but still within that Christian sensibility which locates some innermost meaning of the self in knowledge of (sexual) desires. Montaigne extends what can be said about

---

[9] 'The man who presumes to know, does not yet even know what knowledge is; and man, who is nothing, seduces and deceives himself if he thinks he is something' (p. 449).

[10] Jameson, 'On the Sexual Production of Western Sexuality', in Salecl and Žižek (eds), *Gaze and Voice as Love Objects* (Durham, NC and London, 1996), pp. 154–78.

no guilt, no shame?

(sexual) desires and reaches beyond this culture, by coupling its ways of thinking with those of other cultures, not least, ancient Greek thought as represented by Plato and embodied by Socrates, and Latin writers such as Virgil and Lucretius. Whether his misgivings not about sexual desire so much as about the desire to *possess* knowledge in all its forms, including the desire to possess (knowledge of) another human being, are bounded by the culture which formed him or whether he can think this in terms which push further, remains to be seen.

The meaning of sexuality, as Jameson among others points out, is not inherent; rather, it always 'leans' on other systems of meaning – even when, or perhaps in order for it, both meanings are to be constructed after the fact; for instance, in Christian culture, the way in which sexuality and guilt lean on one another:[11] the 'symbolic significance' of sexuality can only be 'deciphered in terms of what it opposes or resists' (p. 160). In 'Sur des vers de Virgile' Montaigne's stated absence of guilt is striking, as is his desire to free sexuality and its representation from not only guilt but also shame. Sexuality thus would need to be understood not in relation to guilt but to its absence; not impossible, but here his writing rather belies this, for it restlessly goes on searching for, and accreting, all kinds of meanings. These meanings – identified in other times and places, in a hybrid and volatile flow of classical and anthropological instances – may be less answers in themselves than decoys or lures. But are they distractions/diversions from the possibility that the truth of Montaigne's (sexual) desire may go on eluding him? Or are they invitations to the reader to keep searching, along with the writer, despite only glimpses of understanding, by offering enjoyment along the way? In the multiplication of instances, Greek, Roman, Indian, or other, what is clear is that Montaigne's writing pushes against the *binary* logic that Jameson identifies when he locates the potential meaning of sexuality in terms of what it 'opposes or resists'.

However, this turns out not to be the case: resist, as a reader, the lure of the array of detail, and something which could be described as binary still remains: the search to locate meaning in an imagined other, whether Greek, Roman, Indian, the feminine, or indeed the Huguenot. The form of resistance which will not settle, representing a desire to move beyond opposition, even if it is not ever quite realized, is the 'but' – the 'no, wait, that's not quite it', the correctives, precisions, resistances, reroutings, and so forth, which keep Montaigne's confession moving. In due course my discussion will focus on what it potentially moves towards, having first analysed what holds that movement back, suggesting hesitations and resistances along the way.

Neither guilt nor shame: if one is without shame, what other than acculturated habit motivates confession? Montaigne is shameless, insofar as it is not what drives his confessing here; but shame is not absent from his representation. It, or related terms, occur 109 times in the *Essais*, 20 of which are here. None associates shame with sexuality except to repudiate it, particularly when it

---

[11] Jameson, 'On the Sexual Production', pp. 160–1.

derives from religious doctrine. For instance, to treat the genitals or sexual inter-course as shameful is dismissed as being stupid, 'sotte' (p. 878). When shame is associated with sexuality it is with failure to perform; the significance of the term here is robustly secular. Earlier in the chapter, Montaigne mocks himself for latterly adopting tastes which in his youth were alien to him ('s'amus[er] à choisir le goust du vin et des sauces' (to spend one's time tasting wines and sauces) (p. 843)); but this 'shaming' inconsistency is not reproached as if it were self-betrayal, and although the word 'honte', shame, is used, it implies not a jot of repentance. Along with these examples are more, all of which remove a fixed moral or religious significance from shame, even undermining it so far as to deem it stupid.

As for ignorance: Montaigne often rails against it, even allowing himself to generalize in his condemnation of it, as in the following instance: 'il s'engendre beaucoup d'abus au monde ou … tous les abus du monde s'engendrent de ce qu'on nous apprend à craindre de faire profession de nostre ignorance' (many abuses are engendered in the world, [indeed] all the world's abuses are engen-dered by our being taught to be afraid to admit our ignorance) (p. 1030). All abuses, our ignorance; yet not quite so. Not ignorance *per se*, but our relation to our ignorance, for it is our fear of revealing it that causes wretchedness and wrongs; a learned fear, embedded in our culture, which leads to denial of it. What passes for knowledge or what we recognize as knowledge may prove misrecognition, fear of what we cannot allow ourselves to know, although we already have that knowledge (which always returns to the fact that our condi-tion is mortal). At issue here are the consequences of denial. What Montaigne does not spell out in this passage from 'Des boyteux' is the link between denial and self-deception: but he does so elsewhere, in his analyses of 'cuider', the vanity in which self-deception is rooted. When it comes to ignorance, who is to say who knows, or does not know, how willed or knowing our denial of ignorance is? To pretend that one knows, when one does not, and to opt for self-consoling misrecognition when different knowledge might be possible or even be what is at stake, is another form of not knowing, if fear and vanity conceal to us our absence of knowledge, allowing us not to know that our knowledge is a pretence. Not knowing, through 'cuider', that one does not know: here, 'knowing' and not knowing oneself merge. If ignorance is castigated, it is as much ignorance of one's ignorance of oneself as of what one is called upon to know and do if one is to 'live well' in the world.

So, ignorance in Montaigne's text comes to meet the passion for ignorance, that is, for the absence of knowledge, the knowledge of ourselves we cannot bear, so much so that we prefer self-deception. This ignorance may still be caught up in a desire to possess, to maintain the illusion that we are in full possession of ourselves. We need, for clarification, to turn not to the past, but to what is in the future for Montaigne, to what Lacan suggests about our desire to remain deceived, in contradiction with the classical and continuing ideal-ized version of ourselves, as seekers after knowledge and enlightenment. While Montaigne opens 'De l'experience' ('On experience') with what seems a confident reassertion of Aristotle's emphasis on the desire for knowledge ('il n'est desir au monde plus naturel que le desir de connoissance' (there is no desire more natural than the desire for knowledge) (p. 1065)), throughout the text a weight of evidence challenges this and also calls for precise understanding of the relationship between desire and knowledge. This 'most natural' desire is no more immune than any other supposedly 'natural' given from sceptical questioning and from being tested, lest it prove self-deception rooted, perhaps, in one's condition of lack – not only lack of (desired) knowledge, but lack *per se*, and lack of the desire to know, unafraid, one's lack. Now this *would* be something about which one might wish to confess …

'Frases dangereuses'

Montaigne anticipates that his confession will be thought dangerously explicit, 'indiscretion' (p. 846), 'cette sorte de parler scandaleux' (this kind of scandalous speech) (p. 889). He courts this; for it is just such a stance that his words are designed to test, asking, why make a scandal of sex? Is the scandal not, rather, the hypocrisies which multiply as a result?

> Qu'a faict l'action genitale aux hommes, si naturelle, si necessaire et si juste, pour n'en oser parler sans vergnongne et pour l'exclurre des propos serieux et reglez? Nous prononçons hardiment: tuer, desrober, trahir: et cela, nous n'oserions qu'entre les dents? Est-ce à dire que moins nous en exhalons en parole, d'autant nous avons loy d'en grossir la pensée? (p. 847)

> (What has the sexual act, which is so natural, necessary and just, done to mankind, that we cannot speak of it without shame and exclude it from serious and decent conversation? We boldly speak of killing, robbing and betraying, but about it, we only dare mutter. Does this mean that the less we breathe a word about it, the more we can allow our thoughts to dwell on it?)

His preference is a seemingly perfect fit between action and words: 'oser dire tout ce que j'ose faire' (to dare say all that I dare do) (p. 845); his chapter, its example. But is it? Setting aside the conceptual problem which Montaigne here seems to bypass, namely, what do words inevitably fail to convey, we should ask: who has such full knowledge of their actions and the desires that drive them that they can be sure of being able to 'tell all'? What does how he speaks of everything in his confession tell us about the possibility of consistently doing what he has said he wants to? Also, what does the recurrent use of 'but' reveal about how an unorthodox confession can be articulated?

There are some seventy occurrences of the word in this chapter, over twenty of which begin a sentence. Some are unremarkable, straightforwardly synonymous with 'however'. But some have much more force, are more complex than just hinges or pivots in the movement of the ideas in the text. For instance: 'de mon dessein, j'eusse fuy d'espouser la sagesse mesme, si elle m'eust voulu.

Mais, nous avons beau dire, la coustume et l'usage de la vie commune nous emporte' (had I had the choice, I would have fled from marrying wisdom herself, had she wanted me. But say what we will, the usual customs of life are what carry us) (p. 852). Montaigne is not the marrying kind: 'but' is a measure of the gap between what he wants and what is required of him. It also works elsewhere in the confession to mark out the difference between Montaigne's position and customary thinking, or generalized abstractions.

After outlining what philosophy says about moderation as an ideal in relation to 'les voluptez naturelles' (natural pleasures), and against dwelling on what might intensify one's erotic longing, he counters:

> mais ay-je pas raison d'estimer que ces preceptes, qui ont pourtant d'ailleurs, selon moy, un peu de rigueur, regardent un corps qui face son office, et qu'à un corps abbatu ... il est excusable de le rechauffer et soustenir par art, et par l'entremise de la fantasie, luy faire revenir l'appetit et l'allegresse, puis ce que de soy il l'a perdue? (p. 892)

> (But am I not right in thinking that these precepts, which, moreover, are still, in my view, too rigorous, concern a body which is doing what it should, and that we are allowed to warm up a worn-out body, helping it out by using artful skill and, by using our imagination, to restore its appetite and joy, because by itself it has lost them?)

This 'but' articulates a sceptical singularity, insisting no, that's not how I see it. However, another instance, in which 'but' is repeated, conveys resistance that is neither sceptical nor respectful of singularity to a (philosophical) view of love too preoccupied with its spiritual dimension. Here 'but' counters an abstract generalization with just as much generalization, albeit citing experience instead:

> je leur oy souvent peindre cette intelligence toute spirituelle, et desdaigner de mettre en consideration l'interest que les sens y ont. Tout y sert; mais je puis dire avoir veu souvent que nous avons excusé la foiblesse de leurs esprits en faveur de leur beautez corporelles; mais que je n'ay point encore veu qu'en faveur de la beauté de l'esprit, tant prudent et meur soit-il, elles vueillent prester la main à un corps qui tant soit peu en decadence. (p. 896)

> (I often hear women portray this relationship as wholly spiritual, dismissing the interest our senses have in it. Everything plays its part: but I can say that I have often seen us excuse the weakness of their minds because of the beauty of their bodies; but I have yet to see a woman willing to give a hand to even a slightly declining body because of its owner's beautiful mind, however wise and mature it may be.)

Whilst there may be some ordinary truth in these (ungenerous) observations, and whilst it matters to test abstractions with examples drawn from experience, these 'buts' allow Montaigne to test one position with another which patently requires just as much testing; but here he declines to be sceptical. They express resistance, not open-mindedness, lapsing from the attitude that Montaigne wants to demonstrate. As will be seen in my next section, it may be no accident that, in these instances, his resistance is, in some ways, towards women and what he thinks women want.

'But' also often acts as a way to persist. For instance: 'la police feminine a un trein mysterieux, il faut le leur quitter. Mais, si je ne me trompe ...' (the workings of the polity of women are mysterious, we must leave it to them. But if I am not mistaken ...) (p. 856). The declared mystery must be demystified, open to or opened up by Montaigne's analysis. Elsewhere, on the subject of cuckoldry and the culture of concealing it, there is resistance to what Montaigne knows: it is ascribed to others, broadly; to 'opinion', to 'what people say', that is, to imaginary interlocutors, who Montaigne can then counter: 'mais le monde en parle ... Mais jusques aux dames, elles s'en moqueront. Et dequoy se moquent elles en ce temps plus volontiers que d'un mariage paisible et bien composé?' (yes, but people talk. But even the ladies laugh at me. And what do they laugh at more freely, these days, than a peaceful, well-made marriage?) (p. 870). These imaginary interlocutors are a rhetorical device, designed to inscribe resistance so as, paradoxically, to keep the text moving, in relation to a topic about which thinking was inhibited by prejudices and anxiety. Moreover, this is only a semblance of difference; it allows the absorption of difference back into the dominant perspective. It stages it in order to cover it over again: shows, to hide. As the chapter's only instance of the device apart from the imagined critic of his writing, who matches his own critical afterthoughts, this example signals the function of 'but' as recoil, resistance to listening openly to what is being opened up.

It is therefore all the more interesting that 'but' is also used so often in the confession on the side not of resistance but of the flow of ideas. For often 'but' simply, and rather loosely, connects the ideas expressed, frequently translatable as 'but', or 'however'; sometimes, rather, it means 'or, to be more precise', or 'moreover', or 'and there's still more to say'. In a negative context it differentiates: not this, but that. At other times, it differentiates Montaigne's opinion from others'. All of these possibilities circulate, along with more forceful and punctual instances such as those discussed above; so the reader is engaged by the structure of the representation along with its themes, and has to keep clarifying for herself which particular meaning is in play, noting as she does so the comparative absence of more rigorously logical argumentation or articulation. It is as if this new material needs a different kind of articulation than Montaigne used elsewhere. So we pause, often, on a 'but'; thus, while this conjunction functions to connect ideas, and is a mark of the mobility of Montaigne's thinking, it is also punctual and indicative of the 'jolting' movement 'à secousses' (p. 842), to which Montaigne alerted the reader at the outset.[12] Whilst ideas are in flux in this chapter, their flow is not uninterrupted; at times the flux meets with resist-

---

[12] For further discussion, see chapter 5.

ance, or hesitation, or is channelled. As will be seen shortly, this mimics ways in which Montaigne's confession proves not an unmixed search for self-knowledge and its authentic representation but rather, along its way, may resist its stated desire for this to be out in the open.

'Je suis affamé … je n'ay faim … je crains mortellement'

Although in the opening pages of the chapter there have been plenty of citations from Latin poetry, albeit of no more than a line or two, there is no reference to poetry or Virgil, no literary appreciation or interpretation. But already, some of the fundamental themes, structures, questions or doubts and affects of the chapter are gathered in the following passage, which occurs quite early, some six pages in, without this being the first mention of confession.

> En faveur des Huguenots, qui accusent nostre confession privée et auriculaire, je me confesse en publicq, religieusement et purement. Saint Augustin, Origene et Hippocrates ont publié les erreurs de leurs opinions; moy, encore, de mes meurs. Je suis affamé de me faire connoistre; et ne me chaut à combien, pourveu que ce soit veritablement; ou, pour dire mieux, je n'ay faim de rien, mais je crains mortellement d'estre pris en eschange par ceux à qui il arrive de connoistre mon nom … Ceux qui se mescognoissent, se peuvent paistre de fauces approbations; non pas moy, qui me voy et qui me recherche jusques aux entrailles, qui sçay bien ce qui m'appartient. (pp. 846–7)

> (In honour of the Huguenots, who condemn our private and auricular confession, I make my confession publicly, scrupulously and purely. St Augustine, Origen and Hippocrates have publicly admitted the errors of their opinions; I go further, and include my errors of conduct. I am hunger-starved to make myself known; to how many, I care not, so long as I do so truthfully. Or, to put it better, I hunger for nothing, but I am mortally afraid of being mis-taken by those who come to know my name … Those who do not know themselves can feed on false approbation; I cannot. For I see myself and search my very entrails, and know well what is mine.)

In its themes, lexis, specificity, and affective force, the passage veers sharply away from the chapter's title, swerving far from literature, the classical past and its ideals, to the immediate present, to the theme of confession, and to Montaigne's desire and anxiety, conveyed with acute intensity. What Montaigne confesses he wants, and what may be made possible by making a confession of it, is to be known, truly known ('me faire connoistre … veritablement'). More accurately, he wants to make himself known (not quite the same), and he not only *wants* this, but – 'je suis affamé' – he is, if we draw on Cotgrave's range of English translations, 'famished', 'starved', 'hunger-starved' for this. He cannot live without it. The use of a metaphor of intense appetite in this context is electric; not only because it is so unusual a use of the adjective – Huguet's dictionary lists no figurative instances of use – but also because, even if it were

hunger → [Euch.] → Hunts

not already a dramatic way of describing his desire, it is all the more so in this context.[13]

For reference has just been made to Huguenots, and to conflict between Huguenots and Roman Catholics, even if, as if to mitigate, the Roman Catholics are not explicitly named; and even if here the site of conflict is forms of confessional practice, nonetheless when this conflict was at the time inseparable from that over the interpretation of the Eucharist, the nature of sacramental 'food', what 'hunger' means is indissociable from those conflicts. Nor, moreover, can his confession be considered independent of prevailing spiritual practices, and conflicts, however secular it might wish to be.

In all the complexity of its assertion and retraction, in its structure as well as in its use of figuration to give form to what otherwise might be too hard to symbolize, the sentence beginning 'I am hunger-starved' seems an impeccable account of anxiety, a representation in a different form of the statement: this is my desire, but this is also my anxiety. Once again, Montaigne might be described as 'décollé de son existence' (existentially unglued).[14] All the more so if that existence is prolonged in the form of a textual representation over which the author will lack control.

Recourse to metaphor alerts us to the difficulty of the ideas and affects that the text attempts to convey. The use of so overdetermined a series of metaphors in the passage amplifies the difficulty, and acts as a reminder that, whilst what predominates is the troubling affect they conveyed, this is not to be understood as exclusively private, but rather as also embedded in complex and complicating social and religious systems of meaning. This all has to do with the cultural complexity of knowledge of the body, especially as a site of knowledge of our being – perhaps, as Montaigne's knowing himself in his 'very entrails' suggests, of our innermost being.[15] The meaning of entrails here is ambiguously literal and figurative, identifying Montaigne's desire for self-knowledge as of his self as an embodied being, as well as acting as a measure of how far his search risks going. It also signals how visceral is Montaigne's fear of the outcome of his – vital – desire to communicate his self-knowledge for others to make of what they will.[16]

This is thematized, though less dramatically, in the course of the chapter, through Montaigne's own reading, his literary appreciation, particularly of Virgil and Lucretius. His enjoyment is uncomplicated: his response open, generous, sensitive to formal detail, and his interest particularly held by the

[13] Unusual but not unique: for instance, there are several instances of the figurative use of the word in Ronsard's love lyric, all of which intensify a Petrarchan topos, the sight of the beloved as vital food.

[14] Lacan, *Le Séminaire IV*, p. 226.

[15] 'Descouvertes jusques au fin fond des entrailles' (revealed our innermost being) (p. 190): for discussion of this phrase in the earlier chapter, which echoes here, see above, pp. 101–2.

[16] I leave it to the reader to decide whether there is also a hint of the divinatory power of entrails in the use of the term here.

relation between these sublime forms of representation and what they actually represent. Thus of poetry such as Virgil's he comments: 'elle represente je ne sçay quel air amoureux plus amoureux que l'amour mesme' (it represents something indefinable about love, more amorous than love itself) (p. 849). This raises two questions: firstly, if the representation of 'love' takes the form not of poetry but of prose, and if it is not sublime but allows something different besides – something more ambiguous – what kind of writing, and moreover reading, will be produced? Montaigne 'knows how to read' writing such as Virgil's; but will others know how to read his, particularly if it takes a form which does not translate readily into recognized conventions, indeed even resists them – at the same time as being interlaced with their poetry's traces, as here? Secondly, what is love itself, beyond its discursive representations? Does this chapter give the reader a version of this, always supposing that it is possible? It may be that this is quite as elusive as writing a representation of oneself which could be described as being precisely oneself, rather than like oneself in recognizable ways. I shall return to these questions later.

The drama signalled and also made tolerable for the reader is heightened when the text then recoils from the overweening hunger to which it has just confessed: it retracts being famished, replacing it with a claim to hunger for nothing, 'je n'ai faim de rien', oddly going back immediately on a 'true' connection between wanting and knowledge. There is, of course, no going back: even though here we have an emphatic instance of the 'buts' that pulse through the chapter, the representation of the starving Montaigne still haunts the version that comes after, or is in fact produced by it. From starving, excessive hunger, to anorexia: from the alarm of excessive hunger or appetite to its disavowal, or the desire for no desire, the move in terms of the psychic economy is clear: that which seems different turns out to be more of the same. To hunger for nothing may be the place into which one is driven by the anxieties associated with hunger that feels excessive – for excess speaks not only of the sensation of overwhelming lack which needs to be met, but also of intolerable anticipation that the lack will not be met: how could so intense a hunger or lack be satisfied? In preferring to hunger for nothing, Montaigne does not set aside desire; he still speaks of desire, with anxiety, and the 'but' which follows does not override this. Instead, he makes a precise point about the relationship between anxiety and desire, about the way in which speaking of his desire has alerted him to the anxiety with which it is freighted and which can now be more precisely understood ('pour dire mieux', 'to put it better'). But if, as in anorexia, anxiety is such as to lead to the desire for no desire, or for no-thing, the outcome is death …

The first awareness of anxiety is amplified and made more explicit by the revelation of a fear he describes as *mortal*. 'Mortellement', mortally, is not an adverb he uses frequently. It occurs five times only, mainly in the third book, both literally and figuratively, or ambiguously. Its use is not always grave, even when combined with a verb such as 'haïr': as in, 'il … hait mortellement le goust' (he utterly loathes the taste) (p. 780) of wine used as medicine, meaning 'utterly', but it leaves a paradoxical aftertaste. A certain amount of (serious) play and ambiguity is also evident in some of the uses of the adjective 'mortel': for instance, 'tout contentement des mortels est mortel' (all mortals' pleasures are mortal) (p. 518). But the use of this adverb here, with 'craindre', in the context of expressions of anxiety, and written in the context of wars which will continue after Montaigne's death, when the commandment 'thou shalt not kill' is in abeyance, is grave.[17] The future of Montaigne's textually 'immortalized' name is at stake; he knows he lacks control over the uses to which that name will be put, and has no guarantee of authentic interpretation or benign understanding. Here it seems that it is his name that is at stake, not his being; a distinction upheld in a reference a few lines later to Socrates: 'Socrates, à celuy qui l'advertissoit qu'on mesdisoit de luy: Point, fit-il, il y a rien en moy de ce qu'ils disent' (Socrates told the man who informed him that people were speaking ill of him: not at all, there is nothing of me in what they say) (p. 847). However, as will be seen shortly, perhaps the imagined or desired relation between Montaigne and his text is more intricated than this, and even if he can reflect with some irony on his desire for his textual self to be perfectly, exactly his, this does not remove the desire.

What if his confession is mistaken, misunderstood, abused by those who hear it? From having initially dealt lightly with the question of how his confession will be heard, the fall into doubt as to whether he cannot but be misheard is searing. Yet this is no more than commonplace: we may be disposed to believe that confessing to a priest carries some guarantee of being rightly heard, but we know that beyond that privileged setting there is no guarantee; rather, every likelihood of being misunderstood – even if, or and so, precisely, we go on yearning for the perfect listener. Here there is not so much doubt or scepticism about what will be understood by the listener: anxiety, traceable not only in the movement of Montaigne's ideas, but also in the use of the phrase 'estre pris en eschange': not 'ne pas estre compris', to be misunderstood, but more forcefully, to be mis-taken: his confession is at risk of capture, his identity mis-taken: taken, what – over? away? hold of? His anxiety is that those who come to know him and his name may abuse it. 'They', his potential abusers, are 'ceux qui se mescognoissent' (those who do not know themselves); who can feed (those metaphors of appetite and ingestion continue) on false approbation. That is, those who, unlike Montaigne, a visceral self-analyst, persist in misunderstanding and misrecognition of themselves. In their 'passion for ignorance', for that is what it is to persist in misrecognizing oneself when one could do

---

[17] 'Thou shalt not kill … the interdiction against murder produces anxiety and desire'; there is a 'constant tension between the fear of undergoing violence and the fear of inflicting violence. I could put an end to my fear of my own death by obliterating the other … I could put an end to my anxiety about becoming a murderer by reconciling myself to the ethical justification for inflicting violence and death' (Butler, *Precarious Life*, pp. 136–7). For all that Butler here gives an account of Levinas, in all his abstraction, this resonates very precisely with what takes hold in a time of civil and religious war, and what Montaigne was so determined to set himself apart from.

otherwise, the risk to Montaigne is that they will also mis-recognize him, which means, if we give serious weight to Montaigne's fear of how they will 'take' him, persist in misidentifying him as being like them. They will exchange his truth for their own.

This takes us towards questions relating to the nature of address and the addressee in this chapter, to be explored in more detail shortly. For now, one further precision is relevant: think back to the context of this confession, which opens with Montaigne, a Roman Catholic writer, seeming, 'in their honour', to align himself temporarily with Huguenot practice while simultaneously using confession in a seemingly secularizing way; at the very least, a liberal, tolerant gesture. But at the time, what possible guarantee does Montaigne have of tolerant hearing on the part of any listener, let alone one identified as Huguenot? If Montaigne particularly reproaches the Huguenots for what in his view are excessive claims as to the power of human knowledge of God's will, he might very well also wish to keep his distance from their attitudes to sexuality. And more particularly, how can Montaigne give his words over to a Huguenot listener without anxiety, given what he knows about the fate of La Boétie's words? Huguenot misappropriation of the pirated essay's implications exemplifies what it might mean to be 'mis-taken'.

To understand the significance of the theme of recognition and misrecognition, and associated anxieties, enough weight needs to be given to the time of writing. The kinds of utterance that might be described as authentic or ethical – and presumably confession would be just such – require that even as we speak we allow that our words will be taken on and away from us by whoever we address; and that beyond an idealized abstraction or theoretical version of how this give and take of words works at its best, we risk, precisely, not being recognized as we want. For that meaning is not in our possession. So for one's words to be of the order of a confession (particularly when the confession in question is not orthodox and therefore will not be heard according to the usual modes of recognition) is conditional upon the speaker accepting the possibility of misrecognition. Indeed, that the odds are in favour of misrecognition. Whether or not the truth of what is being confessed is taken or mistaken is a matter over which one's judgement can only be suspended.[18]

Setting aside for now the question whether and how the speaker knows the truth of what he or she confesses before, or independent of, his or her words being heard by the addressee, we can now begin to understand something further about why Montaigne, who might more than many be able to suspend judgement, should instead suffer such anxiety here as to disable that ability. For this model of ethics to be viable, there has to be enough of a possibility of the addressee being open and benign, capable of putting herself in the place of the speaker, the other, and prepared to address the other in turn; this would be an addressee whose world has not collapsed into bare opposition, in a world in

---

[18] For a fuller inquiry into this kind of ethics, see Butler, *Giving an Account of Oneself.*

which the violence of imaginary relations which allow only that which is like has taken hold; who does not kill or figuratively 'kill' the other but can allow that the other being different does not threaten her sense of identity and the beliefs which form that identity. Not, that is, an addressee caught up in civil and religious war. So what Montaigne's mortal fear speaks of here is, not least, the extreme difficulty of going on suspending judgement, risking misrecognition, at the time of writing; at a time when suspending judgement is most urgently needed for any resolution of conflict to be imaginable.

It is not only the prospect of being taken over, wrongly taken hold of, that provokes anxiety, although this is where it is most marked; we should not overlook the weight of 'eschange' in the phrase: the nature of exchange, and exchange value, are recurring issues in the chapter, with fluctuating force. Sometimes the existence of exchange values, as in marriage, for example, is criticized; but elsewhere Montaigne needs objects of exchange to prop up his arguments, or as decoys. Focus on women as objects of exchange can lure us away from what is fundamental, namely, that they primarily represent fantasy objects, give form to his desire, the location of it and of much of what he struggles to know about. Not until very close to the end of the chapter is an alternative economy to that of exchange proposed. This may turn out to be no resolution; even after so much open talk, a different economy, free from exchange value and therefore one in which who I am, what is mine, how I am represented and how I am 'taken' perfectly coincide, may not have been secured. Indeed, it may turn out to be nothing more than the exchange of one form of fantasy for another.

The intensity of the metaphorical verb, I am hunger-starved, coupled with the reflexive verb, to make myself known, seems to convey something both acutely desired and known about himself, which will become part of what will be made known to others, truly. Rather than reading the swift corrective as undermining the truthfulness of what had just been confessed, perhaps we should understand the corrective as another truth, an insight reached only through the utterance of the first desire, and with it the realization of its related anxiety; these are different, developing, truths about what he wants, as well as what he knows. In the first statement, the question, to whom does he want to become known, is almost suspended, because Montaigne's syntax does not specify where the truthfulness of the representation lies. Does it lie in his words, or with those who hear them, or between the two? For all that Montaigne claims, unlike some, to know what is his: 'qui sçay bien ce qui m'appartient' ([I] know well what is mine) (p. 847), that knowledge will not safeguard what is his as his; and as language does not belong to him in the first place, any more than it belongs to anyone, an uneasy, risk-filled sharing of words is all that is possible at the best of times.

But these are not the best of times; on the contrary, it is a time of crisis of interpretation. It is by giving full weight to all the detail of Montaigne's introduction of his confession that we shall understand the intensity of his anxiety about how it will be interpreted.

The detail also includes the names of others who have risked confession of their 'erreurs', and of being misunderstood: Augustine, Origen, Hippocrates.

Augustine's place here, in the context of a confession of sexual habits and knowledge, has already been mentioned; but what of Origen? Montaigne's sensibilities seem to differ greatly from his, given Origen's recoil from the flesh; but his association of food and eating with *greed* not just for food, but symbolically for property, in other words, the desire to possess, rather than other sorts of relation to that which is 'not mine', or 'other', may be pertinent here. For it has acute bearing on textual interpretation, how others' words are heard: to what extent do they remain the other's? But (how much) were they ever the other's in the first place? The fantasy that self-representation in writing can coincide perfectly with its writer, 'estre exactement mien' (to be exactly mine) (p. 875), is as much in question as the vicissitudes of the text when taken on by future readers.

The link between eating and sexuality has already been discussed, and will return shortly. For now, the aspect that resonates most urgently is that of excess: whether for Origen, an infallible association between eating and greed (excess), or for Montaigne, an anxiety-freighted intensity of desire. In 'affamé', 'hunger-starved', we recognize both lack and desire, both experienced as excessive.

It is perfectly mundane to associate anxiety with fear of excess. The theme of excess runs through Montaigne's chapter, and no amount of confessing seems to free him of it. The chapter opens in a restless mood, as he explores his ageing. His thoughts twist and turn, never settling, remembering what it was to be young, regretting what it is to be old: 'je ne suis ... que trop rassis, trop poisant, et trop meur' (only too sedate, too heavy, too mature) (p. 841). That repeated 'trop', too, or excessively: more than a rhetorical nicety; but in youth, on the other hand, there was also excess, 'excez de la gayeté' (excess of gaiety). Young or old, the capacity for steady 'bien vivre et bien croire' (right living and belief) (p. 841) is difficult to achieve; we prefer to distract ourselves from the painful knowledge of death, illness, poverty. We need to balance pain and pleasure, thought and enjoyment, our minds and bodies working in tandem. For even wisdom can lack balance: 'la sagesse a ses excés' (wisdom has its excesses) (p. 841). How, then, may we read: 'or je veus estre maistre de moy, à tous sens' (now, I want to be master of myself in all respects) (p. 841)? Self-mastery would be the achieving of a state of perfect balance between 'volupté' (sensual pleasure) and 'temperancc' (temperance); fair enough, but it is difficult not to read in the desire for self-mastery the excesses of Stoic voluntarism ('la sagesse a ses excés'), the illusion that mind should conquer body rather than be attentively attuned to it (and vice versa), and the excessive investment in human will and reason of which Montaigne is usually so critical. The desire for self-mastery is readable, perhaps, as an instance of the kind of idea that is described at the start of the chapter as being solid and 'onereux' – excessively weighty. Over against what is excessively solid, this chapter seems to propose a form of 'lightness' of being – not that this will not go on eluding Montaigne.

However, as the chapter unfolds, perhaps a strategy emerges: if Montaigne wishes to be on the side of balance, one means is to identify excess with the other rather than with oneself. In this instance, with women. Montaigne will avow that men do this to women, construct them – as women know – as objects for their own use, misrepresent them wholesale as the locus of excess, as distinct from men. In his corrective inclusion of what Plato's *Timaeus* (91b–c) has to say about men being subject to desire quite as much as women, Montaigne is unusual for the time of writing. He seems to confess the injustices done to women by men; but if he is even-handed it is unsustained and oddly negative: 'nous sommes, quasi en tout, iniques juges de leurs actions, comme elles sont des nostres' (in almost all things, we are unjust judges of their actions, as they are of ours) (p. 885). This is a semblance of doing women justice, a decoy. There is a repeated recoil in the writing from developing this thinking about the relation between the genders and a reversion to identifying excess with 'them'. A somewhat anxious pattern, then; and perhaps Montaigne is less interested in really knowing about women or doing them justice, than in what he does not know about who he is as desired by them. So, less interested in correcting his understanding of them and of what they mean to him than in what he means to them – so that 'they' still remain 'them', while he pursues his most authentic particularity.

What it means to have knowledge of women and women's desire remains a vexing question, one to which Montaigne's knowledge of his own desire takes precedence. At one point he refers rather nonchalantly to Tiresias as the authority on women's desire: 'ce prestre ancien l'a … tesmoigné, qui avoit esté tantost homme, tantost femme' (that priest of antiquity, who was first a man, then a woman) (p. 854). A commonplace; but to offer a mythical figure, who embodies the fantasy of being both genders, having and being it all, as a witness (and therefore implicitly as an authority) is only to problematize what it means to have knowledge of, or have any basis for knowing about, feminine desire – other than by being a woman. Two pages later, there is more of the same, albeit couched as a question: 'seroit-ce ce que dict Platon, qu'elles [sc. les femmes] ayent esté garçons desbauchez autresfois?' (could it be that, as Plato says, they were once debauched boys?) (p. 857): dream on … Less a philosophical insight than a masculine fantasy, a reminder of the ways in which (Montaigne's) fantasy and desire inflect what passes for knowledge.

Perhaps the most extreme instance in the chapter of the ways in which not only fantasy but also anxiety can inflect 'knowledge' of women's desire is Montaigne's mistranslation, misreading, or misremembering, no matter, of an anecdote from Herodotus. 'Les femmes Scythes crevoyent les yeux à tous leurs esclaves et prisonniers de guerre pour s'en servir plus librement et couverte-ment' (the Scythian women put out the eyes of all their slaves and prisoners of war so they could use them more freely and secretly) (p. 866). Savage desire – misascribed. In Herodotus, the women blind their slaves (who had been pris-oners of war) to stop them stealing milk. The blindness here is Montaigne's, allowing him to use this as an example of the excesses of feminine desire. This is a wonderful instance of the anxiety triggered by what the other (here identified not only as feminine but barbarian) wants of me; if this were one's fantasy, one might very well fear it mortally. It is the reader's, Montaigne's, fantasy that is in play; and in being so, it produces mistranslation. These savage

the reader 'we' excludes women

women figure here as a symptom of Montaigne's anxiety: this is to be read less as another anthropological/classical anecdote about women than about women as figuring the other when Montaigne is faced with a question, what does the other want of me, to which he does not (yet) know the answer. Montaigne mis-takes the meaning of the text – as he fears his own will be vulnerable to being mis-taken by other readers.

For whom do you write?

Elsewhere in the *Essais* Montaigne makes his expectations of the reader clear.[19] Although they are high, and expressed with assurance, they are also rooted in a melancholy awareness that the ideal reader does not exist, for this is less an abstract awareness of a conceptual impossibility than a reflection on the loss of his 'best', even idealized, reader, La Boétie. All other readers are substitutes. Their – our – strength is in our having distinct identities, for as a writer quite as much as an interlocutor Montaigne enjoys the possibility of engaging with different perspectives. Up to a point: his expectations make it clear that his kind of reader should be rather like him.[20] But with this chapter being couched as a confession, the questions, who is the reader? and, to whom is it addressed? take a specific turn. Perhaps the answers to the questions change over the course of the confession.

The chapter (not yet declared a confession) starts with a general reflec-tion before the first-person subject enters at the start of the second paragraph (according to the conventions of modern critical editions of the text). A singular perspective and intimate tone, in keeping with the confessional mode that will follow, holds for a while, after which the first-person plural form takes over. The plural form continues to make its presence felt, even when the first-person singular returns and dominates. But who precisely is included in the apparently general plural form? It is not, in fact, open or welcoming to all. Women (as if all women were the same) feature as the object of the writer's reflections: whether they are inquired into, desired, feared, they are always imagined others. If they from time to time occupy the place of the subject, it is only as mediated by Montaigne, so they still remain dependent on his representing them, and their function is to represent something of him. The 'nous', we, is a plurality grounded in likeness; we are complicit by being not like them – women.

Not that these are 'real' women; whoever they are in this chapter, from Messalina to Montaigne's daughter, they function as fantasy objects; they have

---

[19] On the reader, see, among many studies, Sayce, *The Essays of Montaigne*, ch. 3, Bauschatz, 'Montaigne's Conception of Reading in the Context of Renaissance Poetics and Modern Criticism', in Suleiman and Crossman (eds), *The Reader in the Text* (Princeton, 1980), pp. 264–91, and Cave, 'Problems of Reading in the *Essais*', in McFarlane and Maclean (eds), *Montaigne: Essays in Memory of Richard Sayce* (Oxford, 1982), pp. 133–66.

[20] See his comments in Book III, chapters 3, 5 and 9.

gender – balance? (in)justice   women fantasy objects

their place in his confession as sites of his desire in all its shapes, whether intensely erotic, intensely anxious, frustrated, mild, or translated into textual pleasure, as in his readings of Virgil and Lucretius. Just a few examples serve to show something of their function: 'on les leurre … et acharne par tous moyens: nous eschauffons et incitons leur imagination sans cesse, et puis nous crions au ventre' (we bait and harass them with whatever means we can: we overheat and excite their imaginations, and then bellyache about it) (p. 860); 'nous et elles sont capables de milles corruptions' (both men and women are capable of thousands of corruptions) (p. 861): whether the subject of the statement is masculine or feminine, these are both exclusively observations about Montaigne's, and heterosexual, masculine, desire. This is also the case in the next instance: 'vrayement c'est trop d'abjection et de bassesse de coeur de laisser ainsi fierement persecuter, pestrir et fourrager ces tendres graces à des personnes ingrates, indiscrettes, et si volages' (it is beyond abject, beyond despicable to let these tender qualities be so cruelly hunted, pawed and plundered by ungrateful, indiscreet and inconstant people) (p. 863) – that is, men. The rhetorical balance between the three verbs and three adjectives produces an illusion of balance between the genders; both are roundly criticized. However, in fact women are more harshly condemned: 'c'est trop d'abjection' (it is beyond abject). Elsewhere in the chapter Montaigne acknowledges women's subjugation to men is culturally determined: nothing natural about it – and therefore by implication, this is an injustice which should be righted.[21] Here, however, these women are figures of fantasy rather than subjects of sociocultural inequity, and if they are masochists, it is insofar as they are imagined to be caught within the circuit of sadomasochistic heterosexual desire, represented from a masculine perspective for other men. The intricacy of Montaigne's syntax obscures who does or says what to or about whom, and whose behaviour is being classed as abject.

However – but – women can be more than the fantasy objects they are throughout the confession. The confession's uses of 'we' and 'one' do not include women; but although the confession is not addressed to them, it may be that it is, nonetheless, made to them – in that if they give themselves licence to take up the place of the reader or listener, they can supplement the chapter's most ready meanings. Even if Montaigne seems to think that 'il y a naturellement de la brigue et riotte entres elles et nous' (there is naturally scheming and strife between them and us) (p. 854), even if the genders are divided rather than complementary, with some continuity between them, women's reading of these confessions need not necessarily ('naturellement') be adversarial, or oppositional. Besides, it may take the perspective of those who are not 'like' to see the ways in which self-deceptions or veering away from knowledge remain, when a confession is addressed only to those who will (be) like the confessant. Indeed,

---

[21] On the other hand, remember Montaigne's comment (p. 885) about both being unjust judges of each other. However unjust men may be, he will not concede that women are any less so. The fluctuations in the representation of gender injustice means that each comment needs to be understood only locally, and some scepticism may be in order.

as suggested earlier, it may be essential, if any 'truth' is to be aired, for these to be the addressees: whether the addressee is 'real' or not, he or she needs to be able to listen differently – even if the speaker may find it hard to recognize him or herself in what this other hears. How to hear a confession is a question to which I shall return in the following section, in terms of what it might have to do with love.

But if 'we' are masculine, this is not all men. Despite what reads at first sight like an inclusive gesture, 'in honour of the Huguenots', the men addressed by Montaigne seem less likely to be Reformers than to be like him. If, that is, their existence independent of Montaigne is acknowledged. Early in the chapter, a desire to escape dulling solitude and for good company is expressed:

> la tranquillité sombre et stupide se trouve assez pour moy, mais elle m'endorst et m'enteste: je ne m'en contente pas. S'il y a quelque personne, quelque bonne compaignie aux champs, en la ville, en France, ou ailleurs, resseante ou voyagere, à qui mes humeurs soient bonnes, de qui les humeurs me soient bonnes, il n'est que de siffler en paume, je leur iray fournir des essays en chair et en os. (pp. 843–4)

> (there is plenty of sombre, dulling tranquillity to be found, but it puts me to sleep and benumbs me: it is not enough for me. If there is anyone or any good company, in country or city, in France or elsewhere, settled or inclined to travel, who likes my humours and whose humours I like, they need only whistle for me, and I shall give them flesh and blood 'essays'.)

'Who likes my humours and whose humours I like': nice rhetorical balance, but in reality a fragile illusion of symmetry. Which said, the kind of reader the text addresses in its use of the first-person plural seems to be one who is like the writer. But a confession to a listener who sees things 'just like me' would probably be an exercise in self-deception: a false confession. So if Montaigne's is not false, a different interpretation emerges; these listeners are not constructed as being like him so much as being listeners with whom he identifies. He does not seem to presume to speak for them, nor wish to, as this is about him, but he can imagine that he will be recognized by them. Either way, what prevails is division into like and unlike, more than the coexistence of a range of differences. This speaks of anxiety, falsely cured by the reductive symbolization of things in terms of what is like, and not, of us and them.

However, the confession is not static. When or how does it open up towards a different kind of listener? The frequent use of 'but' noted above, at times disjunctive rather than connective, is one indication of a more open perspective, requiring a (real) reader's engagement. It signals that something other, different, is needed: if, reader, you (like the writer) thought that was it, you were mistaken, you need to keep revising your ideas.

A few pages from the end of the chapter there is a hint of a different relation with the listener or reader. After a set of general reflections on the relation between body and mind, he comments: 'je n'ai point autre passion qui me tienne en haleine' (I have no passion but love to keep me alive) (p. 893). This remark about love seems addressed to no one in particular; the question, who listens, is as if suspended here. The listener who matters is perhaps Montaigne himself.

But what if we then turn to the end of the chapter, with its observation that we are all cast in the same mould? Who is addressed here? We know who addresses us: 'je dis' (I say) (p. 897); one who knows that, rather than women being men's other, as culture would have it, the genders are in fact alike – he has this on Plato's and Antisthenes's authority. He knows, moreover, that we attack the other gender to protect or justify our own. Here what he has resorted to during his singular confession is now cast as a general commonplace, even given proverbial form: 'c'est ce qu'on dict: Le fourgon se mocque de la poele' (as they say: it's the pot calling the kettle black) (p. 897). They, who? And this leaves suspended who is being addressed: everyone, alike? A semblance of openness only, for whoever is being addressed, they are caught within the restrictive circuit of 'on dit', hearsay, a world of speakers and listeners ruled by convention, the hidebound certainty of proverbial utterances and the dulled, levelling acceptance of 'the way things are'; there seems no place for scepticism here. So a world of speakers and listeners, then, who would probably fail the test for the kind of reader Montaigne wants for his writing, and far from Montaigne's own resistance to such misleading certitudes.

These are speakers and listeners who remain bound up in either misrecognition or in the passion for ignorance: either accepting imaginary understanding – associated, not least, with a habit of seeing the world in terms of what is like (therefore wanted) and not like (therefore rejected); or refusing to allow unpalatable or anxiety-provoking realities as being too painful to bear. So, it seems, not an open ending, but rather a collapse into the closure of 'having the last word'. Here genders are reduced to dead metaphors, inert forms and function;[22] when only a few lines earlier there was emphatic recognition that things (such as models of gender) congeal through cultural habit, not because of intrinsic qualities. With that recognition also came the possible recognition of injustice, pain, deprivation; without it, indifference or futile aggressivity seems to take hold.

In order not to find a perverse ending to a confession which has represented itself as daring to challenge habit and speak out, we need to test this reading. Perhaps the point is more oblique, and is about what reaching for such proverbs represents? That only those who accept the reductive fixities of such utterances would fall into the trap of treating gender this way, believing there is nothing more to be said. Proverbs are often on the side of fear and self-deception. Thus the ending should be read as a challenge to readers in their responsibility to go on interpreting, more sceptically. The same holds for the apparently irresponsible acknowledgement of the injustice of gender inequality just a few lines earlier. Not necessarily an abdication of the responsibility that comes with knowledge

---

[22] An example of the 'metaphores desquelles … la couleur s'est ternie par maniement trop ordinaire' (metaphors whose colour is tarnished by being handled too frequently) (p. 874).

but an unpossessive offering to the reader, for her to take responsibility for as she chooses, and to give an ethical turn to the ending of the chapter. To be ethical, it needs to be identified with interpretation which recognizes and does not judge the fear that induces the reduction of what is complex and beyond our control to the poverty of proverbs; for neither the fear nor denial of it sits with an ethical stance, which offers fear a place in which, rather than being denied, it can be acknowledged, learned from and then moved beyond.

This reading, which brings a generous irony to rescue the ending of the chapter from its initial seeming-collapse, gives much weight to the place of the kind of knowledge that love brings. This was marked out towards the end of Montaigne's confession. It also recognizes the vulnerability that is a part of it – although largely missing from much of what went before – except, of course, for its avowal not long after the outset (see pp. 130–5). But there, vulnerability was all Montaigne's and his text's, rather than a fundamental aspect of all human relations. My next section will explore how vulnerability enters the confession in other ways, and how, along with it, a different form or site of knowledge emerges.

This is not to disregard women's vulnerability to men, as represented here: where in so many other chapters the identity or place of the reader could be occupied by female or male readers alike, here, for over fifty pages, women have not been directly addressed, and figure, rather, as objects. Not excluded as readers, but not the addressees of the confession, so that should they choose to read this chapter, they are cast as listeners-in: 'ce chapitre me fera du cabinet' (this chapter will get me inside the boudoir) (p. 847). They, according to Montaigne (though how does he know?), refuse to read his other writing, but rather treat his books as objects – 'mes essais servent les dames de meuble commun seulement' (my essays serve the ladies as just an ordinary piece of furniture) (p. 847). This, however, they will pore over in private. That is, he imagines that he is revealing what women want to know about him – or imagines his text being treated as a form of soft porn; so here still women are objects within his psychic economy rather than beings with autonomous existences. Their (imagined) desire is presented as if demonstrating what he knows about them; in fact, it demonstrates nothing about them at all, but signals his anxious fantasy about women's desire and the vulnerability which would follow from women knowing too much about his own. Their vulnerability, that is, is to how they are imagined, and to what Montaigne (and perhaps other men) want to know about them, but cannot. In this respect they are the ones vulnerable to being listened-in on and misrepresented.

From 'tout asseché que je suis et apesanty' to the 'flux de caquet'

This section has two convergent focuses: what Montaigne has to say about his own text, and how that helps us understand the ways in which his confession develops. As suggested earlier, that it is a confession does not preserve it from self-deception at times: self-deception associated particularly with the either/ or, like/not like habits of a self-knowledge that remains only imaginary and addresses itself to an equally imaginary reader; both are instances of misrecognition. Such an addressee, 'like me', is designed to recognize me as I want to be recognized. However, the confession does not remain caught in these illusions; rather, it vacillates, hesitates, but moves towards a more ambiguous and less self–deceiving understanding.

Figuratively, this is represented as a move from a state of dryness and weighty solidity, a state of (excessive) fixity, to one of fluidity and mobility of a particular kind, namely the shitty flow Montaigne calls his confession as he ends it. Not the self-evidently positive fluidity that we remember from, say, 'Du repentir' ('On repenting'), but one which is ambiguous and requires counter-intuitive revaluation of messy shit and incontinence. We can trace this out by exploring aspects of what Montaigne says about his own writing here: we find, obliquely, directions for readers as well as an acknowledgement of the illusory nature of what he wants of his writing. Secondly, in an anecdote which is a scene of reading, we find suggestions as to how to read differently and allow different kinds of knowledge, which open us towards ways of making our condition more tolerable, and less self-deluding.

Montaigne's writing reverberates with the enjoyment Lucretius's language gives him: it is transformative, 'parolles (:) non plus de vent ains de chair et d'os' (words which are wind no longer: they are flesh and blood) (p. 873). The reading gives him pleasure and prompts reflections on his own desire for his writing. Just as, earlier, much grew out of his reading of Virgil, so again, here, the power of texts is generative – and regenerative, if the pleasures they lend the reader include remembering past enjoyments which would otherwise be out of reach. Texts are like the bowl of water in which Japanese paper flowers unfurl and float. Others' poetry, in all its vigour, richness and specificity give rise to Montaigne's desires for his own words, even though they form prose: from initially wishing (prosaically) that his writing will have 'quelque chose du mien' (something of mine) (p. 873), within two short pages this has grown into the dream of producing a work which will be 'exactement mien' (exactly mine) (p. 875): this is to be its 'fin principale et perfection' (chief aim and perfection). When for other texts (Ficino, Leone Ebreo) it is enough for the reader to recognize himself in them (p. 874), for his text, the recognition will be all his: 'tout le monde me reconnoit en mon livre, et mon livre en moy' (everyone recognizes me in my book, and my book in me) (p. 875), without danger of misreading: everyone.

Even before Montaigne has gone on to puncture this fantasy of a text which is perfectly like its author, the recourse to symmetry and the concept of recognition together should warn the reader that this is slipping into illusion. A slipping, moreover, already inscribed by the gap between the text being exactly his and the preposition 'en', in: what is in the text and the text being completely his are not totally commensurate. In this version of the pleasure and value of reading, it is not what the reader recognizes of herself that matters; rather, self-recognition is transcended. But the problem remains that the concept of recognition is still in play, along with the question, what is meant by a text being exactly his (and no one else's). Less than a page earlier Montaigne had reminded the reader how porous he is as a reader, how readily others' words affect him: 'quand j'escris, je me passe bien de la compaignie et souvenance des livres, de peur qu'il n'interrompent ma forme' (when I am writing I like to do without books and what I remember of them, for fear of them intruding on my style) (p. 874). This from a writer who elsewhere seems entirely open to accepting the intertextuality of all writing, not least his own. That one's writing is traced through with others' words does not disqualify it from being described as being one's own; but it does make the idea of it being exactly one's own problematic. It may be one's owned, but that is different. That acknowledges something of the way in which 'selves', as Montaigne's exploration of his 'self' accepts, are constituted by their relations with others, who leave their sometimes unknowable traces in and on us. Moreover, the self as represented in writing also will in some unknowable ways be constituted by future others, not only the readers who are explicitly addressed but also by unaddressed others.

Recognition of such intersubjectivity should be a basis for tolerant human relations, and is so when it acknowledges the risk always run when one individual asks for another's recognition in all his or her difference (as a Reformer or Huguenot might, before the time of writing, have asked of a Roman Catholic, without fearing for his or her life, or vice versa). But recognition is a sham when in fact it is misrecognition, bound up with valuing what is like: I think something in the text is like me, and so I like it. Recognition that is misrecognition, identification, imitation cling together. But how, then, does difference have its place? Montaigne's fear of others' words getting in the way indicates the difficulty of negotiating likeness and difference, and even wanting to be different from that which seems (too) like.

According to Montaigne, the words of Ficino or Leone Ebreo have no value for his page, even though those writers 'parle de luy, de ses penseés et de ses actions, et si il n'y entend rien' (they talk of him, his thoughts and actions, and yet it means nothing to him) (p. 874); he understands *nothing* because he does not recognize himself; because he does not recognize himself, for his language of love is not like that of the text, he has no interest in the text, in all its difference. Montaigne may be a more sophisticated reader, able to value Aristotle despite not recognizing himself: 'je ne recognois pas chez Aristote la plus part de mes mouvemens ordinaires' (I don't recognize most of my ordinary actions in Aristotle) (p. 874). Even though this comment can be read as a preference for ordinary language rather than the more rarefied discourse of philosophers such as Aristotle, still the operative concept initially is a version of recognition which is too close to its travesty form of only seeing what is like. And it has reductive force: for Montaigne elsewhere acknowledges that 'Montaigne' includes what he has absorbed from his reading of Aristotle, and Plato, and Heraclitus, and many more besides: a complexity, fluidity and diversification of identity that the travesty of recognition has difficulty with. Like the page who only likes what is like him, the danger when this (mis)recognition prevails is that it goes on wanting and liking only what is more of the same, and struggles when it encounters difference – which is where authentic recognition is called for.

Put this way, we arrive at themes beyond those of literary appreciation, closer to those running throughout Montaigne's confession in which, despite an anxious fascination with what is different (primarily the feminine), on the whole, the difficulty of valuing difference tends to have prevailed. Likewise the difficulty of thinking not in terms of like and not like, but in more fluid terms of difference, has been palpable. Recognition is misrecognition in disguise, so long as it is a version of what is like (me, and what I like in me), rather than a desire to know more about what I do not recognize about myself, in terms of who I am for the other, and what I do not know about myself – for that is for the other to know.

If Montaigne really wants to make himself known, he must accept a model of listening or reading which really is grounded in recognition, rather than misrecognition, which is a desire for how one is known to be just what one imagines one knows. So in fact, in terms of knowledge rather than misrecognition, 'quelque chose du mien' (something of mine) turns out to be more precisely what is 'exactement mien' (exactly mine) than the fantasy of a text which is perfectly like its writer, free of anxious reliance on the reader's account of that representation.

Montaigne does not underestimate the power of imitating – not least, his own, and at this point, although he still focuses on linguistic imitation, he also expands the theme. 'J'ai une condition singeresse et imitatrice' (I am an aper and imitator) (p. 875); imitation may equally well be called usurpation; he continues: 'ce que je considere, je l'usurpe' (whatever I consider, I usurp). The inclination to ape opens into a lengthy anecdote, which dramatizes the *deadly* power of imitation: 'imitation meurtriere comme celle des singes' (murderous imitation, like that of apes). What becomes clearer in the course of the anecdote is that what is 'killed' by imitation is not something of that which is imitated (as the verb to usurp suggests), but the imitator, in this instance the terrifying apes encountered by Alexander and his forces as they pushed east towards India. The only way to save themselves was to lure the apes into harm by harnessing their tendency to imitate – that is, turning their self-protecting mimicry against them:

> ils en prestarent le moyen par cette leur inclination à contrefaire tout ce qu'ils voyoyent faire. Car par là les chasseurs apprindrent de se chausser des souliers à leur veuë à tout force noeuds de liens; de s'affubler d'accoustremens de testes à tout des lacs courants et oindre par semblant leur yeux de glux. Ainsi mettoit imprudemment à mal ces pauvres bestes leur complexion singeresse. Ils s'engluoient, enchevestroyent et garrotoyent d'elles mesmes. (pp. 875–6)

> (They got the idea from their tendency to imitate every action they saw. The hunters worked out they should put their boots on in front of them with lots of knots in the laces, put on headgear with nooses dangling and seem to daub birdlime round their eyes. So these poor beasts were led to their destruction

through their apish natures. They birdlimed their eyes, got hopelessly tangled up, and garotted themselves.)

The apes' (ascribed) tendency to imitate, to behave like others who are different to them (in this instance, as a species), is their undoing; they are undone by their own 'inclination' and 'complexion', or we might say their instinct, but just as much by their lack of knowledge of what is different between them and others.

In the confrontation between nature and culture, ape and human, there is a missing term: knowledge. The anecdote itself does not match Montaigne's 'condition' in that his imitating is an aspect of culture and cultural knowledge, whereas the comparison confronts knowledgeless instinct and human *savoir faire*. The anecdote exemplifies an economy which operates in terms of misrecognition, imitation, being like, and of identification collapsing into identity, without the apes having a counterbalancing knowledge of difference as both a coexisting array of identities – apes are not humans – and a necessary element in identification – but there are ways in which apes and humans seem like. It therefore ends in a deadly binary: kill or be killed.

Apes or Macedonians; Roman Catholics or Huguenots/Reformers; men or women. The first is a simplified example which demonstrates the destructive potential of imitation without difference; the other two are more complex, and demonstrate the destructive potential of the refusal of recognition for, or intolerance of, the other's difference (experienced as refusal to be like), leading to the demand that the other be like one's own overvalued sense of one's different identity. In the first two instances, it is literally deadly; in the third, figuratively so, but still powerfully destructive.

Much of Montaigne's confession focuses on how men behave towards women, and what they want of them, and on how women behave towards men, not least as a result of men's behaviour. That painful affects such as jealousy, fear or anxiety are part of this economy, as is injustice, is acknowledged, but until they can be understood not in terms of the genders being like or unlike (with the privilege given to likeness), but in terms of what it is that each gender does not know of the other, beyond the limited logic of like or not, and of what each is for the other, neither knowledge nor the self-knowledge which drives the confession will be much enhanced. Grounds, then, for preferring an economy in which difference, ambivalence and ambiguities survive, whether this has to do with how literary texts are interpreted, sectarian differences tolerated, or the different genders value each other.

The figure of 'flux' by which, towards its close, Montaigne describes his confession, keeps these values in circulation. Fluid, so evading the limits of damaging fixity; but an image of the fluid from which a reader might well recoil, for it suggests neither health nor value. Nor creativity: its 'matter' is incontinent mess, not creative substance; and yet, because it is a figure, it *is* creative. It opens up into a number of different interpretations, all of which coexist, thus exemplifying the different kind of economy towards which Montaigne's confession has been leading, albeit intermittently and at times reluctantly. It does not direct the reader's interpretation, but rather takes the risk of allowing the reader to find her way towards interpretations, plural. So here perhaps we have a recovery from the anxiety expressed earlier in the confession about how it would be interpreted and a return to a frame of mind in which scepticism, openness and a suspension of judgement might now be possible.

To bring all these different readings into the open, we first have to revalue 'shit': not disgusting, nor waste matter, but rather in the context of a confession which disavows customary shame, matter which contains something that is still mine, for it has passed through me, and in the process has been transformed by me. Transformed into a figure for something other than matter and its customary denotation, without losing these utterly. Rather, it encompasses what is both like it and yet not it, allowing a more open and ambiguous relationship than, say, that of imitation which is akin to simply being like. Its value is particularly its being fluid, rather than solid or dry: the latter are the sorry qualities of old age and of the excesses of wisdom which Montaigne's confession sought to counter, by allowing the body and physical pleasures, and the self-knowledge that comes through them, their place. With fluidity comes the possibility of keeping ideas moving, and of possibilities being sustained rather than rigid or closed positions being upheld. And because of the kind of matter it is, there is not a simple opposition between solid and fluid, or negative and positive; far from it, the ambiguity and instability of the relation between the two terms is paramount. With this particular flow, a clear distinction between what is inside and what is outside is unsettled: for what comes out had been inside, but before it was inside, ingested, it had been outside. If here it emerges from the body as shit, a few pages earlier what was at issue were words: others' written words read and re-emerging as one's writing.

Of course, we could decline all these suggested meanings, and instead interpret the 'flux de caquet' (shitty flux) in the light of Montaigne's emphasis on his thoughts, in age, working 'à reculons' (backwards) (p. 842), and on his desire to amuse himself, give himself something to play with: 'je ne puis moins, en faveur de cette chetive condition où mon aage me pousse, que de luy fournir de jouets et d'amusoires, comme à l'enfance' (the least I can do for the feeble state forced on me by age is give it toys and playthings, as we do for children) (p. 843): perhaps the choice of metaphor is just a childish joke about poo to be enjoyed ... Of course the child's joke is not free of the embarassments that the body acquires even before the child has consciously learned to articulate them and defer to them; but it is at least a creative response, which allows for ambiguity rather than solely a negative attitude. But why not allow the metaphor all its fluidity and all its potential meanings, for then the richness of the body as a site of meaning will come into play?

body

Un attouchement

In terms of the emergence of different sites of knowledge the body still has more to say when Montaigne's confession moves beyond both misrecognition and the passion for ignorance. Consider the following passage, a scene of reading:

> Et Socrates, plus vieil que je ne suis, parlant d'un object amoureux: 'M'estant, dict-il, appuyé contre son espaule de la mienne et approché ma teste à la sienne, ainsi que nous regardions ensemble dans un livre, je senty, sans mentir, soudain une piqueure dans l'espaule comme de quelque morsure de beste, et fus plus de cinq jours depuis qu'elle me fourmilloit, et m'escoula dans le coeur une demangeaison continuelle.' Un attouchement, et fortuite, et par une espaule, aller eschauffer et alterer une ame refroidie et esnervée par l'aage, et la premiere de toutes les humaines en reformation! Pourquoy non, dea? Socrates estoit homme; et ne vouloit estre, ny sembler autre chose. (p. 892)

> (And Socrates, older than I am now, speaking of a love object said: 'Leaning my shoulder against his, our heads close, reading a book together, I felt what I can only call a jab in my shoulder like some animal's bite; it went on stinging for five days, and my heart itched constantly.' A chance touch on the shoulder would warm and alter a soul cooled and weakened by age – the most reformed of human souls. And why not? Socrates was a man, with no desire to be or seem anything else.)

This is an account of a philosopher falling in love. Here a text, rather than being vulnerable to destructive misreading, plays a part in producing not only knowledge but a different, extended form of knowledge. Neither Montaigne nor the original Greek text, Xenophon's *Symposium*, identify the text that has such creative power; what matters is that texts can have such power, in the hands of readers who are open to them.

It is not reading (together) that in itself leads to love; but reading is integral to its emergence. In the anecdote no single element acts as a cause, or as the source of understanding of what is taking place: neither whatever is read in the text, nor all the philosopher's accrued knowledge are alone, or together, enough; a different site of knowledge and source of apprehending must join them for there to be understanding of love: the (philosopher's) body. This underscores the fact that love, even soul-love (*âm-our*), involves the body, and without the body love may not be known or understood, which is consonant with the emphasis throughout the *Essais* on the essential interrelation of all aspects of human being. It seems that philosophy alone is not enough, but depends on a different kind of understanding if it is, belatedly, to gain insight into what would otherwise remain unknown about love or through love.

Curiously here we have another instance of Montaigne mis-taking his classical source: not, this time, misrepresentation or mistranslation, but the omission of something in the original: namely the role played by Socrates's friend.[23] The

---

[23] See Xenophon, *Symposium*, 4, 27–8, in *Xenophon: The Shorter Socratic Writings*, trans. Bartlett (Ithaca and London, 1996), pp. 133–72 (p. 150).

philosopher did not know that it was love that touched him: it took his friend
Charmides's teasing for him to realize this, five days later. The philosopher did
not know, for realization came through the body; and also, he needed a friend to
help him towards understanding. It seems that philosophy depends on different
kinds of understanding if it is, belatedly, to gain insight into what it would
otherwise fail to recognize. Here we have a scene in which reading, knowledge,
love, the body and friendship are linked.

So what are we, its readers, to know about Montaigne? Friendship is brack-
eted out in his version, as if a combination of a certain kind of philosophical
knowledge (it is not for nothing that the anecdote is about Socrates, who along
with Plato has figured most recurrently in this chapter) and an attunement with
the body, an acceptance of the body's place and of the body as a site of self-
knowledge, as well as the predisposition occasioned by reading, taken together,
were enough. The reader then – in place of the friend? – is invited to reflect on
what she knows of the text now being read and what it has been communicating
(not without difficulty) about the body, love and knowledge.

This is borne out by the comment shortly after on love being the only passion
keeping Montaigne alive. In a chapter which has drawn on Plato, and referred
to Socrates so frequently, not least here, may we not hear an echo of Socrates
again: 'the subject of love is the only one I claim to understand'?[24] But what
matters as much as there being perhaps an echo is that there is also a difference:
Montaigne's comment is couched in terms of a physical metaphor, 'qui me tient
en haleine', which keeps me going, which gives me oxygen, breathes life into
me … So something of the body is emphasized again here, rather than (just)
the intellect: passion is enlivening and – if we allow that Socrates hovers here,
albeit unidentified – it is what I want to understand, as well as being a source of
understanding. Philosophy needs love's knowledge and also the body's.

However, this being Montaigne's writing and his represented body, we cannot
understand the body without its relationship with the spirit or soul. Indeed, the
various uses of the phrase 'tenir en haleine' in the *Essais* illuminate just this.
The phrase occurs nine times, and there is a tenth, similar usage, 'remettre en
haleine'. Only two of the examples, on maintaining physical fitness, seem simply
literal, and one of these two may well have figurative significance also, as it
refers to the Roman practice of provoking wars.[25] To keep their men fighting fit
to be sure, but perhaps also to promote their 'Romanness', their *virtu*, a masculine identity encompassing moral and mental strength as well as physical. All
the other instances, related to virtue, love and desire, keep the literal, physical
connotations of 'haleine' and its figurative potential in play together. Two examples suggest the range of significance and force of Montaigne's usage.

Firstly: 'te souvient il de ces gens du temps passé, qui recherchoyent le maux
avec si grand faim, pour tenir leur vertu en haleine et en exercice?' (do you

[24] Plato, *The Symposium*, 177d, trans. Gill (Harmondsworth, 1999), p. 9.
[25] See p. 638.

remember those men in the past who sought out suffering so avidly, to keep their virtue alive and in practice?) (p. 1091). These testers of virtue were those Stoics who appear in the *Essais* in anecdotes of physical pain nobly endured, whose will, reason, moral and physical courage ideally converged. The 'maux' were not necessarily physical challenges, but here the relationship between mind, will and body does matter, because its context is the discussion of how to live (well) while enduring such chronic pain as Montaigne's kidney stones. More immediately, the inseparability of moral, psychological and physical desire and courage is emphasized by the use of metaphorical appetite: avidly, with such keen hunger.

The other example plays in a rather different direction. It occurs in 'De la præsumption', in a passage in which Montaigne comments on his powers of narration:

> je ne sçay ny plaire, ny rejouyr, ny chatouiller: le meilleur conte du monde se seche entre mes mains et se ternit. Je ne sçay parler qu'en bon escient, et suis du tout desnué de cette facilité, que je voy en plusieurs de mes compaignons, d'entretenir les premiers venus et tenir en haleine toute une troupe. (p. 637)

> (I know not how to please, delight or tickle; the best story ever dries up, dulled, in my hands. I can only speak genuinely and completely lack the skill, which I see in several of my acquaintances, of entertaining whoever is listening and holding the attention of a whole group.)

Here it means to keep a crowd spellbound or in suspense. We recognize that the spellbound crowd is holding its breath, in breathless anticipation of what will happen next ... But as well as this, even before it, we are also imaginatively attuned to the physical aspects of the process of storytelling: the words leave the mouth of the speaker and enter the ears of the listener, and affect the listener's body. We have been gentled towards this by the use already of tickling and drying up in his hands which have brought Montaigne's body and those of his listeners in already. Making sense is here grounded in materiality and embodiment.

In the instance in 'Sur des vers de Virgile', Montaigne's description of Socrates's discovery of love seems a faithful translation of the original. But the reality of the experience nonetheless seems only obliquely representable, as a puncturing of the skin, a bite, a rash – terms ambiguously both figurative and literal. To emphasize what is disturbing here, let us put this in psychoanalytic terms: the surface of the Symbolic order is punctured; the Real makes itself felt. Anxiety is like a rash; desire bites, it eats you up. This materialization in figurative language is a signal of an 'edge phenomenon', a communication which disturbs the sense of a clear boundary between inside and outside, and lingers without its meaning becoming any clearer expect insofar as it prevails, insists, troubles. Montaigne's version translates the original into French and additionally translates it, giving it another turn; it adds pathos to the sting with the addition of 'un attouchement' (a touch) and seems to assimilate the translation seamlessly into his own text: 'pourquoy non, dea?' (and why not?). But perhaps this is another lure, which averts from the sharp otherness of the moment of desire's bite and instantaneous entering which Socrates seems paradoxically slow to understand, as well as distracting the reader from Montaigne's excision of the friend from his version of Xenophon's text. What we need to hold in mind, however obliquely it is represented (and indeed it is such that it can only enter representation obliquely), is the anxiety of a difficult desire. Montaigne's account seems to run a line between him and Socrates, through the comparison of their ages, and to palliate the sting of desire; nonetheless, the sting's vivid forceful otherness is not fully assimilable, a still disruptive presence, the truth of which eluded Socrates and the 'true' significance of which for Montaigne remains veiled. The potential meaning of this scene of reading as an activity which might incubate such other knowledge, both feared and desired, remains to be discovered by being read, in another, later scene of reading – ours, of Montaigne's confession.

The next chapter broadens out these questions of knowledge, anxiety and interpretation in terms of the psychic economy of the thinking subject who grapples with such questions. Throughout the *Essais*, in Montaigne's search for self-knowledge and, through it, knowledge of the world he inhabits, the significance of the body is an indispensable site of inquiry. So next, the discussion will develop from the reading of aspects of the body's meaning and the body as a source of insight as just suggested, and explore further its place in Montaigne's self-knowledge, particularly when his inquiries involve extreme doubt. That is, when working towards the edges of his understanding, and when the suspension of judgement and acceptance of uncertainty is not free from anxiety.

doubt

5

Tickling, Shaking, Shitting

> We only exist through the others who make up the storehouse
> of the mind: models in our first tentative steps towards identity,
> objects of our desires, helpers and foes. The mind is a palimp-
> sest in which the traces of these three figures will jostle and
> rearrange themselves for evermore.[1]

This chapter explores the psychic economy of doubtful thinking and of the self
and the self in the world, a self which is narcissistic, although as much a subject
of doubt as everything else: Montaigne is 'autant doubteux de moy que de toute
autre chose' (as doubtful of myself as of all other things) (p. 634). Doubt may
be a condition and principle of thinking, both desirable and creative; it may also
be troubling, hindering thinking; and, both troubling and creative, it may unsettle self-regard. At its most troubling in his text, 'cette extremité de doubte qui
se secoue soy-mesme' (doubt at its extremes, which shakes itself up) (p. 503)
is on the 'limites et dernieres clotures' (limits or edges) (p. 588) of intellectual
and psychic sustainability; or is in the internal limits represented as a 'pli sans
nostre sçeu' (a fold of which we have no knowledge) (p. 633), that is, aspects of
self that are not known or even knowable. And this combination of doubt, limit
or extremity, and shaking pulls away from tranquil doubting, or the tranquillity
to be achieved by accepting doubt in preference to certitude.

We can understand this kind of thinking in terms of scepticism, and, particularly, the kind of attitude associated with Pyrrhonism. The shaking up of one's
thinking, which open-minded suspension of judgement requires, may only arise
by chance – '*tukhikôs*' – as exemplified in the *Hypotyposes* by analogy with
the painter Appelles's sponge. Frustrated by his failure to represent a horse's
foaming breath, Appelles threw the sponge on which he wiped his brushes
at his painting, and happened to achieve the effect of foam.[2] Montaigne does
not reproduce this anecdote. In 'La fortune se rencontre souvent au train de la
raison' ('Fortune is often encountered in reason's way') he chooses what seems
a comparable anecdote, that of the painter Protogenes; but it is not, as in the
Hypotyposes, an example of the accidental discovery of a desired effect, and
tranquillity attendant upon suspension of judgement: it merely illustrates the

---

[1] Rose, *The Last Resistance*, p. 62.
[2] See p. 221. For further discussion of the Appelles passage and its significance for
sixteenth-century scepticism, see Cave, *Pré-histoires*, ch. 1.

title of this brief early chapter. We are still some distance from Montaigne's more sceptical thinking and more complex and ambiguous perspectives and writing effects. The anecdote is engaging, but does not shake up the reader's thinking or invite change of direction; nor is its potential significance fully exploited. It remains a story of the creative power of the unexpected, unsettling gesture without further performative or conceptual purchase.

Here I shall focus on the affective and psychic impact of such doubtful thinking as that of scepticism. The metaphor of shaking in the quotations in my opening paragraph associates shaking with doubt and limits; but to doubt is not only or always to shake or be shaken. Given the original importance of the association between suspension of judgement (a version of doubt) and tranquillity, tolerance for unsettling, untranquil doubt seems particularly revealing of Montaigne's own inflection of scepticism. How the subject might come to want to shake and be shaken, and also, what shakes one's capacity to think productively, is traceable in a range of examples of the kind of thinking that Montaigne encourages and demonstrates: particularly, its edges or limits. These shed light on the relationship between these edges and the space for thinking that they delineate. Limits, boundaries and folds may not demarcate clearly and stably; sometimes they shake the reader by producing gaps and indeterminacy, ambiguities and doubt. As we shall see, doubting, materiality and vulnerability are folded together in the *Essais*, in the play of figuration such as shaking.

Death is one limit, or extreme, of which the existence is certain. Neither the defining meaning of a life, nor even fully known; as Montaigne argues, with increasing force over time, death tends to limit the potential meaning of how we live. 'Nous troublons la vie par le soing de la mort' (we trouble our lives with our concerns about death) (p. 1051). Fear, whether acknowledged or in unacknowledged conversion into certain forms of thinking or misdirected striving, makes our dying the 'end', that is, final aim, of our living. 'C'est bien le bout, non pourtant le but de la vie; c'est sa fin ... non pourtant son object' (it is indeed the end of life, but not the aim; it is its end ... but not its object) (pp. 1051–2). Were freeing ourselves from the 'desir ... crainte ... doubte qui ... trouble' (desire, fear and doubt that trouble us) (p. 1112) as simple as that 'bout/but' pun suggests, there would not perhaps be so many pages of Montaigne's writing. Yet the reduction of death's significance or dreadfulness to a pun and to the sliver of difference that is the absence of one vowel is one way of conveying an acceptance of the randomness of one's own death.

'De la moderation' presents religious belief as having catastrophic consequences. Far from reducing hate, violence and delusion, it incites them; it fails to help us live together peaceably and equitably. Nor is religion represented as offering consolation for death; in the ongoing wars it works on the side of death. So, if religion is not a reliable source of morality and justice, the more secular formation of the equitable subject who will live well and wish the good of the collective becomes all the more significant. How is this subject who is capable of doubtful thinking, self-knowledge and living well to be formed? My epigraph indicates the direction that my exploration of such questions will take;

narcissism

but it needs to be supplemented by the proposition that whatever else 'we' are, we are both desiring and narcissistic. Tracing the workings of narcissism in the *Essais* will help shed light on areas of opacity in Montaigne's representation of the subject in relation to himself, to others and to ideas and phenomena that he encounters.

Montaigne explored the relationship between his desire and his knowledge, testing how the process of inquiry – one in which there was no secure basis for knowledge – changed both him and his objects. What limited what he could know of this? And in what sense was the desire to communicate his knowledge a desire for what is good, for both himself and others? All of this plays through what follows here, concerns what I am calling narcissism, and also relates to the use of figuration.

Bearing in mind, once again, that Montaigne wrote during a time of disillusionment and crisis, because in the wars the enemy was not external but the fellow Frenchman, let me turn to Jacqueline Rose for a trenchant summary of the importance of narcissism in the development of Freud's thinking about the complexities of the relations between the individual and all the other individuals who form his culture or nation, and questions of aggressivity, hate and violence. I shall quote at some length because the details in Rose's account are so relevant to Montaigne's thinking.

> In 1914 Freud ... set out the basic terms of ... his second 'topography'. A previous distinction between love and hunger, the drives of desire and those of self-preservation, between the other and the 'I' breaks down when he alights upon the problem of narcissism, the subject's erotically charged relationship to her- or himself. If you can be your own object, the neat line between impulses directed towards the self and those tending towards the other starts to blur. But it is no coincidence that this discovery of subjects hoist on their own self-regard should bring him up so sharply against the question of how we connect to the others around us. How indeed? No longer is it the case that what we most yearn for in others is the satisfaction of our drives: what we are no less in search of, and passionately require, is to be recognised and acknowledged, seen. Freud is often wrongly taken to be interested only in the sexual drives ... but that is half the story. If we need others, it is not so much to satisfy as *to fashion* ourselves. And in this struggle to conjure, and hold fast to, our identities, there is no limit to what we are capable of. From the outset, identification is ruthless; we devour the others we wish to be: 'Identification ... behaves like the product of the first *oral* stage of libido organisation in which the coveted, treasured object was incorporated by eating and was annihilated as such in the process.' Overturning his model of mind in the face of war, Freud thus arrives at the problem of collective life.[3]

³ Rose, 'Mass Psychology', in *The Last Resistance*, pp. 62–92, including a quotation from Freud, *Mass Psychology*, in *Mass Psychology and Other Writings* (London, 2004), pp. 57–8 (p. 63). See also Freud, 'On Narcissism', in *A History of the Psycho-Analytic Movement* (London, 1957), pp. 73–102.

In another essay in the same collection Rose comments further: 'Freud's study of narcissism ... obliged him to transform completely his model of the mind. It was impossible for him to hold on to his early distinction between love and hunger, the move towards the other and towards the self, once he discovered that people can be their own preferred object, that our most passionate commitment might be to maintaining our own best image of ourselves.'[4] Together these comments illuminate ways in which Montaigne tries to explore the making of identity, the workings of the mind, and how one identity and another or others live together. Rose's Freud and Montaigne illuminate each other in ways extending beyond cannibalistic metaphors. The causes of the blurring of lines remarked on here will help us with opacities in Montaigne's representation of the subject's thought processes, doubts and desires, and the role of passionate attachments in our psychic investments will also be a useful analytic tool. To offer just a taste of this for now: the following passage from 'L'histoire de Spurina' ('The story of Spurina') suggests an acceptance of the power of narcissism in our ethical decisions and actions, to which only the most exceptional individuals are not subject:

> mais de nous foitter pour l'interest de nos voisins, de non seulement nous deffaire de cette douce passion qui nous chatouille, du plaisir que nous sentons de nous voir aggreables à autruy et aymez et recherchez d'un chascun, mais encore de prendre en haine et à contre-coeur nos graces qui en sont cause, et de condamner nostre beauté par ce que quelqu'autre s'en eschauffe, je n'en ay veu guere d'exemples. (pp. 733–4)

> (but to whip ourselves for the good of our neighbours, and to not only give up that sweet passion that tickles us and the pleasure we feel in realizing that we are attractive to others and loved and sought after by all, but even to hate and abhor what it is in us that draws others, and to condemn our beauty because someone is aroused by it – of this I know scarcely any instances.)

Montaigne's desire for knowledge at the limits of conventional thinking, 'hors les bornes ordinaires' (beyond the usual limits) (p. 346), and the thinking it involves, match his exceptional capacity both to tolerate extreme doubt, even so extreme as to be anxiety-laden and 'shake' him, and to write that doubt into the *Essais* in ways which invite the reader to engage with it rather than retreat or resist. This is doubt which seems neither to threaten, nor, paradoxically, to be a symptom of, the subject's narcissism – and becomes in turn the reader's doubt. As the diverse forms of desire and doubt to be considered here, primarily through analysis of patterns of figuration, will suggest, Montaigne encourages different kinds of thinking, in which affect and imagination play their part.

In the field of questions to do with Montaigne's desire for knowledge and self-knowledge and where it leads, understanding the cognitive and imaginative

---

[4]   Rose, 'Freud and the People, or Freud Goes to Abu Ghraib', in *The Last Resistance*, pp. 159–67 (p. 161).

potential of figures *per se* is important, as is particular figurative vocabulary: both inform our interpretations. I have already discussed the first in some detail, suggesting the productivity of figures in conveying difficult, ambiguous and testing ideas, so here can focus on the second, more specific, aspect. All the figures to be discussed relate to processes by which ideas and phenomena are encountered, absorbed (or not), and in turn communicated, and such encounters help form the subject we come to know as Montaigne.

The concept around which much of this turns, which is often also called internalization, or psychic investment, is incorporation, used by Montaigne with particular force because it is so potently associated with his network of symbolic social, political and religious bodies, as well as emphasizing the interrelationship of mind and body: 'l'estroite couture de l'esprit et du corps s'entre-communiquants leurs fortunes' (the tight stitching of mind to body, communicating what happens to each of them to the other) (p. 104). Moreover, he represents mind, judgement and spirit as figurative bodies and therefore their working as being expressible by analogy with the body.[5] His figurative practice here simultaneously reminds the reader of the materiality of the human body's interior, and indicates imaginative connections between physiology, intellect and what would now be called psychology and psyche.[6] But in so doing, the further salutary effect of such figuration is to destabilize such oppositions as material and immaterial, and to imply questions about the nature of the body's interior, if it is not to be understood in terms of, say, Galenic or Vesalian models.

Symbolic and imaginary bodies, which also include the conventional trope of the 'body' of the literary text, have such cultural and conceptual significance for Montaigne and his contemporary readers as to offer foundations strong enough to bear complex figuration conveying an array of reflections on the relationship between the external world and his self. This is of course an embodied self, and so the significance of that body, which is material and figurative, at times undecidably both, will also be important here, as will be, intermittently, questions of pleasure and pain, and their relationship with thinking and understanding. 'La douleur, la volupté, l'amour, la haine sont les premieres choses que sent un enfant; si, la raison survenant, elles s'appliquent à elle, cela c'est la vertu' (pain, sensual pleasure, love, hate are the first things a child feels; if when he gains reason these things work closely with it, that is virtue) (p. 1111): an interesting observation, but precisely how does reason's sway develop?

Montaigne states that the soul should incorporate knowledge; however, not everything is to be incorporated, and it should learn what properly concerns it: it 'ne se doibt paistre que de soy' (it must feed only on itself) (p. 1009). The soul's education is governed by nature, 'les loix de la nature nous apprenent

---

[5] Incorporation is a more appropriate term than internalization which seems to presuppose a clear, and pre-existing, distinction between what is internal and external, which is not a given in Montaigne's representation of self or the text which represents it.

[6] For the Latin dimension of Montaigne's psychological vocabulary and imagery, see Clark, *The Web of Metaphor*, ch. 4.

ce que justement il nous faut' (the laws of nature teach us what we rightly need) (p. 1009). But unless we accept that this is a process of *re*-education, *re*discovery of what was already 'naturally' ours but not yet 'known', we reach a paradox, indicated in the tension between incorporation and feeding only on itself: does this self now constitutively include that which has been incorporated? Does incorporation fully transform whatever has been incorporated into its own substance? This echoes a paradox in 'De la gloire' ('On glory'):

> des ma plus tendre enfance, on remarquoit en moy je ne scay quel port de corps et de gestes tesmoignants quelque vaine et sotte fierté. J'en veut dire premierement cecy, qu'il n'est pas inconvenient d'avoir des conditions et des propensions *si propres et si incorporées* en nous, que nous n'ayons pas moyen de les sentir et reconnoistre. Et de telles *inclinations naturelles*, le corps en retient volontiers quelque pli sans nostre sçeu et consentement.
>
> (pp. 632–3, my italics)

(from my tenderest childhood, people noticed something in the way I held myself and certain gestures which revealed a form of vain, stupid pride. The first thing I want to say about it is, that it is not unseemly to have characteristics and propensities that are *so much our own and so incorporated* in us that we have no way of sensing them or recognizing them. And without our knowledge or consent, such *natural inclinations* form a fold in the body of which we have no knowledge.)

Natural, and yet acquired; one's own, incorporated; one way or another, not knowable. This limit to the understanding of the formation of the subject and knowledge of it will need further exploration. Perhaps it is not so much a matter of a limit in understanding, as that to understand requires knowing what in being human is beyond the limit of what is called 'natural'; that is, all that is required 'pour vivre à nostre aise ... Toute cette nostre suffisance, qui est au delà de la naturelle, est à peu pres vaine et superflue' (to live at ease, all our abilities which exceed what is natural are more or less futile and superfluous) (p. 1039). This equally has to do with desire, mortality and what we call the unconscious. I shall return to these issues later.

Incorporation is not one-way; we also need to consider Montaigne's representations of ways in which the world can threaten to consume him, and the permeability of the boundary between inside ('Montaigne') and outside ('the world') which such transit suggests.

Montaigne conveys key aspects of processes of incorporation, of what he calls digestion, and of communication, through an array of figures of the boundaries of the body, forms of impact on them, or processes which involve crossing them or even unsettling the relationship between internal and external that those boundaries supposedly demarcate, giving rise to agitation, perturbation, pleasure, pain, or pleasure-in-pain. Take tickling, shaking and shitting. As figures, they dramatize difficulties as well as enjoyment in our relations with desire, knowledge and understanding, and the possibility of their changing. However, they *narcissism ≠ sl   what exceeds All's int^n*

may also be used more literally to stage both the vulnerability of the body and the complexity and ambiguity of pleasure and its proximity to pain.

Montaigne's use of shit and shitting suggests that the ambiguities of pleasure and pain, good and bad, outside and inside (of the body) may have been uncomfortable for him, but necessary, and not, through anxiety, to be prematurely resolved. They also relate to consequences of appetite and what has been eaten, which equally have to do with narcissism. Take Montaigne's quotation from Erasmus's *Adages*: 'Stercus cuique suum bene olet' (everyone loves the smell of his own shit) (p. 929): seemingly a criticism of self-love, its roots in Aristotle and Plato. However, narcissism and the philosophical and theological concept of self-love are not simply the same. Here I want to suggest the productivity of narcissism (as well as its inevitability), without ignoring instances in the *Essais* which are value-neutral, ambiguous or negative. Also, let us recall the frequently used metaphor of the body that is writing, as in: 'donner corps' (p. 665), to put into writing. When, rather than settling for this conventional figure Montaigne calls his writing shit or excrement, one consequence of the choice, which could trigger disgust or at least puzzlement, but equally might launch laughter, is that it lends interesting freedom to the reader to make of it what she will, because the range of reactions is unusually unpredictable.

Tickling is even more unpredictable; this may even be its critical quality for Montaigne, again in terms of what is given to, and asked of, the reader. Furthermore, unpredictability also hints at erotic excitement; and we may discover that what tickles Montaigne or what he thinks would tickle someone else is revealing of his (or any subject's) narcissism, 'the erotically charged relationship to her – or himself' (Rose, p. 63). It also pinpoints that if the aim is pleasure, another person's knowledge and desire to play must be involved, making tickling a metaphor for the relationship between Montaigne's writing and its readers, as is shaking. Each of these verbs and the relationships they help us to analyse involves unreliability or uncertainty of outcome. Likewise, no guarantee that the process or outcome is simply enjoyable: just enjoyable enough, or surprisingly so, and always potentially painful. This element of uncertainty in these processes and the relationships within which they figure is consonant with the doubt and irresolution of Montaigne's thinking: engagingly, pleasurably so. If at times pain overtakes or replaces pleasure, it is such as to be tolerable and helps enable a kind of thinking or understanding that might otherwise not emerge.

The strategic, but risky, use of such figuration sits alongside Montaigne's awareness of what in the text is not accessible to his own understanding: 'les graces et beautez qui s'y treuvent non seulement sans l'intention, mais sans la cognoissance mesme de l'ouvrier' (the grace and beauties in it not only without the worker's intention but without his knowledge) (p. 127). Which is where, tickled, shaken, impassioned, perturbed … the 'suffisant lecteur' (good-enough reader) (p. 127) comes in, as the following readings illustrate.

My earlier chapters focused on one or more of Montaigne's chapters; here interpretation is structured around key instances of the use of these figures. Both what is said and how need analysis: so, for instance, I shall explore a range of examples of what shakes us and instances of the effects of shaking the reader, which may not involve a verb such as 'secouer' (jolt) or 'esbranler' (shake), but which nonetheless jolt or dislocate the reader out of habitual or comfortable thinking or patterns of response and interpretation. Such terms are used so often that my analysis is illustrative rather than exhaustive, focusing on ways in which doubt and its attendant unsettling affects and effects pulse through the writing.[7]

'Il en demeurera en doubte'

A model for education reveals much about how cognition, judgement and their nurture are understood; so, as a preliminary to analysing doubtful thinking in the *Essais*, let's consider 'De l'institution des enfans' ('On the education of children'). The kind of engagement and enlivening implied by tickling and shaking play a part, not least in ways in which the pedagogical relationship recognizes and uses the impulses of narcissism. But for instances of extremely difficult or disturbing ideas, we shall, unsurprisingly, need to look elsewhere; this education prepares the (male) child for such tests but does not include them.

The aim is to teach the individual how to live well: to value freedom, be autonomous, love virtue, be just, speak freely; to instil 'une honeste curiosité de s'enquerir de toutes choses' (an honest curiosity fuelling the desire to inquire into all things) (p. 156), and a critical attitude: 'qu'il ... ne loge rien en sa teste par simple authorité et à credit' (let him lodge nothing in his head simply on authority; let him not borrow) (p. 151). So far so very good; but how? Socrates's name keeps recurring, an alternative to traditional models, the flaws of which are clear in what is prized: rejection of authoritarian monologue, of the presumption that the passive child is an empty container for the teacher's wisdom, and of the priority assumed by what matters to the latter.

Instead, there is to be a relationship, interaction, dialogue – as with Socrates, a form of love – as a means to helping the pupil develop his own judgement and understanding; the idealized teacher works with his pupil's desire not simply for knowledge but for *his* knowledge, and to be like him. The substructure of this relationship is a network of figures of the desire for knowledge and of a creative response: the child's appetite for learning, the food that is offered by nurturing teaching, the child's digestion or incorporation of that food. The connection between these and Socrates is the *Symposium*. For Montaigne, learning is not a harsh discipline, the preserve of the schoolroom, but can take place anywhere, any time; all interaction can be instructive. Philosophy is as welcome a dinner guest as anyone; witness the *Symposium*: 'Platon l'ayant invitee à son convive,

---

[7] Among the numerous illuminating discussions of doubt that shakes and life-threatening shaking, in 'De l'exercitation' ('On practice') and the 'Apologie', see Aulotte, *Montaigne: Apologie de Raimond Sebond* (Paris, 1979) and Brahami, *Le Scepticisme de Montaigne*, pp. 5–57, Jenny, *L'Expérience de la chute* (Paris, 1997), pp. 30–7, and Kritzman, *The Fabulous Imagination* (New York, 2009), pp. 87–103.

nous voyons comme elle entretient l'assistance d'une façon molle et accom-
modée au temps et au lieu, quoy que ce soit de ses plus hauts discours et plus
salutaires' (Plato having invited her to his table, we see how she entertains the
guests; she is relaxed and suits her words to the time and place, although she
speaks of the most sublime and salutary things) (pp. 164–5).

But this is to move too fast: what precisely is the link between the metaphors
and Plato's text? In French, in which *Symposium* becomes *Le Banquet*, it *seems*
clearer; also, Rabelais's feast of words, thought and play, and the humanist
concept of 'innutrition', the process whereby others' wisdom and linguistic
prowess read in texts is absorbed by the reader, were still culturally influential.
Underwriting all of this, and reappearing in Montaigne's chapter, is the metaphor of the body that is the text.

Montaigne can rely on his readers to recognize the network of metaphors,
and can elaborate his nurturing educational model through them; we still intuitively understand them, even if we lack knowledge of the classical or humanist
traditions that determined and sustained them. But they can prove disarming,
as if we can all simply agree on there being 'food for thought'. As metaphors
go, these have affective force: readers of the *Essais* have all been nurtured
and educated (albeit in diverse ways), and we come to the chapter with our
own experience and strong ideas as to what works. If this were not enough to
induce a particularly strongly identificatory reading, Montaigne's framing of his
educational model with passages on his own reading experiences, pleasures and
preferences is a further invitation to this kind of reading: look, reader, I share
what I care about and what I value with you, and share how I came to have these
pleasures and tastes. This appeals to the narcissism in each of us as readers. The
'personal' relationship is a powerful force in this writing; it stages it as part of
what persuades us of the central importance of the interrelational in the learning
process (if we needed any persuasion).

Reading, and the relationship in which he learned to read and to enjoy it,
displaces the relationship between the child and his parents, particularly the
relation to the maternal: thematically or ideologically this has to do with the
claim that the child must be removed from the 'giron de ses parents' (lap of
his parents) (p. 153) if he is to be educated effectively. Parental love fails the
child in being too tender – not toughening up the 'tender' child, whose body
and soul must be stiffened, 'roidir' (p. 153). Soft and hard or firm, and clusters
of associated qualities, is one of the structuring contrasts of the chapter; and the
trajectory from soft to hard or firm is what makes the child a man.

Formation, in other words. A rather premature, but not culturally atypical,
version of what is, after all, one of the aims of good-enough parenting: to enable
the child to become independent. However, if we focus precisely on what is
happening at the edges or borders of the child's 'body' – whether the soul's
and mind's figurative body or his material body – we find more ambiguity and
tension between 'tender' and 'firm' (and associated qualities) than clear differentiation. I note this first cut to suggest that for qualities associated with tenderness to be allowed, revalued, they have to be dissociated from first love, and

particularly from the maternal. This becomes even clearer later, in a passage about Montaigne's own language acquisition and the relationship with literature that ensued. 'Nous nous Latinizames' (we Latinized ourselves) (p. 173): his father judged that for his son to develop a great soul and understanding, on a par with classical ideals, he had to learn Latin as early as possible – 'en nourrice et avant le premier desnouement de ma langue' (before I was weaned or had said my first words) (p. 173).

The process is recounted in a passage which is both tender and at times tense, although Montaigne ascribes any failings of his father's programme to his own 'softness' and a lack of alertness that is associated with softness: 'poisant, mol, et endormi' (heavy, soft and half-asleep) (p. 174). What stands out (for a reader here and now) is the reference to Latin as his mother tongue: 'la mienne maternelle' (p. 175). It is only maternal figuratively, dislocated from the 'real' mother's tongue – which his mother had had to abandon in order to speak to her child ('nous nous Latinizames'). With that, tacitly, seems to go a symbolic identification with the form of culture that Latin articulated: all that is identified with Romanness. However, the effects of this dislocation of the mother tongue from the substantial maternal prove more complex and ambiguous: on the side of Latin is not only the ideal symbolized by Rome but also form and culture, which in turn are associated with what is superior and masculine. The maternal feminine, traditionally associated with matter, nature and what is inferior, here is absorbed into the masculine: we *all* Latinized ourselves. Lack of firmness is also absorbed, not only a negative value, as in the instance cited, but also potentially positive – by virtue of its traditional gender associations having been subsumed or veiled by the emphasis on language as if divested of associations other than cultural superiority.

The relationship that results, floating free from real bodies, enables, at times, *but not always*, something soft to persist. It is still categorically and anxiously excluded in the formation of masculinity: 'endurcisssez-le … ostez-luy toute mollesse et delicatesse … Que ce ne soit pas un beau garçon et dameret' (harden him … rid him of all softness and delicacy … don't let him become a pretty boy, or girly) (p. 165); but although ideal speech is similarly 'masculine' – 'vehement et brusque' (vigorous and brusque), not 'delicat' (delicate) (p. 171) – the ideal pedagogical relationship works through a fusion of 'masculine' and 'feminine' in oxymoronic 'severe douceur' (severe gentleness) (p. 165). This is possible because of that dislocation of this relationship from the parental, maternal feminine. While it is here that the new masculine subject is produced, if soft 'feminine' qualities are at times admitted or even essential – for it is gentleness that is transformative according to Montaigne, writing against the unremitting severity of most teachers at the time – it is only because they have been, on the one hand, incorporated into the masculine, and, on the other, dislocated from their origins in the maternal, in matter and the love associated with it.

There is a dissonance in the use of so affectively powerful an adjective as 'maternal' in relation to his first, but artificial, language; there is also an unexamined confusion of becoming Latinized with 'maternal', which indicates another obscurity in Montaigne's thinking about subject formation. I shall return later to such themes as origins and the relations between others' desires for the subject and his coming into being, through examination of Montaigne's reflections on the relationship between 'inside' and 'outside'; this is where tickling, shaking and shitting will supplement the less defined ideas of appetite and meeting it.

Beyond recognizing the power of such overdetermined figures as those that have to do with appetite and nurture, we also need to be a little more alert to the inclusion of the *Symposium* in the chapter: in it there is some of the most satisfying food for thought we may encounter – about love.

I shall approach this in two steps. First, the presence throughout the chapter of both Plato and Socrates as models. For all that there are many reminders of 'Rome' in Montaigne's Latin citations and references, Plato and Socrates and their Athens prevail. Increasingly so, insofar as several instances of both Socrates's and Plato's names are later additions.[8] Socrates is the ideal citizen, not only virtue's 'mignon' (dearest) (p. 162), and one whose inquiring spirit ranges to the horizons, not limited by local interests;[9] Socrates's teaching is invoked as a model, as is Plato's, and it is Plato who underwrites Montaigne's insistence that the child should come to occupy the position that suits him rather than one determined by his father's rank and wealth (p. 163).

One reference to Plato sums things up: 'Ce n'est non plus selon Platon que selon moy, puis que luy et moy l'entendons et voyons de mesme' (this idea is no longer Plato's or mine, as he and I see and understand it in the same way) (p. 152): here, to be well educated and well formed seems to mean to have fully identified with the (ideal) other, to have completely internalized or *incorporated* the other's knowledge and views – not for nothing are those slippery verbs 'entendre' (hear, understand) and 'voir' (see, understand, have insight) used here.

This prompts my second step, which is to bring more precision to the relationship between incorporation, embodiment and the body in this chapter. Not only is a dislocation between the maternal/paternal and pedagogical relationships introduced; it seems almost as if the (ideal) teacher displaces the father … (although of course, if it were a shared ideal, it would end up being what the father wanted, and Montaigne's learning Latin is a case in point). The dislocation is not between the father's values and those to be acquired from the teacher; rather, it is between different forms of love, and different versions of the body, given that the link between the child and the maternal has been cut. Not a natural body, but one to be formed, made masculine;[10] above all, despite the emphasis

---

[8] See (Plato) pp. 152 and 167 and (Socrates), pp. 150, 159 and 169.

[9] 'On demandoit à Socrates d'où il estoit. Il ne respondit pas: D'Athenes; mais: Du monde' (They asked Socrates where he was from. His reply was not, 'Athens', but 'the world') (p. 157).

[10] On the formation of the masculine body, and changes in sociocultural practices over time, see for instance Vigarello, 'The Upward Training of the Body', in Feher (ed.), *Fragments for a History of the Human Body*, vol. 2 (New York, 1989), pp. 149–96. For the making

on the need to attend to the body as well as the mind, that cut made, the body thereafter is the figurative body of the mind, judgement, memory and spirit; figurative appetite, figurative digestion.

This child's body provides a network of readily manipulated potential figures; its ears, eyes and mouth are the orifices that matter. The body serves incorporation, rather as the teacher's love serves love of knowledge, philosophy and virtue, which is now free to take the place of mother: 'c'est la mere nourrice des plaisirs humains' (she is the breast that feeds human pleasures) (p. 162). The relationship between teacher and pupil, disembodied despite the emphasis on incorporation of learning and embodiment of it ('il ne dira pas tant sa leçon, comme il le fera' (he will not recite his lesson so much as enact it) (p. 168)), can have as its ideals Plato and Socrates – minus the body. For all the approving reference to the *Symposium*, to Plato and Socrates, this chapter thus avoids any of the more culturally unacceptable dimensions of the relationship between the Athenian teacher and learner. Both 'masculine' and 'feminine' in this chapter are voided of their association with sex; desire and love are all for knowledge and philosophy, virtue and truth ('science', 'connaissance', 'philosophie', 'vertu', 'vérité', in French all nouns of feminine gender). Thus disembodied, liking and wanting to be like are powerful tools in this programme; reading Montaigne's account of how his teacher worked *with* his love of reading (p. 175) you might say, what's not to like? This has its place. Indeed, and that is not quite the point; the point is how unclear the formation of the autonomous subject still remains.

The body- and appetite-related figures are not precise about how a child's desire to learn is best developed. But if we move from desire to love, then perhaps we have a clearer idea of how Montaigne's pupil would learn – to love knowledge, which is, after all, where the chapter seems to end: 'il ne faut pas seulement loger [la science] chez soy, il faut l'espouser' (we must not only allow [learning] to lodge within us, we must wed it) (p. 177). But once again, precision is needed: is to wed, to love? We are led towards this by a reference just before to the need to 'allécher l'appétit et l'affection' (arouse the appetite and love) (p. 177), by instances earlier in the chapter of the pupil's 'affection' for virtue being encouraged,[11] and throughout, by Montaigne's liberalism and understanding: education requires a good relationship between teacher and pupil, which suggests empathy, trust, respect and sufficient understanding if not necessarily love. Is there not a tension between arousing or tempting appetite and love, and being wed – associated at the time of writing with reproduction, not love? If the ideal is in fact transmission, for the well-taught learner to reproduce what he has learned, all well and good; but this does not altogether account for the metaphor here. It seems that exciting emotions and enjoyment are allowed in the service of education, but then cede to something more tram-

---

of the courtly body, the *production* of *artless* civility, see Castiglione, *Il Cortegiano*, to which Montaigne's 'nonchallante de l'art... dressé à la façon d'un cortisan' (deliberately artless ... trained as a courtier) (p. 172) alludes.

11 The tutor should encourage love of virtue, not just high regard for it (see p. 161).

melled. So what remains unclear at this end of the process is, why would you want to give those excitements up: who would you then be?

The chapter travels from infancy to adulthood, from entry into education just after weaning, to 'marriage': education for 'life'. But precisely 'how' one person's learning, culture, experience and values are transmitted to another is not clear. Nor, for it is the formation of the subject that is at issue, is precisely the nature of the relationship between the *potential* subject and the other. So, does Montaigne's educational alternative help us understand how the subject emerges, and how his desires become his own rather than those of someone else (parent, teacher, friend, Other, that is, the set of options available to the subject within the cultural framework in which he is born)? This model seems to want to challenge the status quo: 'nostre ame ne branle qu'à credit, liée et contrainte à l'appetit des fantasies d'autruy, serve et captive' (our minds owe their movement to others, bound and constrained by others' fantasies, their slaves and captives) (p. 151); but how? And also, what precisely is the outcome?

The outcome is to live well (that theme again); to produce a good citizen and person, whose understanding and judgement are his own: so how does this sit with the need, also, to produce a conforming subject? 'Tout estrangeté et particularité en nos meurs et conditions est evitable comme *ennemi* de communication et de societé et *comme monstrueuse*' (in our manners and habits we should avoid all strangeness and singularity, for these are *enemies* of communication and social relations: they are *monstrous*) (pp. 166–7, my italics). It is too simple to invoke the historicist reminder that, at the time, not individuality but conformity to the ideals of the place or position into which one was born was desirable.[12]

The hyperbole of Montaigne's statement has curious effects. It is an instance of performative 'shaking', one of the textual strategies that interest me here. Its excess, coming after a brief, bland account of the entertainment and arts favoured by Plato, is unsettling, it demands a different kind of attention, as if this is particularly significant; but it also undermines the seriousness of the assertion rather than emphatically underlining it. It makes it shaky, unreliable.

It troubles a shrewd and far from excessive observation. Montaigne invites us to think about the way in which culturally, how fractional (while how greatly divisive) the difference may be between those who belong and those who are alien. This is particularly the case during troubled times in which what secures the social order has become precarious, and fundamentalisms cause strife, so this might very well be called a 'monstrous' fraction.[13] What he recognizes is

---

[12] On this topic, see such new historicist studies as Greenblatt, *Renaissance Self-fashioning* (Chicago, 1980).

[13] Žižek's example is *Invasion of the Body Snatchers*; he comments on the 'tiny detail' that gives away the alien, who otherwise looks and acts exactly like humans. He continues: 'are we not dealing with the same in our everyday racism? Although we are ready to accept the Jewish, Arab, Oriental other, there is some detail that bothers us in the West: the way they accentuate a certain word, the way they count money, the way they laugh. This tiny feature renders them aliens, no matter how they try to behave like us' (Žižek, *How to Read Lacan* (London, 2006), p. 67).

the fragility of what forms and delineates the culturally acceptable subject and allows him to hold his place. What is less clear are the details of the model underlying his account of what it is to be (like) one of us, other than in terms of social and symbolic norms and values that are internalized or 'incorporated' during one's education.

Forming the subject is partly a process of figuratively giving him the desired shape and surface (clothes, manners, gestures and so forth); *as if* he *naturally* had all the qualities and values he comes to embody. As for the mind's figurative body, the chapter focuses quite frequently on shaping it, attending to its borders, their edges knocked off through interaction with others' minds ('frotter et limer nostre cervelle contre celle d'autruy' (to rub our brains against those of others, to smoothe their rough edges) (p. 153)). The process of internalization corresponds to the network of digestive metaphors already mentioned, notably the classical analogy with bees making honey from nectar. However, the proliferation of digestive metaphors, and particularly this analogy with instinctive animal behaviour, ignores the gap between animal learning and behaviour, so-called 'natural processes', and human learning and subject-formation. The flexibility of the teacher's feeding plan for the learner is welcome (sometimes the learner has to eat a text whole, at others he is given the pulped essence 'toute maschée' (already well chewed) (p. 160)): simple educational principles of appropriateness of material to the learner's level and adaptations accordingly; but the figures do not shed light on the more complex dimensions of human learning.

They cannot account for the desire to 'form' and correspondingly to learn or be formed. Not only in terms of how something becomes 'sien' (one's own), not least because whatever 'sien' may be, it seems to be produced by this process rather than being its foundation; also, how would this learner deal with really difficult questions? What would sustain his desire to go on learning and coping with its consequences? That doubt may be difficult to bear is bypassed: 'qu'on luy propose cette diversité de jugements: il choisira s'il peut, sinon il en demeurera en doubte' (let these different judgements be presented to him; he will choose if he can, and if not, he will remain in doubt) (p. 151).

Neither what happens to the shape or surface of the figurative body nor how it digests and grows strong through figurative food sheds light on cognitive processes or development of memory and verbal skills; but before setting these metaphors aside let us briefly consider other ways in which this body is treated, in case they suggest more about how things are absorbed. Slightly more purchase is provided by forms of impact associated with shaking and tickling, which I am provisionally aligning with aggressivity and unpleasure, and pleasure, respectively. Aspects of the chapter which figuratively shake the reader reveal what shaking might induce.

The 'follastre' (carelessly playful) (p. 160) quality of philosophy can be aligned with tickling. Philosophy is lovely, alluring, joyful, both enlivening and soothing, and transformative: 'elle fait estat de serainer les tempestes de l'ame, et d'apprendre la faim et les fiebvres à rire' (her role is to still the tempests of the soul, and to teach hunger and fever to laugh) (p. 161). While this still may not

poetry shakes. unpredictably

help us understand precisely how we establish a relationship with philosophy, what tickles our curiosity and shapes reading is the writing's playful seductiveness, as much as the idea that when the relationship flourishes, affect and imagination are engaged along with intellect and judgement.

We can also align dancing with tickling. Dancing is the antithesis of teaching that pours facts into a passive, silenced pupil, treating what is transmitted as if it is unchanging and unchangeable, whereas dancing can only be learned by dancing, and by engaging the learner fully: experiment and experience. 'Je voudrois que le Paluël ou Pompée … apprinsent des caprioles à les voir seulement faire, sans nous bouger de nos places' (I should like Paluel or Pompey to try to teach us our dance-steps simply by having us sit and watch them perform) (p. 152). Laughter, light-footed movement, seductiveness: these are a far cry from troubling doubt. On the other hand, without the play and movement to which Montaigne draws our attention here, in the dance of ideas that is thinking there might not exist the precondition for doubt. And without the presence of a 'dancing partner', that is, without openness to response, or without dialogue, doubt would not flourish.

However, Montaigne in fact aligns thinking that dances with shaking: 'l'esbranler' (p. 152). Perhaps tickling and shaking are less divergent than they first seem? Tickling potentially shakes us in unpleasant ways as well as pleasant; some shaking (but not all) is beneficial … Interpretative precision is needed to allow words to be open to further nuance or even definition – all part of the more sceptical approach that is required of Montaigne's readers, and encouraged by the play of figuration.

The first instance of shaking in the chapter is poetry's capacity to shake Montaigne. Poetry speaks to him more powerfully than prose through the effects of rhythm: it 'me fiert d'une plus vive secousse' (strikes me with a much greater jolt) (p. 146). Read aloud, its power is transformative, and listening, we remember, is an embodied activity and pleasure; poetry's form is not only enlivening but initiates our specific enjoyment of it. This comment comes even before Montaigne has begun to lay out his educational programme, but instruction has already started: value what shakes you in a piece of writing. This may also take the form of being open to chance and the unexpected; the effects of a chance encounter ('s'il m'advient … de rencontrer' (if I happen to encounter) (p. 146)) shake us up, surprising us into engaging fully with the text's potential. Moreover, chance and incalculability continue to play their part, because if shaking, and indeed also tickling, figure the processes involved, each of these involves an element of unpredictability as the process develops.

Other examples of shaking as a textual effect also demonstrate unpredictability. What is to be done with an unteachable, 'diverse' or odd boy, with no (masculine) appetite for warfare and a preference for frivolous pleasures? The boy who will not be man enough? 'Je n'y trouve autre remede sinon que *de bonne heure* son gouverneur l'estrangle, *s'il est sans temoins*' (I see no other remedy than for his tutor to strangle him *early, if there are no witnesses*) (p. 162, my italics). Montaigne is not really advocating murder, of course, but using stylistic shock tactics – and they work: that hyperbole of strangling rather than, say, 'give up on him' or 'get rid of him', and, shaking the reader further, those two stipulations. How early risks being premature? And the absence of witnesses? An act which is not shameful does not need secrecy. These additional precisions throw us, cutting across the impression of a throwaway comment, or a satirical joke to relieve frustration. That it may be, but the excessive specifi-cities are disorienting, shaking our otherwise tranquil and trusting relationship with the text.

What is also shaken is the reader's – my – narcissistic delusion that I am not, of course, and unlike others, potentially capable of killing. Montaigne rips away this illusion here, and actively educates us out of self-idealization, also reminding that he sees self-idealization (a negative facet of narcissism), the boy's insistence on the primacy of his difference, as one of the limits of educability. He forces the issue: what *should* happen to those who deviate from cultural expectations (here, of gentlemanly masculinity)? And at what point is faith in the power of education to be lost? But the text meanwhile has moved on, apparently authorizing itself by appeal to Plato's principle that we earn our place in the world through our own qualities rather than our father's prestige ...

A second example is much less troubling; it is similar to Montaigne's comments on poetry, and illustrates what reading with that honest curiosity and omnivorous spirit of inquiry (p. 156) would be. Using Livy and Plutarch as his examples, Montaigne reflects on the rich variety of potential interpretations of their writing, not only among different readers, but also beyond the author's knowledge and interpretation: 'j'ay leu en Tite-Live cent choses que tel n'y a pas leu. Plutarque en y a leu cent, outre que j'y ay sceu lire, et, à l'adventure, outre ce que l'autheur y avoit mis' (I have read a great many things in Livy that no one else has. Plutarch has read a great many that I have not seen, and which perhaps go beyond what the author included) (p. 156). He goes on: Plutarch's reader needs to be alert to clues and cues. Unexceptional perhaps, other than the use of figuration, for a shaking injunction follows: 'il les faut arracher de là et mettre en place marchande' (rip them out, put them up for sale, display them). His example is: 'que les habitants d'Asie servoient à un seul, pour ne sçavoir prononcer une seule sillabe, qui est Non, donna *peust estre* la matiere et l'occasion à La Boitie de sa Servitude Volontaire' (that the inhabitants of Asia were slaves to a one man because they could not pronounce that one syllable, No, *perhaps* inspired La Boétie to write his Servitude Volontaire) (p. 156, my italics). Why such violence towards the other's text? And why the extraneous vocabulary of commerce? Particularly in the context of so exemplary a text as his friend's? These questions risk detracting from the force of the 'No', first in Plutarch's *De la mauvaise honte* (79B), then here. What further tests the reader is the tension between the cryptic drama of that decisive 'No' and the conces-sive 'perhaps'; but constructively so, luring her to reflect further on how she reads, particularly when the text's moves are unsettling and if she has doubts about how to interpret.

In a chapter on education instances of how to read, or tests for the reader, are unsurprising. None too troubling, except perhaps the fate of the ineducable boy. However, a capacity for doubt and critical reflection is fundamental to the programme, and here and there the generation of doubt is one of the performative strategies of the writing. It is to this more generally that I shall turn shortly. But first, incorporation: Montaigne's chapter has worked with the metaphors of knowledge as food or nutrition, and the process of learning as digestion; but how the process works, and what it is to 'incorporate', are matters about which there is still more to learn.

'Mais comme une impression spirituelle face une telle faucée dans un subject massif et solide, et la nature de la liaison et cousture de ces admirables resorts, jamais homme ne l'a sçeu'[14]

The verb 'incorporer', to incorporate, is not used as frequently in the *Essais* as some of the other metaphors that interest me here; but while it occurs less than 'digerer' (to digest) used figuratively, it has more force and lability. More than once Montaigne uses it in relation to the soul or mind, thus lending them a figurative body. For instance: 'il ne faut pas attacher le sçavoir à l'ame, il l'y faut incorporer' (knowledge must not just be attached to the mind or soul, it must be incorporated) (p. 140): fully integrated. But even when the verb is used with apparent precision (see p. 157), in fact, opacities or impasses tend to remain. Distinction between 'proper, its own' and 'incorporated' is not clear (other than it matters that it exists); nor is the justification for describing that which has been incorporated as 'natural'.

Its meaning seems more evident in a consistently clear distinction between symbolic or public identity and personal, intimate identity: 'si quelquefois on m'a poussé au maniement d'affaires estrangieres, j'ay promis de les prendre en main, non pas au poulmon et au foye: de m'en charger, non de les incorporer; de m'en soigner ouy, de m'en passionner nullement ... le Maire et Montaigne ont tousjours esté deux' (if people have insisted that I take on others' affairs at times, I have promised to take them in hand, not breathe or metabolize them: to take charge of them, not to incorporate them; to attend to them, yes, but not to care about them ... the Mayor and Montaigne have always been two different people) (pp. 1004, 1012).

Here the limb and gestures of the figurative body contrast clearly with the internal organs, lungs and liver; these figure emotional or vital engagement (the liver being, moreover, associated with passion in Galenic physiology), and are

---

[14] 'But how a purely psychological event can have such an impact on the solid mass of bodies like ours, and the nature of the relation and connections between such stimuli, no one has ever known' (p. 539).

the locus of his intimate subjectivity.[15] But this is only a temporary and specific clarity, as two further examples show.

The first has a paradoxical trajectory: 'cette habitude qui *nous incorpore au vice*, et y conforme nostre entendement mesme … ce vent impetueux qui va troublant et aveuglant à secousses nostre ame, et nous precipite pour l'heur, jugement et tout, en la puissance du vice' (this habit which *incorporates us into vice*, even making our powers of understanding conform with it … this gusting wind which buffets, unsettles and blinds our soul and for a while casts us, judgement and all, into the sway of vice) (p. 812, my italics). Vice subsumes the subject, rather than the habituated subject becoming inured to vice; 'incorporation' suggests the connection between our corporeality and our inclining towards vice rather than virtue, but it also figures in relation to vice, in a much less substantially corporeal way while simultaneously lending vice material force.

The second has to do with the imagination, and, with it, desire and fantasy. 'Car si l'imagination peut en telles choses, elle est si continuellement et vigoureusement attachée à ce subject, que, pour n'avoir si souvent à rechoir en mesme pensée et aspreté de desir, elle a meilleur compte d'incorporer une fois pour toutes, cette virile partie aux filles' (for if the imagination has any power in such things, so constant and energetic is its attachment to this subject that, in order to avoid having to return so often to this unremittingly acute desire, it would do better to incorporate, once and for all, the penis in girls' bodies) (p. 99). Such is the supposed force of feminine desire that, if the imagination could work such a wonder (and let's not forget that Montaigne had ascribed impotence and hysteria to imagination), women would simply have their own penises.

Here 'incorporation' seems literal; yet the passage is much more interesting if it is read in terms of an inchoate theory of sexual difference and desire, not too remote from Freud, according to which the little girl's 'problem' is that she lacks a penis, and wants to have one. Montaigne's (humorous?) fantasy of feminine desire and fantasy is over the top. His understanding of the imagination is that its supposedly uncanny powers rest not least on a failure to recognize that it is in play. Thus an explicit request to the imagination would deprive it of its 'magic' potential. Moreover, if, as in the case of Marie Germain, exceptionally, and fascinated, Montaigne encounters a case of spontaneous 'sex change' (the emergence of the 'virile partie'), logically and epistemologically he would not extrapolate from the singular case to the set of all women.

And what would result? For Freud, in wanting to have a 'virile partie' she refuses the reality of castration and therefore her femininity; but here, is the figure of the Androgyne the determinant fantasy? Moreover, as this is as much Montaigne's fantasy about feminine desire as any woman's desire, what does

---

[15] On Greek and Roman influences on early modern thinking about the body's organs see Onians, *The Origins of European Thought* (Cambridge, 1951).

it say about what his desire incorporates? To speculate further labours the text; what matters is the complexity of the apparently simple use of 'incorporation'; this example confirms that the body in the *Essais* is not natural or unmediated but a complex site with mutable imaginary, symbolic and also real significations.

Here the impulse driving incorporation is desire which might equally be called imagination. In some other instances there seems to be an intentional relationship with the good of the soul; elsewhere, it seems to have more to do with intuitive, unconscious or unknowable processes, or indeed with a process to which the individual is subject. This suggests that incorporation is a process which is not fully understood, needing more investigation if we are not to remain in too much doubt as to how Montaigne understands subject formation and what can be known of phenomenal self-experience.

Such uses of 'incorporation' suspend the questions, who, originally, incorporates, and how is that subject, or potential subject, who goes on incorporating all manner of phenomena, formed and transformed by that process? Does what is incorporated become wholly 'them'? If, as the 'De la præsumption' passage suggests (see p. 157), there is a gap between what, having been incorporated, come to be called 'inclinations naturelles' and some dimension of unknowable natural subjectivity, then the validity of maintaining that clear line between personal and symbolic identity becomes questionable. If all that can be known is already that which is incorporated, then 'private' identity is no less a matter of intersubjectivity and of becoming one's 'self' in response to others' desires for us than symbolic identity. 'Our "psyche" is a social space.'[16] So, while it is understandable to want to maintain a distinction between the two, this difference seems to rest on fantasy and on a certain not knowing about oneself.

Montaigne may insist: 'j'ay peu me mesler des charges publiques sans me despartir de moy de la largeur d'une ongle' (I have managed to engage in public duties without departing a nail's breadth from myself) (p. 1007); but who is to know the extent to which a fantasy as to who he is, already involving the incorporated desires of others for him (as evident, say, in his father's desire to 'Latinize' him), plays in what he believes he knows himself to be. It may be more accurate to say, as he does elsewhere, that he is 'autant doubteux de moy que de toute autre chose' (p. 634), his version of himself a retroactive construction: 'n'en suis instruict qu'apres l'effect' (I understand only with hindsight) (p. 634). It seems that, once again, we need to return to doubt.

'La volubilité et incomprehensibilité de toute matiere'

Montaigne's educational ideals are not only expressed in 'De l'institution'. In 'Des boyteux' we find a powerful performative statement: 'si j'eusse eu à

---

[16] Rose, p. 62.

dresser des enfans, je leur eusse tant mis en la bouche cette façon de respondre (C) enquesteuse, non resolutive: (B) Qu'est-ce à dire? Je ne l'entends pas, Il pourroit estre, Est-il vray?' (If I had had children to raise, I would have given them a taste for this inquiring, open-ended way of responding: What does it mean? I don't understand it, it could be, is it true?) (p. 1030).[17] The forms taken by inquiring, sceptical open-mindedness are questions, concessives, admissions of lack of understanding – the inclinations of the writings of Pyrrho and Zeno: 'branler, douter et enquerir, ne s'asseurer de rien, de rien ne se respondre' (to shake, doubt and inquire, to have no certainty, to vouch for nothing) (p. 502); also, forms such as dialogue, of which the paradigms are Plato and Socrates. Dialogue stages the coexistence of a range of different possible perspectives; moreover the dialogue is not only in the text, between Socrates, who kept the discussion moving, and others, as 'midwife' of their ideas, but also between the text and the reader.

Such writing, metaphorically, plays (with), tickles, dances (with) and moves the reader. Montaigne celebrates play: 'si quelqu'un me dict que c'est avilir les muses de s'en servir seulement de jouet et de passe-temps, il ne sçait pas comme moy, combien vaut le plaisir, le jeu et le passe-temps. A peine que je ne die toute autre fin ridicule' (if anyone tells me that it degrades the muses to use them just as playthings and pastimes, he doesn't know – as I do – the value of pleasure, play and pastime. I'd almost say that any other aim is ridiculous) (p. 829). Play is a state of mind which is not preoccupied with, or oriented by, outcome: outcome can remain unknown, or beside the point. All of which makes this kind of text and the questions with which it engages the reader, seem lovely. We can't wait to play; and this can be imagined as an expansive and enjoyable form of doubtful thinking, or tickling before it suddenly becomes painful or threatening. Of course, however playful Montaigne may be (and he is), there is no underestimating the seriousness of the need for play and doubt – and for doubt even when it is no fun any more.

His stance on the need for doubt is underwritten by Christian authority as much as by classical Greek thinkers. 'Et suis l'advis de sainct Augustin, qu'il vaut mieux pancher vers le doute que vers l'asseurance és choses de difficile preuve et dangereuse creance' (and I follow St Augustine in thinking that it is better to lean towards doubt than certitude in matters which are difficult to prove and dangerous to believe) (p. 1032). Doubt not dogma or wrongful condemnation; doubt and with it tolerance rather than religious and civil wars. Doubt, and self-doubt, because we cannot trust our own reasoning or judgement: 'la raison va tousjours, et torte, et boiteuse, et deshanchée, et avec le mensonge comme avec la verité ... les moindres choses du monde le [sc. nostre jugement] tournev-irent' (reason is always crooked, lame, and lopsided, in falsehood as in truth ... the slightest thing can send [our judgement] flying) (pp. 565, 564).

---

[17] For further analysis of the passage in question in 'Des boyteux', see Sellevold, *'J'ayme ces mots'* –, ch. 4.

This figuration of our hobbling reasoning suggests that it is not much good at play, or doubt; and the least trifle sends our judgement spinning. A shaky gait, easily shaken. This seems remote from the tranquillity that is the ideal of sceptical thinking, apparently embodied instead by aboriginal Brazilians unburdened by the desire for knowledge. It seems to belong on a distant horizon (if it even exists), not to the here and now of Montaigne's France, or to any culture of writing. So is tranquillity only possible without the desire for knowledge? The capacity to suspend belief and to doubt and to remain uncertain requires the capacity to tolerate not knowing, but nonetheless, folded into that is the desire to go on questioning, which may pull against tranquillity. For Montaigne, suffering and disquiet are the excessive price we pay for our capacity to reason: 'certes, nous avons estrangement surpaié ce beau discours dequoy nous nous glorifions, et cette capacité de juger et connoistre, si nous l'avons achetée au pris de ce nombre infiny de passions ausquelles nous sommes incessamment en prise' (indeed, we have paid strangely too much for this fine faculty of reason we are so proud of, and also for the capacity to judge and know, if the cost of its purchase has been the countless passions to which we are ceaselessly subject) (p. 486).

The context of this comment is a much longer set of reflections on what differentiates humans from other creatures. Not for Montaigne the inert belief that reason and language distinguish us from other animals, or that we are superior in being conjugal and political animals. He worries away at the traditional distinctions, unsettling them; a catalogue of what emerge in the *Essais* as particularly human qualities would include: sadism, self-destructiveness, envy, resentment, shame, anxiety, self-deception and consciousness of mortality, not to mention (sexual) desire.[18]

At the heart of this list are consciousness of mortality and self-deception, which can usefully be aligned with that comment on reason's exorbitant cost. Consciousness of mortality is that which we suffer, a source of both (excessive) certitude and (excessive) doubt, the price, or trap – 'pris' and 'en prise' are put into play together – of our desire for knowledge. But we are also subject to self-deception, a trap into which we constantly fall: the illusion of our superiority over other creatures, our illusions about who we are or might be, about all the ways in which we (don't) fail, and also about what we know of ourselves. 'Nous nous attribuons des biens imaginaires et fantastiques, des biens futurs et absens, desquels l'humaine capacité ne se peut d'elle mesme respondre, ou des biens que nous nous attribuons faucement par la licence de nostre opinion, comme la raison, la science et l'honneur' (we attribute imaginary, fantastical goods to ourselves, future, absent goods which we lack the capacity to answer

---

[18] The last is extrapolated from the ironic comment immediately following the one just quoted, that humans can be distinguished from animals in that, unlike the latter, they want sex anywhere, any time, not just when in season. That is, the human sexual drive is decoupled from reproduction, which implies the existence of what we could call desire, along with instinct.

for, or which we wrongly claim because of how we want to see ourselves, such as reason, knowledge and honour) (p. 485).

We cannot simply, in an act of rational will, decide to free ourselves from our illusions and self-deceptions; the problem is more involuted, in the absence of sufficient secure self-knowledge to guarantee against self-deception. 'C'est merveille que, sauf nous, aucune chose ne s'estime que par ses propres qual-itez' (it's astonishing that while everything else judges itself according to its own qualities, we do not) (p. 259): but how do we know what is really our own? To what sense of individual self-hood or identity are those qualities to be ascribed? Is not 'self'-doubt – doubt to do with our shaky reason and judgement, with the unknown-ness folded into our embodied being, with what may be only imaginary or fantasied – called for, as a greater challenge to self-deception than reasoning can muster: 'cette apparence de discours que chacun forge en soy' (that show of judgement that we all fabricate for ourselves) (p. 565)?

To demonstrate just how insecure this 'self' is, let's consider four of its prop-erties about which Montaigne seems to know something. First, his porousness: 'quelque odeur que ce soit, c'est merveille combien elle s'attache à moy, et combien j'ai la peau propre à s'en abreuver' (whatever the smell, it's wonderful how it clings to me, and how my skin just drinks it in) (p. 315). Montaigne's skin, he says, is very permeable; it drinks in smells, it absorbs what touches it, as if it were a porous membrane linking 'inside' and 'outside' rather than demarcating them; even undecidably both inside and outside. Similar perme-ability is also suggested by this second instance: 'le veue des angoisses d'autruy m'angoisse materiellement, et a mon sentiment souvent usurpé le sentiment d'un tiers' (the sight of others' anguish causes me real anguish, and my feelings have often usurped someone else's) (p. 97). Total identification may seem a form of compassion but involves violent alienation; he has 'usurped', wrongly taken over, another's feelings. Although the first example is from 'Des senteurs' ('On smells'), its significance extends beyond smells; and neither instance should be read only as a comment on the complexities of our senses. What happens on the surface or through the body's orifices are aspects of what makes processes of 'incorporation' so opaque, because the 'self' doing the incorporating seems to lack the clear, fixed boundaries needed to define it as an identity.

Two further examples confirm this, from different perspectives. Firstly, Mont-aigne identifies the lack of difference between real emotion and the semblance or performance of it. What was not mine becomes mine; the orator will be both genuinely moved and tricked by ('se lairra piper') his own performance ('cette farce') of the passions of which he seeks to persuade his audience: 'il s'imprimera un *vray* deuil et *essentiel*, par le moyen de ce battelage qu'il joue' (he will be imprinted with the *true essence* of the grief he merely enacts) (p. 838, my italics). Montaigne continues:

> comme font ces personnes qu'on loüe aus mortuaires pour ayder à la ceremo-nie du dueil, qui vendent leurs larmes à pois et à mesure et leur tristesse: car, encore, qu'ils s'esbranlent en forme empruntée, toutesfois, en habitant et

rengeant la contenance, il est certain qu'ils s'emportent souvent tous entiers et reçoivent en eux la *vraye* melancholie. (my italics)

(it is like those people for hire at funerals to help with the rituals of mourning, who sell their tears by weight and measure, their sadness too. For although their emotions are borrowed show, nonetheless, the habit of wearing the expression of grief often quite carries them away and they are inwardly affected by *genuine* melancholy.)

The lexical tensions mark the strangeness of the transformation described here. From semblance, performance and faking, a suspect means to an end, to the real thing; the real thing derives from a corrupted copy? The point is that repetition of ritualized gestures, of a performance which begins as empty or compromised (because) fake, acting 'as if', has the power to produce the emotion it initially only represented. The real emotion may be felt, and who are we to rule out this possibility; but Montaigne intimates that we are not in a position to know if it is real or feels as if it is. Here he pursues the slippery power of self-deception, along with the paradox that the authentic may derive from the fake. Such are the constituents of the 'self' that we become. My last instance is: 'je n'ay rien mien que moy et si en est la possession en partie manque et empruntée' (I own nothing but myself, and my possession even of that is lacking and partly borrowed) (p. 968). When it comes to knowing what is mine, my own, I may be all I have but I have to know that I do not fully own even that: I lack something in what I own of myself, and some of what is mine is borrowed.

These four examples separately and cumulatively argue for doubt as an essential element in our relation with our objects of knowledge, the self included; yet none conveys the difficulties, the intense affects that may be associated with doubt, whether stirring it or being stirred by it. Nor do they directly clarify how we engage with whatever we are thinking about, in such a way as to form a judgement of it. How do we understand that which cannot be comprehended so as to arrive at a judgement such as 'I agree' or 'I disagree'? When 'I disagree' is expressed in the form 'je ne digere pas bien' (I don't digest well) (p. 136) it loops us back to the ingestive/digestive model but does not explain the process, other than to imply that what is voiced as a matter of judgement may conceal a constitutional resistance or incapacity towards something indigestible – or incomprehensible?

The metaphor matters; it recurs in 'De l'experience' in relation to Socrates: 'rien ne m'est à digerer fascheux en la vie de Socrates que ses ecstases et demoneries' (in the life of Socrates nothing is so difficult for me to digest as his ecstacies and his dæmons) (p. 1115). The metaphor may be an instance of the 'limites et dernieres clotures des sciences' (limits and furthest edges of our knowledge) (p. 558), that is, the limits of human understanding of the human; but the second half of the sentence perhaps takes us in a different direction: 'rien si humain en Platon que ce pourquoy ils disent qu'on l'appelle divin' (nothing in Plato is so human as the qualities for which he is called divine). Montaigne can understand this so-called 'divine' in 'human' terms, identifying it with what his understanding of the human encompasses, which suggests that digestion has to do with recognition; what is distinctive is his desire to go on trying to understand, rather than rejecting as indigestible, whatever tests his understanding to its limits.

These examples represent some causes of doubt, not least because of absence of forensic understanding: what makes skin 'breathe' conveyed by the personification of 's'abreuver', drinking in; the curious way in which one person can identify or even over-identify with an other's suffering captured by the homophony of 'angoisses' and 'angoisse', which allows an impression of identity in repetition while simultaneously marking difference (first plural noun, then singular verb); performance producing real emotion, oscillating between negative and positive valency and coming to rest on the production of what is true. Lastly, an absolute assertion, with charged terms, 'rien' (nothing) and 'mien' (mine); the juxtaposition is aurally rather diminishing but raises the significant question whether what is mine (or what I can call 'me') is nothing. It is then undercut by the heavier cadence of 'manque et empruntée' (lacking and borrowed), terms which mark imperfection and the limits to what is own of what is owned. By the use of different linguistic strategies, including figuration, all these sentences hold the reader's attention, and prompt speculation and further analysis, initiated by the need to linger over the formal effects. This is the kind of play in which this text engages the reader; engagement in the exploration of meaning without it being driven by the need for outcome; indeed only possible by setting that aside, in favour of the production of the kind of space within which thinking can play freely.

'Ces mouvemens qui se gouvernent sans moy'

Doubt *plays* if it is tranquil. However, it is often associated with agitation, perturbation, shaking, the effects of which on play need further analysis. But let's note, as a preliminary, that they involve some play of meaning, for their connotations may be emotional and psychological, or physiological, or both.

Agitation, which is akin to shaking, belongs with the illusion of knowledge. According to Montaigne such self-delusion produces not tranquillizing false certitude, but 'agitations' (p. 503), it troubles us; doubt, on the other hand, seems to be on the side of calm – Pyrrhonist *ataraxia*? Montaigne is interested in the theory, and he favours doubt, but his self-representation is saturated with instances of his being troubled, such as: 'il se faict mille agitations indiscretes et casuelles chez moy' (I feel the turmoil of a thousand rash, unexpected emotions) (p. 566); writing is not a tranquil process: 'je ne fay qu'aller et venir' (all I do is come and go) (p. 566); his style aims to be lively, edgy, invigorating: 'nerveux, court et serré … vehement et brusque' (sinewy, brief and compressed … vigorous and brusque) (p. 171); and he values writing which wakes you up and you can get your teeth into: 'vous esveille l'esprit … l'ame trouve où mordre' (p. 160). Nor is the kind of reading he desires necessarily tranquil, as in the examples already discussed, for instance of tearing key ideas from the text. Doubt, trouble and agitation seem to have creative value.

But not always: indeed, 'agitation' is markedly mobile and ambiguous in its connotations. These include natural energy and motion, such as that of waves, and the transit of stars and planets; the effects on the individual of love; the sensation of sexual desire; thought processes – how they are triggered, develop and are subject to change; but also, exceptional and destructive natural force, for instance a river in flood; forms of mental or emotional agitation which impede thinking or even provoke collapse into madness. Its destructive natural, emotional and psychological connotations are not consistently cases of extreme 'agitation', but tend towards excess and violence (breaking of river banks, psychological breakdown, or immobilizing conflict). The complexity of the processes it connotes, as well as the plurality of contexts, is well illustrated by the following passage, in which Montaigne reflects on how he deals with changes in his health:

> je consulte peu des alterations que je sens, car ces gens icy [that is, doctors] sont avantageux quand ils vous tiennent à leur misericorde: ils vous gourmandent les oreilles des leurs prognostiques; et me surprenant autre fois affoibly du mal, m'ont injurieusement traicté de leur dogmes et troigne magistrale, me menassant tantost de grandes douleurs, tantost de mort prochaine. Je n'en estois abattu ny deslogé de ma place, mais j'en estois heurté et poussé: si mon jugement n'en est ny changé ny troublé, au moins il estoit empesché; c'est tousjours agitation et combat. (p. 1090)

> (I rarely seek advice about my physical symptoms, for when those people [sc. doctors] have you at their mercy they dictate to you: they bully you with their prognoses; and once, when they caught me weakened by illness, I suffered their injurious treatment: dogma, magisterial frowns, threats of terrible suffering, even imminent death. They neither floored me nor dislodged me from my position, but I was bumped and jolted: my judgement was not changed or troubled by this, but as a result, at the very least, it felt stuck in a state of constant agitation and conflict.)

Dogmatic authority and excessive certitude opportunistically inflict injury, and they play on fear; they so shook his capacity to think about himself that the resulting internal conflict hindered his own judgement. Here 'agitation' loses its creative potential, fuelling, instead, self-consuming conflict – not doubt. Dogma is here identified with what is deadly or deadening, as is 'agitation'; but whilst 'agitation' in many other contexts is animating, and constructively associated with creative doubt, dogma is never enlivening. It is on the side of death, violence, abuse of power, and provokes the kind of 'agitation' that intensifies into disorder, fracture and disintegration.

The comment relates not only to Montaigne's ailing body. These symptoms are all associated in the *Essais* with the disease and disintegration of the body politic in war, the effects of fear, the 'dissipation et divulsion l'extreme de noz craintes' (our worst fear, dissolution and disintegration) (p. 962), and the effects of dogmatic beliefs that are blind to their limits and flaws: 'en ces desmambre-mens de la France ... chacun se travaille à deffendre sa cause, mais jusques aux meilleurs, avec desguisement et mensonge' (in the current dismembering of France ... each man strives to defend his cause, but even the best of them use deceit and lies) (p. 993).

The disguise and lies, at best, may not have been conscious, but rather, were symptomatic of the self-delusion that is Imaginary knowledge, *méconnaissance*. In the dimension of the Imaginary, that of binary structures and of the false clarity and certitude that believes that 'mine' and 'thine' are distinct, likewise 'self' and 'other', 'friend' and 'enemy', 'right' (mine) and 'wrong' (thine), the solution to differing views will be, if not the delusion that one view subsumes the other, violent antagonisms. Montaigne's question is urgent: 'apres avoir establi le doubte, vouloir establir la certitude des opinions humaines estoit ce pas establir le doubte, non la certitude?' (having established doubt, was not to then want to establish the certitude of human opinions in fact to establish doubt, not certitude?) (p. 964). For doubt, which operates in the Symbolic dimension, to cede to certitude would be precisely to retreat into Imaginary *méconnais-sance*, misrecognition or misunderstanding.

Montaigne conveys the fragility of the Symbolic order itself – as figured repeatedly in the text by metaphors of disease, dismemberment, infection and fever as well as destructive or futile agitation. He remains in the Symbolic; witness a question posed in the middle of a long passage on the current state of France and its violently polarized factions: 'faut-il, si elle est putain, qu'elle soit aussi punaise?' (because she is a whore must she smell bad?) (p. 1013) – and this from a man who emphasized the delicacy of his sense of smell.[19] In the Imaginary, the individual whore is denied Symbolic recognition, thus: all whores are the same, smell bad (and are one of society's metaphorical 'bad smells'), and therefore none deserve either respect or recognition, least of all of their vulnerability. This traumatically denies each and every whore the possibility of her individual difference and capacity, presumably, for reform or redemption (smelling good), and it denies our invaluable recognition of vulnerability, not least our own, as that which an equitable system should protect.

To develop this analysis of 'agitation', let us consider the following further examples. Our 'condition de nature' – character – emphatically needs 'agita-tion': 'si elle va toute seule, elle ne fait que trainer et languir. L'agitation est sa vie et sa grace' (left to find its own way, it will drag along listlessly. Agitation is its life and grace) (p. 40). The precise context matters: the topic is verbal fluency. If we are to speak well, and to appeal to others, we need to be emotion-ally engaged by, alive to, our material, be impassioned. So here, 'agitation' is associated with passion, and with positive value. A literary text which fails to engage the reader, which Montaigne ascribes to the writer's lack of sufficient

---

[19] Montaigne is playing on the uncertain etymology of *putain*, from the Latin adjec-tive *putidus*, rotten, stinking, foul: the prostitute's body was not just a site of moral rot; her humoral constitution was associated with a foul smell.

passion for his theme, similarly 'traine languissant ... ne vous donne point de coeur, car luy mesmes n'en a point' (drags it out languidly ... he does not hearten you, for he has no heart) (p. 716). Thus to agitate is to 'put heart into' a text, speech, particularly when the form is poetry, and into the writer, speaker, reader or listener, or viewer; this also holds for painting.[20]

We might conceptualize the particular movement and energy that is 'agitation' in terms of the role of the unconscious in creative production; Montaigne already uses adverbs such as 'elsewhere' and 'beyond' to locate it. The association between 'agitations' and what we do not or cannot know is important, as the next example, more neutral than positive in value, confirms. 'Nostre sagesse mesme ... suit pour la plus part la conduicte au hazard. Ma volonté et mon discours se remue tantost d'un air, tantost d'un autre, et y a plusieurs de ces mouvemens qui se gouvernent sans moy. Ma raison a des impulsions et agitations journallieres et casuelles' (even our wisdom ... for the most part is led by chance. My will and my reasoning move this way and that, and many of these movements are independent of me. There are daily changes in my reason which are contingent and unsettling) (p. 934). The explicit cause here is chance, but it is neither a sufficient nor exhaustive explanation; so let us keep the possibility of unconscious factors in play for now, and explore other more troubling examples of 'agitation' before concluding.

The need for 'agitation tumultuaire' is characteristic of those who, unlike Montaigne, depend on societal approval and recognition: 'voyez les gens appris à se laisser emporter et saisir, ils le font par tout ... à ce qui ne les touche point comme à ce qui les touche: ils s'ingerent indifferemment où il y a de la besogne et l'obligation, et sont sans vie quand ils sont sans agitation tumultuaire' (observe the people who have learned to let themselves be seized and carried away; this is how they always behave, whether touched or not: they get involved indiscriminately, wherever there is business and obligation, and are not alive without agitation and turmoil) (p. 1004).

This form of 'agitation', imaginary recognition, is a form of flight from a different kind of 'agitation' we suffer, which makes us anxious: 'l'agitation de nostre esprit nous apporte de maladies' (mental agitation makes us ill) (p. 491), 'agitations que nous recevons par l'impression de l'opinion et science que nous pensons avoir des choses' (the disturbances caused by the impression we have of knowledge of things) (p. 503). 'Agitation' associated with the knowledge we only imagine we have, self-deluding failure to understand, fearful ignorance taken for knowledge – and paradoxically, without (equally false) calm resulting. So it relates both to self-deception and to that which does not deceive, namely, anxiety, which signals the presence of what we can neither bear nor put into words.

My last example of the force of this term is even more traumatic and more closely linked to limits and edges; here, the edge of reason. In the 'Apologie'

---

[20] See I, 24, p. 127.

'agitation' is twice linked to madness and means passion or strong emotion; it shakes or disturbs the figurative body of the soul – or psyche: 'chez un philosophe, une ame devient l'ame d'un fol, troublée, renversée et perdue: ce que plusieurs occasions produisent, comme une agitation trop vehemente que, par quelque forte passion, l'ame peut engendrer en soy mesme' (a philosopher's soul becomes that of a madman, troubled, disordered, lost: there are many causes for this, such as the excessive disturbance that the soul can engender in itself through some strength of passion) (p. 551). Montaigne's reflections on madness earlier in the chapter were more acutely focused: why is there such a danger of exceptional wisdom and creativity disintegrating into madness? 'Des rares et vifves agitations de nos ames [sc. naissent] les plus excellents manies et les plus detraquées' (the most intense and unhinging of manias are born of the most rare and lively disturbances of our souls) (p. 492): so close were the antithetical qualities in his example, Tasso, that this closeness requires an oxymoron, the 'vivacité meurtriere' (murderous vivacity) of his mind.[21] The limits to his understanding of the problem are conveyed by the trajectory from the chaotic mobility of figurative 'agitations', the intuition of there being only a fine line between wisdom and madness, to their collapsing together, as conveyed by the oxymoron: but Montaigne does not understand why or how that line is crossed. That he thinks it a line seems clear: Tasso, he says, no longer knows himself, 'mesconnoissant … soy' (not recognizing himself), but is no longer himself, 'survivant à soy-mesmes' (surviving himself) (p. 492). Montaigne has arrived at a limit to his understanding and to what he thinks it is to be a human individual – or is the latter a misunderstanding produced by the former? This would be uncharacteristic of Montaigne: precisely because he accepts the limits of what he can know, his thinking is not constrained by the need to seem to know, but rather can remain in play without driving towards an answer. Limits free.

However, the questions which proliferate without anwers here suggest some anxiety, particularly when taken in conjunction with that drawing of a line, which suggests the excessive certainty that is equally symptomatic of anxiety. Montaigne is not prone to anxiety, but does acknowledge when he feels it. Again, 'agitation' is in the frame: 'la plus penible assiette pour moy, c'est estre suspens és choses qui pressent, et agité entre la crainte et esperance' (for me the most painful situation is to remain in suspense about pressing matters, torn between fear and hope) (p. 644): anxious ambivalence when confronting an unpredictable outcome – but not anxiety about death. He has no doubt he will die; this knowledge does not unsettle him, and he has come to have no desire to live or think differently so as to alter his relationship with his mortality.

---

[21] This is not the place for detailed analysis of this topic, and, in particular, how melancholia, genius and madness are conceptualized in the *Essais* and in the early modern period more generally. For discussion see for instance Screech, *Montaigne and Melancholy*, and for more general studies, see Klibansky, Panofsky and Saxl, *Saturn and Melancholy* (London, 1964), Kristeva, *Soleil noir* (Paris, 1987), Schiesari, *The Gendering of Melancholia* (Ithaca, 1992), and Dandrey, *Les Tréteaux de Saturne* (Paris, 2003).

What provokes anxiety is not mortality but encounters with phenomena which seem deadly. Take hatred: 'ce qu'on hait, on le prend à coeur. Cettuy-cy nous souhaitoit du mal, estoit passionné du desir de nostre ruine' (we take what we hate to heart. That man wished us harm – he passionately desired our destruction) (p. 304); but we might equally well include dogma, which is deadly in its *excess* of certitude. He recoils from Reformers' questioning of the traditional criteria of religious 'truths': 'on a mis aucuns articles de sa religion *en doubte et à la balance*' (articles of their religion have been *called into doubt, their validity weighed up*) (p. 439, my italics). Illegitimate scepticism, being directed against what he believed to be beyond human reason. The use of 'en doubte et à la balance' identifies the Reformers' appeal to individual conscience (which might void any standard of truth) in matters of belief as a misdirected form of scepticism. But Montaigne's criticism of their thinking (which is simultaneously tacitly a defence of his own, legitimate scepticism) slides the terms of the discussion away from epistemology. The problem as stated here identifies the affects and self-deception to which these believers were vulnerable: 'se laissant emporter à la fortune et aux apparences … la hardiesse de mespriser… il jette en incertitude … secoue comme un joug tyrannique' (let themselves be carried away by chance and appearances … the excessive boldness of despising … cast into uncertainty … shake off, like a tyrannical yoke) (p. 439). The violence and excess in their 'reasoning' seems symptomatic of the self-deceptions that taint and give excessive scope to human reason. The problem of individual conscience for Montaigne can be understand as being, as much as a problem of standards of truth, a problem of narcissism at its most self-deceiving – excessive love of one's own position at the cost of hatred for the other's. Either way, a problem of intolerance.

I shall return shortly, in the context of tickling, to the wars and to the attendant themes of excess and also of *méconnaissance*, that is, alienated misunderstanding and imaginary illusion of knowledge of the kind that Montaigne rails against, particularly Reformers' dogmatism: the specific, fundamentally problematic instance of imagining that one's own human reason can make claims to know, let alone with certitude, that which belongs only to God to know. This matters, not least, as a clear example of Montaigne not working with a simple opposition between reason and illusion: he is as interested in the illusion of reason and also in locating both reason and illusion in relation to what belongs beyond human reason.

Before turning to the theme of tickling, it is more logical to explore further the notion of shaking, turning from 'agitation', which is quite diffuse, to the more precise 'secousses' (jolts) and and 'secouer' (to jolt), along with 'esbranlements' (shaking) and 'esbranler' (to shake). Let us see how instances of these figures work at the limits, whether of the 'body' or of thinking itself, and also their performative significance as textual effects.

staccato   *joking the ?d??*

'Nostre vie n'est que mouvement. Je m'esbranle difficilement'

In a discussion towards the end of 'De la vanité' Montaigne draws attention to ways in which his writing tends to shake the reader: ways in which it goes adrift, and how disruptive his changes of subject can be (p. 994), as can the shortness of his early chapters. His rationale is twofold: the kind of writing he prefers, namely poetry's jumping and leaping ('à sauts et à gambades' (p. 994)), and classical prose which shares such 'viguere et hardiesse' (vigour and daring) (p. 995); and the kind of reader he has in mind, with the agility and energy to follow the movement of his ideas: a reader who, like him, enjoys the 'vive secousse' (lively jolt) (p. 146) of poetry. Another simple example of this textual effect is the recurrence of chapter titles without direct bearing on what follows. While their relevance may subsequently emerge, the initial effect may be dislocation or deviation; the well-trained reader is not introduced as she expects to what will follow, and so must be more self-sufficient and alert.

As Tournon's edition of the Bordeaux copy of the *Essais* so compellingly demonstrates, another site of examples is Montaigne's use of punctuation marks in keeping with what is sinewy, compressed, vigorous and brusque in his writing (p. 175). Their effects include giving additional salience to paradoxes and contradictions as they unfold in the text. Compare for instance: 'si je parle diversement de moy, c'est que je me regarde diversement. Toutes les contrarietez s'y trouvent, selon quelque tour et en quelque façon. Honteux, insolent; chaste, luxurieux; bavard, taciturne; laborieux, delicat; ingenieux, hebeté; chagrin, debonaire; menteur, veritable; sçavant, ignorant, et liberal, et avare, et prodigue' (I speak about myself in diverse ways because I look at myself in diverse ways. This turn, that quality … I find every kind of contradiction in me. Sheepish, insolent; chaste, lascivious; talkative, taciturn; tough, delicate; clever, dull; glum, congenial; lying, truthful; learned, ignorant; liberal, and miserly and prodigal) (Villey and Saulnier, p. 335), and: '… Honteux insolent, chaste luxurieux, bavard taciturne, laborieux délicat, ingénieux hébété, chagrin débonnaire, menteur veritable, savant ignorant et liberal et avare et prodigue' (sheepish insolent, chaste lascivious, talkative taciturn, tough delicate, clever dull, glum congenial, lying truthful, learned ignorant and liberal and miserly and prodigal) (Tournon, p. 21).[22] Or: 'qu-iray-je choisir? Ce qu'il vous plaira, pourveu que

[22] *Montaigne Essais II*, ed. Tournon (Paris, 2003). See Tournon's articles on Montaigne's singular practice: 'Un langage coupé', in La Charité (ed.), *Writing the Renaissance* (Lexington, Ky., 1992), pp. 219–31, 'Syntaxe et scansion: l'énergie du "langage coupé" et la censure éditoriale', in O'Brien, Quainton and Supple (eds), *Montaigne et la rhétorique* (Paris, 1995), pp. 117–33, 'La Segmentation du texte', in Blum and Tournon (eds), *Éditer les Essais de Montaigne* (Paris, 1997), pp. 173–83, 'L'Inquiétante Segmentation des *Essais*', *Le Discours Psychanalytique* 18 (1997), pp. 277–306, and '"Ny de la ponctuation": sur quelques avatars de la segmentation autographe des *Essais*', *Nouvelle Revue du seizième siècle* 17/1 (1999), pp. 147–59. For discussion of Tournon's edition together with others' (such as Simonin and Céard), see O'Brien, 'Are we Reading what Montaigne Wrote?', *French Studies* LVIII/4 (2004), pp. 527–32.

vous choisissez! Voilà une sotte response, à laquelle pourtant il semble que tout
le dogmatisme arrive, par qui il ne nous est pas permis d'ignorer ce que nous
ignorons' (what shall I choose? Whatever you like, so long as you choose! What
a stupid answer, and yet this is where all dogmatism, which does not allow us
not to know what we don't know, seems to lead) (Villey and Saulnier, p. 504)
and: '"qu'irai-je choisir? – Ce qu'il vous plaira pourvu que vous choisissiez."
Voilà une sotte réponse. À laquelle pourtant il semble que tout le dogmatisme
arrive. Par qui il ne nous est pas permis d'ignorer ce que nous ignorons' ('what
shall I choose? – Whatever you like, so long as you choose.' What a stupid
answer. Yet this is where all dogmatism seems to lead. It does not allow us not
to know what we don't know) (Tournon, p. 274).

Finally for now we might consider the effect of the list of customs in 'De la
coustume' which stretches extravagantly over some three pages (pp. 112–15),
and includes many instances that were shocking or strange to Montaigne's
contemporary readers. However, it is the proliferation of such instances without
perspective or comment, with neither logic nor guidance, and no structuring
indication of what the limits to the catalogue might be, which jolts the reader,
example after example. This performatively makes Montaigne's point about the
anaesthetizing effects of our own culture's habits and the need to shake up our
torpid judgement, preparing it to extend its horizons.

If thinking is not to congeal, the narrow limits of habitual reasoning and
the desire for certainty should be resisted. At times in the *Essais* it seems that
scepticism is called for: 'toute presupposition humaine et toute enunciation a
autant d'authorité que l'autre, si la raison n'en faict la difference. Ainsin il
les faut toutes mettre à la balance: et premierement les generalles, et celles
qui nous *tyrannisent*' (every human presupposition and every enunciation has
as much authority as any other, unless reason differentiates between them. So
they must all be weighed on the scales, starting with general assumptions, and
those that *tyrannize* us) (pp. 540–1, my italics). That is, as Plutarch via La
Boétie and Montaigne remind us, we need to be able to say 'no', to resist and
open-mindedly question. However, the phenomenology of thinking represented
in the *Essais* emphasizes the difficulty of sustaining that capacity to suspend
judgement: it cannot be done without our being shaken or jolted, and without
engaging our shaky powers of understanding and reasoning. 'Mon entendement ne va pas tousjours avant ... c'est un mouvement d'yvroigne titubant,
vertigineux, informe' (my understanding does not always make smoothe onward
progress ... it moves like a drunk, staggering, dizzy, all over the place) (p.
964).[23] It is all very well for Socrates, say, to keep thinking moving; but moving
turns out to be uncomfortable to the point of perturbation and dislocation, even
when these effects are given positive value in the text. So how do we sustain
the disquiet as well as pleasure of thinking? Or in the psychic economy, such
affects as anger and fear, which is closely linked to desire?

---

[23] For a similar representation of reason's emphatically shaky gait see above, p. 171.

continued movement vs discont[?]

To keep thinking moving means allowing affect and thought to combine and for thinking to be in accord with the principle of being in the *Essais*: 'nostre vie n'est que mouvement' (our life is nothing but movement) (p. 1095). This principle is eloquently laid out in 'Du repentir' but given abyssal form at the end of the 'Apologie': 'et nous, et nostre jugement, et toutes choses mortelles, vont coulant et roulant sans cesse ... quant et l'estre tout un, change aussi l'estre tout simplement, devenant tousjours autre d'un autre' (we and our judgement, and all mortal things, go on flowing and rolling ceaselessly ... that which changes, while being the same, changes its simple being, an other always becoming other) (pp. 601, 603). But where 'couler' and 'rouler' suggest that our essential mobility is fluid and continuous, elsewhere discontinuity, gaps and fragmentation dominate Montaigne's representation.[24] His writing, which is 'tousjours un' (always one) (p. 964) and 'consubstantiel' (consubstantial) (p. 665) with its writer, is nonetheless only 'une marqueterie mal jointe' (a piece of clumsy marquetry) (p. 964), and to think as one should, and therefore also to live well, is to be shaken, dislocated and perturbed. For the soul to be moved to act well, it must be shaken out of its tranquillity, and for us to become virtuous our already shaky powers of reason must be dislocated: 'les secousses et esbranle-mens que nostre ame reçoit par les passions corporelles, peuvent beaucoup en elle, mais encore plus les siennes propres ... sans leur agitation, elle resteroit sans action ... par la dislocation que les passions apportent à nostre raison, nous devenons vertueux' (the jolts and shaking that our soul receives from the corporeal passions have great impact on her, but her own, even more so ... without their agitation, she would remain becalmed ... it is the passions' dislocations of our reason that make us virtuous) (pp. 567–8).

---

[24] One might also align this with the symbolic system of language as theorized by Lacan: mobility, difference, gaps and incompletion are its features, and there must always be another 'move in the game'. Thus mobility is fundamentally connected with doubt and scepticism in Lacan as well as in the *Essais*:

> vous ne savez que trop ... la manifeste discordance entre les différents systèmes symboliques qui ordonnent les actions, les systèmes religieux, juridique, scientifique, politique. Il n'y a ni super-position, ni conjonction de ces références, il y a entre elles béances, failles, déchirures. C'est pourquoi, nous ne pouvons concevoir le discours humain comme unitaire. Toute emission de parole est toujours, jusqu'à un certain point, dans une nécessité interne d'erreur. Nous voici donc amenés, en apparence, à un pyrrhonisme historique qui suspend la valeur de vérité de tout ce que la voix humaine peut émettre, la suspend à l'attente d'une totalisation future.

> (you know only too well ... the manifest discordance between the different symbolic systems which prescribe action, the religious, juridical, scientific, political systems. There is neither superposition nor conjunction of these references – between them, there are gaps, faults, rents. That is why we cannot conceive of human discourse as being unitary. Every emission of speech is always, up to a certain point, under an inner necessity to err. So we are led, it would appear, to a historical Pyrrhonism which suspends the truth-value of everything which the human voice can emit, suspends it in the expectation of a future totalisation.) Lacan, *Le Séminaire I*, p. 291.

Productive shaking takes the form of the kind of performative textual effect discussed above; or, given the overestimation of reason's dignity and power, the personification of understanding as staggering, dizzy, all over the place, is designed to shake the reader out of complacency by dint of dramatic belittling. Similarly, disillusioned recognition of the shakiness of understanding is called for – but here, its fragility and vulnerability are also acknowledged, along with its lack of power, by the comparison which follows, with 'des joncs que l'air manie casuellement selon soy' (reeds that the wind stirs haphazardly, as it wills) (p. 964).

In order to underline what is at stake let's turn to the example of Montaigne's critique of Luther, and then to a possible antithesis, Socrates. According to Montaigne, Lutheran ideas are redolent of the desire that 'suborns' the subject (p. 1013). They are the product of, and incite to, 'le zele' (zeal) (p. 1013); they claim the monopoly on truth. They disguise mixed motives and difficult passions, 'leur cholere et leur haine' (their anger and hatred), and 'un autre principe plus caché' (another more hidden origin) (p. 1012); Montaigne figures this state of being as fever and infection, as are the extremist alignments he eschews: 'd'une si violente obligation que mon entendement s'en infecte' (with so violent an obligation that my understanding is infected) (p. 1012). What is 'wrong' is lack of balance, that is, the lack of capacity to see both or all sides (and in humoral medicine, it is lack of balance that produces disease). Luther's failure is to sufficiently doubt his own thinking, his false certitude disguised by identifying tyranny with what he attacked, rather than recognizing that of his own position: 'c'est tousjours un aigreur tyrannique de ne pouvoir souffrir une forme diverse à la sienne' (it is always tyrannical ill humour to be unable to tolerate a position different from your own) (p. 928). Unshakable conviction or dogmatism; Luther exemplifies the dangers of failing to doubt, and of the unfreedom that is the tyranny of certitude, in its refusal to allow other views and in the limits imposed by the desire for certitude and its persistence on the certitude-seeker's freedom to think differently. If the beloved self-ideal requires certitudes, this is not only an unfreedom for the subject but also diminishes others' freedom – not only in their views but, as in this war, to worship differently, to inhabit the same place, even to live.

Allowing one's ideas to be shaken, on the contrary, is disillusionment, openness to dialogue and to the possibility of change, and self-doubt, as embodied by Socrates. 'Apres que Socrates fut adverti que le Dieu de sagesse luy avoit attribué le surnom de sage, il en fut estonné; et, se recherchant et secouant par tout, n'y trouvoit aucun fondement à cette divine sentence' (when Socrates was told that the god of wisdom called him wise, he was astonished; he searched his mind and shook himself thoroughly, but could find no basis for this divine judgement) (p. 498). Montaigne, 'moy qui la [sc. la raison] secoue vivement et attentivement' (I who shake my reason energetically and attentively) (p. 815), enacts a similar self-shaking: 'les faux pas que ma memoire m'a faict si souvant … ne se sont pas inutilement perduz: elle a beau me jurer à cette heure et m'asseurer, je secouë les oreilles' (the missteps my memory has so often taken

fear

have not been lost on me: there is no point her swearing loyalty now and assuring me she is trustworthy, I shake my ears) (p. 1074). I shake my head and refuse to believe my ears.

Socrates, too, could be shaken, in such a way that his judgement and virtue were blocked; this demonstrates not weakness so much as the limits to human wisdom:

> on luy voyoit estonner et renverser toutes ses facultez par la seule morsure d'un chien malade, et n'y avoir si grande fermeté de discours, nulle suffisance, nulle vertu, nulle resolution philosophique, nulle contention de ses forces, qui la peut exempter de la subjection de ces accidens; la salive d'un chien mastin, versée sur la main de Socrates, secouër toute sa sagesse et toutes ses grandes et si reglées imaginations, les aneantir de maniere qu'il ne restat aucune trace de sa connoissance premiere. (p. 550)

> (they saw all its [sc. the soul's] faculties stunned and turned upside down simply by the bite of a sick dog; no amount of firmness of judgement, good qualities, virtue, philosophical resolve or tensing of its powers could save it from such accidents. The slaver of some mastiff on Socrates's hand could shake all his wisdom, all his great, disciplined ideas, wiping them out so that no trace would remain of his former understanding.)

Not even a bite, just a lick: at the limits, when the fear of death takes hold and shakes us,[25] wisdom lacks force, and what is only a form of touch to the skin, the limit of the body, is experienced as annihilation. Fear is itself already an eloquent example of the psychic economy of human understanding and its limits, and of ways in which Montaigne thinks about the power of affect. His chapter on fear opens with an admission of how little he knows about it, and goes on to describe its effects as follows:

> je ne suis pas bon naturaliste ... et ne sçay guiere par quels ressors la peur agit en nous; mais tant y a que c'est une estrange passion: et disent les medecins qu'il n'en est aucune qui emporte plustost nostre jugement hors de sa deuë assiette. De vray, j'ay veu beaucoup de gens devenus insensez de peur: et aux plus rassis, il est certain, pendant que son accés dure, qu'elle engendre de terrible esblouissemens. (p. 75)

> (I am not a good natural philosopher ... and have very little understanding of how fear acts in us; but I do know that it is a strange passion; and doctors say that there is nothing like it for violently unseating our judgement. Truly, I have seen many people driven out of their minds by fear; and it is certain that, while it grips us, it engenders terrible astonishment in even the most grounded of people.)

---

[25] See 'Que philosopher c'est apprendre à mourir' ('To philosophize is to learn how to die') for the association between death and being shaken (p. 91).

In the absence of understanding, fear. It acts in, not on, us, and is 'estrange', that is, alien, in us but not of us (or not in a way that we can recognize as being ours), and alienating: here the dislocation is such as to displace our judgement and drive us out of our minds. The description seems to presuppose a proper place within the person for such faculties as judgement and mind, that powerful affect has the force to dislodge or dislocate them, and in consequence they lose their function. English also offers these kinds of figures – out of our minds, beside ourselves; but whilst both French and English figures speak to us in-tuitively, how fear 'gets in', or is already 'in', us, and whether it is, rather, an aspect of ourselves which is 'ours' even if it feels strange or alienating, remain unexplained.

An apparently similar limit in relation to desire and hope helps us take the analysis a step further: 'nous ne sommes jamais chez nous, nous sommes toujours au delà. La crainte, le desir, l'esperance nous eslancent vers l'advenir, et nous desrobent le sentiment et la consideration de ce qui est, pour amuser à ce qui sera, voire quand nous ne serons plus' (we are never at home; we are always beyond. Fear, desire and hope propel us towards the future, and rob us of feelings and concern for what is, diverting us with what will be, even when we shall be no more) (p. 15). First, the idea of our having a proper place is problematized: if we are always 'beyond', then does this beyond not become our place?[26] And if our proper place is experienced as being at home (insofar as we are ever there), is there not already a sort of gap or difference between the subject qua articulating consciousness and the place recognized as being his or her own? A similar point echoes this later in the *Essais*: 'chacun court ailleurs et à l'advenir, d'autant que nul n'est arrivé à soy' (everyone rushes elsewhere, into the future, for no one has reached his own self) (p. 1045). The self is always still being sought, in a way of being that seems both teleological but not, in its actuality of constant movement in the present without arrival at the desired goal. The subject is in fact caught between the past (having failed to arrive) and the future; in other words, between lack and desire.

By locating what complicates the subject's relationship with him or herself in terms of fear, lack and desire, Montaigne identifies what is specific to being human in terms of human temporality and our relationship with our mortality, when we are no more. The text invokes Plato at this point: 'fay ton faict et te cognoy ... Et qui se cognoist ... refuse les occupations superflues et les pensées et propositions inutiles' (do what you must and know yourself ... And whoever knows himself ... rejects superfluous issues and useless thoughts and proposi-tions) (p. 15). Apparently a cure for such dislocations; however, self-knowledge also involves acceptance of the force of fear and desire, which are not thoughts or resolutions but have to do with different aspects of our being, and may not even fall within our conscious knowledge of, or consciously knowable, self.

[26] The quotation is from the chapter entitled 'Nos affections s'emportent au delà de nous': all our feelings, it seems, 'get carried away beyond us' (tr. Screech, p. 11).

Later in the *Essais* there will be tranquil acceptance of 'inquietude et ... irresolution. Aussi sont ce nos maistresses qualitez, et praedominantes' (disquiet and ... lack of resolution. These are our dominant, ruling qualities) (p. 988). Disquiet is not fear, but the notion that disquiet is an essential part of being human is far from the version of the self to be known in that earlier chapter. It implies the presence of the unknown or unknowable in the subject or in the subject's relationship with the world. What is key is the difference between when we are no more, as what preoccupies us, and 'irresolution'; this is the Montaigne who is so emphatic that death is the end of life but not the end that governs life. This way of (thinking about) living is more consonant with his non-teleological writing, with the capacity for desire to be present-oriented rather than a way of imagining the future, indeed that there is a future, and sets the conditions in which doubtful thinking can be enjoyed, even when it shakes us up or brings us up against unsettling limits: 'je ne l'entreprens ... pour le parfaire; j'entreprens seulement de me branler, pendant que le branle me plaist' (I do not undertake it ... to complete it; I undertake it solely to move around, while I still enjoy moving) (p. 977). Without this, it would be impossible to sustain the doubtful play of his thinking and writing: 'je ne trace aucune ligne certaine' (I trace no fixed line) (p. 985).

Tranquillity is both an apparent good, to be reached by certain forms of doubt, but also that which needs to be sacrificed for living well, mobility and doubtful thinking to be possible. Shaking is a necessary and productive process but can nonetheless also flag danger and failure to live well. The problem addressed by this array of figures, and the text's interest in different forms of impact on the capacity to reason and understand or judge, had already frequently preoccupied critics of scepticism: the relationship between suspension of judgement and living.[27] In Montaigne's hands, what is it really like to be a doubtful thinker, and what is its impact on the person? In his exploration of the issues that shake humans, he does not offer a clear taxonomy; instead, the text gives shaking a therapeutic and performative dimension. Textual shaking keeps unsettling the reader by the mobility and lack of predictability of its functions, and invites her to develop her own awareness of different kinds of shaking, productive and unproductive, pleasurable or painful or a combination of the two, as part of the process of developing her knowledge of herself as a doubtful, but, when appropriate, also impassioned reader and thinker.

'(Why) can't you tickle yourself?'[28]

Tickling, used figuratively, is as mobile as the vocabulary of shaking. For instance: 'la pluspart des plaisirs ... nous chatouillent et embrassent pour nous es-

---

[27] See Burnyeat, 'Can the Skeptic live his Skepticism?', in Burnyeat (ed.), *The Skeptical Tradition* (Berkeley, 1983), pp. 117–48.

[28] Blakemore, Wolpert and Firth, 'Why Can't You Tickle Yourself?', *Neuroreport* 11/11 (3 August 2000), pp. 11–16 (my brackets).

tickling

trangler' (most pleasures ... tickle and embrace us only to strangle us) (p. 245) and: 'il y a quelque contentement qui me chatouille à faire une action juste, et contenter autruy' (when I act justly, and make others content, a certain pleasure tickles me) (p. 63). It figures the dangerous seductiveness of pleasure and, by being linked with the verb 'to embrace', erotic pleasures which are singled out as being particularly addictive; but it also can convey the pleasure of doing good. Both appeal via the subject's narcissism, which makes the second example ethically ambiguous: the prospect of the other person's contentment that encourages me to do good is matched by my own. It is not developed into a reflection on the ethical implications of mixed motives, particularly if the self-interest is not conscious, but has the potential to raise such questions.

This is a hallmark of figurative tickling: it gestures towards ambiguities or different interpretative possibilities, as well as conveying an array of connections between pleasure and knowledge. Its mobility is increased, as is that of shaking, by its use as a reflexive verb and in such constructions as 'se laisser chatouiller' (to let oneself be tickled). But these, particularly the reflexive verb, may be more complex when used of tickling than of shaking. After all, as cognitive neurologists now assert with utter confidence: 'It is well known that you cannot tickle yourself.' Why? 'Such attenuation of self-produced tactile stimulation is due to the sensory predictions made by an internal forward model of the motor system.'[29] To translate: if we already know what being tickled feels like, our anticipation means we cannot reproduce the effect, for it relies on surprise and unpredictability.[30]

Cognitive neurology's answer seems precise and certain. Nonetheless tickling is on the minds of over seven million of us and rising – just Google: 'can one tickle oneself?', or variants: 'why can't I/you/one tickle my/your/oneself?' Perhaps we do not know our neurology, or are not quite persuaded, despite its assertions and supporting data; or perhaps the questions that tickling and tickling oneself raise for us are not those of neurologists, important though theirs are. For them it is a way of developing understanding of 'sensory feedback', the roles played by the somatosensory cortex and/or the cerebellum, that is, how the brain registers sensations; but further questions remain, all the more so if tickling is figurative as well as literal, as in the *Essais* – where at times it even plays between its literal denotation and its figurative connotations. Here it touches on predictability and unpredictability, but is also related to the desire for knowledge, to the pleasure of thinking, and to ways in which it may be possible to think and understand oneself differently.

Before returning to the *Essais* let us turn to a different source of insight, one perhaps more attuned than neurology to the kind of thinking Montaigne offers: children can tell us a thing or two about what we do and don't know – or have

---

[29] The two sentences quoted are the first two sentences of the abstract of the Blakemore, Wolpert and Firth article.
[30] See Phillips, 'On Tickling', in *On Kissing, Tickling and Being Bored* (London, 1993), pp. 1–4.

forgotten we know. Children know that you can only successfully tickle yourself on your tongue – and then not always.[31] They remind us that there are many ways of knowing things, including knowing their idiosyncracy and uncertainty, and that one of the obstacles to remembering what one knows is to want too much to know it, in the belief that one does not. Instead of striving and Googling and turning to cognitive neurology, let's be open to remembering, to being at the disposition of our knowledge, able still to be surprised by it – that is, able to be tickled. What children's thinking about tickling also reminds us is that it has to do with shared knowledge, and how knowledge is used: children know who knows, and who doesn't, where they are ticklish, and also know who they trust to tickle them. Tickling may be playful, but it is always a seductive game. In the hands of Montaigne, this opens onto questions of reading and being read, the relationship between writer and reader, and what makes knowledge and thinking alluring.

If for current neurologists tickling is an important experimental site which extends understanding of neurological function and dysfunction, this does not account for why questions to do with tickling fascinate the millions who Google it and doubtless many more besides. Let's suppose both that early modern subjects were in their own ways fascinated by it, that Montaigne's play with it appeals to existing interest and questions; also that, because tickling has to do with what is idiosyncratic and seems very intimately personal, in terms of what an individual knows about his or her sensations and pleasures, to be interested in tickling is a way of puzzling narcissistically over not only the particular relationship between one's own sensations, pleasures and self-knowledge but also over the relationship between what is particular and what is generalizable. Tickling dramatizes this relationship, whether as a problem for philosophy or as an issue in erotic life. Moreover, it raises the question: to whom might I trust this idiosyncratic and intimate knowledge about myself? The risk of the result being disappointing, futile or, worse, painful, is high – what child does not know how unpleasant it is to be tickled too much? If we imagine tickling as an analogy for the play of conversation as we enjoy it, and then think of the climate in which Montaigne, a lover of conversation, wrote, when knowing whom to trust was a more complex (because potentially more dangerous) issue than for us, we can see why the exchange of ideas might seem to be a ticklish business. Not only in conversation; also in print – witness the vicissitudes of *De la servitude volontaire*, the risk to the *Essais* of Papal censure, and also, to cite just one other instance, the reception of Castellio's *De Haereticis*, a sceptical questioning of the grounds for killing heretics. The implications of its scepticism for Calvinist certitude in matters of religious belief may have been radical, but it was not an attack on Reformation. However, Bèze quickly published an

---

[31] My thanks to Emily and James for this. (Unknown virtual others, however, claim instead that tickling oneself is only possible on the roof of the mouth.)

attack on Castellio: such certitudes were those of the true Christian. Castellio's response was not published.[32]

In the *Essais* the significations of tickling, being tickled, tickling oneself and what is ticklish range from enlivening and unmixed enjoyment, through the paradoxical subjective reality of fantasy, and painfully excessive experiences (including what had been pleasure initially), to premonition of death. In all instances, the association between tickling and eroticized pleasure is strong: not just explicitly erotic pleasures but also the pleasures of reading and thinking. It may be that the precariousness of tickling – the idiosyncrasy of it combined with that split-second shift from pleasure to unpleasure, that too-convulsive laughter that signals that enjoyment has become *jouissance* – is an index of the erotic.

Tickling is mobile enough to figure positive, negative or ambiguous experience, and also functions as a way of testing certain givens, not least philosophical ones, as well as, via the dimension of enjoyment, opening up how we think about what we want to know, or know differently. What this mobility suggests is that one reason for its effectiveness in the text is precisely the unpredictability of its meaning in any given context: it tickles the reader into alertness to the play of meaning and the pleasures of the text, and to what the enjoyment of reading has to do with desire and embodiment.

Montaigne uses tickling very simply at times. It is in the more specific uses of tickling in relation to erotic enjoyment that its complexities have more resonance. It conveys something about the nature of desire: 'les dames ne chatouillent celuy qui en joyt à coeur saoul' (ladies do not tickle the man who enjoys them to excess) (p. 264). Or, we might say, desire is always the desire for something else, not for what one has; as for tickling, its elusive pleasures may be greater in anticipation than in the event (the principle of deferral) and nonstop tickling would cease to give pleasure, but would instead be painful or lose its charm and become indifferent. It also speaks of Freud's pleasure principle, as the trajectory towards indifference hints.

> Ce mesme chatouillement et esguisement qui se rencontre en certains plaisirs et semble nous enlever au dessus de la santé simple et de l'indolence [that is, lack of suffering], cette volupté active, mouvante, et je ne sçay comment, cuisante et mordante, celle là mesme ne vise qu'à l'indolence comme à son but. L'appetit qui nous ravit à l'accointance des femmes, il ne cherche qu'à chasser la peine que nous apporte le desir ardent et furieux. (p. 493)

> (That same tickling and jab of enjoyment that we find in certain pleasures, which seems to lift us beyond mere health and lack of suffering, that active, stimulating, inexplicably burning, biting voluptuousness, even this only aims, in the end, at freedom from sensation. The appetite that drives us so avidly to desire women seeks only to chase away the pain caused us by ardent, fierce desire.)

---

[32] For further discussion, see Popkin, *The History of Scepticism from Erasmus to Spinoza*, pp. 8–14.

'"Enjoy as little as possible" (which is why Freud originally called it the *unpleasure* principle). Pleasure is the safeguard of a state of homeostasis and constancy which *jouissance* constantly threatens to disrupt and traumatize.'[33] Tickling is only enjoyable when the tickler knows when to stop (before it switches to being the painful excess that is *jouissance*), and the aftermath of being well tickled is languid contentment. So tickling, at its most erotically or relationally effective, relies on certain kinds of good judgement and attunement, precise understanding of the complexities of the process involved – whether it be literally tickling, or sexual pleasure, or the communication and exchange of understanding, whether in writing and reading or in conversation (which is, after all, also a form of intercourse – in the *Essais*, 'commerce'). In other words, knowing one's desire.

Tickling also enables Montaigne to convey the paradoxical power of another aspect of psychic economy, fantasy, which also challenges entrenched overvaluations of human reason. Consider this passage at the end of 'De la diversion' ('On diversion'):

> une resverie sans corps et sans sujet la [sc. nostre ame] regente et l'agite. Que je me jette à faire des chateaux en Espaigne, mon imagination m'y forge des commoditez et des plaisirs desquels mon ame est reellement chatouillée et resjouye. Combien de fois ... nous inserons en des passions fantastiques qui nous alterent et l'ame et le corps. (p. 839)

> (a reverie with neither body nor subject rules and agitates it [the soul]. If I get caught up in building castles in the air, my imagination conjures up comforts and pleasures there which really tickle and delight my soul. How often ... we are drawn into fantastical passions which transform both our souls and our bodies.)

For all that we are substance and soul, our fantasy or daydream, in which the usual laws of logic, time and space, accountability and probability do not apply, has a subjective reality with the power to alter our sense of who we are. As a way of staging our desire it tells us something fundamental about ourselves, about the relationship between the soul and other aspects of our being, and, in so doing, alters us and how we understand ourselves and our souls – our psyches. Castles in the air, far from being trivial distraction, are a valuable source of self-knowledge. The strangeness of fantasy is concisely conveyed by the unmotivated shift from castles in the air to tickling – no logic in this, just as there would not be in a dream's shifting scenes, but within a remembered dream, this would not be epistemologically troubling.

The importance of the precise qualities of the tickling process is indicated by the comment in 'De la solitude' on pleasures tickling us in order to strangle us. Montaigne reflects not only on the 'price' of pleasure – his example is hangovers – but also the need to be skilled in distinguishing between 'pure' pleasure

---

[33] Evans, entry on 'pleasure principle', *An Introductory Dictionary*, p. 148.

('les vrays plaisirs, et entiers' (true, full pleasures)) and 'mixed' ones ('plaisirs meslez et bigarrez de plus de peine' (mixed pleasures, traced through with pain) (p. 245): we need to know when to stop and also to know what is enjoyable but self-destructive. The use of tickling gives us a conceptual difficulty which compounds the other problem in what is encouraged here: the apparent assumption that humans seek their good and shun what is destructive, and that they even necessarily can tell the difference. Given the omnipresence of narcissistic delusion and the limits to what the subject can know of herself, we arrive at an impasse. To which we have to add that tickling is so specific an experience for each individual that generalizations about the nature of enjoyment cannot readily be made through it – unless, that is, Montaigne is relying on an identificatory reading according to which each reader supplies the specific coordinates of her own tickling pleasure.

That example also suggests Montaigne's alertness to the temporality of fear. In the psychic economy, memory plays its part in generating dread: past experience tells me that it is always possible that what I have experienced, or already have an intimation of, will happen again. Dread or fear are ways of imagining the future, and can be harnessed to help deter us from going on seeking that which causes us danger or pain – 'nous estrangler' (to strangle us). But also, as Montaigne's coupling of tickling and strangling intimates, fear and desire are intimately connected, and we may in fact seek that which causes us pain, desire what we fear, or, as those to whom the theory of the death drive is persuasive would say, we desire our own destruction, the 'indolence' that is a state of inertness.

The instance of tickling in which fear is most pressing is in 'De la physionomie', in which terrain is described as ticklish: 'je m'acheminai à un voyage, par pays estrangement chatouilleux' (I set out on a journey through a particularly ticklish region) (p. 1061). Here, ticklish means where something dreadful has happened, and where, therefore, it may be anticipated, although not with any certainty, that awful things will happen again. The adjective is Janus-faced: it insists on the past while looking to the future, and its presence in the sentence stirs the reader's dread that something terrible would happen, a dread reinforced by the intensifying adverb, 'particularly, strangely'. Montaigne's journey was through death-filled territory in which battles had been fought between Huguenots and Roman Catholics and which was still not secured: dangerous terrain, as Montaigne's narrative will recount. He was captured and robbed, his life at risk for some time. The use of ticklish is concisely, precisely effective, for it conjures up the history of terrible events and heightens the reader's anticipation of them (cushioned by the fact that Montaigne lived to tell the tale). Yet this is the writer who elsewhere declared his inability to tell a good story: 'je ne sçay ny plaire, ny rejouyr, ny chatouiller: le meilleur conte du monde se seche entre mes mains et se ternit' (I don't know how to please, delight or tickle: the best story in the world dries up in my hands and becomes dull) (p. 637).

Two further examples signal the limits of philosophy and of Stoicism in particular, revealing something of Montaigne's model of mind in relation to will, affect and embodied being, and therefore form part of the foundations for his thinking about reading, writing and reader-relations.

First, Stoicism, which had some intermittent appeal to Montaigne. Its significance for him has been widely debated already.[34] Here I need not engage with that debate, as I want simply to consider a critique of Stoicism in the 'Apologie', and what figurative tickling has to do with this. Montaigne is questioning Stoic indifference to physical pain, to pleasure, and to the sublime in the form of religious architecture and ritual. He instances the power of music to move us: 'il n'est coeur ... si dur, que la douceur de la musique n'esveille et ne chatouille' (there is no heart ... so hard that the sweetness of music will not awaken and tickle it) (p. 593). No specificity or idiosyncrasy here; indeed, this is a quite unusually generalized observation. The point is clear, not least because of tickling's play between its more literal and more figurative force, linking the sense of hearing to affect, to the heart that is moved, and refusing to allow that mind voluntarily operates independently of sensation and affect: the will cannot effect this separation. To posit that it does embraces a philosophical stance that cannot really recognize how affect and embodiment may be in play, which restricts both the scope of thinking and its potential as a guide to living well, and one's understanding of what it means to think.

The second comment which brings tickling to bear on philosophy is: 'sentez lire un discours de philosophie: l'invention, l'eloquence, la pertinence frape incontinent vostre esprit et vous esmeut; il n'y a rien qui chatouille ou poigne vostre conscience; ce n'est pas à elle qu'on parle, n'est-il pas vray?' (listen to an example of philosophical reasoning: its invention, eloquence and pertinence immediately strike you and move you; there is nothing that tickles or pricks your conscience; it isn't addressed to her, is it?) (p. 989). Ideas in rhetorically polished form may engage intellect and emotion, but despite moving ('esmeut') the hearer, do not yet tickle, that is, seduce, and so engage the conscience. The kind of thinking that tickles Montaigne involves mind, emotion, conscience and imagination (as the recourse to figuration suggests), but perhaps also something more ambiguous, a touch of eroticism, perhaps? It is not clear how striking, engaging, tickling and pricking are connected; a sequence, on a continuum of increasingly intense effects, or is there a conceptual distinction implied between the first two (a pair?) and the second more dramatically figurative two verbs? The reader is drawn in, to puzzle over the potential meaning and ponder how her own thought processes are engaged and enriched by the force of figuration.

Tickling is a labile term in Montaigne's text, particularly in his literary criticism. At times it figures his enjoyment, but it can equally be used negatively; Montaigne works with tickling's potential to turn from pleasure to unpleasure.

---

[34] See Schmitt and Skinner (eds), *The Cambridge History of Renaissance Philosophy* (Cambridge, 1988), passim; on aspects of Stoicism in the *Essais* see for instance Goyet, 'Montaigne and the Notion of Prudence', and Schneewind, 'Montaigne on Moral Philosophy and the Good Life', in Langer (ed.), *The Cambridge Companion to Montaigne* (Cambridge, 2005), pp. 118–41 and pp. 207–28.

Comparing contemporary Spanish and Petrarchan poetry's fantastical flights of fancy unfavourably to classical poetry, such as Catullus's and Martial's, on the grounds of excessive ornamention, he comments: 'ces premiers là, sans s'esmouvoir et sans se picquer, se font assez sentir: ils ont dequoy rire partout, ils ne faut pas qu'ils se chatouillent: ceux-cy [sc. his contemporaries] ont besoing de secours estrangier: à mesure qu'ils ont moins d'esprit, il leur faut plus de corps' (the former make themselves felt without getting overwrought or over-heated; they are full of laughter, they don't need to tickle themselves; the latter need outside help: the less spirit they have, the more body they need) (p. 412). The metaphors here have immediate force but prove quite unstable: 'outside help' suggests the practice of imitation. But if 'estrangier' is understood to imply estranging, then we can coordinate the terms here: those fantastical flights are extraneous in that they distract from whatever the 'meaning' of the text may be, as well as not being fully integrated into its body (as classical rhetoricians such as Quintilian required). Self-reliance, a form and spirit all their own, is what is valued in the classical texts, and found wanting in the contemporaries'; so too is 'knowing when to stop'. Excess is the flaw in this writing, figured in terms of what the classical ideals do not involve: overwrought, overheated, they have to tickle themselves. Tickling has crossed the limit, moving from pleasure to unpleasure.

Perhaps Montaigne was considering these texts' capacity to give him eroti-cized pleasure, which the overdressed contemporaries fail to do. He had already quite explicitly associated tickling with this form of reading pleasure: 'cette vieille ame poisante ne se laisse plus chatouiller, non seulement à l'Arioste, mais encores au bon Ovide' (my heavy old soul can no longer be tickled, not just by Ariosto but even by an old favourite such as Ovid) (p. 410). The texts he had in mind may well have been *Orlando Furioso* and the *Amores*, which would make it a comparatively simple, although poignant, comment on the reduction, with age, of erotic reading pleasure. However, it is more complex and more revealing about what constitutes the pleasure of the text. The text that tickles – appeals seductively, holds out the promise of intense engagement, unpredictable enjoyment, all in a playful spirit – does so particularly by its language and style; for the sentence ends thus: 'sa [sc. Ovid's] facilité et ses inventions, qui m'ont ravy autrefois, à peine m'entretiennent elles à cette heure' (his fluid inventive-ness, which once entranced me, now scarcely entertains me) (p. 410).

This sorrow over the loss of the seductive pleasures of poetic language echoes his lament elsewhere about the mortifications of age. 'Je merquois autrefois les jours poisans et tenebreux comme extraordinaires: ceux-là sont tantost les miens ordinaires; les extraordinaires sont les beaux et serains ... Que je me chatouille, je ne puis tantost arracher un pauvre rire de ce meschant corps' (in the past, I only rarely experienced dark and difficult days; now they are the norm, and the fine serene ones are rare ... though I tickle myself, I can scarcely wrest a laugh from this wretched body) (p. 842).

Unlike Plato, whose prescription for old men was the vicarious pleasure of watching the beauty and suppleness of the young, his only consolations may be 'fantasie et … songe' (fantasie and daydreaming) (p. 842), or writing. Here tickling – and it seems that Montaigne may believe you can, all being well, tickle yourself – is situated in an interesting texture of physical sensations and moods: serenity, pain, joy, tickling, ending with absence of response. It has both literal and figurative force here, bridging between body and affect, and represents a test of his diminishing sensuality, but with the implication that even his most specific enjoyment eludes him.

The figure returns many pages later, with even greater force, connecting questions of sexual pleasure, desire and also knowledge, in a narrative line linking Montaigne, 'sage Anacreon' and Socrates. Thus Montaigne binds his thinking about the relationship between body, desire, learning and living well to that of a revered Greek lyric poet (who knew a thing or two about love) and to a philosopher he admired greatly, who declared (in the *Symposium*) that: 'the subject of love is the only one I claim to understand'.[35] 'Pendant que … le pouls bat encores … nous avons besoing d'estre sollicitez et chatouillez par quelque agitation mordicante … Et Socrates, plus vieil que je ne suis, parlant d'un object amoureux …' (while we still have a pulse, we need to be entreated, touched and tickled by some intense agitation … And Socrates, older than I am now, speaking of an object of his love …) (p. 892). The thinker and writer in old age needs to be tickled. That is, he needs sexual and sensual pleasure and with it – and this is the critical difference between this passage and the one just cited previously, in which he tickled himself – the relationships in which such pleasures take place. But he needs analogous pleasures also, chiefly the intercourse of conversation or intercourse with texts which combine seduction with bite, pleasure with pleasure-with-a-painful-edge, a paradoxically entertainable and enlivening danger: tickling that knows precisely when to stop.

Tickling, therefore, is a figure which enables Montaigne to convey the complexities of his thinking about desire and self-knowledge and about thinking as a process saturated with aspects which philosophers had tended to insist had no proper place in the kind of thought they valued. It also travels with the subject represented in the *Essais* from childhood to old age, enlivening and giving valuable specificities to Montaigne's representation, underlining that this subject, with whose formation he was so preoccupied, was desiring and not fully knowable; acknowledging this is fundamental to his search to become an understanding and ethical subject.

[35] Plato, *Symposium* (Harmondsworth, 1999), p. 9. On Plato, Socrates and love see, for instance, Dover, *Plato: Symposium* (Cambridge, 1980), Nussbaum, 'The Speech of Alcibiades', *Philosophy and Literature* 3 (1979), pp. 131–72, Vlastos, 'The Individual as an Object of Love', in Vlastos (ed.), *Platonic Studies* (Princeton, 1981), pp. 1–34, and Sheffield, *Plato's Symposium: The Ethics of Desire* (Oxford, 2006).

'Pourquoy non ces excremens'

I seem to have left narcissism a little way behind. However, with shitting, it returns: an aspect of the subject as the sceptical thinker and also the citizen holding public office; of Montaigne who was these and also chronically ill with kidney stones, the subject in pain; moreover, he was the writer representing all the other aspects of himself, alert to the complexities of the relationship with his readers, to whom he gave – his shit.

The aspect of figurative shit to which I shall attend least here relates to public office and the necessary difference between symbolic, public identity and the personal. In English, polite enough metaphors such as 'mud sticks' and 'dirty hands' often figure the compromises of public and political office; Montaigne's version is more robust and also has an impeccable pedigree – 'Platon, maistre ouvrier en tout gouvernement politique' (Plato, past master of all political government) (p. 952). 'Platon dict que qui eschappe brayes nettes du maniement du monde, c'est par miracle qu'il en eschappe' (Plato says that it is a miracle that anyone escapes from handling the world's affairs with clean breeches) (p. 992). The metaphorical 'dirt' here scarcely needs explication, but Montaigne's use of Plato's comment vigorously specifies what dirt might be, in the context of a notion of the 'body politic', and particularly a body politic that was as 'diseased' as was France at the time.

Here the body of the subject involved in government is infected by that disease, his body leaks (loses integrity) and his clothing bears the stain of that loss; it may also symbolize the effects of fear; moreover it brings into play questions about the relationship between what is, or has come to be inside, and what appears outside the (body of) the subject. This is clearer in a passage in 'De mesnager sa volonté' ('On directing your will') already mentioned (see p. 168) in which Montaigne, distancing himself from his contemporaries and insisting on clear separation between his symbolic and his private identity ('le Maire et Montaigne ont tousjours esté deux' (the mayor and Montaigne have always been two people) (p. 1012)) contrasts himself with others. 'J'en vois qui se transforment et se transsubstantient en autant de nouvelles figures et de nouveaux estres qu'ils entreprennent de charges, et qui se prelatent jusques au foye et aux intestines, et entreinent leur office jusques en leur garderobe' (I see people transforming and transubstantiating themselves into as many new shapes and beings as the roles they take on, and who are prelates down to their liver and intestines, taking their status with them even when they go for a shit) (pp. 1011–12). Shitting symbolizes the private and personal, distinct from performance, indeed a last vestige of an identity not yet consumed by public office. And yet, as the comment reminds us, for Montaigne and Plato, only exceptionally would the role not be so incorporated/internalized that the two had become one.

The use of this figuration makes 'perfect sense' in terms of the already dissected figuration of digestion: identification, internalization, psychic investment, incorporation of knowledge and of the others who form 'me' as eating or devouring. The digestive model gives narrative form to figurative eating, one which, as has already been observed, works readily with predominant humanist theories of reading and writing, in which the reader cannibalistically devours the words that form the bodies of his ideal texts. However, this figurative narrative then veers towards that of (equally figurative) reproduction: the resulting writing is the textual child. The fusion of cannibalistic and procreative vocabularies suggests a kind of inchoate prehistory of later psychoanalytic and anthropological theories which equate fantasies of cannibalism and incest (desire for the same) and the societal taboos they represent.

Montaigne also works with the metaphor of the textual child to convey his relationship with his published words and their meaning, as well as his fantasy of the text's independent life, outliving him.[36] But at times his figuration is more strictly coherent; what is produced by reading and thinking, by the digestion of all he has eaten, is figured as excrement. These passages, unsurprisingly, given their paradoxical quality (writing is no more than waste matter? 'nihilité' (nullity) (p. 664)? diseased waste matter at that? something to joke about?) have already been discussed by others.[37] Not only is excrement associated with the changing nature of Montaigne's ideas (by its changeable consistency, hard or soft), but also with 'agitation', which connotes uncontrollability as well as unsettledness: 'ce sont icy … des excremens d'un vieil esprit, dur tantost, tantost lasche, et tousjours indigeste. Et quand seray-je à bout de representer une continuelle agitation et mutation de mes pensées?' (this is an old mind's excrement, sometimes hard, sometimes loose, always undigested. And when will I ever finish representing the continual agitation and mutations of my thoughts?) (p. 946). But this bodily function figures the relationship between reading, thinking, living and the desire to write, and also the relationship between inside and outside, and the identity of the subject: 'there is no clear borderline between what is "inside" and what is "outside" in the *Essais*. The linking thread that is the first-person-singular subject connects them together as the objects of a constantly travelling gaze; things seen, things read and things lived are all transmuted into experience.'[38]

In this comment on 'outside' becoming 'inside' and on the fluidity of the relationship between the two, Cave works with first, perceptions, and then experience, via 'transmutation'. Figurative shit – what is expelled from the body, waste matter, but equally an index of digestive health; things which had been outside, then inside and subsequently outside again – supplements Cave's point interestingly. It conveys the complexities of the relationship between inside and outside and also its implications for this first-person-singular subject's 'singularity'. I have already explored, via tickling, something of the complex singularity of the subject in the *Essais* and also ways in which Montaigne develops

[36] See, for instance, II, 8, discussed in chapter 7.

[37] See for example Mathieu-Castellani, *Montaigne: l'écriture de l'essai* (Paris, 1988), ch. 4.

[38] Cave, *Montaigne*, p. 96.

the reader's engagement with that subject. But shit also has something to tell us about singularities and about shifters.

'Stercus cuique suum bene olet' (p. 929): everyone loves the smell of his own shit. A point about narcissism, and about valuing one's own words more than another's, hence failing to have a genuine dialogue; moreover a point about what is one's own, and how that singularity works in words. The comment is about something intimately known, perhaps a shameful secret as well as a private pleasure. Or even, an expression of some innermost 'truth'? What is interesting is the way in which the revealing little point is made: in a quotation, in Latin, from Erasmus who already calqued his comment on Aristotle and Plato (on self-love).

So this exposure of an aspect of self-knowledge which is not usually acknowledged but instead experienced as singular, even idiosyncratic (I know this about me but does anyone else share this?), is not made directly in the first-person singular. On the contrary: while the first-person-singular subject 'connects' Erasmus, Aristotle, Plato, Latin and French, he disappears, and that which is experienced as a form of singularity (but apparently by 'all' subjects) is communicated as an impersonal statement in an other's words. But the words nonetheless are integrated into Montaigne's 'own' writing, to nail the point he has been making. For it implies all of what I have suggested above, and also, self-deluding attachment to the rightness of our own views; therefore the other must be wrong. So, a singular subject who has incorporated others' words, whose 'own' use of them contains a plurality of meanings; theirs, his and potentially others produced by readers who enjoy the punctual figure, recognizing something they intimately knew but may not have read before – that enjoyment becomes each reader's enjoyment of what is now her own shit as well as Aristotle's, Plato's, Erasmus's, Montaigne's ... Interpretative pleasures tend to have a narcissistic tinge.

That which feels singular at the moment of reading or of utterance or writing might be described as being like a shifter. A shifter, linguistically (after Jespersen and Benveniste), signifies the subject but does not define it, being purely indexical and context-dependent; the most familiar shifter is the first-person-singular pronoun, 'je'/'I'; it functions because it can be 'incorporated', used by everyone (it shifts between or among one and any other one). The moment in which I speak or write as if most myself, using 'je'/'I' is equally open to being each and everyone else's her- or himself; this should be troubling, but we are so habituated to using 'je'/'I' as if it were that which is really most mine that we go on doing so undisturbed.

This is how shit operates in this quotation, because of the singular intimacy of the substance and our relationship with it: had Montaigne chosen, instead, to write 'I love the smell of my own shit', this would be directly read and experienced as a point about, primarily, his singularity, albeit nonetheless (it is said) equally everyone else's. Displaced into someone else's Latin, but with a different context, it alerts the reader to the complexities of claims to singularity, and to singularity being inseparable from others: not different and therefore outside, but different and already inside.

Shitting troubles boundaries, as Montaigne's use of it exploits. Its more conventional power to unsettle – being associated with shame or disgust, or being improper – is relevant through its punctual use as a figure, which may shake the reader at the same time as it intrigues and invites her to reflect on conventions of propriety, which may map onto the anthropological model of purity and danger.[39] In Montaigne's *Essais* there are often concerns that could be categorized as anthropological, for instance those of 'De la coustume'. How different cultures deal with waste, and what this says about them, are questions tackled there not least with reference to blowing one's nose and to urinating, which feature in a long catalogue of customs endemic to one culture and challenging for those of another.

In anthropological terms, in the 'total structure of thought' that is a culture's pollution beliefs, the concepts of purity and danger may be fundamental;[40] they subtend such cultural distinctions as proper and improper, private and public, concealed and revealed, shameful and not. In the 'Apologie' Montaigne pursues this as a point about specifically human behaviour. After a (rather conventional) comment on women never being seen (by men) without the disguise of make-up, and the wisdom of such concealment, his attention shifts ('là où ...' (whereas)) to our taste for all the parts of animals: as well as the more obvious liking for their skins and flesh, we even like their waste matter, and eat them (take them inside) as well as decorating our outside with them: 'là où en plusieurs animaux, il n'est rien d'eux que nous n'aimons et qui ne plaise à nos sens, de façon que de leurs excremens mesmes et de leur descharge [that is secretions, presumably milk] nous tirons non seulement de la friandise au manger, mais non plus riches ornemens et parfums' (whereas there are many animals which wholly appeal to our senses and we love all their parts; we even turn their excretions and secretions into delicacies to eat, rich ornaments and perfumes) (p. 485).

Scent from the civet cat, for example. Other species' excrements are readily transmuted, metamorphosed into valuable commodities and objects of desire. Humans may remain disgusted by their own, but transmuted into figures, they have great value in this writing, where it is, moreover, released from its destiny of figuring only 'rubbish', that which is unpleasant or unwanted, or of which to be afraid or ashamed.

At the start of 'De la vanité' Montaigne introduces his own 'shit' via a Buñuel-like recollection of a nobleman who: 'ne communiquoit sa vie que par les operations de son ventre' (only expressed himself by the movement of his bowels) (p. 946), as if others would be as interested in his shit as he was, and enjoy what he enjoyed. He had no other way of 'expressing' himself, making external what was internal. Montaigne's final comment on him is both the hinge

---

[39] See Douglas, *Purity and Danger* (London, 1966).
[40] See Douglas, Introduction and p. 41.

between him and the description of his own expression that follows, and encapsulates what the man failed to understand: 'tout autre propos luy puoit' (to him,
all other words stank) (p. 946). All other topics (in words) 'stank'. Montaigne
leaves suspended the question: literally? or metaphorically, were worthless and
unpleasant to him? This ambiguity opens up the issue here: this man failed to
accept the metaphorical function of language, whereby words stand for things;
thus he equally failed to understand communication, and that to successfully
convey meaning requires the mediation of shared, rule-governed language.

Told that words stink, we intuitively understand, and recognize that a metaphor is in play. Not so this nobleman: he refused to play the game of language,
particularly the translations it involves, of thing into words, of figures into
something else. Montaigne's anecdote is also about a form of dogmatism, which
he challenges partly via the non-dogmatic power of comedy. The man is a bit of
a joke. But more seriously, this use of metaphor indicates what the man lacked,
what happens if we inappropriately confuse the literal and figurative meanings
of words, and also the power as well as necessity of words, with their potential
to open up meaning. Besides, the cultural dimensions of all bodily functions or
practices, including pissing and shitting, are exposed by Montaigne and inquired
into; for instance, that the supposedly 'natural' is not, but is already cultural, is
a factor in apparently 'natural' processes (such as eating, digesting and so on)
having such open figurative potential.

On the other hand, let's not forget that 'shit sticks': it *is* matter which remains
particularly strongly associated with its materiality, as confirmed by the use of
the word to curse. The nobleman's impoverished 'language' has none of this
ambiguous power, whereas Montaigne's primarily figurative use of the word
fully recognizes how its materiality remains, generating tensions and ambivalence which are productive of meaning.

This anecdote and Montaigne's writing practice combine to raise questions
about the signifying force of figuration. The gentleman's currency was shit,
lacking exchange value. What Montaigne enjoys is language the economy of
which differs from, and may be said to exceed, an economy of exchange which
operates by A standing for B. His densely figurative language unsettles this and
is part of a much more productive economy of meaning.

Moreover, these particular metaphors suggest a use of figuration which is
particularly apt in the writing of a sceptic. Figures of shit or shitting have an
affective and ideational power in the text akin to the sceptical image of purgatives, which 'displays the near-simultaneity of sceptical self-inscription, in
which arguments inscribe themselves "together with" (Gk. *sumperigraphein*)
the arguments they oppose'.[41] The use of 'shit' unsettles the reader, who may
recoil but is simultaneously propelled into exploring the potential meanings of
the figure; recoil is transformed into the pleasures of interpretation, and thus

---

[41] Nussbaum, *The Therapy of Desire*, p. 311. '*Sumperigraphein*' refers to the term used
in Sextus Empiricus's *Adversus Mathematicos*, which would have been known to Montaigne
in Gentian Hervet's Latin translation, *Contra mathemiticos*, published in 1569.

suspension of judgement is encouraged. In other words, the reader's thinking is loosened by the figure (as by purgative arguments), aiding digestion of that which is 'indigeste' (undigested), making way for new thinking and ideas.

It is only after this anecdote of eccentricity, with its layers of meaning, that Montaigne turns to his own writing, as excrement – constipated, runny, undigested. This echoes the descriptions of his writing at the end of 'Sur des vers de Virgile', as being an uncontrolled and potentially painful 'flux de caquet ... impetueux parfois et nuisible' (verbal diarrhoea ... [which is] sometimes acute and severe) (p. 897), but the contexts are rather different. In the latter, this ironic self-mockery is apt for the chapter drawing to a close and the loving humiliations to which he had exposed his ageing but still desiring self; in the former, the metaphor is pre-emptive. It could of course be read in the light of the theme of human vanity: all writing, and fantasies of surviving after one's death in writing, are worthless, self-deluding. If writing is shit then the demand on the reader is: 'love my shit (as I do)'. This returns us to the fantasy of communication as a symmetrical relationship belonging equally to speaker and listener (see p. 65). Only a fleeting hope, and the overdetermined use of shit, which causes the reader to pause and take a bit of distance, reminds of the improbability of that symmetry.

The figuration of shit also articulates something about the relationship between experience and writing. It presents this writing as unhealthy, a product of the failure to digest; yet it becomes clear that indigestion is symptomatic of the excess and volatility of his thinking – those constantly agitated and mutating thoughts he refers to in 'De la vanité'; perhaps the digestive process is not compromised so much as incomplete. The process is continued by writing and reading; continued also, without ever being completed, by a reader who is ready to accept an old man's 'shit', and engage with all its figurative play and complexity, even when tested by a metaphor such as this.

This discussion of the psychic economy of encounters with all manner of others and otherness that are significant for the formation of the subject and its sustained sense of identity cannot end without returning to the incorporation of La Boétie. In love and identification, the desire for the other who is just like me/ who I want to be just like (the two being inseparable), the vocabulary of eating and incorporation has been crucial. La Boétie: eaten, internalized, incorporated after his death, as loss, quite as significantly as he had been while alive. So incorporated that dead, he became life-threatening: 'je m'y fusse perdu à l'aventure' (it might very well have destroyed me) (p. 835). Montaigne's self-cure was to decide to fall in love with someone else; to distract himself. More persuasive perhaps than this cure-by-will (think of his scepticism about Stoic attitudes, as in the example in the 'Apologie' discussed above (see p. 193)), is the idea of writing as a way of evacuating that which is no longer vitalizing. Expelled, that which had been experienced as life-threatening comes to be acknowledged as being vital still, in its turn incorporating treasured aspects of his own self.

Matter and experience undigested, not yet understood, required Montaigne to go on digesting, thinking and writing. As well as being undigested, it has other particularities, already noted, which are more salient than ever at this point of my argument: hardness, loosesness and 'flux': its fluidity is of a piece with the mobility and fluidity of being. On the other hand, where that conveys continuity, 'dur tantost, tantost lasche' speaks of change and discontinuity. Montaigne's 'shit' mimics his fluctuating experience of being, as both discontinuous and yet also continuous.[42] It also – hard, morbidly fluid – expresses pain which is associated with loss; yet at the same time as always being a form of loss it is, also, a vital part of the digestive process and of sustaining a healthy body.

We need to allow Montaigne's figuration to shape and inform how we interpret it; but now it is important to resist the veiling that figuration also offers, such as the use of 'indigeste' (undigested). Whilst that is Montaigne's own word, together with the use of 'se perdre' in 'De la diversion' just quoted, meaning 'to be destroyed', 'undigested' needs to be translated uncompromisingly into the words for which it substitutes: dead and to die. That which goes on being 'digested' but which remains that which is indigestible is not only the death of his beloved friend but death itself, which inhabits the 'body' of the *Essais* – and yet, as the use of figuration also suggests, there is much more besides this theme.

This is not 'shit' that represents the end of a process – which indicates how puzzling or misleading a metaphor this may seem. To call it 'shit' is an index of intimacy and personal value and a way of pushing the reader to ask what, if not just shit, it is. And, just as shitting is part of the digestive process, not its end but an aspect of a cycle, so this writing engages the reader in a cycle designed to keep questions moving on, past answers, not ends but a means towards generating further questions.

And let us not forget that this is not only shit: this is his word-child.

---

[42]   Elsewhere, without this figuration: 'impossible de voir deux opinions semblables exactement … en mesme homme à diverses heures' (it is impossible to find two opinions exactly alike … in the same man at different times) (p. 1067).

6

The Place of the Brother

Je sçay bien ce que je fuis, mais non pas ce que je cherche.

'Je me trouve quasi tousjours en ma place'

In June 1580, having published the first two books of the *Essais*, Montaigne left his home for over a year, to travel, via Germany and Switzerland, around northern Italy.[1] His account, the *Journal de voyage*, records things and people seen in places visited, customs and beliefs, as well as considerable detail about his experience of different spas, and about the illness and pain that led him to try out the waters as potential sources of cure. It also conveys Montaigne's curiosity about the other, such as courtesans, Jews, those thought to be possessed, or those required to convert.

The direction of travel is towards openness and possibilities. The most significant places visited – Venice, Ferrara, Rome and Bains della Villa – have symbolic potential; likewise Montaigne's body, a different kind of place. The journey and these places gain significance when the *Journal* is read with chapters in the *Essais*, primarily 'De la vanité', which reflects on the desire to travel and on metaphorical journeying. It traces an arc from the vanity (futility) of writing about himself to the vanity (self-delusion, false perspective) of the place of humans in the world. The *Journal* and this chapter also need to be read together with Montaigne's letter to his father on the death of his friend La Boétie; for his 'brother', as Montaigne so insistently calls him in the letter, has a place in Montaigne's journey and his writing about it.

In 'De la vanité' Montaigne explains why he left home: to see what he might find by travelling; because his home had become intolerable to him, a place of burdensome responsibilities, his property under threat of attack during prolonged confessional conflict locally; and because of the lawless discord that had overtaken his country and its people. This was no place for free or open thinking. Moreover for two years he had been suffering the agonizing pain of kidney stones. Conventional medicine offered no cure; perhaps the more 'natural', gentle effects of spa waters might bring some relief. No guarantee, of

---

[1]   My focus is on Montaigne in Italy; for discussion of the earlier months of his travels, see Blum, Deredinger and Toia (eds), *Montaigne: voyage en Alsace et en Suisse* (Paris, 2000).

course, and Montaigne does not declare that he seeks a cure: what folly (vanity) to seek a cure´for what he believes incurable …

No longer at home in his home, 'je me trouve quasi tousjours en ma place' (I am nearly always in my place) (p. 811). As Montaigne's next sentence reveals, this place is a metaphorical home: 'si je ne suis chez moy, j'en suis tousjours bien pres' (if I am not at home, I am always very near it). Metaphorical place makes a good point of departure for my analysis, which focuses on the relationships between different kinds of places important to him: topographical, culturally resonant, symbolic and figurative; and, particularly, on the more enigmatic and troubling aspects of his desire for travel, which can be productively explored in terms of place and displacement, and in terms of the perspectives opened up by holding two different or alternative places in mind, for instance Rome and/or home. Also, guided by Montaigne's sense of metaphorical place, connoting (being) in place, in one's place, or in one's own or proper place, I shall explore what he discovered about that kind of place by travelling, and through his encounters and experiences away from home.

These figurative places are almost synonymous with the other figure with which Montaigne puts place to work: 'chez moy', instances of which in the *Essais* help to define the range of meanings of place. 'Chez moy' often denotes 'at home' in the simplest, most common sense. But it also frequently denotes the subject, or the self – not least Montaigne himself: the changeability of the disjunctive pronoun allows the phrase to be, variously, particular or plural and general in scope. For instance in the 'Apologie': 'que les choses ne logent pas chez nous en leur forme et en leur essence … nous le voyons assez' (we see clearly enough that things do not lodge in us in their own form and essence) (p. 562), or in 'De l'experience': 'le jugement tient chez moy un siege magistral' (judgement holds a magisterial seat in me) (p. 1074). Affect is also experienced, received or contained 'chez moy', in the place that is the subject, thus: 'sous cette parfaicte amitié ces affections volages ont autrefois trouvé place chez moy … Ainsi ces deux passions sont entrées chez moy en connoissance l'une de l'autre' (during this perfect friendship these fleeting affections did once find a place in me … Thus within me these two passions came to know each other) (p. 186). Elsewhere, the place of the subject is Montaigne's embodied self: 'on doit donner passage aux maladies; et je trouve qu'elles arrestent moins chez moy, qui les laisse faire' (we should allow illnesses their course; and, as I let them be, I find that they stay with me less long) (p. 1088). It is also the text: 'j'ayme bien autant voir Brutus chez Plutarque que chez luy mesme' (I am as happy to see Brutus in Plutarch as in his own text) (p. 415). Home, subject, embodied self and text all need to be explored in relation to the place for which La Boétie, his 'brother', asked Montaigne – the meaning of which seemed to elude him.

Despite being chronically ill, Montaigne was keen to set out, without a fixed, final destination, both literally and figuratively: travelling, like his thinking and his writing, had to be non-teleological: 'je ne trace aucune ligne certaine, ny droicte ny courbe' (I follow no fixed line, either straight or crooked) (p. 985).[2] This open adventurousness was secured by his sense of always being more or less 'chez moy'; but let's not underestimate the difference between being happy to start writing without a project ('je commence volontiers sans project' (I willingly start without a plan) (p. 253)), or to keep a discussion open, and leaving a home feeling displaced by meanings which have gathered in it, without knowing what you want instead. '*Quasi* toujours', *nearly* always in my place, articulates hesitation, makes the statement of security insecure, and reintroduces a more vulnerable version of Montaigne, as in the phrase: 'c'est chose tendre que la vie, et aisée à troubler' (life is a tender thing, easily troubled) (p. 950).

The troubled nature of Montaigne's movement will predominate in my discussion. Movement towards 'choses nouvelles et inconnues' (new and unknown things) (p. 948), but not altogether free from the return of known but unwanted things, to which he was all the more vulnerable when not anaesthetized by routine and habit: '*nous nous durcissons* à tout ce que nous accoustumons ... l'accoustumance ... endort nostre sentiment à la souffrance de plusieurs maux' (*we grow hardened* to whatever we are used to ... habit anaesthetizes us to much suffering) (pp. 970–1, my italics). However, vulnerability and trouble may well be both the condition and the cost of the undefined, open state of being which Montaigne sought: and movement may be unsettling, rather than a source of freedom.

Montaigne's physical, emotional and psychic economy was also troubled. My second section will return to the troubled calculus and calculation of the subject (see chapter 3), focusing on pain. Kidney stones are also called 'calculs', from the Latin *calx*, pebble: a hard concretion troubling the body's tender organs (the kidneys, also the genitals), causing excruciating pain, disturbing the balance of the body, its healthy economy, troubling Montaigne's capacity to think and be, and his capacity to communicate. When what is hard is present in what should be 'tender', the relationship between the body and what is not it (whether because it should not exist or should be outside it) is troubled. Moreover, what disturbs the organic economy of the body incurs attempts to cure which produce additional trouble.

Places

As Montaigne's 'quasi' warns us, place can be elusive or unreliable: displacement and dislocation may not be far away and, 'ma place', as he discovered at

---

[2] For an invigorating discussion, see Cave, 'Le Récit montaignien', in Samaras (ed.), *Montaigne*, pp. 125–35. There are many studies of the movement of his thinking, to which he himself drew attention, its zigzagging, its non-linearity, its involutions. Among the most illuminating are: Tournon, *Montaigne en toutes lettres* (Paris, 1989), Nakam, *Montaigne: la manière et la matière* (Paris, 1991), Charpentier, 'Ecriture de l'errance, errances de l'écriture', in Samaras (ed.), *Montaigne*, pp. 243–52, McKinley, *Les Terrains vagues des 'Essais'* (Paris, 1996), and Jeanneret, *Perpetuum mobile*.

one point on his travels, in a place in which he felt perfectly at home,[3] can even be the site of the most unhomely experience, in Freud's sense of the *Unheimlich*. We shall arrive at this particularly troubling place, Bains della Villa, shortly, but first, let's consider what place has to do with metaphor and figuration.

In chapter 1 I set out the connections between figuration and place: figure, trope, meaning turning (Gk *trepe-*); topos: motif, meaning place (Gk *topos*). The textual turning that is figuration produces a space of potential, in which different perspectives can emerge; a place in the text in which thinking may be structured differently. Take three places: home, Rome, Bains della Villa. The first two were already highly charged symbolically for Montaigne; the last a new discovery for him. What interests me here is how Montaigne turns the existing symbolic significance of places so as to explore his own questions: in this respect, he *did* know where he was going, but not what meanings would emerge from his own experience of place. Also, it remains to be seen how places not yet so fixed as Rome on public symbolic maps, become charged in his writing with symbolic significance because of what he brought with him, because of what happened to him in those places, or a combination of the two.

Montaigne seemed to know why he wanted to travel: 'je sçay bien ce que je fuis' (I know well what I am fleeing) (p. 972). By using such a complicating verb as 'fuir', to flee, associated with fear and anxiety as well as danger, Montaigne suggests that his courage lies in his lack of self-deception. But the associations of flight with fear – a slight on his virtue – cannot be set side; they slip towards the question whether his direction of travel is not also morally unsound. Is it errancy, an erring and deviation from his 'proper place' rather than, as wished, a wandering free from both loathed obligation and from any preordained destination – without which free and open thinking would be at risk. Montaigne resolves this tension: what leads him astray is, already, obligation, which ties and binds: 'l'estre tenu et obligé me fourvoie' (p. 962); so if to stay in place is to lose one's place, to go astray, then to leave (even if in flight) may be a form of recovery, not an erring so much as a rediscovery of one's *own* way and place – by being free to move. How figuration (also for some classical thinkers an erring or deviation), place and mobility work together in Montaigne's writing is one strand of my analysis, my hypothesis being that figuration is in Montaigne's thinking and writing what moving freely without a fixed destination is in his attempts to live well. This has implications for his travels and also for his scepticism and his freedom of expression.

But let's also suppose that he knew that *flight* from never altogether soars free from what it seeks to leave behind. If Montaigne acted on his desire to be free of obligations by leaving home, he was still not unburdened. He carried with

---

[3] 'Il semblait en vérité que je fusse de retour chez moy', *Journal de voyage*, p. 327. The *Journal* has generated much critical discussion; see for instance Moureau and Bernoulli (eds), *Autour du 'Journal de voyage' de Montaigne* (Geneva, 1982), Garavini, *Itinerari a Montaigne* (Florence, 1983), Samaras (ed.), *Montaigne*, and Schneikert, *Montaigne dans le labyrinthe* (Paris, 2006).

him to the places he had never been before (except in his mind and imagination) three other places: the first, a real location but also an emotionally charged place (topos), home, the property inherited from his father; the second (not altogether unrelated to the first) the figurative place in his heart and memory of his dead friend, his figurative 'brother'. My analysis will trace the connection between the brother's place and the significance of the place that is figuration in Montaigne's writing. The third place is that which is really beyond representation, no place whatsoever: imaginable as a void, or that which is beyond, namely one's own death. For Montaigne, however, it took form in his experience of the deaths of the two most formative men in his life, his father and his friend, and in the place within him occupied by pain, by kidney stones, an illness he believed he shared with his father. Two of these places are inhabited by ghosts: his father, haunting him at home, and La Boétie, his symbolic brother, haunting him wherever he was.

The place of the brother within Montaigne's psychic economy and his writing and his travels is spectral. It is that for which his dying friend asked him; but it might also symbolize what was both missing and impossible at the time of writing, the antithesis of 'fratricidal' civil war: a healthy polity in which all are connected fraternally, rather than subjected to an authoritarian hierarchy, a democratic ideal. As well as a political and ethical ideal, it also represents an alternative to the ties that bind, on the one hand, father and son, and on the other, man and wife, bonds which Montaigne wanted to leave behind.

Even if Montaigne travelled away from home, from France, driven by a desire to free his future from the bonds of the past, nonetheless, as we shall see, his father had bound his future to the past, with a prediction of ruin. Nor could he leave behind two forms of pain: the physical suffering of his illness, and the psychic and emotional desolation of the loss of La Boétie, which make their presence felt in the *Journal*. Both forms of pain challenge Stoicism and the Christian precept of patient acceptance, a – figuratively – 'philosophical' attitude. It is also often claimed that physical pain is that about which there cannot or should not be scepticism; even Montaigne writes of it as being that which, exceptionally, is not a matter of *opinion*, and therefore not open to sceptical debate. True, the experience of pain is one of certitude for the sufferer; however, this does not necessarily make of pain a site of challenge to scepticism. It is more ambiguous. For it resists communication; we doubt we can understand another person's pain with any certainty – perhaps least of all when we identify with it; something of their pain remains uniquely theirs. We can understand a groan, a howl, a cry perhaps better than pain put into words, grammar or syntax. The gap between the certitude of the sufferer (here Montaigne, but it could be you or me) and the uncertainty of the other's understanding seems to make sceptical doubt a required perspective: I must doubt my understanding of what I think I comprehend of the other's pain. Moreover, it is a radical challenge to the sufferer, here, the writer, to communicate it to the reader, despite the limits of words – and perhaps despite the reader's reluctance to know about his pain.

Flight, loss, pain, illness and scepticism can all be approached via two aspects of travel: place and perspective. Movement between places, the different perspectives that new places offer, what it means to be between places, to travel with no fixed destination, to be out of place, and what happens when two places or planes coexist in such a way as to profoundly trouble perspective (anamorphosis); all of these cluster in Montaigne's phenomenal journey and his reflections on it. They also keep returning us to Montaigne's scepticism, and to why his open 'irresolution', uncertainty, remains both troubled and desirable. Suspension of judgement and the ideational potential of figuration converge in the symbol of 'balance' (Fr.): for 'balancer' means both to balance and to hesitate – as one might not only if the balance of arguments were equal. 'Balance' is, then, both a symbol of sceptical thinking, a form of scepticism about formal scepticism, and a figure of figuration, when more than one meaning is kept in play.

'C'est une plaisante imagination de concevoir un esprit balancé justement entre-deux pareilles envyes' (it is amusing to imagine a mind perfectly balanced between two equal desires) (p. 611). That two arguments, or wishes, might hang evenly in the balance is a fantasy; there is always, according to Montaigne, 'quelque difference, pour legiere qu'elle soit' (some difference, however slight) (p. 611). The symbol of the scales of judgement in which the balance of arguments is weighed seems appropriate for this weighing up of different places; however, in Montaigne's practice, the other sense of the verb 'balancer', to hesitate, is just as telling. Montaigne hesitates, without this implying any failure (to choose, to judge or to commit himself), and uses the power of figuration to allow a space of productive hesitation. The hesitation with which the reader responds to a figure might stem from uncertainty in the face of opacity; equally, figuration can act as an unexpected opportunity, taking her unawares, and offering a turning away elsewhere ('ailleurs') from fixed direction. The effect is similar to those textual jolts ('secousses') explored earlier. In this sense, hesitation is a way of momentarily suspending the direction of one's reading or interpretative impulse so as to open up the possibility of an other direction. So figuration and scepticism work together; and figuration is a particularly productive textual device for a writer like Montaigne.

All these themes keep returning him and us to the place of the brother. In the three sections that follow here, the themes intertwine and recur, rather as they do in Montaigne's text, but in each section, one takes central place. We shall move from leaving home and travelling, to pain and scepticism, to haunting; from why and what Montaigne left, what travels with him, and how this affects his experience of certain places; to pain and how it informs his thinking and self-representation – from seeing, to calculating (in and out), to subtraction, to incalculability; to loss and the relationship between past and future. In the next and final chapter the desire to communicate all of this in a form of writing which might enable a different economy, not governed by calculation, will be explored.

'Je fuis à me submettre à toute sorte d'obligation'

In 'De la vanité' Montaigne reflects on, and at times justifies, his reasons for travelling, such as his repeatedly expressed desire for what is new and unknown (pp. 948, 973), or the possibility of some alleviation of his pain by taking the waters in various recommended spas. The early pages of the chapter lament that the material place that was home is no longer a place he wants to be. He puts it rather obliquely: 'j'arreste bien chez moy le plus ordinairement, mais je voudrois m'y plaire plus qu'ailleurs' (I stay at home most of the time, but I wish I enjoyed being there more than anywhere else) (p. 952): what is missing is his feeling most at home there. His reasons seem clear. Given how fully others have already discussed the reasons such as the 'desolation' (p. 947), 'corruption' (p. 956) and 'desmambremens de la France' (dismembering of France) (p. 993),[4] I shall focus instead on the various 'obligations' from which Montaigne wanted to be free, and the presence of which, or association of which, with home, constrained his desire to be there, as did the prolonged wars. The two leading and intertwined causes of this constraint were his father, and the home having become his property on his father's death in 1568, and with them, other associated bonds that he found irksome: 'c'est pitié d'estre en lieu où tout ce que vous voyez vous enbesogne et vous concerne' (it is miserable to be in a place where everything you see is work and worry for you) (p. 951).

The everyday worries ('abjection', 'importunité', 'aigreur' (ignominies, persistent bother, bitterness) (p. 954), especially those of, or caused by, dependents, eat away at him ('me mangent' (p. 951)); they are not what he hungers for. He dislikes paperwork (p. 953). The economy of ownership and management is troubled. Montaigne is more aware of what goes wrong: 'je suis, chez moy, respondant de tout ce qui va mal' (at home, it is I who am responsible for whatever goes wrong) (p. 954), than able to enjoy what goes well, not least because the conventional compensations of this kind of life and of being in charge do not appeal to him: 'c'est un plaisir trop uniforme et languissant' (it is too unvaried and dull a 'pleasure') (p. 948). His burden is as much one of guilt as of actual responsibility; guilt induced by anxiety that he is failing his father, despite following his example in how he runs the estate.[5] What he lacks, he says, and what he wishes above all he had inherited, is his father's *love* of the place (pp. 951–2). His care for the property is driven by duty, by doing what his father would have wanted, rather than by love or his own satisfaction: 'ce que je me suis meslé d'achever … et de renger … a esté certes plus regardant son intention qu'à mon contentement' (what I have bothered to complete … or repair, has definitely been more to satisfy his intentions than for my own

---

[4] See, for instance, Nakam, *Montaigne et son temps* (Paris, 1982).

[5] For a suggestive reading of Montaigne's representation of father and father's house here, which identifies *Ecclesiastes* as the intertext above and beyond the allusion to 'vanity of vanities' at the start of the chapter, see McKinley, *Les Terrains vagues*, pp. 120–44.

pleasure) (p. 951). His enjoyment does not derive from being like his father, or how his father would have liked.

I shall return shortly to his guilt and its relief by travelling, but first need to clarify what Montaigne berates himself for,[6] and also what he suffers. For his father he tries to be a good son and steward of the estate for its future: 'si je pouvois mieux pour luy, je le ferois' (if I could do better for him, I would) (p. 951). As a father himself, he is at a loss, for he has no surviving son; and his hope that France in future will be a place of well-being is fragile. He sees, instead, a country reverting to savagery, future generations continuing the present destruction: children (a topos for the future) as 'bestes furieuses comme nostre siècle en produit à foison' (savage beasts, of which our century produces all too many) (p. 392). But perhaps as difficult to bear as his own vision was his father's prediction of his future: 'celuy qui me laissa ma maison en charge *prognostiquoit que je la deusse ruyner*, regardant à mon humeur si peu casaniere' (he who left me responsible for my house *predicted that I was bound to ruin it*, for I am so far from stay-at-home) (p. 998, my italics). France in ruins, past ideals ruined – and with this, future potential also reduced to ruin. Here the father is identified only as the one who bequeathed him (responsibility for) the property – and with it, cast a long shadow over his future. 'Have this, which you will destroy for the future'; 'have this, which you do not want, and which will destroy the future you would rather have'.

It is a particularly problematic version of an economy of giving that is in fact exchange and tie. Family relations entailed duty and rivalry, as well as the inequities of inheritance, which Montaigne condemns in 'De l'amitié' (see p. 185) for tainting the emotional economy of the relationship between blood brothers.

'De l'amitié' indicates that Montaigne wanted no part in such an economy, preferring the ideal of his relationship with his symbolic 'brother'; yet he could not be completely free of it. Themes of the burden of family ties, closely related to lack of freedom and openness, as well as of obligation, circulate in 'De la vanité'. The father–son relationship, about the complexities and ambiguities of which Montaigne reflects so movingly in 'De l'affection des pères aux enfans' ('On the affection of fathers for their children'), is here stripped down to property inheritance. To be bound, by his father's bequest, to be caught in relations of exchange, obligation and dependency was a 'cruel garrotage' (a cruel ligature) for one whose ideal was to neither need nor be needed: 'j'essaye à n'avoir expres besoing de nul' (I try to have no express need of anyone) (p. 968), and preferred an economy of giving. His desire for independence could scarcely be clearer: 'j'ay prins à haine mortelle d'estre tenu ny à autre ny par autre que moy' (I have a mortal hatred of being beholden to or through anyone but myself) (p. 969). The impassioned ferocity of the adjective and noun, 'mortal hatred', suggests a trace of anxiety, an awareness of the vulnerability of his subjective

---

[6] Or appears to. His self-reproach over his poor grasp of administrative issues seems excessive, 'negligence inexcusable' (p. 953), suggesting irony: only the kind of person Montaigne would not want to be would judge this in such terms.

freedom. I shall return to this and to an alternative economy in the next chapter, in the course of discussion of what writing made possible.

When the place called home becomes one's property, with ownership come limits to freedom and entanglement in ethical and existential problems, which were exacerbated by France being in the grip of war. Montaigne would have preferred not to own, for possession reduces the potential of place to be a locus of free or open thinking and also makes him subject to the kind of binary – mine, thine – which his thinking so sought to escape. This is not the place described in 'De trois commerces' ('On three kinds of social intercourse'), in which Montaigne could while away time in his library: 'tantost je resve, tantost j'enregistre et dicte, en me promenant, mes songes que voicy' (sometimes I wool-gather, sometimes I walk to and fro, dictating and noting down these musings) (p. 828). The possibility of this kind of writing, associated with untroubled reflection and gentle pace is under threat also.[7] The writing symptomatic of the time is 'escrivaillerie' (scribbling) (p. 946), incontinent outpouring, lacking composition and order; or corrupted and constrained by factional interests and pressures, no longer able to represent openly or accurately the situation on either side. Home and France had become no place for Montaigne's kind of writing.

Home had also become too occupied by expectation, obligation and worry: 'je n'ai rien cher que le soucy et la peine' (nothing really costs me other than care and trouble) (p. 954); there he could no longer be the hospitable gentleman, his doors open, welcoming guests. With civil disorder, uninvited guests became not potential friends but probable enemies. Property was under threat, envied by others. As Montaigne wrote to M. de l'Hôpital, the Chancellor, in 1570, this was: 'un siecle si grossier ou si plein d'envie ... ceste vilaine traficque qui se couve sous l'honorable tiltre de justice' (a century so brutal and so full of envy ... this ugly traffic which grows under the honourable name of justice).[8] Justice is a response to the consequences of envy (wanting the good that is not mine); France in a state of civil war was lawless; the risk of envy having free reign was high, and also, this being 'fratricidal' war, France was in a state in which envy, atavistically, too often motivated events – think of those primitive brothers, Cain and Abel. It is important to recognize these passions: these were wars which Montaigne described as 'monstrueuses en inhumanité ... je n'ay point le courage de les concevoir sans horreur' (monstrous in their inhumanity ... I am unable to think of them without horror) (p. 956).

Walking, dreaming and writing are closely and creatively associated in that comment in 'De trois commerces'; but the kind of being that Montaigne sought by travelling is symbolized by being able to just walk: 'et me proumeine pour me proumener' (I walk for walking's sake) (p. 977) or dance: 'quand je dance,

---

[7] For interesting revision of this version of Montaigne, see Hoffmann, *Montaigne's Career*, ch. 1.

[8] Dedicatory letter by Montaigne for La Boétie's *Poemata* addressed to Monseigneur, Monsieur l'Hôpital, Chancellier de France (1570), *Montaigne: Oeuvres complètes*, ed. Thibaudet and Rat, pp. 1363–5 (p. 1364).

je dance' (when I dance, I dance) (p. 1107). That is, being fully engaged in the present moment, rather than caught between past and future; mobility is the figure of openness and freedom that is destroyed by both war and possessiveness – a 'cruel garrotage'.

This version of Montaigne – 'mes qualitez plus favories: l'oisifveté, la franchise' (my preferred qualities: enjoyment of free time, freedom) (p. 969) – is at odds with the forms of subjectivity crowding in on him at home: his father's version of him, his version of himself for his father, his own version of himself. The version of himself, meditatively pacing, playing with ideas, writing when the fancy took him, is how he would like to be – an idealized self-image. Montaigne the hospitable gentleman is a different version again – his symbolic identification, the generous and judicious Montaigne who others respect (which, while reproducing an attractive ideal, might be a form of 'vanité'). To prove his father's prediction wrong requires an ideal version of himself, a symbolic identification, seeing himself through his father's eyes: 'je me glorifie que sa volonté s'exerce encores et agisse par moy' (I glory in the fact that his will still operates and acts through me) (p. 951). Also, as all that self-berating about his failings – 'et accuse ma faineance' (I reproach my laziness) (p. 951) – suggests, it is a version of himself which is more subject to a punishing internal agency which, already cruel in the demands it makes, is insatiable: the more one tries to meet its demands, the more exacting and endless they become. One might well think one wanted to be free of this. So perhaps Montaigne's capacity to leave, despite the reproaches of those who saw it as abandoning his responsibilities, indicates less flight than the ability to act on his own desire, to be understood as a different form of ethical responsibility; the responsibility not to conform to others' desires for one, that is, the person they imagine or want one to be. Not an easier option, or way out: to leave, because that is one's desire, without any justificatory, reasonable or culturally valid motive, may be more difficult than to stay.

Travel is imagined as the antithesis of irksome versions of himself and unwanted obligations: 'quand je voyage, je n'ay à penser qu'à moy' (when I travel I have only myself to think about) (p. 955), enabling a different 'self', or so the fantasy might go. The statement is interestingly unapologetic, willing to transgress others' expectations and the norm that one not think (only) of oneself. I shall return to this theme of being true to one's desire, what others can know of it, and how troubling it may be, later, in terms of Montaigne's encounters on his journey with those who seemed to be able, or not, to be true to theirs, as well as with more intimate encounters with himself. Also, even if Montaigne left behind some unwanted bonds and burdens, he travelled haunted by others, primarily losses; these spectres returned over the course of his journey, and make their presence felt in his writing. But before considering these aspects, spectral and troubled, of Montaigne's experience away from home, we should pause and explore two other reasons for his leaving, both interrelated and related, as we shall see, to what haunted him.

These are his illness; it was not impossible that taking the waters at certain spas might relieve some of his renal pain, even temporarily; and, to travel was to act as if one were not afraid of dying.[9] Most precisely for Montaigne, afraid of dying anywhere other than one's birthplace or far from one's loved ones: 'si je craingnois de mourir en autre lieu ... à peine sortiroy-je hors de la France; je ne sortirois pas sans effroy hors de ma parroisse' (if I were afraid of dying anywhere else ... I would scarcely leave France; I would be terrified to leave my local parish) (p. 978). Here the theme of unwanted bonds with others, the illusions fostered by those bonds – that their presence might ease one's dying – and the need for a symbolic rather than material, geographical sense of one's place in the world combine. What mattered to Montaigne was not to be lured by such culturally (or paternally) valued ideas of identity and place, not to be captured by family ties, and not to fear death. Lucid awareness of one's mortality brings freedom from the delusion that one setting (such as one's home) is any better than any other. Death travels with us: 'elle m'est une par tout' (death is the same for me everywhere) (p. 978). There is a hint of momentary vanity (pride) in Montaigne's distinguishing himself from others' vanity (self-deception) in this: 'je suis autrement faict' (but I am made differently).

In 'De la vanité' there is not much reference to his illness, despite it being a reason for leaving. So let's turn to his representation of his illness elsewhere for further insight into it and into what the experience of pain led him to realize; then, and only then, we can explore further what his other experiences of mortality, through the deaths of his father and, particularly of La Boétie, his 'brother' taught him. Today both his pain and his losses might be described as forms of trauma. But in preference to that vocabulary, let us work here with that of disorientation, dislocation, loss of place. Also, we should focus on the economies deployed by Montaigne in his descriptions of the body in pain, such as the ways that what is hard affects what is tender, the sensation and rhythms of illness and also of attempted cures. The calculation of loss, and of loss of balance – humoral or physiological equilibrium – and his ambivalence about the value of such calculation, when subjected to so disorienting a pain as renal colic, give us more insight into Montaigne's knowledge of himself as subject to pain, than today's vocabulary. So too do the ways in which the loss of his friend fractured his writing. 'C'est chose tendre que la vie, et aisé à troubler' (life is a tender thing, easily troubled): others' deaths, and the hard pain of kidney stones and their expulsion from his (tender) body, are the troubles on which the following pages will focus.

---

[9] It is also to act as if one were not afraid of melancholy, which is a loss of desire for what is one's home; even, to act in the knowledge that no object that can be possessed can assuage the loss of the object we never had.

pain incommunicable

'C'est une sotte coutume de compter ce qu'on pisse': pain, calculus and incalculability

How do you describe pain? How am I to imagine your pain? In 'De la ressemblance des enfans aux peres' Montaigne describes his illness as 'vivre coliqueux' (colicky life) (p. 759), his 'qualité pierreuse' (tendency to stones) (p. 763) and his 'subjection graveleuse' (subjection to gravel) (p. 779). Each emphasizes a different aspect of his condition: that it affects how he lives, that (kidney) stones are so much a part of his being that they become one of his identifying qualities, and that his pain subjects him. It is perhaps the last condition that most precisely conveys the quality of pain: it is that to which one is subject, and being so subject makes it difficult to put it into language. How does Montaigne try to communicate the nature of his pain, the relationship between pain and imagination, his attitude to potential cures and the consequences of being in pain?

In Montaigne's ontology there is an early link between pain and scepticism. Pyrrho's pig makes his first appearance in the *Essais* in 'Que le goust des biens et des maux ...' ('The taste of good and evil things ...'), perhaps written in 1572, as an example of the difference between death, which is only comprehensible insofar as it is imagined, and pain. 'Ici tout ne consiste pas en l'imagination. Nous opinons du reste, c'est ici la certaine science qui joue son role ... Le pourceau de Pyrrho est ici nostre escot ... si on le bat, il crie et se tourmente' (there is more than imagination at work here. We have opinions about everything else, but here it is for certain knowledge to play its part ... in this respect Pyrrho's pig is one of us ... beat it, and it squeals and squirms) (p. 55). Pain is *known* through the senses; but we increase it, as we do pleasure, by the 'pointe de nostre esprit' (acuity of our minds) (p. 58); that is, how we conceive of it and amplify it in our imagination-infused thinking about it. Imagining is also involved in the communication of pain: how to put it into words rather than an 'animal' cry like the pig? It is notable that in this early chapter Montaigne also wrote: 'la douleur ... le pire accident de nostre estre ... je suis l'homme du monde qui luy veux autant de mal, et qui la fuis autant' (pain ... the worst thing that can happen to us ... of all men in the world I am that one who wishes it most ill and who most flees from it) (p. 56) – and this before suffering renal colic. A gesture towards the value of patience in suffering which follows this comment is no match for its intensity.[10] Read again many chapters later, after the onset of his illness and after his scepticism had become marked, it reads more like an unconscious intimation of his later frustrations with the forms of Stoicism that appealed to his Christian contemporaries. *His* pain will challenge such influential philosophies and discourses of pain, his power as a writer and his conception of himself; it 'essays' him and he may come to learn from it, although it may elude his ability to write about it.

An already strong sceptical tendency might well have been intensified by

---

[10] 'Mais il est en nous, si non de l'aneantir, au moins de l'amoindrir par la patience' (But we have it in us, if not to wipe out pain, to lessen it by patience) (p. 56).

suffering pain and attempting to communicate it. Experiences of medical practice and of not only the culture of spa treatment he tested in Italy but also other
cultural encounters along the way might equally have effected this; notwithstanding which, at this point in my argument, pain and its incommunicability
have most claim on our further attention to the development of Montaigne's
sceptical attitude. The secondary point is that being subject to pain cannot be
isolated from other aspects of being, but informs, dislocates, deforms them – at
the same time as isolating the sufferer. I shall now explore Montaigne's attempts
to describe his pain in, first, his *Journal*, then in 'De la ressemblance des enfants
aux peres' ('On the resemblance of children to their fathers') and 'De la vanité'.
In the first, it takes what seems to be its simplest descriptive form; nonetheless, its power to 'unmake', to use Elaine Scarry's vocabulary, is palpable;[11]
elsewhere 'unmaking' persists, along with a more reflective attitude towards
his pain.

Along with this unmaking which is the subjective loss experienced in pain's
incommunicability, and to supplement this vocabulary's lack of cultural specificity, I shall work with the French word 'calcul', variously meaning calculation
and calculus, in its mathematical as well as medical or pathological senses. This
echoes my exploration in chapter 3 of what it means to live well and how the
economy of living as ethically interrelated subjects is to be calculated, Derrida's
'calculation of the subject'. Pain and the subject's fragility that is so accentuated
by bodily suffering extend our understanding of living well and of our relations with others in all their vulnerability. But it has more immediate, pressing
significance here also: calculation (Eng.), 'calcul' (early modern French). In
Cotgrave's *Dictionary of the French and English Tongues* we find: '*calcul*: a
calculation, computation, reckoning; an accompt or casting of accompts; also,
the Stone in the bladder, or (more properly) in the reines'. Huguet's *Dictionnaire de la langue française du seizième siècle* gives us a little further precision. *Calcul*, see *calcule*, 1. a 'caillou servant au vote', that is, a pebble with
an already symbolic function; and 2. calculation (citing Rabelais for usage).
The entry on *calculeux* gives a 1540 medical usage, the 'maladie non pareille
de nefresie calculeuse' (the worst illness of all, renal stones). Let us hold that
'maladie non pareille' in mind and return to it shortly, in relation to Montaigne's
descriptions of his illness.[12] The early modern use of 'calcul' corresponds to
current usage in medicine or pathology, namely: calculus, an abnormal concretion in the body, usually formed of mineral salts, in the gall bladder, kidney or
urinary bladder.

That convergence between the stone, 'calcul' (from the Latin *calx*, pebble),
and 'calcul', reckoning, the 'casting of accompts', matters. For, as will be seen,
among Montaigne's experiments in his *Journal* in ways of describing the expe-

---

[11] Scarry, *The Body in Pain* (Oxford, 1985).

[12] Others have been more interested, instead, in the symbolism of the stone, with its
potential for archaeological assocations. See Mayor, 'Montaigne's Cure', *MLN* 97 (1982),
pp. 958–72, and Kritzman, 'Le Roman de la pierre', *BSAM* 13–16 (1988–89), pp. 119–26.

pain incalculable

rience of pain, is his sceptical, even caustic, response to forms of calculation in the treatment of the illness and the body's response to it. Is the mark of pain, rather, its incalculability – for the other? This question opens out into issues to do with the 'balance' and health of the subject's physical, emotional and psychic economy, and how well-being can be reckoned, despite pain's capacity to confound linguistic expression. If pain 'unmakes' the subject, then it seems likely that in the attempt to convert this disintegration or dissolution into the terms of a balance sheet, the essence of the experience of being subject to pain will be lost.

Montaigne had already suffered from renal colic for some two years before setting out for Italy. As the *Journal* records, despite this being a chronic condition, he had periods of respite, and some months pass without any record of pain. The descriptions or notations of pain are most frequent between May and October 1581; he was often preoccupied with the impact of different spa waters on his kidneys, and recorded the different ways in which, periodically, stones were expelled from his body in his urine; although this was excruciatingly painful, even more tormenting for him at times were his migraines and toothache. Forms of pain which, it might be imagined, are common enough to need little description to be comprehensible: we remember, we think we recognize our own experience. And yet no one person's pain is identical to another's, and these are notations of the problem of expressing such singularity. Classical persuasive rhetoric offered Montaigne little help: Quintilian's strategies, for instance, seem to presume that identification is the solution, our response depending on 'our being able to identify ourselves with the persuasive representation, for a brief space feeling their suffering as though it were our own'.[13] 'As though' simultaneously acknowledges the problem and evades it. How, then, did Montaigne find the words for his pain that would enable others to imagine it in its particularity?

There is much in Scarry's extraordinary and extensive analysis of the body in pain that resonates with Montaigne's ways of thinking and writing about his experience, as well as with his aversion to torture and the pain inflicted by cruelty.[14] I do not have space here to do justice to the exceptional richness of her discussion; so rather, I shall extract three aspects of her argument that are particularly congruent with what we discover in Montaigne's text. These are, her insistence on the singular power of pain to resist articulation, and on its therefore remaining unreal to others than the sufferer, generating doubt or a gap in comprehension, which is where the connection suggested between pain and scepticism originates.

> Nothing sustains its [sc. pain's] image in the world ... From the inarticulate it half emerges into speech and then quickly recedes once more. Invisible

---

[13] See Vickers, *In Defence of Rhetoric* (Oxford, 1988), p. 79.
[14] For discussion of the significance of pain in early modern France see Silverman, *Tortured Subjects* (Chicago and London, 2001).

imag^ c pein

in part because of its resistance to language, it is also invisible because its own powerfulness ensures its isolation, ensures that it will not be seen in the context of other events ... Though indisputably real to the sufferer, it is, unless accompanied by visible body damage or a disease label, unreal to others.

(pp. 60–1, 56)

The third aspect that is particularly useful for reading Montaigne is her investigation of the connection between pain and imagination. Hers is a complex argument, developed minutely over many pages, to do with the nature of (philosophical) intentionality: 'pain is an intentional state without an intentional object ... in isolation, pain "intends" nothing, it is wholly passive; it is "suffered" rather than willed or directed'; imagining, on the other hand, is, for Scarry, an 'intentional object without an experienceable intentional state'; that is, it 'is only experienced in the images it produces' (p. 164). She argues that imagining comes to the aid of pain, as a kind of 'intentional counterpart' (p. 164), that is, it gives pain a form, an object-ive existence in the world outside the body of the sufferer. She is not suggesting that they are in a supplementary relationship; what matters for her, rather, is to conceptualize pain and imagining as the 'framing events within whose boundaries all other perceptual, somatic, and emotional events occur; thus, between the two extremes can be mapped the whole terrain of the human psyche' (p. 165): from unmaking to making, from losses and trauma to its creativity. My aim, now, is to suggest ways in which Scarry's position resonates with Montaigne's writing about pain and the part he gives to imagining. We have not only his various attempts to put his inner physical pain into words, but also, as will be seen in a later section of this chapter, we have the dislocation of his being by psychic pain, and the communicability of that experience – or not.

Migraines, renal colic and toothache, as described in the *Journal*, are distinct types of pain. Montaigne notes headaches, at times describing them self-referentially in comparison with his own previous experience, and kidney stones are frequently notated in a vocabulary of calculation and transit (to which I shall return), rather than consistently that of pain, as in the following example: 'j'avais les reins fort douloureux: mes urines étaient abondantes et troubles' (my kidneys were very painful: my urine, of which there was a lot, was cloudy) (p. 329). But toothache, experienced less constantly than colic, is described more than once as cruel torment, and more: 'je fus cruellement tourmenté de la douleur des dents ... la force du mal me donnait des envies de vomir. Tantôt j'étais tout en sueur, tantôt je frissonnais ... je passai la plus cruelle nuit que je me souvienne d'avoir passé de ma vie: c'était une vraie rage et une fureur' (I was cruelly tormented by toothache ... the pain was so fierce I wanted to vomit. I had alternating sweats and chills ... as far as I remember, this was the cruellest night I have ever passed; a night of real rage and fury) (p. 335).

How does this demonstrate Scarry's intuitively persuasive argument about pain's incommunicability? By only being able to describe one form of pain in terms of another; by its registering only in terms of Montaigne's own remembered experience, and by the level of generalized abstraction of such terms as 'real rage and fury'. These do not communicate precisely the nature of his own pain that particular night. True, the accumulation of details helps the reader to produce a version of that pain; but the problem remains, that this will be the reader's version. Appeals to identification or imagination are problematic when it comes to pain. That this would be an appealing problem for Montaigne as a writer seems probable, and shortly I shall explore the ways in which he chose to represent his pain in the *Essais*, to see if he develops other linguistic strategies to help address problems of imagining and identification. First, though, let us return to his colic as represented in the *Journal*.

The place of much of the representation is Bains della Villa, a spa near Lucca he visited twice in 1581, first in May and June, and again in August and September. It was here, on 7 September, that he received the news that he had been elected Mayor of Bordeaux; he would have to return home. At that moment political exigency intruded into this *locus amoenus*: his use in the *Essais* of the phrase 'amenité de lieu' (beauties of the location) (p. 777) to describe spas and Bains della Villa in particular summons up the Latin idiom, with all its literary associations.

The basis of his *Journal* account is, indeed, an accounting: water drunk, urine passed. To give just two of many instances: 'si fus cinq heures depuis boire jusques au dîner, et n'en rendis une seule goutte' (I drank it five hours before dinner, and did not pass a single drop of it) (p. 272); 'à compter tout ce que je rendais en 24 heures, j'arrivais à mon point à peu près' (counting everything that I passed in twenty-four hours, it was almost as much as I had drunk) (p. 277). The ideal is balance: in, out, in equal amounts; 'good' fluid in, harmful matter flushed out. Montaigne writes of his fear of not urinating enough (according to this model): 'le jeudi matin, j'en rebus cinq livres, craignant d'en être mal servi et ne les vider' (on Thursday morning I again drank about five pints, fearing they would do me no good and that I would not get rid of them) (p. 277). He notes the colour of his urine; thus, his description of his bodily functions is consistent with existing medical models.[15] He also notes the presence of what he calls 'sable' (sand), gravel in his urine, that is, when particles of his kidney stones are excreted. He experiments with how much he drinks, how much he bathes, and tests the prescribed practices of the spa; he enjoys this spa and its social life; but this descriptive and prescriptive model (in, out, restoration of 'balance') says little about his pain.

The language for pain has to disrupt such calculation, such an economy, and to erupt in an attack on it: 'c'est une sotte coutume que de compter ce qu'on pisse' (measuring what you piss is a stupid practice) (p. 276). Such calculation is foolish, when it comes to kidney stones – 'calculs', calculus – and the physical, emotional and psychic economy of the subject, his 'calcul', calculation. 'Sotte',

---

[15] For a clear introduction to early modern medical practices and the diagnostic and prognostic functions of urine, see Siraisi, *Medieval and Early Renaissance Medicine* (Chicago, 1990).

stupid, here has something of the force it has in two of its many instances in the *Essais:* futile, self-deluding – vain, in the sense it has in 'De la vanité', a chapter to which I shall return shortly. In other words, the practice seems to have no bearing on, and to be incommensurate with, what it is to suffer such pain, whether the stone is an invisible foreign body within the body, a hard concretion in tender tissue, or is in transit. While Montaigne can convey something of the acute pain of toothache or migraine in his *Journal*, the experience of renal colic eludes expression, and he continues to use primarily a vocabulary of quantity, for instance: 'la quantité extraordinaire de sable que je rendais continuellement' (the extraordinary amount of gravel that I passed continually) (p. 295), until the middle of August 1581.

Fittingly what introduces a shift in his vocabulary is the recurring use of the adjective 'trouble' of his urine (pp. 321, 327, 328, 329): this is pain which cannot be 'measured' or calculated – such vocabulary is a decoy, a fictional rendering of, or accounting for, the pain. This affliction troubles him physically and troubles his capacity to communicate its specificity, even to himself, apparently. For despite his familiarity with his illness and the pain he suffers, and therefore some capacity to notate it, new suffering can still surprise him, as the following passage shows:

> La nuit je sentis au côté gauche un commencement de colique assez fort et même poignant, qui me tourmenta pendant un bon espace de temps, et ne fit pas néanmoins les progrès ordinaires … Le 21, je continuai mon bain après lequel j'avais les reins fort douloureux: mes urines étaient abondantes et troubles, et je rendais toujours un peu de sable. Je jugeais que les vents étaient la cause des douleurs que j'éprouvais alors dans les reins parce qu'ils se faisaient sentir de tous côtés. Ces urines si troubles me faisaient pressentir la descente de quelque grosse pierre: je ne devinai que trop bien. Après avoir le matin écrit cette partie de mon journal, aussitôt que j'eus dîné, je sentis de vives douleurs de colique; et pour me tenir plus alerte, il s'y joignit, à la joue gauche, un mal de dents très aigu que je n'avais point encore éprouvé. Ne pouvant supporter tant de malaise, deux ou trois heures après je me mis au lit, ce qui fit bientôt cesser la douleur de ma joue.
>
> Cependant, comme la colique continuait de me déchirer … (pp. 329–30)

(During the night, in my left side, I felt a violent and very acute attack of colic start; it tormented me for quite a while, and did not run its usual course … On the 21st I continued my bathing, after which my kidneys were very painful: I passed a lot of cloudy urine, and some gravel. It seemed to me that the pain in my kidneys was caused by wind, because I felt it all over. The cloudiness of my urine made me expect some large stone to appear; I was only too right. After writing my journal the next morning, just after eating I felt sharp colic pains; and lest their pain not be lively enough for me, they were joined by a very acute toothache in my left jaw; I had not felt the like before. Being unable to endure such discomfort, two or three hours later I went to bed, and the pain in my jaw eased soon after.

However, since the colic still tore into me …)

Twice he is overtaken by a new, unanticipated form of pain, reminding him that although he is the expert in his own illness, he remains subject to the pain it inflicts; knowledge is not mastery, and predictive imagining and articulation do not reduce the power of pain. The descriptive indices of pain also stand out from other passages in the *Journal*. 'Very acute attack ... tormented me': already this is not his usual quantification. It diminishes and then rebuilds: 'very painful ... cloudy ... so cloudy ... sharp pains ... very acute ... unable to endure': such pain can only be conveyed in terms of its being unbearable, until the passage reaches its maximal intensity: this is pain which tears him apart, tears into him.

The phenomenology of the pain is not precise here; but as the sole occurrence of the verb 'déchirer', to tear, with reference to his suffering, this suggests an attempt to convey the specific intensity of the pain. Against this, the momentary return three days later of an attitude of composed, Christian-Stoic acceptance of suffering and mortality is both impeccably orthodox and strangely remote from his pain again – until he allows that suicide might be justified: 'le seul remède ... c'est de se résoudre à les suffrir humainement, ou à les terminer couragueusement et promptement' (the only remedy ... is to be determined to suffer them humanly, or to end them promptly and courageously) (p. 331). Heretical – equally a recurrence of how pain *tears*: attacks tissue, organs, breathing, thinking, one's relationship with the external world; textually, it disrupts, dislocates, and throws the reader.

'De l'experience' offers versions of an acceptance of mortality which develop a more *seemingly* conventional stance. But his comments there do not demonstrate the power of physical pain to, in Scarry's term, 'make', not least because the focus is not on pain so much as on illness in relation to health. The communication of his pain is not the issue. Rather, he elaborates the ways in which, appealing to his imagination, he rationalizes the experience of illness and, when he mentions pain, the terms are deliberately general. What is offered here is an undifferentiated catalogue of more and less convincing attempts to convert illness into an experience of value for the individual – without Montaigne seeming very convinced himself: 'par tels argumens, et forts et foibles ... j'essaye d'endormir et amuser mon imagination' (by such arguments, strong and weak ... I try to soothe and beguile my imagination) (p. 1095). On the other hand, psychic or emotional pain may prove to be the source of 'making', that is, creative redefinition of the individual's relationship with the world beyond. I shall return to this question in my last section; before that, questions relating to the representation of pain remain to be explored.

How is Montaigne's pain represented in the *Essais*, specifically in 'De la ressemblance des enfans aux peres' and 'De la vanité'? Let us bear in mind that Montaigne begins 'De la ressemblance' with a reference to his writing; reflections on his illness and his relationship with his father follow from this. I shall return to the intrications of these themes shortly: once again, in order to discuss the place of pain in Montaigne's text, patterns of recurrence and deferral need to be part of the approach.

Here Montaigne represents the onset of his illness: from becoming acquainted,

to habituation, to struggle and subjugation by pain. 'J'ay pratiqué la colique
... j'entre des-jà en composition de ... je suis aus prises ...' (I have become
familiar with kidney stones ... I am already reconciled to ... I am struggling
with) (pp. 759, 760). It tests him: 'je suis essayé' (I am tested) (p. 762); and
he explores himself, 'je me taste' (I probe myself) (p. 762). What tests him
here is translation: how to put such pain into words. He reaches for repeated
superlatives, as if such extreme pain is not (quite) beyond communication: 'je
suis aus prises avec la pire de toutes les maladies, la plus soudaine, la plus
douloureuse, la plus mortelle et la plus irremediable' (I am struggling with the
worst of all illnesses, the most sudden, the most painful, the most fatal and the
most incurable) (p. 760). Such a chain of superlatives is unusual in his writing,
and seems symptomatic of the difficulty of conveying pain – it relies, in effect,
on the reader's identification and imagination, as well as fear. Thus it continues
to evade precise expression.

A similar device is used shortly after; he writes of his life having become
'la plus doloreuse et penible qui se puisse imaginer' (the most intolerable and
painful imaginable) (p. 763). Here the appeal to, even demand on, imagination
is explicit: it even is given an absolute turn. But this is still something of a
representational impasse: imagination is notoriously fickle, and that which we
imagine is perhaps only generalizable insofar as we imagine it to be. So, appeal
to imagination invites an identificatory reading while simultaneously exemplifying the limits of such a perspective and underscoring pain's singularity and
resistance to, or exceeding of, calculability and communicability: 'cette douleur
excessive' (this excessive pain) (p. 762).

This problem is inscribed here more intensely than in the *Journal* with its
vocabulary of calculation, as three further examples confirm. The first accen-
tuates the problem for knowledge as well as for communicability that is this
pain. Montaigne wants not only to convey its nature but also to understand its
– incomprehensible – cause: 'parmy les choses que nous voyons ordinairement,
il y a des estrangetez si incomprehensibles qu'elles surpassent toute la difficulté
des miracles. Quel monstre est-ce, que cette goutte de semence' (among the
things we see every day, there are things so strange and incomprehensible that
they are even more mysterious than miracles. What a prodigious thing is that
drop of semen) (p. 763). Secondly, he comments directly on pain's capacity
to dis-articulate him: 'je me taste au plus espais du mal et ay tousjours trouvé
que j'estoy capable de dire, de penser, de respondre aussi sainement qu'en une
autre heure; mais non si constamment, la douleur me troublant et destournant'
(I probe myself when the pain is most engulfing and have always found that I
was able to speak, think and reply as soundly as at any other time; but not so
steadily, for the pain troubles and distracts me) (p. 762).

The vocabulary of 'trouble', being troubled and distracted, is milder than
that sequence of superlatives designed to work on the reader's imagination and
fear, but no less resonant when we remember: 'c'est chose tendre que la vie et
aisée à troubler'. In the third instance, only three sentences later, Montaigne's
'trouble' is dramatized: 'les miennes me desgarsent estrangement!' (my kidney

stones estrange me from my desire, unmanning me) (p. 762). This pain takes away desire, and what is more, strangely: the 'trouble' that is the pain to which he is subject unmakes him and is a form of self-estrangement, his body occupied by 'foreign', inhospitable bodies.

In the same chapter conventional medicine comes under attack for failure to cure, and also for the violence of its methods, 'les violentes harpades de la drogue et du mal' (the violent struggles between the medicine and the illness) (p. 767) or for even worsening the patient's condition: 'on va troublant et esveillant le mal par oppositions contraires' (we aggravate and arouse the illness by attacking it with contraries) (p. 767). 'Trouble' recurs, and again the theme of the *tenderness* of life and the body returns; so too, the link between pain and scepticism, in two respects. Firstly, the abusive authority of doctors who, he says, tyrannize those weakened by pain and fear (see p. 769), is antithetical to the kind of more *balanced* relationship in which free and open thinking – here, attentiveness to the patient, sympathetic diagnosis and treatment, and respect for the patient's self-understanding – might flourish. That is, medical practice proves the need for a different form of thinking and relating – therapeutics. This without beginning to take into consideration the voiding of its presumed authority by its failure to cure ... Secondly, this form of treatment by contraries is a perverted version of scepticism, because the contrary is imposed and moreover imposed as the 'last word'. Thirdly, intellectual purgatives may appeal to Montaigne, as in the practice of scepticism, but not physical ones: 'faictes ordonner une purgation à vostre cervelle, elle y sera mieux employé qu'à vostre estomach' (order a purge for your brain, it will be more use there than in your stomach) (p. 768).

Here there is a clear distinction between mind and body. Elsewhere in the chapter, the impact of the body affected by pain on the mind is much more evident – the one 'troubles' the other, in an interrelation of mind, psyche and body more characteristic of Montaigne's epistemology. He insists on his 'condition' being 'mixte' (mixed) (p. 1107). If at that particular moment he distinguishes between them, he is thinking of them as organically distinct at the same time as they are intricated, and wants doctors – whose knowledge he clearly thinks is primitive and limited – to acknowledge how little they understand physiology, let alone the mind, which may be creatively purged, but only figuratively. Medicine, for Montaigne, is an 'art' full of unacknowledged 'confusion et incertitude' (confusion and uncertainty) (p. 777), inflated claims and promises, ignorance: 'la totale police de ce petit monde leur est indigestible' (policing this whole microcosm is too much for them to digest) (p. 774). Thus medicine is a paradigm of 'vanité', self-delusion and futility, and its dangers: 'la vaine chose que c'est que la medecine' (how futile and overrated medicine is) (*Journal*, p. 277).

In both 'De la ressemblance' and the *Journal* the possibility that spa waters might relieve his pain is clearly a motive for his journey. But when his reflections circulate around the theme of vanity, as enacted or identifiable in the structuring motif of the desire to travel, the absence of discussion of his pain

is striking. A rather detached passage, well into 'De la vanité', begins: 'je represente mes maladies, pour le plus, telles qu'elles sont' (I represent my maladies,
at most, just as they are) (p. 979): by referring to illness rather than pain, the
still problematic issue of conveying pain is avoided, although the claim that his
representation is 'telles qu'elles sont', as if he has found a form of linguistic
correspondence, leaves the reader in doubt.

Three hypotheses present themselves as to why detail of his pain, a phenomenon so closely associated with the 'vanity' of the human condition, is missing
from this chapter. 1. the comment, 'les souspirs de ma cholique n'apportent
plus d'esmoy à personne' (the groans of my colic no longer move anyone) (p.
981). Without taking Montaigne at face value, we might still wonder whether
his 'silence' is a disillusioned recognition of the impossibility of *his* pain being
expressible to anyone else? 2. illness is required in the chapter for its symbolic
force, namely, the catastrophic illness of the French body politic that Montaigne
was so eager to flee? Or 3. pain and illness here undergo a further turn, and are
integrated in reflections on his mortality.

The first of these possibilities returns us to those connections between pain
and writing with which 'De la ressemblance' opens; 'De la vanité' also has a
long reflection on writing towards its close, but it is not linked to pain. Contrary
to those arrogant doctors' claims, the body is 'indigestible', incomprehensible
largely because of the cruelty of the pains to which humans are subject – this
is its unpalatable, unwanted reality. But that which is indigestible may also be
transformed into writing; it is the antithesis of 'les plus delicieux plaisirs' which
'se digerent-ils au dedans, fuyent à laisser trace de soi' (the most delicious pleasures are digested inwardly, and avoid leaving any traces) (p. 665). The excess
of this pain which Montaigne feared most: 'en plus grande horreur, des mon
enfance ... que je craignois le plus' (held in the greatest horror since childhood
... which I feared the most) (p. 759), and which unmans, dislocates, isolates and
robs of desire, is also pain which challenges the sufferer to make it understandable to others, to want others to feel it. If others lose interest in it – a cruel dread
for chronic sufferers – then the failure of, or imagined by, the writer, becomes an
additional form of pain. However, it still continues to raise questions to do with
suffering and its expression. Not for Montaigne Stoic or Christian resignation;
pain is an affront to philosophy as well as to language. 'En accidents si extremes
c'est cruauté de requerir de nous une demarche ... composée' (in such extreme
misfortunes, it is cruel to require us to remain composed) (p. 761). Instead, a
howl, a cry: 'pousser hors la voix avec plus grande violence ... qu'il crie tout à
faict' (to cry out more violently ... let him really shout out) (p. 761).

In a passage altered in posthumous editions of the *Essais*, Montaigne both
differentiates and connects 'philosophy' and 'poetry':

> comme si elle [sc. la philosophie] dressoit les hommes aux actes d'une
> comedie, ou comme s'il estoit en sa jurisdiction ... qu'elle empesche donq
> Socrates de rougir d'affections ou de honte, de cligner les yeux à la menasse
> d'un coup, de trembler et de suer aux secousses de la fiévre: la peinture de la

Poesie, qui est libre et volontaire, n'ose priver des larmes mesmes les personnes qu'elle veut représenter accomplies et parfaictes. (p. 761)

(as if she [sc. philosophy] were rehearsing men to act in a play, or as if it were
in her jurisdiction … let her stop Socrates blushing with affection or shame,
blinking when a blow threatens, trembling and sweating when fever grips; the
descriptions of Poetry, who is free and acts as she wills, do not dare to deprive
of tears even those she wishes to represent as complete and perfect.)

Beyond 'philosophy', that is, the conventions of Stoicism and Christianity; in
their place, the ideal of Socrates, so not altogether beyond philosophical 'jurisdiction'; and via Socrates, a line runs between another form of philosophy and
poetry. In Montaigne's last revision of the passage explicit mention of poetry and
Socrates is lost. Instead it focuses on allowing the sufferer to express his pain, so
long as it is 'sans effroy' and 'sans desespoir' (without fear, without despair) (p.
761) – either a perverse injunction or a belief in philosophy's power to diminish
such passions. No poetry, but this is nonetheless a poetics of pain: 'preste ces
plaintes volontaires au genre des soupirs, sanglots, palpitations, pallissements
que Nature a mis hors de notre puissance' (let [sc. philosophy] consider these
voluntary laments as she would the sighs, sobs, shaking, loss of colour, which
are Nature's and beyond our control) (p. 761). Pain can be articulated, it seems,
by setting aside current 'philosophy', by invoking Socrates – as long as fear and
despair do not taint it. They must be managed, or, for the writer, silenced or
veiled: indeed, returning to the *Journal* we shall now see that, for Montaigne,
their place seems beyond verbal representation, until they make their presence
felt in strange dislocations. Montaigne is not alone in thinking that profound
emotional pain must be conveyed by veiling or transforming it – figuring it.
In 'De la tristesse' ('On sadness'), reflecting on representations of unendurable
griefs, he recalls the covered face of Agamemnon grieving over the sacrifice of
his daughter Iphigenia, and the metamorphosis of Niobe, insensible at the deaths
of her fourteen children, turned to stone.

'Ne desmentir l'image de mes conditions'

Now my focus moves from what troubles the representation of physical pain
to less constantly felt, but more profoundly troubling, sources of pain and their
effects on Montaigne's subjectivity. Some are not unconnected to his physical
pain, but what undoes him is the emotional and psychic pain of loss – of his
father, of his 'brother'. The phenomenology of both forms of pain is to be both
desolating and isolating, and to saturate the subject's experience of being in the
world. Physical and psychic pain are linked in the text by the motif of haunting
or ghosts and spectres, thus associated with ways in which the past informs the
present and future.

I shall turn shortly to the ways in which pain haunts Montaigne's body, how
his father haunts him, and how his spectral 'brother' makes his presence felt. As

a preliminary, let us pause and consider ways in which, in his *Journal*, Mont-
aigne's representations of place involve displacements and dislocations; troubling perspectives, whether jarring narrative shifts, descriptive disjunctions, or
disturbing conjunctions, unsettle representation. These aspects of the representation of more literal, geographical place are symptomatic of, and on a continuum
with, the instances of Montaigne's psychic and affective geography or place, as
the following citation obliquely suggests: 'j'y ay pratiqué la colique par la liberalité des ans ... Je voudray bien, de plusieurs autres presens qu'ils ont à faire à
ceux qui les hantent long temps ...' (I have become familiar with kidney stones,
which the passing years have generously given me ... I could wish, out of all the
other gifts the years hold for those who haunt them long ...) (p. 759). To live is
to 'haunt' time; one's symbolic place in time is that of a spectre. Living, one is
already a ghost, in the traces of one's past that continue to shade one's present
and future being, of others' pasts, and of one's own mortality which are already
everywhere in one's life: 'je sens la mort qui me pince continuellement la gorge
ou les reins' (I feel death's pinch constantly in my throat and kidneys) (p. 978).
One's own dying, as envisaged here, haunts one's living. The fear that haunts
Montaigne, his greatest dread, is becoming ill like his father. What haunts are
traces of fear and anxiety, unfinished business, and loss. In 'De la vanité' the
word that gathers these aspects of the place of the past in the present and future
is 'image'. Thus what haunts is also an aspect of 'true representation': 'l'image
de mes conditions' (representation of my qualities) (p. 980) – which by implication may also have a spectral dimension.

There are just five occurrences of 'image' in the chapter. Another, removed,
still haunts the text; I shall come to it shortly. Two of the five refer to Rome, its
polity and Empire; the first anticipates its fall, by describing its originary lack
of polity: 'à peine reconnoit-on *l'image* d'aucune police soubs les premiers
Empereurs' (you can scarcely find any trace of polity under the first emperors)
(p. 960), or, no ghost of a polity, which must be the (in a sense impossible)
ghost of what was to come. The second finds some trace still of what Rome
was, after her 'death': 'encore retient-elle au tombeau des marques et *image*
d'empire' (even in the tomb she still retains some signs and trace of empire)
(p. 997). Another instance conjures up the way in which his father's desire and
identity haunt Montaigne and the place called home, as anxiety: 'Jà, à Dieu ne
plaise que je laisse faillir entre mes mains aucune *image* de vie que je ne puisse
rendre à un si bon pere' (God forbid that I let fail in my hands any ghost of life
that I could give back to so good a father) (p. 951). This instance will haunt the
term's return, referring to his self-representation, the '*image* de mes conditions'
(representation of my qualities) (p. 980). The fifth occurrence of 'image' refers
to what remains of traditional law: ghosts that bind Montaigne to the French
monarchy. 'Autant que l'*image* des loix receuës et antiennes de cette monar-
chie reluyra en quelque coin, m'y voilà planté' (while the ghost of accepted,
ancient laws of monarchy still remains in some corner, that's where I will be)
(p. 994) – implying that much of what Montaigne considered to be 'good law'
had already 'died'.

To stay with place, for a while, let us return to Rome, to consider the presence of the past together with other forms there of what we might call the other, who captured Montaigne's attention. This will be a brief outline, only enough to support my interpretation of the place of haunting in his *Journal* as well as in 'De la vanité'.

The *Journal*'s first section, written by a secretary, relies on the convention of the eyewitness record, 'nous vîmes' (we saw) being the predominant verb and subject pronoun.[16] This suggests confidence in the validity of empirical description, of an account as a (selective) catalogue of things seen. But already before Montaigne took over the writing, there are unsettled or unsettling moments, such as in this description of Verona: 'ce que nous y vîmes de plus beau … ce fut le lieu qu'ils appelent l'Arena … Nous y vîmes aussi les Juifs' (the finest thing we saw there … was the place they call the Arena … We also saw the Jews) (p. 158): the apparent commensurateness of the sights, ancient amphitheatre, object of cultural prestige, and sequestered humans, is odd. Nonetheless the visual descriptive mode, seemingly incurious about the complexity of the temporal, spatial and cultural relations between the different phenomona seen, prevails – until Montaigne's overall authorship, which begins in Rome. At once there is a shift; the nature of what can even be seen is an aspect of the first experience recorded. Montaigne happened to witness, with lively curiosity, an exorcism; his quite detailed description has the effect of calling the practice into question: the devil's failure to manifest himself is presented to Montaigne as 'evidence' of his tenacity, but Montaigne's representation suggests, rather, the failure, or questionable validity, of the practice.

For Montaigne (unlike others) Rome is not a place of pilgrimage or the culmination of his journey; he is fascinated by religious practices but from what might be called an anthropological perspective. He enjoys Rome as a city inhabited by strangers, eternal city in which much is transitory: 'c'est la … ville du monde … où l'étrangeté et différence de nation se considère le moins' (of all cities in the world it is the one in which strangeness and differences of nationality matter least) (p. 231). He is particularly curious about traces of the past, not only ruins but, say, inscriptions and routes, and about the others he encounters there: Jews, *conversos* (p. 223), the humanist scholar and poet Muret (who had taught him) exiled from France for homosexuality (p. 214), a heterodox Portuguese 'belle secte' (fine sect) (p. 220) which he records as practising same-sex marriage, prostitutes … The otherness which teems in Rome is noted when encountered, not analysed; but that this Rome is a site of challenge to conventions of travel

---

[16] The Leydet copy of Montaigne's *Journal* suggests that Montaigne had other secretaries besides this one, with whom he parted company in Rome, to whom he dictated. See Brush, 'The Secretary, Again', *Montaigne Studies* 5/1–2 (1993), pp. 113–38, and Hoffmann, *Montaigne's Career*, ch. 2.

writing such as existed at the time[17] and to his own expectations and under-standing seems clear.[18]

Rome visited, as recorded, is haunted by its potential to be anatomized, archeologized and anthropologized, its present re-presented by his focuses and by his being free from it symbolizing an ideal for him, or the end (telos) of his journey. The symbolic Rome of revered texts is invisible: 'il disait qu'on ne voyait rien de Rome' (he said that one saw nothing of Rome) (p. 200).[19] The Vatican may dominate the city, but Montaigne's Rome is peopled by those who are displaced, exiled, denied authentic identity and belief, subjugated, or those such as prostitutes whose role is to service the more complex and unsanctioned desires of Rome's citizens, including her cardinals (p. 231). His otherness is not theirs, except insofar as some (Jews, homosexuals) are in a form of flight. To say that theirs was forced, but his not, is true in terms of cultural and religious realities of the time; however, when it comes to unconscious reasons for flight, the distinction between what is forced or unforced is less straightforward. While in 'De la vanité' Montaigne gives clear reasons for wanting to travel, that he may have been in flight from his unsettling awareness of mortality (his own, and as felt in the continuing pain of the loss of his father and 'brother') is not so explicit. The determination to travel may demonstrate that one is not afraid of dying (see p. 213 above), but that is not to say that pain and some fear do not stay with one: why else, arriving at almost each new place, his preoccupa-tion with whether he could die as he wished there?[20] Just one of his 'foibles humeurs' (frailties) (p. 983)? It is not for nothing that it is presented: would it not be vanity, that is, self-delusion, to believe oneself fully free of such fear?

Least of all in Rome. The past ideal is dead: 'ce n'était rien que son sépulcre' (nothing but its sepulchre) (p. 200). The humanist ideals that gave intellectual vigour to his generation had already lost their lustre: they are thinkers whose vision of the present and the future had been built on nostalgia for a lost past, and many of whom, in the decades of desolation and primitivism of war, were increasingly at a loss to envision a positive future. Montaigne's curiosity and sense of possibility, in Rome, sometimes feeds on the company of the cultur-

---

[17] On the embryonic conventions of early modern accounts of travel in the 'old' world as well as towards the 'new' see: Atkinson, *Les Nouveaux Horizons de la Renaissance française* (Geneva, 1935), Campbell, *The Witness and the Other World* (Ithaca, 1988), and MacPhail, *The Voyage to Rome in French Renaissance Literature* (Stanford, 1990).

[18] For a rich analysis of Montaigne's handling of challenges in the Rome that is also the site of the Vatican, see Boutcher, 'Le Moyen de voir de Senecque escrit à la main', in O'Brien (ed.), *(Ré)interpretations*, Michigan Romance Studies 15 (Ann Arbor, 1995), pp. 177–214.

[19] This is, of course, already a nostalgic humanist motif; see, for instance, in Du Bellay, *Les Antiquitez de Rome* (1558), sonnet 3: 'Nouveau venu, qui cherches Rome en Rome/ Et rien de Rome en Rome n'aperçois' (Newcomer, seeking Rome in Rome/ But seeing nothing of Rome in Rome) (lines 1–2).

[20] 'J'advoue qu'en voyageant je n'arrive gueres en logis où il ne me passe par la fantaisie si j'y pourray estre et malade et mourant à mon aise' (I admit that when I travel, I hardly ever arrive at my lodgings without it crossing my mind to wonder if I could be ill and die there in comfort) (p. 983).

ally powerful, but also, importantly, on those who are displaced or inhabit the margins: 'tous ces amusements m'embesognaient assez; de mélancolie, qui est ma mort, et de chagrin, je n'en avais nulle occasion' (all of these amusments occupied me well enough; I had no occasion for melancholy, which is the death of me, or for upset) (p. 230).

His relationship with Rome was not theirs: his was on the one hand a long-standing imaginary city and civilization, a humanist fantasy, a source of intellectual *nourishment*: 'j'ay esté nourry dés mon enfance avec ceux icy [sc. les Romains]' (from childhood I was raised with those dead [Romans]) (p. 996).[21] On the other, his was comparatively free, in that Rome was not the aim of his travels and he had no desire to stay. Nonetheless, he was subject to Rome in terms of the Vatican censors' power to suppress his text or force him to alter it. Punishment of ideas was not new in Rome, he knew. In 'De l'affection des peres aux enfans', written shortly before his travels, he already mentioned the first death sentence in Rome against writing and learning;[22] he was also prepared to encounter the censors. Montaigne was fortunate, in that his writing was neither put on the Papal Index, nor was he forced to make changes intolerable to him. The censors allowed his freedom as a secular thinker and writer, while leaving it to him ('ils me remettaient à moi-même' (*Journal*, p. 237)) to make revisions to aspects of his text that ran counter to theological doctrine, such as his concept of 'fortune'.[23] Whilst they may not have constrained his freedom, their power to inhibit the free expression of ideas was growing, as was that of the Inquisition. Nor were the wars that threatened his own home any closer to resolution: a form of censorship also, in their primitive enactment of the refusal of a just or open hearing to those whose religious beliefs differ – 'enemies', therefore. Montaigne's refusal to excise his account of Julian the Apostate from 'De la liberté de conscience', but in fact to give it more prominence in the Bordeaux edition, seems symptomatic of his understanding of the link between censorship and war, given that freedom of conscience continued to be denied in France.

As his secretary noted (p. 190) and as Montaigne's own account of his dealings with the censor also makes clear, Rome was not an ideal or place of intellectual freedom for him; Venice, the city associated closely with La Boétie by virtue of being a republic, was preferable. But Montaigne was nonetheless very

---

[21] With the metaphor of nourishment, we return to the figures of 'De l'institution', not least those relating to his appetite for Latin texts, among others (see p. 175). It is, moreover, a chapter in which travel is promoted, as being culturally and socially enlivening and a good introduction to human diversity (see p. 153). On Montaigne's Rome see McGowan, 'Contradictory Impulses in Montaigne's Vision of Rome', *Renaissance Studies* 4/4 (1990), pp. 392–409, and McKinley, 'Poétique du lieu', in *Montaigne e l'Italia* (Geneva, 1991), pp. 339–50.

[22] The case is that of the writer Labienus (see p. 400).

[23] For details of the censors' report on the *Essais*, based on recently discovered archival evidence, see Legros, 'Montaigne face à ses censeurs romains de 1581', *BHR* 71/1 (2009) (pp. 7–34). Scholar's discussion (*Montaigne*, pp. 166–80) of the complexities of Montaigne's dealings with the censors while in Rome and the effects traceable in his text is fascinating.

determined to gain Roman citizenship. Why? The reasons he offers, 'l'ancien honneur et religieuse mémoire de son autorité' (the ancient honour and religious memory of its authority) (p. 232), are opaque, given that Rome had become a site of nostalgia and loss. To be persuaded we would have to take at face value the comment that Rome was 'la plus noble [ville] qui fut et sera oncques' (the noblest [city] there ever was or will be) (p. 1000). Montaigne does not usually parrot such unqualified hyperbole about any place, nor readily use an adjective of such conceptual complexity as 'noble'; never mind what his own account of Rome already revealed. (Perhaps the elision of Rome present, in that 'fut et sera' – the intervening 'est' (is) is missing – is a surreptitious unsettling of the superlative?) Is this not the hollow hyperbole of public rhetoric, as required in, say, a speech of acceptance? Once again, an instance of 'vanity'? The 'bulle' (bulla) conferring citizenship ends up in full in 'De la vanité': as McKinley has already noted, *bulla* and 'bulle' connote illusory vanity, like a bubble.[24] Indeed, Montaigne cannot use the word without this resonance, for this was already a classical trope. Montaigne delights in precisely its vanity; his own vanity is 'fed' by it: 'se paist' (p. 999) – those metaphors of appetite again. Supposedly wanting to satisfy readers' curiosity, he presents a transcription of the full Latin text; thus (Papal) Latin is subsumed by (his) French, Rome's prestige encased in his comments on illusion, and Rome now takes its place within the 'chez moy' of his own text.

This subsuming is an act symbolic of the freedom that survives for Montaigne as *writer*. The relation between Montaigne's personal psychological identity and his symbolic identity ('Mayor of Bordeaux' 'citizen of Rome' 'son of Pierre Eyquem' ... among other signs of status) resolves into this third term; in his writing he finds a way of putting into place these different aspects of his subjectivity. He admits to his desire, at the same time admitting to its being illusory, allowing a set of more complex reflections on his identity and also using his freedom as a writer to represent Rome's under-represented inhabitants. It was in their company that he escaped his melancholy, not in that of cardinals and Rome's elite, and by commemorating these encounters in his writing, as well as responding in his own way to the censors, his writing remains the site of a form of freedom and freer identity.

This can be retold as a narrative of place. Montaigne, travelling, is out of place in the eyes of those who see him as property-owner, public official, son, husband, father, family man. Montaigne's route is never direct; he is always ready to make a detour; and of course, if his journey has no end, then the absence of this symbolic place disturbs the relationship between direct and indirect or detour. Montaigne in Rome is curious about those whose place is ambiguous, conflicted, unorthodox, prohibited. But that in Rome everyone has a place proves a complicated notion. 'Chacun y est comme chez soi ... la consi-

---

[24] See McKinley, *Les Terrains vagues*, p. 118. McKinley develops a very interesting reading of the intertext with Erasmus's *Ciceronianus*, both as regards the *bulla*/ 'bulle' of vanity and more broadly in the chapter: see pp.120, 128–30.

dération d'origine n'a nul poids' (everyone is as if at home ... origin is not a consideration) (p. 231). In 'De la vanité' he repeats this – almost: 'chacun y est chez soi' (everyone is at home there) (p. 997). So long, that is, as they are Christian. The 'comme', as if, of the *Journal*, has disappeared, as has mention of origin. In the *Journal* Montaigne is not out of place, or no one is in place: the distinction between 'in' and 'out' of place is obscured if origin is disregarded. The limits are also obscured, absent the reference to Christianity in the later version; it however does not allow the complexity of the earlier, with its 'as if', which renders the relationship between subject and place more contingent.

There is no resolution to these differences, but in Montaigne's thinking and self-representation, place is freed from what it had meant in the eyes of others, and in the end, while it is – and this is important – not a resolution, it is by writing and in his written version of himself that an alternative 'chez moi' is produced. What is particular about this place, true to the logic of more fluid identity and resistance to place-holding, is that the meanings it contains are not altogether fixed; a form of freedom is handed over to the reader, over time, to find further meaning. I shall return to the relationship between place and writing in my final chapter.

There is another dimension to these encounters with others that we should not overlook: the association between the other and death, or awareness of mortality. For instance, his account of hearing a converted rabbi preach, excellently, is followed by a reference to also hearing Padre Toledo, a Jesuit, and a few lines later, a comment on the Jesuits (whose eloquence he has just praised), as the branch of his church that most threatened those thought heretic (see p. 223). To give up one's religious belief and culture may be the only way to escape death, whether one is Jewish or a Reformer. The issues that drove the troubles of France (and also of Germany and Switzerland, as noted in the earlier part of his *Journal*) have not been left behind; they haunt the Roman experience. In a long passage written by his secretary, but which seems to closely follow Montaigne's responses to Rome ('il disait que ...' (p. 200)), the destruction wrought by contemporary religious schism is recalled by the Rome that is built over its ruins:

> les bâtiments de cette Rome bâtarde qu'on allait asteure attachant à ces masures antiques, quoiqu'ils eussent de quoi ravir en admiration nos siècles présents, lui faisaient ressouvenir proprement des nids que les moineaux et les corneilles vont suspendant en France aux voûtes et parois des églises que les Huguenots viennent d'y démolir. (p. 201)

> (the buildings of this bastard Rome which they were now joining to the ancient ruins, may very well seem wondrous here and now, but they reminded him exactly of the nests that sparrows and crows suspend from the arches and walls of churches in France recently demolished by the Huguenots.)

In this city which in the present seems open to all, Montaigne remembers the ruin of monuments and other symbolic structures, and layers of destructive an-

Lacan: only sustained by O, wh confers image wholeness
= Thg, lost obj. (mother) Real

tagonism, akin to that of Roman Catholics and Huguenots – not in Rome's case
religious schism, but enmity with the same binary structure.

Rome is describable as a 'ville rapiécée d'étrangers' (a city pieced together
from foreigners) (p. 231), inhabited by foreigners, everyone each other's other;
but Montaigne seems keenly aware of a different dimension of otherness. His
curiosity about religious practices and rituals, particularly exorcism, flagellation
or purported miracles, is of this order: these are ways of exploring belief in the
power of God, as the Other whose power confers wholeness and coherence on
the subject. Montaigne does not doubt God's existence, but he is sceptical (in
an ordinary sense) about Catholic practices such as exorcism and worries away
at the significances ascribed to God, particularly in such rituals; elsewhere he
insists on the power of human fantasy and imagination in such domains. He
does not look to God to confer a sense of self-recognition.

That God might be the locus of the Other for Montaigne in Rome is unsurprising, given the symbolic significance of the Vatican. But this converges on
another version of the Other inescapable here: the aspect of human desire entangled with vanity, of which the fall of Rome was a paradigm. Let me turn to
Lacan, briefly, to suggest what a symbol of political and cultural ambition and
its undoing has to do with God.

Each can be conceptualized in terms of the Other. The Other (God, Roman
ideal, those such as the father who occupy the place of the Other in one's
psyche), whatever the subject imagines as conferring wholeness, integrity and
coherent meaning on him or her, is what sustains the subject.[25] The originary
Other is also what Lacan calls the Thing, and is *the* lost object, the mother,
fantasized as the source of bliss and plenitude – to possess whom would in
reality be catastrophic. Not simply because it is a cultural taboo, but because to
possess her would be to discover that she was not the whole and perfect being
of fantasy. The Thing is at once what is most wanted and most to be feared, in
terms of the possible consequences of the subject's desire. Never either really
possessed, nor ever recoverable, and not symbolizable; its substitutes may exist
in the Imaginary, but its place is in the Real.

One effect of casting the Other as the source of recognition is that the subject   *recog.*
sacrifices his or her (authentic) desire in order to have the Other's (fantasized)
acknowledgement. For example, the child who chooses not the career he or she
dreams of but the one his or her father wants for him or her: this desire is to be
as I am in the Other's eyes. Thus Montaigne, struggling with his father's bequest
of the Montaigne estate, along with his other bequest, his anticipation that his
son would ruin it (p. 998): he wants to look after the property as well as his
father had, to be as the Other wanted. He did not ruin it: 'il se trompa' (he was
wrong) (p. 998). However, this does not mean that his father was wrong about
his being 'peu casanier' (far from stay-at-home) (p. 998); this is how his father

---

[25] Much of my account of the gaze is drawn from Lacan, *Le Séminaire XI*, pp. 65–112.

we sacrifice desire for recog.

saw him, and Montaigne's account of himself bears this out. The father/Other is revealed as in fact less than ideal, not a source of coherence and integrity.

The relationship between the subject and the Other is figurable as a gaze: not literally how one is seen but, rather, seen in the sense of how one imagines oneself to be perceived or acknowledged, recognized, and how this operates intersubjectively and culturally. For the subject to be able, via a belief in the Other (whether it be God, or an Imperial ideal, or the Lady, or death), to sustain a sense of self as more than an illusion or hopelessly lacking, this Other must itself lack nothing. If or when the moment of realization comes that the Other does lack – and come it must, for it is a product of our imagination, an effect of our need for illusory coherence rather than the cause – the subject will be traumatized, but (vitally) disillusioned.

In sixteenth-century terms, this way of thinking about God was not available; nor is that what concerns us here, except in terms of understanding the ways in which secular versions of the Other developed in relation to its religious form. But the Other that was the Imperial ideal is an eloquent example of the Other as lacking, and sustaining not political and cultural greatness but always already sustaining an illusion and disaster. *This* is what Montaigne 'saw' in Rome, and with the comment about this 'bastard' Rome and how what he saw reminded him of the consequences of religious schism at home, it is a way of thinking about that too. So perhaps this is the significance of those two interrelated 'images' of Rome in 'De la vanité', its originary lack of polity (p. 960) and its vestiges of empire beyond its grave (p. 997). These 'ghosts' of not-immortal Rome are the spectral reminders of its never having been ideal, but rather always lacking, and of any remaining ideal being illusory. Any striving which cannot recognize its basis in lack of wholeness (this being our condition), but claims exclusive wholeness and integrity as opposed to others' failing and lack, exemplifies such illusion and is potentially catastrophic. The early modern term for this version of our relationship with the Other is vanity, or its Latin form, 'vanitas'.

The Other, and its links with trauma, anxiety and death, are consonant for Lacan with early modern questions relating to subjectivity, desire and illusion. His key example is one of the period's most famous representations of 'vanitas', Holbein's *Ambassadors*, which indicates that their worldly significance and riches ('vanitas') are no consolation for mortality. Let's make a detour to England here (assuming that Holbein's two figures are French dignitaries at the court of Henry VIII) before rejoining Montaigne elsewhere in Italy, in Bains della Villa. Even though the 'gaze' is not to be understood literally, a visualization of what is at stake helps us understand it.

One form of the fantasized Other, that site of wholeness, plenitude, is also *the* lost object of everyone's desire, the *objet a* for which all other objects are substitutes. This is Lacan's Thing, 'la chose' (after Freud, 'das Ding'). It is both most desired and terrifying, and cannot be seen or symbolized, only intuited. It makes its presence felt obliquely, reminding us of the existence of another plane of signification, incommensurate with the Symbolic: the Real. Awareness of it is signalled by anxiety, dread, dislocation: we might say, it is what haunts us.

Thing ← Real

Holbein's composition is busy, the space between the two men full of objects symbolizing their prestige and values; but its strong structure is doubly triangular: as well as the two ambassadors' relationship with the viewer (for they seem to return our gaze), within the painting already is another triangle. They form two of its points, and the third is occupied, famously, by an anamorphic skull.[26] From the perspective which organizes the composition as a whole around the centre and in which the gazes of the painted figures and the viewer meet, this unsettling object is indecipherable; it is only perceptible as a skull when its different plane is given precedence, but to do so distorts the rest. The two planes are incommensurate. We are not dealing with the Symbolic and the Real, for the Real is unsymbolizable; but it makes its presence felt, as in the gap between the two conflicting planes here, and can be intuited via the anamorphic object, the presence of which slices across the plane of the Symbolic.

Let us return to that description of 'cette Rome bâtarde' (this bastard Rome). Of Rome, the classical ideal, Montaigne saw nothing; but in his imagination, the nothing takes on form as its tomb: 'rien que son sépulcre' (only its sepulchre) (p. 200), now reborn in 'bastard' form. For now; for what is seen and what it symbolizes, and the incommensurablity between the two provokes fear in Montaigne of its return to an unsymbolized nothing: 'encore craignit-il à voir l'espace qu'occupe ce tombeau, qu'on ne le reconnût pas tout, et que la sépultre ne fût elle-même pour la plupart ensevelie' (he was also afraid, seeing the space that was the tomb, that not everyone recognized it, and that the sepulchre was for the most part buried) (p. 201). This intimation of what Lacan calls the Real results from two anamorphoses: the radical disjunction between the unseeable nothing that remains and the 'bastard' materialization of Rome beyond its tomb; and the dislocation between the ideal of classical Rome and the present self-destructive state of France which Montaigne suddenly remembers and visualizes, an oblique symbolization of unsymbolizable death.

The anamorphic object which unsettles the gaze that the figures in Holbein's painting seem to exchange with the viewer is likewise an intimation of death. If, like Montaigne at times you consider dispassionately that 'vous estes en la mort pendant que vous estes en vie... pendant la vie vous estes mourant' (you are in death while you are in life ... in life, you are in death) (p. 93), the skull might be an object of aesthetic curiosity and pleasure, a prompt for meditation. But if, also like Montaigne, you know that this dispassion is not the whole story, that your capacity to be 'nonchalant' (careless) (p. 89) about the end of life is cut through by each singular death,[27] for you the skull will reach beyond dispassion, trigger anxiety, remind you of what it is you never really see, or what it is that can only be represented by being veiled or metamorphosed (like Niobe). Death may always be present, but that omnipresence does not reduce the dislocating acuity of particular experiences of it, as Montaigne's experience reminds us.

---

[26] On anamorphic representation, which flourished in the early modern period, see Baltrusaitis, *Anamorphoses* (Paris, 1955).

[27] See chapter 3 above, p. 101, for further discussion.

La B still alive

'L'ombre d'un homme'

It is now time to return to Montaigne in Italy, and to the place of the 'brother'. Already in the 1563 letter to his father on the death of La Boétie Montaigne had described his dying friend's increasingly ghostly presence; not yet a shade, but a shadow, 'l'ombre d'un homme', a spectral presence: 'non homo, sed species hominis' (not a man but a semblance of a man) (p. 1358). Some eighteen years later, we encounter La Boétie's spectral presence again. 'Je tombai en un pensement si pénible de M. de La Boétie, et y fus longtemps sans me raviser, que cela me fit grand mal' (I fell into such grievous, overwhelming thoughts of Monsieur de la Boétie, that it caused me great pain) (p. 277). Sidering grief, but as striking as his pain is the abruptness with which Montaigne's prose changes direction: 'cela me fit grand mal. Le lit de cette eau est tout rouge et rouillé' (it caused me great pain. The bottom of this bath is all red and rusty). Notations of the taste of the water, and of the amount Montaigne urinated (in … out …) follow. The writing recoils into that practice of calculation which, only lines earlier, had been condemned as a futile practice. This pain is beyond calculation and precise representation. But something persists in the gap between these different planes.

Others have already noted this disjunction and the disorientating effects of grief, and have offered phenomenological or psychoanalytic interpretations of Montaigne's dissociation,[28] but there is more to say. It reminds Montaigne of the ways in which he is not fully who he thinks he is, but inhabited by the enigmatic traces of others, here, his lost friend. We might read this as an experience of the uncanny, a spectral call on his body, the experience of which is untranslatable into words and representable only performatively by dislocation: an encounter with the Real, that is, a state of traumatic anxiety.[29]

As Montaigne had put it in the dedicatory letter to M. de Mesmes appended to La Boétie's translation of Plutarch's *Rules of Marriage*, dated 30 April 1570, his lost friend, 'se loge encore chez moy si entier & vif, que je ne le puis croire si lourdement enterré' (he still lodges in me, so whole and alive, that I cannot believe that he is buried so deep in earth).[30] His two previous sentences conveyed his desire to *revive* his friend, and his belief, couched in present tenses, of his awareness of this: 'je … m'essayois … de le ressusciter & remettre en vie. Je croy qu'il le sent aucunement, & que ces miens offices le touchent & resjouissent' (I tried … to revive him and bring him back to life. I think he is somehow aware of this and that my services touch him and bring him joy): less a matter of revival than of still being alive – to Montaigne. This vocabulary anticipates the figures he will use in his later chapter on friendship; he not only haunts him, but he lives in him, as if undead; precisely the conditions for an uncanny encounter,

---

[28] Among these discussions, see Starobinski, *Montaigne en mouvement*, ch. 1 passim.

[29] In *L'Inquiétante Etrangeté* Pot works with the return of the repressed and emphasizes the political implications of the episode, rather than its affective dimension and its uncanniness (pp. 180–1).

[30] *Oeuvres complètes*, ed. Thibaudet and Rat, pp. 1361–2 (p. 1362).

that is, with that which *should* be missing.[31] We may find a reminder here of La Boétie's dying call on his friend to which he had failed adequately to respond (but then, what human response to such a call does not fail?). The call therefore makes its presence felt otherwise.

We might also think about the story Montaigne had just heard, before this spectral experience (pp. 274–5). It is presented as an '*accident* mémorable' (memorable accident) (p. 274, my italics): while this might be translated as an occurrence, we are also reminded that it came to Montaigne's attention unexpectedly, so had that jolting, disruptive power that is relevant here. This is the tale (see pp. 274–5) of an Italian soldier, Giuseppe, who, captured by the Turks, 'se fit Turc' (became a Turk); then, as a member of a Turkish marauding party he was captured by Italians who took him to be Turkish, whereupon he declared himself to be Christian, and thus, after some twelve years' captivity, regained his freedom. Returning to Lucca, he went to see his mother, who at first failed to recognize him, seeing only what was 'étrange' (strange). When she finally recognized him, so great was her shock that: 'elle, ayant fait un cri, tombe tout éperdue' (she uttered a cry and collapsed, beside herself) (p. 274). The moment of recognition was beyond words, she could only cry out. The account is somewhat enigmatic: the recognition killed her, but whether it was shock or joy remains unknown. Giuseppe – now 'nostre Giuseppe' (our Giuseppe), reclaimed for Christians – abjured his Islamic faith and recovered his Christianity – but it was all a sham, for he was, as Montaigne puts it, 'Turc dans son coeur' (Turk at heart), and fled to Venice to join the Turks again, only to be recaptured by the Genoese and conscripted, 'bien attaché et garrotté' (well bound and fettered).

Here is a story which resonates with what will happen to Montaigne in that same place. Giuseppe's story seems to have fascinated Montaigne: what might it mean to give up one identity for another, and discover that one had become, deep down, one's adopted identity? Or was this one's 'unknown' self all along? Where and how are we most ourselves? Can recognition and emotion kill? What is the relation between body and emotion, organic heart and heart that loves? Perhaps such questions preoccupied Montaigne as he drank the waters at Bains della Villa and (however reluctantly) monitored what went in and what came out of his body, and inform possible readings of his uncanny encounter with La Boétie. In me that which is not me.

Giuseppe, Turk at heart, could not give up what he really wanted whatever the cost, even that of becoming an enemy to his own people; we might also say that Giuseppe's story is about the recognition of what is other within us, our own inner strangeness – or, to use Lacan's term, that 'extériorité intime, *extimité*' (intimate exteriority, *extimity*).[32] A story about the possibility of knowing

---

[31] On the uncanny as the presence of that which should be absent, see Freud 'The Uncanny', in *An Infantile Neurosis and Other Works* (London, 1955), pp. 219–52, Lacan, *Le Séminaire X*, and Safouan, *Lacaniana* (Paris, 2001), pp. 231–54.

[32] On 'extimité', see *Le Séminaire VII*, p. 167. For a fascinating, different reading of the same episode, see Cave, 'Le Récit montaignien', pp. 134–5.

ourselves in our strangeness to ourselves rather than this remaining unknown
or unknowable, or knowable only in a momentary sense of the uncanny, the
force of which 'fait littéralement vaciller le sujet' (literally throws the subject
off balance) (Safouan, p. 237): 'je ... fus si longtemps sans me raviser, que cela
me fit grand mal' (such overwhelming thoughts, it caused me great pain) (p.
277). It is also a moment of acute anxiety, Lacan's uncanny moment of feeling
suspended between loss of one's former sense of self and (still disorienting)
discovery of a radically altered version of oneself.[33]

But when we read this story together with the 'pensement de M de La Boétie',
which is not thought at all, but rather an intimation the effect of which is to
make thought impossible, further possible interpretations emerge. Montaigne,
as already noted, is haunted both by what is other or what falls out of knowing
(p. 1029), and also, paradoxically – or it will seem so if we are lulled by the
lyrical evocations of perfect fusion in his chapter on friendship – he is haunted
by the intolerable closeness of his friend's presence at that moment. Also, here is
something of Montaigne's abiding preoccupation with the relationship between
the body and other aspects of being, the body seemingly beyond discourses of
the body available to him and beyond medicine, the body which speaks to him
of what cannot be cured in him, and of what otherwise would remain unex-
pressed and unknown.

This takes us back to the death of his friend, and to the question – for it
remains a question – of the place he wanted. In his letter to his father Montaigne
writes as if he is certain of understanding his friend; to quote one example: '*sans
doute ... j'avais *très certaine* connoissance des intentions, jugements et volontés
qu'il avait eus durant sa vie, autant *sans doute* qu'homme peut avoir d'un autre'
(*without doubt ... I had a *very certain* knowledge of his intentions, judgement
and wishes during his life, *no doubt* as sure as any man can have of another) (p.
1347, my italics). However, this insistent certainty seems, rather, the certitude
that is in fact an awful characteristic of dread. Also, there are two identities at
stake here, not only La Boétie's. Addressing his father, Montaigne is recovering
the place from which he himself can maintain himself and speak; the letter can
be read as his attempt to recover something of himself, Montaigne, from his
loss. The letter ends with La Boétie's last words: 'me nommant une fois ou deux
... il rendit l'âme' (saying my name once or twice ... he gave up the ghost)
(p. 1360); his friend also gives him *his* name. Whereas, strikingly in the course
of this letter, Montaigne only once, and there for instrumental purposes, names
La Boétie (see p. 1357). Instead he prefers the interchangeability of the term
brother, whereby each is repeatedly represented as 'my brother' for the other;
for instance: 'la mort n'a rien de pire que cela, lui dis-je lors, mon frère ... Mon
frère, mon amy, dit-il ... Cela n'est rien, lui dis-je, mon frère ... Vraiment non,
ce n'est rien, mon frère, me répondit-il' (death holds nothing worse than that,
my brother ... My brother, my friend, he said ... That is nothing, my brother,

---

[33] See Lacan, *Le Séminaire IV*, p. 226, and as discussed above, pp. 21–2.

I said … Indeed, it is nothing, my brother, he replied) (pp. 1349, 1353 and 1350).[34] The interchangeability of this identification masks the cardinal reality that no one can die in an other's place. And then from the seeming identity of this relationship of brothers, the letter struggles to retrieve a place for the writer – while at the same time culminating in what some read as a terrible confession, that the writer had failed to give his brother the place he asked for. Or had the brother failed him, by not conforming to contemporary ideals of 'dying well'?[35] Or do both fail each other?

This exchange has already been critically interpreted many times; frequently it is suggested that 'De l'amitié' became that place, or that the *Essais* as a whole were written to be the place of remembrance; or the tomb.[36] I touched on the passage in question earlier (see p. 106), but want to return here, to amplify that interpretation.

At the heart of the passage is the following exchange:

> il se prit à me prier et reprier avec une extrême affection, de lui donner une place … 'Mon frère, mon frère, me refusez-vous donques une place?' Jusques à ce qu'il me contraignit de le convaincre par raison … 'Voire, voire, me répondit-il; lors, j'en ai, mais ce n'est pas celui qu'il me faut …' Étant sur ses détresses, il m'appela souvent pour s'informer seulement si j'étais près de lui. (pp. 1359–60)

> (insistently and with extreme affection he entreated me again and again to give him a place … 'My brother, my brother, do you refuse me a place?' This until he forced me to convince him by reason … 'True, true, he replied; I have one [sc. a place] but it is not the one I need …' Very distressed, he kept calling out to me, wanting to know if I was still near him.)

Montaigne offered La Boétie reason, or the consolations of philosophy; his friend's response was, no, that was not what he needed, lacked or must have

---

[34] In only one of his dedicatory letters, written for the publication of the various texts by La Boétie entrusted to him, does Montaigne use the term again. In letters addressed to, for instance, M. de Mesmes, M. de l'Hôpital and M. de Foix, Montaigne's emphasis is on the public prestige of his friend: 'le plus grand homme de nostre siècle' (the greatest man of our time), 'l'un des plus propres & necessaires hommes aux premieres charges de la France' (one of those most suited to, indeed needed for, the highest offices in France) and 'son extreme valeur' (extreme worth) (*Montaigne: Oeuvres complètes*, ed. Thibaudet and Rat, pp. 1362, 1363 and 1367). Montaigne's rhetoric tends to conform to the discursive conventions of the genre of the dedicatory letter, of course; but it is nonetheless striking that the symbolic brother is reserved for a letter to his wife: 'ce mien cher frère & compaignon inviolable' (my dear brother and inviolable companion) (p. 1371).

[35] On these ideals, see Blum, 'De la *Lettre sur la mort de La Boétie*', and see above, p. 00.

[36] See Charpentier, 'Ecriture et travail du deuil dans les *Essais*', and Desan, *Les Commerces de Montaigne* (Paris, 1992), pp. 146–72. On the text as tomb see Butor, *Essais sur les Essais* (Paris, 1968), and Henry, *Montaigne in Dialogue* (Stanford, 1987).

('celui qu'il me faut' (the one I need)); but, what then was his question, and why did Montaigne not unhesitatingly give him the answer he wanted?

To speculate: 'mon frère, mon frère, me refusez-vous donques une place?' (my brother, my brother, do you refuse me a place?) Will you remember me? Or a disguised injunction, do not forget me? Do you recognize me? What is it to be a brother? Am I irreplaceable? Save me? Do you love me? Or a combination of all these?[37] What was Montaigne called upon to say? If the question were 'do you love me?' then Montaigne's going on writing about his friend, which he will, and about the love he has lost, needs also, simply, to be understood as all that anyone can do. In the face of the absolute, unconditional demand that drives that question, from the place that it puts us in, all that is possible is to never stop responding, because nothing will ever meet that demand. All the more so when the question is asked by someone about to die. Death's proximity reveals as illusory the imaginary identity, symmetry and reciprocity of love, as figured by the words 'my brother' passing to and fro between the two men.

In the *Essais* we find that Montaigne's passage from fantasy of fusion and perfect communication to acknowledgement of lack and of the ways in which language, understanding and love always fall short, was a continuing, unfinished process. Symptomatic of the process of realization is an addition, in 'De l'affection des peres aux enfans' of the question: 'et aura l'on jamais assez dict de quel pris est un amy?' (and will the true value of a friend ever be adequately expressed?) (p. 395), followed by further lament which was removed and then reinstated in the posthumous edition. The subtracted/restored sentences make the significance of 'dire' clear: 'faire à tout jamais les obsèques' (to be for ever performing his obsequies): the text becomes an endless ritual – one which not only can never be completed, but which also is what Montaigne enjoys: 'un pieux et plaisant office' (a pious and pleasant duty). So lack, if it can be admitted, can also become a source of pleasure. On the other hand, if obsequies are endless, perhaps the moment of realization of the absolute loss of the one who has died is always being deferred?

Another reading of this passage in the letter is that when put to the test, philosophy is found wanting. La Boétie is represented as wanting to die in accordance with their shared philosophical principles: 'les discours que nous avions tenus ensemble pendant nostre santé, nous ne les portions pas seulement en la bouche, mais engravez bien avant au cueur & en l'ame, pour les mettre en execution aux premieres occasions qui s'offriroient, adjousant que c'estoit la vraye prattique de nos estudes, & de la philosophie' (the words we had exchanged while we were in good health were not only on our tongues but engraved deep in our hearts and souls, ready to be acted on when the situation presented itself; he added that this was the true purpose of our studies, and of philosophy) (p. 1353). Montaigne also insists that it was something of this order

---

[37] Or again, consider Rigolot's reading, which identifies an echo of Christ's last words. See *Les Métamorphoses*, p. 77.

that his friend called upon him to give him, but what he offered did not meet
his friend's need. He was thrown, unable either to recognize his friend or the
question, except to realize, with hindsight, that it addressed him in a way that
was beyond philosophy and reason, beyond what he knew or knew of himself.

This moment is perhaps key to Montaigne's recognition of what will become
two abiding themes of his *Essais*: the limits to conventional thought systems,
when acutely tested, as by death, and more broadly, the need for the politics
and ethics which guide us in our relations with others in all their differences
to us and when they demand most of us, to be rooted not only in philosophical
reason, but also in an understanding of the things which we only recognize, too
late, when we are thrown by them.

That lack of recognition also marks the end of the deathbed scene. The dying
man was clear; he had been ready to die for three days: 'il y a trois jours que
j'ahanne pour partir' (for three days I have been desperate to leave) (p. 1360).
Yet Montaigne still believed that his becoming calm was a sign of hope: 'nous
confirma encores plus en nostre bonne esperance' (which strengthened our hope
still further) (p. 1360). With this in mind, he left the bedchamber. His friend was
dead within hours, calling his name. That naming is also anamorphic: Montaigne could leave the room, hoping for La Boétie's recovery – because he was
deluded. This is a form of 'looking away';[38] had he looked back, at the last
moment, he might, as one sees the skull in Holbein's painting, have realized the
truth. His name was called from the room which had become a different scene,
it should have broken the silence of his hope, rather as the anamorphic skull
cuts between the planes of symbolization, and as, later, that sudden memory of
his friend would shatter him in Bains della Villa. The difference between the
painted representation and the instances relating to the death of his friend is that
the art-ful representation offers the viewer some consolatory pleasure; the other
two are abyssal moments, even if in the letter the experience seems to have more
coherent narrative form.

It is not, as Montaigne came to be so acutely aware, just about others being
different to ourselves, but also about the knot of relations between what we do
not know in or of ourselves and what that strangeness, which already inhabits
us, allows us to recognize and bear in others, even, or particularly when, they
throw us. There are many instances in the *Essais* that echo this theme of internal
difference; to quote just one: 'nous sommes, je ne sais comment, doubles en
nous mesmes, qui fait que, ce que nous croyons, nous ne croyons pas' (we are,
I know not how, double within ourselves, which means we do not believe what
we believe) (p. 619).

La Boétie haunts Montaigne's writing; he keeps returning, throughout the
Essais, beyond the chapter in the first book. He is perfect friend, symbolic ideal
of 'brother', author of an admired essay, *and* the one Montaigne failed and who

---

[38] 'Vous ne pouvez le savoir – car vous vous détournez' (You cannot know – for you turn
away) (Lacan, *Le Séminaire XI*, p. 83).

perhaps, on his deathbed, seeming to turn from the philosophical ideals he had shared with Montaigne, may have been thought to fail both those ideals and his 'brother'. But the greatest way to fail the loved one is to die. This (as I am not the first to note) not only haunts Montaigne's writing; it is one of the essential reasons for his writing in the first place. As already suggested, the loss of La Boétie was also a loss of symbolic compass, for this man represented so many of Montaigne's ideals. That emotional and intellectual losses combine is a theme that returns in 'De la vanité', where the loss of Rome converges on that of his father and both of these in turn resonate with the death of La Boétie and all that he symbolized. For here, Montaigne recalls his very early acquaintance with classical Rome and its heroes who haunt the Rome he visits who, he claims, he knows better than any in the present day. The next two sentences draw the themes together: 'ils sont trespassez. Si est bien mon pere, aussi entierement qu'eux, et s'est esloigné de moy et de la vie autant en dishuict ans que ceux-là ont faict en seize cens; duquel pourtant je ne laisse pas d'embrasser et pratiquer le memoire, l'amitié et société, d'une *parfaicte union* et tres-vive' (they are dead. So is my father, as completely as them, and after eighteen years is as remote from me and my life as they are at sixteen hundred years' distance. However I do not cease to cherish his memory and know his love and companionship in a *perfect union* that is fully alive) (p. 996, my italics).

Despite earlier differentiations between his love for his 'brother' and any other love, here Montaigne, remembering the textual world opened up to him by his father's insistent desire that Latin be his first language, seems momentarily to put this relationship on a par with that of his and his 'brother': 'a perfect union'. Without this, he would not have had so formative – nourishing – a relationship with these heroes of Roman texts. He remembers them and commemorates them, intimately as well as in his writing: 'il me plaist de considerer leur visage ... je remache ces grands noms entre les dents et les faicts retenir à mes oreilles' (I like thinking about their faces ... I chew over their great names and make them resound in my ears) (p. 997).

'Le soing des morts nous est en recommendation' (the care of the dead is recommended to us) (p. 996): after death, it seems, there is no singularity: father, Roman heroes, all equally ('autant') lost to him, all now described as 'les morts' (the dead). But this is not quite the case. Although heroes now take on an exemplary role, Montaigne still repeats their names to himself, which maintains some singularity. More importantly, father, Rome and brother remain distinct. All haunt the text; but father and Rome are linked in a way that separates them from the brother; that is, both are associated with ruin. The ruins of Rome, perhaps foreseeable in its originary lack of good governance, which will haunt it; his father's prediction that he would be the ruin of his property – another proleptic ruin and haunting; and the more general observation that there are cultures in which father and child, child and father: 'naturellement l'un depend de la ruine de l'autre' (by nature, the one depends on the ruin of the other) (p. 185), in which the use of the present tense conflates past, present and future, implying the inescapability of ruin. The past ruins the future, or the future will ruin the past, unless – or such is Montaigne's untested antidote – by writing about past and present, possible futures can be imagined and the relation between past, present and future reconfigured.

7

Uncertain Futures

> If you place two or three things next to each other that have
> never been next to each other before, this will produce a new
> question. And nothing proves the existence of the future like
> a question.[1]

What is the relationship between Montaigne's questions – not only the questions
he explores but also his preference for inquiring rather than resolving or asserting – and the future, between his writing and its readers? Here I return to the
themes and problems of my earlier chapters, to consider how questions – possibilities raised by new placings of things, new relationships between them (which
we sometimes also call love) – like the effects of figuration in Montaigne's
writing, help build the text's relationship with the future. Whether through play,
seduction, surprise, disquiet or unsettling, what kinds of reading do his questions and reconfigurations engage? I shall focus on what is unsettling, and, as
before, what sustains the reader's relationship with testing material.

Sacrifice: 'une estrange fantasie'

I shall begin with the relationship between sacrifice and the ethics of writing.
Early modern French culture inherited an ethical tradition founded on sacrifice
and self-sacrifice, as required by unconditional belief in God and respect for the
law. Whilst the law retains an unconditional authority for Montaigne, his representation of sacrifice and self-sacrifice in the *Essais* tends to accentuate themes
of ambiguity, illusion, self-deception, cruelty and destructiveness. Sacrifice and
self-sacrifice seem far from a secure foundation for ethical relations, whether
they originate in a Judaeo-Christian doctrine or a more secularized model. But
what else could stand between humans and their 'inhumanité' (inhumanity) (p.
53)? Montaigne's career had moved from law, with all its injustice, in all its
necessity, to writing; perhaps the relations between text and readers produced by
his writing offer a possible form of equitable ethics based on intersubjectivity,
which might evolve?

No idealization here: this relationship is not free of destructive potential;
rather, it rests on the mitigating value of disillusioned acknowledgement of the

---

[1]   Michaels, *The Winter Vault* (London, Berlin and New York, 2009), p. 122.

inescapability of destructiveness and its links with the need to have the last word. An 'open', questioning text, however vulnerable, might be a part of what makes for a different, less belligerent future. This is not a grand theory of writing or art forms as redemptive and culturally transformative; rather, a suggestion about the transformative potential of disillusionment, made contemplatable by the form which writing or other art objects gives it; in particular, via the play of meaning produced by figuration.

The function of writing has centre-stage in what follows. Firstly, the void around which writing is produced and the ethics this signifies; then this ethics' engagement with sacrifice, as represented in the *Essais*; lastly, I shall discuss the ethics envisaged in what the text asks of the reader – and its anticipation that she – we – might fail in this.

Montaigne's instances of sacrifice are drawn from a wide range of sources and contexts, sacred and secular. What they expose reflects the turbulence of the time of writing, including what the wars signify of the troubled emerging of more secular subjectivity out of subjectivity overdetermined by the subject's relationship with the divine; moreover, they concern the place of love, and of knowledge, and the relationship between the past and the future.

Let us return to the void ('vuide') occupied by his writing; this is the description which opens 'De l'amitié'.[2] Lacan's work on art and ethics helps us read this and develop further ideas about the functions of literature (in this instance, Montaigne's writing) in the production of the kind of ethics that corresponds to doubtful thinking.

> Considerant la conduite de la besongne d'un peintre que j'ay, il m'a pris envie de l'ensuivre. Il choisit le plus bel endroit et milieu de chaque paroy, pour y loger un tableau elabouré de toute sa suffisance; et, le vuide tout au tour, il le remplit de crotesques, qui sont peintures fantasques, n'ayant grace qu'en la varieté et l'estrangeté. Que sont-ce icy aussi, à la verité, que crotesques et corps monstrueux, rappiecez de divers membres, sans certaine figure, n'ayants ordre, suite, ny proportion fortuité? (p. 183)

> (Watching how a painter I had employed was working, I felt a desire to imitate him. He chooses the best place, the middle of each wall, for a picture he will compose intricately using all his skill; and he fills the empty space around it with grotesques – fantastical paintings, whose only charm is their variety and strangeness. And what are these things here, in truth, but grotesques and monstrous bodies, pieced together from various different limbs, with no clear form and only fortuitous order, sequence and proportion?)

Others already have noted that, here, Montaigne's writing is rather like the style of painting described,[3] but I shall explore, rather, the relationship between art and the 'void' it frames: Montaigne's painting plus void-now-painting

---

[2] See pp. 91–2 for a first approach to the passage.
[3] Among these studies see Butor, *Essais sur les Essais*, pp. 66–72, Garavini, *Itinerari*

raises questions relating to the location of the frame and its meaning: the frame surrounds the work, or the work's existence reframes the space in which it is located?[4] The void that has become the painting in this passage is, emphatically, filled, as is the surrounding void. But only the latter is termed a void, although both spaces had been; and the emphasis of the description of the latter is less on plenitude than on strangeness and lack. So the reader's attention is drawn to there being a void, produced by art. However full it then becomes, a trace of its having been a void is left.

For Lacan the essence of art is to represent the void – but also to be a form of protection against it. In *L'Ethique de la psychanalyse* he focuses on creation *ex nihilo*: the void that is conceived from nothing and which therefore cannot be represented, is produced, retroactively, by artistic re-presentation, and we are lured into feeling protected from it. This void is Lacan's Real; so we return to death, as in our earlier encounter (see pp. 232–3) with its anamorphic, equally retroactive, re-presentation. This helps us to relate Montaigne's void to Lacan's.[5]

It is not for nothing that this passage opens 'De l'amitié', in which Montaigne mourns and celebrates his lost friend. His emphasis on his failings as an artist intimates that his writing may not completely conjure what threatens in the void. Whilst he may be able to produce those strange, indistinct, disorderly figures he cannot produce the plenitude of that painting within the frame; in this, the 'better' role, he falls short, unable: 'oser entreprendre un tableau riche, poly, et formé selon l'art' (to dare to undertake a rich, polished painting, a work of art) (p. 183). He wanted to use La Boétie's *De la servitude volontaire*: 'plein ce qu'il est possible' (as full as can be) (p. 184) to provide that. He goes on to explain why the essay does not occupy his text's centre. I have discussed this, and the additional dramatization of its absence by the substitution and then subtraction of his friend's sonnets (see pp. 91–7), so need not recap. But in the light of the meaning of the void just suggested, the absence of this 'full' work, together with the subtraction of his sonnets, and therefore their marked absence, takes on further significance, and risk.

The consequence of Montaigne's manoeuvres is that the void is held open as empty; and by drawing attention to the imperfections of his own writing around that void, he seems to offer the reader less protection from the Real than would a text which was rich, full of art or as full as can be. In its place, an incomplete and contingent text, lacking much order, sequence, proportion … It is 'rappiecez' (patched together); but while others patch their texts with 'inventions anciennes' (ancient inventions), the 'armes d'autruy' (others' armour) (p. 148), in what Montaigne calls a 'cowardly' attempt to disguise their own failings, his text has

---

a Montaigne, ch. 4, Tournon, *Montaigne en toutes lettres*, pp. 62–5, and McKinley, *Les Terrains vagues*, pp. 33–40.

   4 See, after Kant, Derrida, *La Vérité en peinture* (Paris, 1978), to which McKinley makes reference (pp. 37–8).

   5 See *Le Séminaire VII*, pp. 139–84.

the courage to refuse to disguise what it lacks and to expose the illusion that artworks fully protect us against the void.

At issue are the need to protect his friend's writing from destruction or from being used for hate-driven, lethal ends, and the rejection of the simulacrum of sacrifice in love lyric – what it means to be willing to die for, to give one's death, is not to be reduced to a conceit; and what writing – *not* a sacrificial gift – is called upon to attempt, particularly in a time of disorder, dogmatism and incoherence.

The context in which Montaigne lived and wrote had thrown into doubt the foundation of ethics in sacrifice and self-sacrifice. Montaigne's experience and understanding of instances of sacrifice and self-sacrifice in the wars raging around him was of the exhaustion and abuse of what passed for sacrifice and, rather than it being a means to preserve against destructiveness, of the deceptions, self-deceptions and inhuman violence sustaining it. Given the specific context of the *Essais* it makes sense to open discussion of sacrifice in terms of the law and religion; thereafter more ambiguously sacred/secular and secular instances can be considered, particularly those relating to love; these considered, we can return to questions of the text.

Montaigne's adherence to the primacy of the rule of law remained constant despite the manifold failings of particular laws. 'Or les loix se maintiennent en credit, non par ce qu'elles sont justes, mais par ce qu'elles sont loix. C'est le fondement mystique de leur autorité' (now, laws remain in credit not because they are just but because they are laws. This is the mystic foundation of their authority) (p. 1072). The insistence on the law's original legitimation being beyond recovery and unaccountable counterbalances the workings of the law in practice, which cannot justify obedience: 'tant il y a de contradiction et d'erreur' (so full is it of contradictions and error) (p. 1070).

However, laws fail citizens for a more specific reason. They are: 'faictes par des sots, plus souvant par des gens qui, en haine d'equalité, ont faute d'equité, mais tousjours par des hommes, autheurs vains et irresolus' (made by fools, more often by people who, hating equality, lack equity, but always by men, vain, deluded, irresolute authorities) (p. 1072). Montaigne had already commented earlier on the difficulty of establishing (just) laws by extrapolation from moral laws or ethical codes. So we are in trouble because of hatred, envy and delusion; laws which should protect the individual from such drives and blindness in others as well as themselves enshrine these very elements. The culture into which he was born had placed sacrifice and self-sacrifice at the heart of ethics and the rule of law, inculcated through unconditional adherence; however, whilst he upholds unconditional adherence, he does not seem to reproduce that emphasis on the essential role of sacrifice and self-sacrifice.

What has happened to that foundational element? The theme is not absent; however, as examples reveal, it is a site of ambiguity, problems, damage and downright inhumanity. Instances of religious sacrifice problematize it, and in consequence, the value of secular sacrifice, or sacrifice that ambiguously bridges the sacred and the secular, is put in doubt.

Montaigne *is* interested in sacrificial structures and subjects; 'Des canni-bales', not least, bears this out. In that culture, each (male) subject accepts that he may be a sacrificial object, may be eaten; but also, symmetrically, that he may sacrifice and eat. The other turns out to be indistinguishable from the same. 'They' are not 'us'? They expose us, naked of our disguise, in that our relations with our others form us and sustain our relations with ourselves. But we are not them, in the asymmetry of our relations, and in sacrifice seeming to be an alibi or disguise.

Montaigne does not dwell on instances of sacrifice and self-sacrifice as what found ethical living: perhaps the epidemic of pseudo-sacrifice that was part of the wars of his time precluded this. One passing reference apart, his writings avoid explicit discussion of the Eucharist, the sacrifice whose significance so divided Roman Catholics and Protestants and was also the source of differences within each doctrine.[6]

These were times, according to Montaigne, of unmatched cruelty, licensed in the guise of sacrifice and just killing.[7] The context of writing is inseparable from Montaigne's attitude to religious sacrifice, without fully accounting for it. Initially the grounds for war may justly have been classified as religious. But over time, perhaps after the Peace of Monsieur in 1576,[8] Montaigne redefines them as civil wars, insisting on religion being a cover rather than legitimate grounds for discord, or worse: on its encouraging the zeal that sustained intrac-table dogmatism and violence. 'Il n'est point d'hostilité excellente comme la chrestienne. Nostre zele faict merveilles, quand il va secondant nostre pente vers la haine, la cruauté, l'ambition, l'avarice, la detraction, la rebellion' (Christian hostility is unsurpassed. Our zeal works wonders when it props up our inclina-tion towards hate, cruelty, ambition, avarice, denigration and rebelliousness) (p. 444). Montaigne's redefinition was not a complete realignment; rather, it demarcates, refusing these wars the name of religion and signalling the need to keep questioning the relationship between faith and secular matters.

At the beginning of 'De la conscience' Montaigne is clear about how confused the situation actually was; indeed he calls this what was worst about the wars.[9] Clear distinction between friend and enemy had evaporated, but also, clear moti-vation – except insofar as it was clear that motives were disguised, perhaps to self quite as much as to others, fellow fighters and 'enemies' alike.

---

[6] On differing sacramental views among Roman Catholics and among Reformers, see Clark, *Eucharistic Sacrifice and the Reformation* (Oxford, 1967), Cameron, *The European Reformation* (Oxford, 1991), ch. 11, Muir, *Ritual in Early Modern Europe* (Cambridge, 2005), ch. 5, and for an earlier history of the Eucharist see Rubin, *Corpus Christi*.

[7] See 'De la cruauté', p. 432.

[8] Peace was not the edict's outcome. Roman Catholics reacted to the concessions granted to Reformers by forming the extremist *Ligue*, and while Henri III tried to ensure that the heavily Catholic *parlement* accepted the edict, by the end of the year the States-General of Blois declared itself against it. Faction and political interest were stacked against peace.

[9] For a brilliant reading of the relevant passage, see Cave, *Montaigne*, ch. X.

Il ne faut pas appeller devoir (comme nous faisons tous les jours) une aigreur et aspreté intestine qui naist de l'interest et passion privée; ny courage, une conduitte traistresse et malitieuses. Ils nomment zele leur propension vers la malignité et violence: ce n'est pas la cause qui les eschauffe, c'est leur inter-est; ils attisent la guerre non par ce qu'elle est juste, mais par ce que c'est guerre. (p. 793)

(We must not – as we do every day – call 'duty' a deeply held bitterness and asperity that is born of self-interest and private passion, nor 'courage', treach-erous and malicious behaviour. They call their propensity for malevolence and violence, zeal, but it is not the cause that incites them, it is their own interests; they intensify the war not because it is just, but because it is war.)

The wars exposed the failure of faith and its rituals to protect us from hatred, cruelty, violence, injustice; instead, it encourages them – or, after Freud, we might say, it gives free rein to the death drive. No matter how many died for their faith, 'sacrificed', 'martyred', this did not dilute the violence driven by re-ligious belief, or the sadism 'licensed' – Montaigne's word – by it.[10] Moreover, one faction's exemplary leader seems, to those on the opposing side, a tyrant: not a man of faith but one who abuses absolute *political* authority.

A longish anecdote about clemency in response to a Protestant attempt on the life of François de Guise represents religion as both alibi for unjustifiable violence and ethical compass in the face of it:

or, suyvit ce Prince, je vous veux montrer combien la religion que je tiens est plus douce que celle dequoy vous faictes profession. La vostre vous a conseillé de me tuer sans m'ouir, n'ayant receu de moy aucune offence: et la mienne me commande que je vous pardonne, tout convaincu que vous estes de m'avoir voulu homicider sans raison. Allez vous en. (p. 125)

(and, the Prince continued, I want to show you how much gentler my religion is than the one you profess. Yours has counselled you to kill me without a hearing, having not been harmed by me in any way; and mine commands me to forgive you, although you are guilty of having wanted to murder me without cause. Go away!)

Guise's interrogation of his would-be assassin translates the act into human terms; he does not consider himself a potential sacrificial victim, and asks: 'ay-je offencé quelqu'un des vostres par haine particuliere?' (has personal hatred led me to wrong a member of your family?) The other's admission that: 'aucuns luy avoyent persuadé que ce seroit une execution pleine de pieté' (people had persuaded him that this would be an act of great piety) (p. 125), smells of fal-libility and manipulation, of the power of rhetoric rather than divine guidance. Guise contrasts how their faiths guide them, demonstrating his clemency in the face of what he deems no more than intended homicide; but quite as much as

---

[10] 'Par la licence de nos guerres civiles' (licensed by our civil wars) (p. 432).

a narrative of mixed motives on the part of Reformers, this is a narrative that raises the questions, are such ambiguities really only on one side of the conflict, and could clemency, supposedly rooted in religious ethics, survive in the face of the mixed motives unleashed in the wars? After all, it was the same Guise who was to be one of the leaders of the extremist *Ligue*, and who was implicated in the Vassy Massacre that started the wars.

In the context of wars that could not be defined as religious, the logic of sacrifice is undermined. Many of the instances of it in the *Essais*, along with the much rarer term 'martyre' (only three occurrences), are not defined as sacrifices but are identifiable as such, whether religious or secular. They tend to demonstrate less heroic self-effacement and unquestionable willingness to die for an ideal, less the value of violent ritual, including killing, as a means of regulating the violence within any community (Girard),[11] than ambiguity, abuse and cruelty. They also underline that sacrifice, far from an absolute ideal, is open to interpretation, entangled with fantasy or delusion.

A few examples from the numerous instances suffice to give a strong flavour of Montaigne's perspective: a desire for tolerance as well as a sharp curiosity about motivations and the fronts (such as 'duty') behind which humans conceal their destructive drives and desires, and about those aspects of ourselves in which we are mistaken. Unsurprisingly, there are trenchant instances in 'De la cruauté' and the 'Apologie'; but also, in chapters which explore the nature of imagination, subjective judgements and ambiguities.

> Amasis, Roy d'Egypte, espousa Laodice tresbelle fille Grecque: et luy ... se trouva court à jouïr d'elle, et menaça de la tuer, estimant que ce fut quelque sorcerie. Comme és choses qui consistent en fantasie, elle le rejetta à la devotion, et, ayant faict ses voeus et promesses à Venus, il se trouva divinement remis dés la premiere nuict d'empres ses oblations et sacrifices. (p. 101)

> (Amasis, King of Egypt, married Laodice, a very beautiful Greek girl; and he was not up to enjoying her, so, thinking it some kind of sorcery, threatened to kill her. This being a matter of fantasy and imagination, she suggested to him that religion held the answer and, having made his vows and promises to Venus, the first night after his oblations and sacrifices he found himself divinely restored.)

Prayer and sacrifice lead to divine intervention and happy ending? Vengeful injustice is averted, true, and impotence seems cured; but the narration turns around the clause: 'comme és choses qui consistent en fantasie' – and her ascribing the matter (cause and/or cure) to supernatural powers. So, less a confirmation of the power of sacrifice than a reflection on how belief and rituals work and on the ascription to divine power of what is not divine but is, rather, what the individual does not understand about himself: here, the unconscious complexities of desire, 'où nostre ame se trouve outre mesure tandue de desir'

---

[11] See Girard, *La Violence et le sacré* (Paris, 1972).

(when our soul is excessively tense with desire) (p. 100), and the role of fantasy in both problem – the tangled relation of fear and desire – and cure. This is also the note on which 'De la peur' ('On fear') ends, with an account of 'terreurs Paniques' (panic terror) (p. 77). This kind of hysterical tumult was 'sans cause apparente et d'une impulsion celeste' (without apparent cause and of divine impulsion): but is this less a simple copula (and) than a statement of cause (and so was taken to be)? These anecdotes and others like them gesture towards a wider inquiry into the nature of the relationship between fear, fantasy and belief, as dramatized by sacrifice.

In these instances, belief and sacrifice appear to cure fear – while Montaigne's account implies illusion. More often, though, Montaigne's focus is the destructive potential of illusion and the savagery committed in the name of sacrifice, across a range of pagan, Christian and secular settings. Examples of pagan practice include instances that horrify him, such as, in the 'Apologie', the sacrifice of children, whether infants or adult, such as Iphigenia. Here Montaigne identifies the desire to sacrifice, that most fundamental and potent ritual, as 'humeur farouche' (savage nature) (p. 522) and 'estrange fantasie' (strange fantasy) (p. 521), and couples this with alienating details such as what was required of the parents. His very use of this word 'fantasie' calls into question the validity of such acts, as does that comment in 'De la moderation' that all religions persist in sacrifice which requires human life, despite Egyptians having already used symbolic offering rather than sacrificial killings.[12]

Christianity, at the heart of which is the sacrifice of Christ, turns to symbolic ritual instead, but does not prevent the 'massacre et homicide' (massacre and homicide) (p. 201) which pass for sacrifice and martyrdom, witnessed by Montaigne. Debates about the presence of the divine in Eucharistic communion and whether it was a sacrifice or not had fractured Christianity and precipitated war, reversion to more primitive acts, to which Montaigne denies the name sacrifice; in his eyes they are neither devout nor required by divine justice.

My last example is of persecution, but so located as to put a series of complicating questions to a rather general assertion about sacrifice which had just preceded it: as the Greeks during the Persian war exemplify, and as Montaigne considers true of all religious belief, who would not give his life for espoused belief or identity, or, as he puts it, 'opinion'?

I shall shortly return to the unsettling use of 'opinion' in this passage from 'Que le goust des biens et des maux ...', but want to turn first to the narrative that follows, a compassionate account of the expulsion of Jews from Castille and then Portugal. Let's not forget that it was more common at the time for Jews still to be represented as threatening, even monstrous figures, sacrificers of Christian children, anthropophagists: Léry's association of Jews and Brazilian cannibals is just one instance.[13] In other words, a fantasy used to reinforce the

---

12 See II, 11, p. 432.
13 The key instance in Léry's *Histoire d'un voyage* is the addition in 1585 of a long passage in which the cruelty of the Tupinamba cannibals witnessed by the author is compared

integrity of Christian confessional identity: but it simultaneously reminds of the violence of the conflicts between Christians – over sacrifice, precisely. In the *Essais* Montaigne avoids both such religious debates and material relating to Jews or Judaism that could be put to this kind of misuse. His narrative here draws quite closely on that of Jeronimo Osorio da Fonseca, but omits the original's anti-Semitism, underlines the inhumanity of the actions of Christians and removes the original's insistence on the 'good faith' of John of Portugal.[14] Montaigne's version is more interested in the tenacity of the persecuted Jews, which bears out the point about willingness to die for one's beliefs, while it remains silent or sceptical about motive on the side of the Christians, rulers and subjects alike. But even more than this, its focus is on the horror of what occurred, on the escalation of cruelty, betrayal, and on the abuses of forced choice.

He recounts the persecutions of the Jews by John, and their preference for slavery over conversion. He goes on to narrate what happened under Emmanuel, John's successor:

> mais ... eux tous [sc. les Juifs] deliberez au passage, [Emmanuel] retrancha deux des ports qu'il leur avoit promis, affin que la longueur et incommodité du traject en ravisast aucuns: ou pour les amonceller tous à un lieu, pour une plus grande commodité de l'execution qu'il avoit destinée. Ce fut qu'il ordonna qu'on arrachast d'entre les mains des peres et des meres tous les enfans au dessous de quatorze ans, pour les transporter hors de leur veue et conversation, en lieu où ils fussent instruits à nostre religion. Ils disent que cet effect produisit un horrible spectacle: la naturelle affection d'entre les peres et les enfans et de plus le zele à leur ancienne creance, combattant à l'encontre de cette violente ordonnance. Il y fut veu communement des peres et meres se deffaisant eux mesmes: et, d'un plus rude exemple encore, precipitant par amour et compassion leurs jeunes enfans dans des puits pour fuir à la loy. Au demeurant, le terme qu'il leur avoit prefix expiré, par faute de moiens, ils se remirent en servitude. (p. 54)

> (But as the Jews were all determined to leave by sea, Emmanuel withdrew two of the ports he had promised them, so that the length and difficulty of the journey would make some of them reconsider; or to crowd them all in one place to make it easier for him to carry out his plan, which was to order that every child under fourteen be snatched from the hands of his or her father and mother and taken beyond their reach, to be brought up in our religion. They say this act produced a horrific spectacle; the natural affection between fathers and children and also their zeal in their ancient faith made them rebel against so violent a decree. It was common to see fathers and mothers killing themselves; or – a more brutal example – in an act of love and compassion,

---

to that of the Jews in the time of Trajan, which was held to be 'encor plus prodigieux' (even more prodigious): see pp. 362–3, n. 4.

[14] See Osorio da Fonseca, *Historia de rebus Emmanuelis Lusitanae Regis* (Cologne, 1574), trans. *L'Histoire de Portugal* (Geneva, 1610), book I, pp. 11–13.

opinion

throwing their young children into wells to escape this law. Meanwhile, their allotted time ran out and, having no alternative, they returned to slavery.)

'Your freedom or your faith': 'your child or your faith': the Jews' acts demonstrated that life without faith was no life. Why does Montaigne not describe their acts as irrefutably sacrificial or self-sacrificial, the gift of death for one's belief? Perhaps he prefers to leave the definition open because they act in response to impossible choices imposed not by God but by the predations of hostile earthly – Christian – powers, and because he is interested in the complexities of this situation, which is less reducible to a question of giving one's death than the Greek and Turkish examples he had just invoked. He is interested in the effect of brutal cruelty and wants to understand in 'human' terms these actions and reactions, in keeping with the chapter's title, and as underlined by his use of that troubling word, 'opinion', in the earlier passage on sacrifice. In Montaigne's writing 'opinion' is indissociable from the desire to possess knowledge and to understand things beyond human comprehension which, according to the Genesis myth, caused the Fall of man: 'la peste de l'homme, c'est l'opinion de sçavoir' (what plagues humankind is the opinion that we have knowledge) (p. 488). Although 'opinion' often has neutral moral value, it is also often strongly negative: set in opposition to truth (p. 957), it is also aligned with 'vanity', that is, self-delusion (pp. 517, 626, 631, 634), its unreliability akin to fantasy (pp. 104, 459). Thus the use of not only fantasy but also opinion in relation to sacrifice insists on not confusing human and secular motives with a claim to divinely willed acts.

Fantasy in Montaigne's lexicon is not identical with its current uses. However, as we have seen, its function can be similar enough for a psychoanalytic reading not to seem belated. While 'fantasie' sometimes means 'idea', it is closely linked with imagination and sense perception; above all, it is a labile term, already historically the subject of philosophical, theological and medical debates.[15] Its meanings range from hallucination, improbable or impossible imaginings, to creativity; it can sit on the border between mind and body in psychosomatic or hysterical manifestations; and because of the inescapable role of sense perception in our grasp of not only external objects but also of our selves as objects of inquiry, its presence in our thinking and knowledge requires that we doubt. Montaigne finds it in Pyrrhonism, and his awareness of its power informs his own sceptical turn of thought. It generates reasons for us to doubt and helps drive our desire to go on doubting: 'si philosopher c'est douter ... à plus forte raison niaiser et fantastiquer, comme je fais, doit estre doubter' (if to philosophize is to doubt ... to fool about and produce fantasies, like I do, must

---

[15] For an overview see Guerrier's entry on 'Fantasmes – Fantasie', in Desan, *Dictionnaire de Michel de Montaigne* (Paris, 2004), pp. 387–90, and for fuller discussion, see Tournon, *Montaigne en toutes lettres*, pp. 138–47, and O'Brien, 'Reasoning with the Senses', *South Central Review* 10 (1993), pp. 3–19, and 'Montaigne and Antiquity', in Langer (ed.), *The Cambridge Companion to Montaigne*, pp. 53–73.

really be to doubt) (p. 350). It is experienced as private and interior and also recognized in collective beliefs and behaviour. If there is no getting beyond it, then we have no access to a pure, objective or irrefutable perception of 'reality' with which to oppose it.

Montaigne intimately associates it with his own writing, which is character-ized as being 'fantasque' or 'fantastique' (fantastic, fantastical, full of fantasy) (pp. 33, 183, 385), and this colours his use of 'fantasie' when its meaning is closer to ponderings or notions: 'je propose des fantasies humaines et miennes, simplement comme humaines fantasies, et separament considerées, non comme arrestees et reglées par l'ordonnance celeste, incapable de doute et d'altercation: matiere d'opinion, non matiere de foy; ce que je discours selon moy' (I offer my own human imaginings and reflections as just that, human, and to be treated as such, not as fixed and formed by divine ordinance, beyond doubt and argument; matters of opinion, not faith; what I figure out in my own way) (p. 323). Writing gives creative form to fantasy and is sustained by it, for if fantasy requires that we question, there is no end either to questioning or to writing.

The hinge with psychoanalytic understandings of the term is the undoing of the idea that our perceptions of reality can be uniform or objective. And though Montaigne insists that his writing does not stray into matters of faith, as if faith were exempt from fantasy, his examples of faith-driven acts suggest otherwise: he repeatedly indicates that supposed sacrifice or martyrdom need questioning in terms of the opacities of human motivation and desire. In Chris-tianity sacrifice and sacrificial love had been essential to faith and ethical belief; but Montaigne witnessed overwhelming evidence of hate taking the lead along with self-delusion, and of self-interest rather than the sacrificial self-effacement associated with Christian culture.

If love is not identified with religion, what about its secular version? If we are to rethink sacrifice in terms of fantasy, and to make a case for a more psycho-analytic reading of it, along the way we must return to what Montaigne suggests about the place of fantasy in secular love.

'Opinion', so closely identified with 'presumption', self-deluding vanity, is more consistently negative in its connotations than 'fantasie', and contaminates it when the two are worked together, as here: 'nature ... ne nous ait donné en partage que la presumption ... l'homme n'a rien proprement sien que l'usage des opinions. Nous n'avons que du vent et de la fumée en partage ... l'homme ... possede ses biens par fantasie' (nature has given us only presumption as our share ... man has nothing that is properly his own but his use of opinion. Our share is only wind and smoke ... man possesses his goods only in fantasy) (p. 489). We enjoy that which is good only in fantasy, or, we only imagine that we enjoy possession of that which is good. Illusion, self-delusion, opinion and fantasy converge on the same point, it seems. The statement about presump-tion is ascribed to Epictetus: this view of humankind is not only Christian. In the 'Apologie' the unacknowledged limits and presumptions of human reason as a means to true knowledge or belief (which comes from faith alone) are at stake. But elsewhere illusion and self-delusion are related to a different form of 'good', namely love, either as an independent issue or as a complicating factor in our failure to understand our relationship with the divine.

We suffer from:

> une trop bonne opinion ... de nostre valeur ... qui nous represente à nous mesmes autres que nous ne sommes: comme la passion amoureuse preste des beautez et des graces au subjet qu'elle embrasse, et fait que ceux qui en sont espris, trouvent, d'un jugement trouble et alteré, ce qu'ils ayment, autre et plus parfaict qu'il n'est. (pp. 631–2)

> (too high an opinion of our own worth ... whereby we see ourselves as other than we are: just as the passion of love lends beauty and grace to its object, and makes the judgement of those who are smitten troubled and confused, so that they find the one they love other – more perfect – than he is.)

The possible cure for these delusions of both love and self-love is secular philosophy, the more sceptical the better:

> la philosophie ne me semble jamais avoir si beau jeu que quand elle combat nostre presumption et vanité, quand elle reconnoit de bonne foy son irresolution, sa foiblesse et son ignorance. Il me semble que la mere nourrice des plus fauces opinions et publiques et particulieres, c'est la trop bonne opinion que l'homme a de soy. (p. 634)

> (philosophy plays her best game when she combats our presumption and vain self-delusion, when in good faith she acknowledges her uncertainty, weakness and ignorance. It seems to me that the breast that feeds the greatest of false opinions, both public and private, is man's excessively high opinion of himself.)

Doubt, then, and self-doubt are required: Montaigne is 'autant douteux de moy que de toute autre chose' (I am as doubtful of myself as of all other things) (p. 634). This secular argument is echoed in the religious context: 'nostre sagesse n'est que folie devant Dieu ... l'homme qui presume de son sçavoir, ne sçait pas encore ce que c'est que sçavoir ... l'homme, qui n'est rien, s'il pense estre quelque chose, se seduit soy mesme et se trompe' (our wisdom is only folly before God ... he who presumes to have knowledge does not yet know what knowledge is ... man, who is nothing, seduces and deceives himself if he thinks he is something) (p. 449).

If we take this conventional statement about human vanity (echoes of Ecclesiastes, St Paul, Aquinas, Erasmus ...) and put it together with Montaigne's required self-doubt, what does this imply for love? Is to seduce oneself or love oneself not to deceive oneself that one is not nothing? Do not both love and self-love find false perfection in their objects, denying lack, which distracts from true understanding of God? Is assertive knowledge not laced with self-love? Are only doubt and self-doubt not prey to self-love and the delusions it supports? Is not all love of human objects deceptive and deceived, and to be doubted quite as much as human reason or knowledge? So, is to be willing to die for love nothing to do with a sacrificial ethical ideal; merely, to be exorbitantly deluded? And should assertions of willingness to die for love not be as subject to doubt as any other claim, lest the self-love in them go unexamined?

The *Essais* are more ambiguous than these sceptical questions imply. While the exclusion of La Boétie's love lyric seems to confirm this orientation, both 'Des cannibales' and 'De l'amitié' allow the possibility of sacrifice as a good. But if the possibility of ethics of sacrifice is not ruled out, it is only insofar as it is not here, not now, and not caught up in an economy of exchange. Even if one were genuinely to give one's life without hope of return, as soon as this – true – sacrifice is represented, it is taken into the economy of exchange that is language, and is no longer the gift without hope of return needed to found ethical relations. But in the disillusioned vision that (I suggest) Montaigne shares with psychoanalysis, this is not so much to betray the sacrificial ethos as to move past fantasy into disillusionment. In religious terms, given his experiences of the destructiveness licensed rather than contained by belief, this means not abandoning his faith but accepting the incomprehensibility of God, and problematizing sacrifice.

Willingness to die for the Reformed or Roman Catholic cause is a fantasy in that it is a collective point of identification and subjection; it is part of the Symbolic, indeed is a support for it. That I am willing to die for my faith is, in times of toleration and in the absence of fundamentalism, a fantasy which secures my identity (rather heroically) and supports the Symbolic in that I do not really believe I shall have to die for it – or ascribe the meaning of martyrdom to my killing of an enemy of my faith. If I do not recognize it for the fantasy it is, I am not protected from the deadly impulse and act on it as if this is really what God wants of me. Montaigne refuses to allow acts called sacrifices by others either the name of sacrifice or their traditional, unchallenged meaning, opens up a gap between motivation, act and meaning, and emphasizes the horror into which such fantasies lure the subject. As fantasies their function is also to protect the subject from horror (the Real); if not recognized as such, their protective function is lost.

In relation to love, the sacrificial fantasy of dying for love (a fantasy that sustains the illusion of the other's wholeness and integrity because it must presuppose it) needs to be rejected. Montaigne seems to allow an exception in the form of his love for La Boétie and what they unconditionally and self-effacingly gave each other, but, by representing it, he veers from the ethics that could, exceptionally, be founded on such a 'free' gift. He also cedes it in his representations of his beloved friend, by allowing some imperfection, for instance in his diminishing description of La Boétie's text, so vital between them, as a form of 'exercise' (see p. 194). The act of writing about this perfect friendship seems to sustain a version of its perfection; but by the end of the chapter, which had opened with a vision of the essay's plenitude, we arrive at this more tempered version of it.

The ethics exemplified by his writing is different. It is sceptical of sacrificial structures (though still longs for them), and combines a desire for a culture in which such an ideal was not impossible and disillusioned recognition of its absence. The gift of the text to the reader denies neither that it is given with hope of return nor that, taking the form of language, it is not outside economies of exchange. Its ideal is openness, a hospitability towards unknown visitors – readers – based on an unpossessive relationship with knowledge and words; and it is also acutely aware of the fragilities of the enterprise.

Let's now focus on this ethics of the relation between text and reader (perhaps the last cannibal to figure in my discussion), the risks and uncertain future of the open text, and what is left of love. 'J'ouvre les choses plus que je ne les descouvre' (rather than discover things, I uncover them) (p. 501); the *Essais* are exploratory, a site of questions left open, and the work of an individual who values his own openness: 'j'ay une façon ouverte … la teste haute, le visage et le coeur ouvert' (I have an open manner … head high, face and heart open) (p. 792). The text's openness, then, identifies it with its author, in whom it means not only honesty but also generosity and hospitability, the qualities of a liberal gentleman. So the text, itself a product of (and therefore opened up by) his inquiring spirit, is honest, accessible, manifest, receptive – open to interpretation.

Montaigne claims to have confidence in the survival of truth, not subject to historical contingencies: 'la naifveté et la verité pure, en quelque siècle que ce soit, trouvent encore leur opportunité et leur mise' (naturalness and pure truth always, even now, find their moment and place) (p. 792). Despite his writing being, he insists, 'laïque non clericale' (lay, not clerical) (p. 323), nonetheless he shores up its lay openness by immediately deploying the complex adjective 'religieux, -euse', which signifies both religious and scrupulous, conscientious and faithful (as in 'true to'); elsewhere likewise the adverb 'religieusement'. Thus, he continues, his writing is 'tres-religieuse tousjours' (always faithful) (p. 323), likened to a confession protected by its authenticity: 'la confession genereuse et libre enerve le reproche et desarme l'injure' (free and generous confession weakens reproach and disarms injuriousness) (p. 980). 'Religieusement' – 'scrupulously' or 'faithfully' – used of obeying the law, or of his or others' writing, reminds us of the traditional cultural associations between obedient faith in the authority of God and the law and how this frames what it means to give one's word. To be scrupulous in all things originated in a God-fearing attitude. Montaigne no sooner separates the lay from the clerical than he reminds the reader that a still 'religious' attitude informs his being and writing. However, this does not fully protect his writing from being misread, from 'la mesdisance' (slander) (p. 980). Open by definition also means unprotected, vulnerable (an open goal) or undefended (an open city), as the anticipation of reproach and injuriousness reminds. Confidence in authenticity and truth, then, needs to be qualified.

Montaigne takes cover behind neither the fantasy of textual plenitude, nor the model of authority that had traditionally secured the prestige of the text, nor again, the *illusion* of stability, coherence and consequence offered by narrative form and its conventions. Moreover his method, writing over many years, making a wealth of changes to the text, enacts a principle of openness and of there always being more to say. The safety of a text which suspends judgement is in doubt: Montaigne's writing, like that of the Pyrrhonists he describes in the 'Apologie', is open in this respect also: 'ils se servent de leur raison pour enquerir et pour debatre, mais non pas pour arrester et choisir' (they use their reason to inquire and debate, but not to conclude and choose) (p. 505), and its vulnerability is increased by its 'façon ... un peu nouvelle et hors d'usage' (ways [being] a bit new and unusual) (p. 980).

He emphasizes the text's 'good faith' when he delivers it, in his opening words, 'Au Lecteur' (To the Reader); he thus raises questions concerning the relation between text and reader. He has his own history and experience as a reader to go on, but is not one to generalize; he is aware that, unlike rituals which operate according to the givens of their proper performance, this is both an unregulated and innovative transaction; moreover, even if he dubs his text 'confession', these are the words of an unrepentant writer who must allow that his reader will be neither repentant nor scrupulously attentive either. This suggests that questions of conscience and responsibility are at the heart of the process of interpretation; it also underscores the vulnerability of the text. I shall shortly explore further Montaigne's desire to write like this, and how his writing addresses and engages the reader; but first, we need to return to a theme touched on in the context of sacrifice, namely forced choice. The forced choice between the life of a child and that of a figurative child, the (Platonic) word-child that is writing, encapsulates a striking aspect of the ethics of writing for Montaigne.

At the end of 'De l'affection des pères aux enfans' we find a set of monstrous challenges to givens about the nature of the good. The metaphor of the text, work, or cultural artefact as child, as what one holds most dear, opens a fantasy in which Montaigne experiments with the reader: the question is not, 'your money or your life?' but 'your child's life or your "child's"?'

> Pensons nous qu'Epicurus qui, en mourant ... avoit toute sa consolation en la beauté de sa doctrine qu'il laissoit au monde, eut receu autant de contentement d'un nombre d'enfans bien nais et bien eslevez, s'il en eust eu, comme il faisoit de la production de ses riches escrits? ... Ce seroit à l'adventure impieté en Sainct Augustin (pour exemple) si d'un costé on luy proposoit d'enterrer ses escrits, dequoy nostre religion reçoit un si grand fruit, ou d'enterrer ses enfans, au cas qu'il en eut, s'il n'aimoit mieux enterrer ses enfans. Et je ne sçay si je n'aimerois pas mieux beaucoup en avoir produict ung, parfaictement bien formé, de l'acointance des muses, que de l'acointance de ma femme. (p. 401)

> (When Epicurus lay dying ... his sole consolation was the beauty of the doctrine he was leaving the world; do we really think that he would have found such happiness in any number of well-born, well-educated children, had he had any, as he found in the rich writings he had produced? ... It would probably be impiety in St Augustine, for example, faced with the choice between the burial of his books, which have so greatly profited our religion, or his children, had he had any, not to prefer to bury his children. And I do not know

if I would not have greatly preferred to have produced one perfectly formed child by intercourse with the muses than with my wife.)

His perspective is that he, and not just he, but also Epicurus (pagan, admired) and Augustine (Christian, admired), or anyone with their ability, would not just prefer, but prefer to save, for the future, his word-child – assuming it were 'fit'. As would, he goes on, Virgil; or Phidias or any other sculptor, who would value his work over his children; or, shifting from cultural artefacts to military triumphs, Epaminondas, Alexander or Caesar … The father-writer's love for his word-child surpasses that natural given, that of the father for the child. Montaigne, of course, feints: Epicurus was childless; he was not aware that Augustine had a son; the lengthy example of Epicurus takes the form of questions, and that of Augustine is couched in the conditional and qualified as probability; he himself had no son to lose, having only had daughters, all but one of whom died in infancy, before his 'amitié vrayement paternelle' (truly paternal love) (p. 387) for them had begun to form; so none of them apparently ever really had to choose. Besides, he himself hedges the question, combining a double negative and a conditional tense, and does not *explicitly* link the perfectly formed child of his brain with the *Essais*. Elsewhere they are said to represent 'un particulier bien mal formé' (a very ill-formed individual) (p. 804) rather than being 'perfectly formed', and at the start of this chapter there is much emphasis on their strangeness and extravagance, both of which are linked with vanity, 'un subject si vain' (p. 385), that is, a subject of illusory value – if any … This is not to say that the choice is purely hypothetical; rather, it may appear to be undecidable but, nonetheless, one must find a way to choose. That the question can be asked, that such a dilemma is even thinkable, stems from the work of the metaphor of the child: authorized by Plato, but charged with renewed force and purpose here, so as to convey to the reader the intensity of the writer's relationship with his creation.

But it has further resonance. The question of relative value – *ars longa, vita brevis* – is dramatized here. Montaigne does not idealize his writing, emphasizing here, and again in 'De la vanité', its tendency to wander, be fantastical and vain: 'l'estrangeté … sotte enterprise … fantastique … farouche et extravagant … je m'esgare … mes fantasies … je vois au change indiscrettement et tumultuairement' (the strangeness … stupid enterprise … fantastic … wild and exorbitant … I lose my way … my fantasies … I am not only changeable, but indiscriminately and tumultuously so) (pp. 385, 994). Nor, unlike Plato, for whom books are 'enfants immortels, qui immortalisent leurs peres' (their fathers' immortal and immortalizing children) (p. 400), does he believe it will have exceptional durability: 'j'ecris mon livre à peu d'hommes et à peu d'années' (I write my book for few men and few years) (p. 982). On the contrary, the condition of his writing is its lack of permanence. He refuses to give it wholeness or exceptional value and authority. Rather, in the extravagant passage with which 'De l'affection' opens, which roams beyond the usually thinkable (Lat. *extra* + *vagari*), the issue staged, and allowed by the exploratory thinking to which metaphor gives access, is the relationship between creativity and the capacity to shake ethical givens, so as to 'act as if to create new principles *ex nihilo*'.[16]

Father and son, 'father' and 'child'; Montaigne is all of these. Scattered throughout Montaigne's writing is warm praise for his father; but it was also from him that he inherited a position he did not want, together with that prediction of disaster (see p. 210). The last decades of Montaigne's life may be read as a narrative of increasingly lucid unburdening of himself – from other's expectations, public identities. He remains 'sans office ... et sans benefice' (without public office and benefice) (p. 999), and frees himself from 'obligation', those ways his place as a subject seemed to be fixed by others; he even fails to fail his father: 'il se trompa: me voicy comme j'y entray, sinon un peu mieux' (he was mistaken: see, I am just as I was at the outset, perhaps a little better off) (pp. 998–9), without this being an issue of psychic winning and losing. Not that he was altogether free: remember, for instance, his being forced to be Mayor of Bordeaux, elected on the presumption that he would be like his father, an identification he immediately, publicly rejected:

> à mon arrivée, je me deschiffray fidelement et conscientieusement, tout tel que je me sens estre ... et par ce que la cognoissance de feu mon pere les avoit seule incitez à cela ... je leur adjoustay bien clairement que je serois tresmarry que chose quelconque fit autant d'impression en ma volonté comme avoit faict autrefois en la sienne leurs affaires et leur ville. (p. 1005)

> (when I arrived I explained myself to them warts and all: me, in my own eyes ... and as they had only wanted to elect me because they knew my late father ... I also emphasized that I would be very unhappy if the affairs of their city made such demands on my will and attention as they had on my father's.)

Even the identities of father, husband and son come to be lived more fully as Montaigne himself desired; Montaigne the wanderer, Montaigne faithful but unengaged husband, Montaigne his father's son but able to live that identity in his own way, and Montaigne to whom his metaphorical child mattered more than anything or anyone. Part of the freedom he reached, and, with it, the capacity to be true to his own desire,[17] rests on his acceptance of the ambiguities and lack inherent in any position, as well as its entanglement with others and the mutual and asymmetrical responsibilities entailed: intersubjectivity and intertextuality are part and parcel of this ethos and ethics. He can take care of his home without being possessive; he is both possessive, and not, of his word-child; that child is not perfect; and he cannot protect its frailties in the hands of

---

16 Kay, *Žižek*, p. 109.

17 Or, to put it in Lacanian terms consonant with the figuration of internalization as eating explored earlier, 'Mange ton Dasein!' Eat, that is, have so understood the ways in which others' desires have structured your existence as to be able to move beyond them, with all the responsibility for your own subjectivity, in all its lack, that this requires. See Lacan, *Le Séminaire II*, p. 240.

unknown others, except insofar as his own example of not taking possession (of meaning) may be persuasive.

'De l'affection' does not avoid the latent psychic aggressivity and destructiveness of relations between parents and children: the whims or perverse transitivity of maternal love (see p. 399);[18] the child's existence at the expense of the father's: 'ils ne peuvent … estre ny vivre qu'aux depens de nostre estre et de nostre vie' (they can neither be nor live … except at the expense of our being and life) (p. 387); a child wishing his father dead – because of his lack of 'bonté et douceur de ses meurs' (goodness and gentleness) (p. 389). All these will be avoided if the instinctual feelings of the father and child are overtaken, diluted by what is on the side of culture rather than nature; reason transforms 'passion' into reciprocal 'affection' (p. 435). However, the provocation of such violent hostility may in fact be on the side of culture: for here Montaigne's theme is the damaging effects of fathers being possessive of their property, at a point when they should share it or pass it on, *unconditionally*. Plato's *Laws* are invoked at some length (see p. 398): a father has no right but to obey the law (of inheritance), because it is the law: the individual lacks sufficient self-knowledge to judge what is fair or even to know what is his to give.

The conflict between father and child turns on possessiveness (and envy), which demarcates and distances to the point of alienation. The error is compounded by fathers' love for their children being love for a version of themselves, 'autres nous mesmes' (our other selves) (p. 399). Here Montaigne draws on the *Nicomachean Ethics*: each holds his own being dear, loving his own being which is within everything he does or engenders (see pp. 386–7). So, identity is far from being clearly demarcated between self (father) and other (child). This is not a symmetrical relationship: the father – who engenders, gives – loves more than the child – engendered, given to; and it is couched in terms of an economy of exchange: 'les choses nous sont plus cheres, qui nous ont plus cousté; et il est plus difficile de donner que de prendre' (we hold most dear what has cost us most; and it is more difficult to give than to take) (p. 387). But in fact the deal on which ethics rests is not so much this willingness to give rather than take (and be more rewarded as a result), as that giving multiplies our being, rather than producing others independent of us. Which is what Plato's Lawgiver recognizes and keeps in place: the other's freedom or guarantee of equity rests on our accepting that we are (both) subject to the Law, the Other.

Similar issues of identity are played out in the writer's relationship with his text; if anything, the problem of possessiveness is more acute. The 'enfantemens de nostre esprit' (children of our mind) are more our own than the 'autres nous mesmes' (our other selves) that are our children; 'toute la grace et pris est nostre' (all their grace and value is ours) (p. 400), they represent the writer more vividly and accurately than his own flesh and blood – being *all* his own, no maternal

---

[18] In 'De la coustume' the roots of cruelty, tyranny and treachery are traced to mothers' and fathers' enjoyment and indulgence of children's ruthless play, such as mistreating animals or what would now be seen as bullying behaviour; see p. 110.

matter involved. What salvages the ethics of the relationship is, once again, an emphasis on the gift: what is given to the word-child is given 'purement et irrevocablement' (purely and irrevocably) (p. 401). As you would give to your child, says Montaigne; in fact though, earlier, he had reserved the right to take back, 'desdire' (p. 392), a material gift to a child. Thus the ethics of this relationship seem purer and freer; the unconditional gift of love, knowledge and self becomes the text's own knowledge and self, and in this, it becomes a stranger to its author: 'il n'est plus en ma disposition; il peut sçavoir assez de choses que je ne sçay plus, et tenir de moy ce que je n'ay point retenu et qu'il faudroit que, tout ainsi qu'un estranger, j'empruntasse de luy' (it is no longer at my disposal; it may know much that I no longer know, and retain things about me that I have forgotten, which I would have to borrow from it, as if from a stranger) (p. 402). However, the demarcation is not quite so clear: the word-child's knowledge was once his and for him still remains identified as his, even if he has lost it beyond recall. The word-child, even if independent, is still called upon to give something in return: to represent and to retain. But in its potential to meet the writer's lack equally lies its autonomy.

Abraham was willing to sacrifice his child, as God willed; would (one's sense of) the potential cultural value of one's writing be such as to justify one's preserving it at the expense of one's child? Less hyperbolically, is one's writing more precious than one's child? Put like that, for Montaigne the question is answerable, and open to all kinds of qualifying clauses; not least that, in the case of Augustine, it is for future cultures to recognize its value is in the eyes of future cultures, not the author. But the drama matters: if I were to sacrifice my child to save my writing, the act might be judged selfish, callous, evil, or just plain wrong, as if good were clearly identified with the life of my child. It is much more troubling to question and act other than in accordance with clear, given moral values, to be true to my own desire and uphold it, whatever the cost: to be condemned as heartless, wicked, evil ... This is the ethics that sustains creativity such as Montaigne's; this is unsettling thinking, on the limits; and it is figuration that both opens up the question and makes this thinking tolerable to the reader.

'Mes ouvrages, il s'en faut tant qu'ils me rient'

My readings of Montaigne's writing about testing ideas and experiences have explored how figuration works to engage the reader and to produce the structures needed for differing ideas to coexist. While we frequently encounter ambivalence and lack of resolution, we also find pleasure in the play of ideas in this open-minded thinking. Forms of linguistic 'turning' open the potential for this writing to be unsettling and for the reader to learn to be unsettled but thoughtful, and for questions to remain.

This suggests that writing is therapeutic: a way of making tolerable the uncertainty or anxiety, which, quite as much as curiosity or sceptical doubt, or detached critical inquiry, drive questions; it produces a place in which the desire to question takes precedence over answers. And as questions imply, it offers even a residual sense of the possibility of the future being different to the past and present. Perhaps. If some hope is involved, this is not to say that what prevails is not, rather, disillusionment and doubt: a courageous venture, therefore, and vulnerable to misinterpretation.

Much has already been written about Montaigne's desire to write,[19] first and foremost by him. From his opening 'Au Lecteur', and repeatedly thereafter, together with passing comments on his taste as a reader and writer, he offers the reader his reasons for embarking on this project of writing which put exploration of what he can know of himself and of what he wants at the heart of the text. Notable among a range of illuminating interpretations are those for which the driving force is the effects of loss; their focuses tend to be melancholy, the death of La Boétie, of Montaigne's father, or of ideals; thus writing is interpreted as a therapeutics, and affect is as salient as philosophical or intellectual issues.[20] Persuasive though such readings undoubtedly are, they tend to overlook the role of anxiety in Montaigne's desire to write and go on writing; and there is also scope for more psychoanalytically informed ideas in exploring the relationship between affect, the unconscious and this writing.

So, drawing on such ideas, I shall now consider the place of anxiety in relation to some of the issues already discussed: the place of the brother, haunting and displacement, and, with them, the theme of incalculability. With respect to writing, the last is fundamental to the way in which the poetics and ethics of Montaigne's text work together. I have already suggested that the place produced by the text is imagined to be a form of freedom, not only in its matter (such as Montaigne's 'confessions' to do with his erotic life) and its innovative form, the 'essai', not yet bound by generic and rhetorical convention, but also in the acknowledgement of the freedom of future unknown readers to interpret what is written as the condition of this writing – its ethics as well as its poetics. This suggests an acceptance of lack, as writer and as constitutive of language.

Acceptance implies that lack has neutral or even creative connotations, and might seem a step towards the tranquillity sought by Montaigne, but this is not the whole story. For, as we shall see, abiding anxieties haunt Montaigne, inhabit his writing, and lead him to declare that he will return to haunt his future readers. The tranquillity that writing might bring proves illusory and inconstant. The balance between his desire and others', as well as others' for him, will not be held by writing any more, perhaps, than it could be held at home; thus

---

[19]   There are studies too numerous to list here. To select just a few: Starobinski, *Montaigne en mouvement*, Cave, *The Cornucopian Text*, Rigolot, *Les Métamorphoses*, and Tournon, *Montaigne: la glose et l'essai*.

[20]   See for instance Starobinski, *Montaigne en mouvement*, ch. 1, Screech, *Montaigne and Melancholy*, Rigolot, *Les Métamorphoses*, Pot, *L'Inquiétante Etrangeté*, and Nakam, *Montaigne: la manière et la matière*.

anxiety, lack and a sceptical perspective will continue to haunt the text, unsettling Montaigne's expressed desire for 'repos' (rest) (p. 33).

In 'De l'oisiveté' ('On idleness') writing is represented as therapeutic. Montaigne needed to find a cure for the restless disorder and disturbance of his thoughts, a state conveyed figuratively as digestive disorder in other chapters. The passage is well known, but still worth reproducing here: 'mon esprit ... m'enfante tant de chimeres et monstres fantasques les uns sur les autres, sans ordre, et sans propos, que pour en contempler à mon aise l'ineptie et l'estrangeté, j'ay commancé de les mettre en rolle, esperant avec le temps luy en faire honte à luy mesmes' (my mind ... gives birth to so many chimeras and fantastic monsters, one after another, without rhyme or reason that, in order to contemplate them at ease, in all their ineptitude and strangeness, I have begun to make a record of them, hoping in time to make my mind ashamed of itself) (p. 33).

In order better to understand the anxiety in Montaigne's writing, rather than discuss the chimeras and monsters,[21] I shall focus on the aspects of excess and its double, lack, in the passage – 'so many', 'one after another', 'without ... without'. These thoughts and imaginings seem to have been exorbitant, insofar as that was knowable without their having yet been symbolized; a first lack, but what made them intolerable was a second lack, the lack of lack, that is, that they flooded him and he could take no distance from their excess. No contemplation without first some distance or perspective, and without symbolization. The state being described is one of high anxiety, lack of lack: 'le manque vient à manquer' (lack comes to lack);[22] and, while the ideas and imaginings – all of which are his own – may have been strange, it is equally anxiety itself that is estranging – to cite Safouan again, it 'fait vaciller le sujet' (throws the subject off balance) (p. 327). Symbolization, writing (or speech) gives form to what is otherwise unassimilable and radically shakes the psychic economy of the subject.

This was what assailed Montaigne, when what he wanted was to live out his life in tranquillity, 'repos'. In the context of his reading pleasures (in 'Des livres' ('On books')) Montaigne also remarks that he wants to spend what remains of his life 'doucement', gently (p. 409). That which is restful comes to meet that which is gentle; is it too far-fetched to connect these qualities with what Montaigne calls the fundamental condition of life, namely that it is 'tendre' (tender)? Easily troubled – by suffering; for Montaigne, by all that 'obligation' meant; by one's own mind, and by anxiety. As we know from the function of phobic objects, anxiety is reduced by being given form and focus, and (which we might say is the same thing as symbolization) by the recovery of a sense of lack.

We find a similar turbulence at the start of 'De l'affection des peres aux enfans'; similar lack of lack also.

---

[21] Among numerous critical discussions of them, see Garavini, *Monstres et chimères* (Paris, 1994).

[22] Lacan, *Le Séminaire X*, p. 53.

Madame, si l'estrangeté ne me sauve, et la nouvelleté, qui ont accoustumé de donner pris aux choses, je ne sors jamais à mon honneur de cette sotte entreprinse; mais elle est si fantastique et a un visage si esloigné de l'usage commun que cela luy pourra donner passage. C'est une humeur melancolique, et une humeur par consequent tres ennemie de ma complexion naturelle, produite par le chagrin de la solitude en laquelle il y a quelque années je m'estoy jetté, qui m'a mis premierement en teste cette resverie de me mesler d'escrire. Et puis, me trouvant entierement despourveu et vuide de toute autre matiere, je me suis présenté moy-mesmes à moy, pour argument et pour subject.

(p. 385)

(Madame, if strangeness and novelty, which usually lend things value, don't save me, I shall never honourably escape this stupid project; but it is so fantastical and looks so far from ordinary that it may just pass. A melancholy humour – so, very threatening to my natural disposition – which grew out of the disquieting solitude I lapsed into some years ago, first prompted me to have a go at writing, strange fantasy that it is. And then, finding myself entirely destitute and void of all other matter, I presented myself to myself as both theme and subject.)

The effect of the tone – reaching for paradox, yet weary of paradox or the desire to invoke it – and the twist within the first sentence from conventional practice and value to even more paradoxical value, in being so far from what is in common usage (source of getting away with it, perhaps), is unsettling. The need to write is now ascribed to sadness and solitude; not that sadness is the product of solitude, but rather, sadness itself isolates and breeds a taste for further isolation. The losses of both his father and his friend were important causes of his disquietude and solitude. However, to read melancholy humour as a reference to failed mourning, and as the driving force behind his desire to write, prematurely narrows our understanding of the relationship between loss and writing. The terms of this passage ask us to recognize anxiety here; not separate, perhaps not separable, from the death of loved ones. The troubled thinking – for it goes beyond worldly paradox – of the first sentence; the sense of being invaded by hostile affect; and again, the sense of lack of lack: entirely destitute and void of any other subject matter. By writing, lack and differentiation (or non-coincidence) are introduced, as the articulation of subjectivity into the syntax of 'je /me /suis presenté /moy-mesmes /à moy' (I/ presented/ myself/ to/ myself) indicates.

We also need to keep in mind the paradoxical expression of this anxious lack of lack, in terms of emptiness, being void. The experience of saturation, and with it anxiety, is intensified by a remaining awareness of the need to think about, have a conceptual and affective relationship with, something other, even if it feels as if there is no space for it. Without this, there is a loss of a sense of differentiation and identity, a loss of the otherness which, far from being strange or estranging, is vital to being at home in the world. Furthermore, this paradoxical resurgence of emptiness within saturation reminds us that full and empty are not in a relationship of stable opposition: neither in the context of affective or relational states nor in terms of speech. Neither ideally full, nor entirely, catastrophically empty …

What then of the place of the other for Montaigne as a writer? We can give the term more specific connotations, both negative and positive. Firstly, to be free to write is to be in a state of freedom from the demands of others' desires for him – 'obligation'. This takes two significant, related forms. The first concerns the social, familial, political constructions of 'Montaigne', against which his retreat into his tower to read, pace, think and write is symbolic. The second is a version of the first, but less tractable perhaps, in that it does not necessarily take material or external form. In 'De l'institution' he comments on our minds' lack of autonomy: 'liée et contrainte à l'appetit des fantasies d'autruy, serve et captivée soubs l'authorité de leur leçon. On nous a tant assubjectis aux cordes que nous n'avons plus de franches allures' (bound and constrained by others' fantasies, slaves and captives of the authority of others' teaching … We have been so reined in that we no longer move freely at all) (p. 151).

Such is the force of cultural expectation (here specifically the education that transmits it), and all forms of authority, religious and secular, that the freedom of movement we imagine we have lost may in fact only be imagined, from within the constrained dimensions in which our subjectivity is formed. As for others' fantasies, it is often even harder to identify the difference between others' desires for us and our own: not for nothing is Lacan's formulation of desire, as always 'le désir de l'autre', ambiguously the desire for and of the other. So it is not surprising if an element of anxiety attaches to the complexity of relations with others' desire – such as to drive one to travel, for instance, enacting what that imagined freedom of movement might be. But as Montaigne was to discover, not altogether free; called back to 'obligation' as elected Mayor of Bordeaux, not free to decline the role. To exercise this freedom was, he was told, to be wrong: 'je m'en excusay, mais on m'aprint que j'avois tort' (I excused myself, but was told that I was wrong) (p. 1005).

'De la vanité' is one of the many chapters in which Montaigne commented on his desire to write, at the outset differentiating his own writing from the 'scribbling' that is symptomatic of the time, 'un siecle desbordé' (a disorderly time). The use of 'desbordé' figures disorder as a river (gesturing towards the topos of the river of time) which has burst its banks ('bords'). Even if Montaigne is adamant that he is a writer not a scribbler, his writing is nonetheless a product of similar suffering, being over-full, overwhelmed: a response to excess. Here it is precisely the lack and imperfections of French that are salvific: his book ('mon livre') is conceived as not being full to perfection of meaning, and the illusion that writing durably preserves meaning is jettisoned: 'il [sc. le nostre langage] escoule tous les jours de nos mains' ([our language] slips through our fingers with each passing day) (p. 982). *My* book, but *our* language and *our* use; the order of language, not just mine but to which we are all subject, is a place of substitution, never coinciding with its object. This is the paradoxical freedom of language: its lack of adequation protects us from both illusions of impossible perfection and from intolerable excess; its flowing through our hands is different from the overflow of inarticulate experience.

The difference between Montaigne's writing and others', he often insists, lies in his 'matter': it is unique, the 'seul livre au monde' (only book in the world) of its kind (p. 385). Yet its matter is not altogether free from others' desires or from contingency: 'c'est un subject que je possede à la mercy d'autruy' (it is a subject I possess at others' mercy) (p. 1003). Even this 'subject', uniquely free of that which is 'estrangere' (strange) (p. 665), is nonetheless full of otherness; as I have already established, Montaigne understands this 'subject' as being formed by and through relationships with others and their desires, not only in terms of his more public identity, but through and through. Internal otherness and difference are no less constitutive of identity than the differences between one person and another: 'se trouve autant de difference de nous à nous mesmes, que de nous à autruy' (there is as much difference between us and ourselves as between us and others) (p. 337).

So, writing is also a way of protecting his relationship with himself; but the relationship between writing – represented subject – and reader needs further analysis, for the freedom that language symbolizes does not simply extend to the imagined relationship with readers. Here, too, despite some idealistic moments, anxiety and ambivalence return, and with them the place of the lost reader, the 'brother'. There are four stages to my inquiry into this relationship: the imagined reader who knows 'how' to read him; the relationship between love, letters, essays and 'correspondence'; the lost reader who haunts the text; lastly, Montaigne's returning to haunt his readers.

Two forms of imagined reader are relevant here: the first, the 'suffisant' (good-enough) reader who appears in an early chapter (p. 127) and again in 'De la vanité', where we encounter his antithesis, the 'indiligent' (inattentive) reader (p. 994). This is the reader who is attuned to Montaigne's thinking, who does not get 'lost', however obscure or dislocated the writing may become (see pp. 995–6). While this version of the imagined or desired reader is also urged to read 'à contre-poil' (against the grain of the text) (p. 1079), all the same, this reader is one who will read as Montaigne does. The second kind of reader, who appears in 'Sur des vers de Virgile' and 'De la vanité', is a more complex variant of the competent reader, because the affective investment in this imagined reader is so much more powerful. 'J'... espere ... que, s'il advient que mes humeurs plaisent et accordent à quelque honneste homme avant que je meure, il recherchera de nous joindre' (I hope that if before I die my humours happen to please and suit some man of worth, he will try to meet me) (p. 981).[23] This fantasy here, which writing might make materialize, is the existence, as in friendship, of someone who 'corresponds' to him, is just like him.[24] So while

[23] Compare this with the description in 'Sur des vers de Virgile'of the other like him to whom Montaigne would give flesh and blood essays; see above (p. 140).

[24] 'La correspondance et relation qui engendre ces vrayes et parfaictes amitiez' (the likeness and affinity which engenders these true and perfect friendships) (p. 185).

Montaigne values the autonomy of his imagined readers, and while his means, language, is imperfect, nonetheless this other fantasy persists.

Elsewhere the fantasy of symmetry between writer or speaker and reader or other speaker is conveyed by reciprocity: 'un parler ouvert ouvre un autre parler, et le tire hors, comme faict le vin et l'amour' (open speech opens up the other's speech and draws it out, as do wine and love) (p. 794), or in the language of (perfect) halves: that 'moitié … moitié' ideal discussed earlier (p. 65). But the version of language in 'De la vanité' pulls against such calculus, for language is such that: 'il fuira et se difformera' (it will run away and change form) (p. 982); added to which, the writer or speaker's condition is one of change and differing. No perfect correspondence between word and object or self; language cannot produce the other half any more than the relationship with the other is ever one of parity or symmetry. Nor does openness prevail: 'si vous venez à les esclaircir et confirmer, ils vous saisissent et derobent incontinent cet avantage de vostre interpretation' (if you happen to clarify and confirm it for them, they seize on your words and steal your interpretation) (p. 937) – this lexis of violence perhaps a reminder of the failure of equitable dialogue to stave off war or conciliate between different factions.

But, despite the vicissitudes during which Montaigne wrote the *Essais*, a fantasy that his writing might produce longed-for symmetry seems to persist: his essays might still have a power akin to the preferred form he had given up, namely, correspondence. 'Et eusse prins plus volontiers ceste forme [sc. de lettres] à publier mes verves, si j'eusse eu à qui parler. Il me falloit, comme je l'ay eu autrefois, un certain commerce qui m'attirast, qui me soutinst et souslevast' (I would have preferred to use the letter form to publish my words, if I had had someone to talk to. But I would have needed a particular relationship to draw me out, sustain and support me, as I once had) (p. 252).[25] This ideal, sustaining listener/reader was La Boétie, after whose death the essay superseded the letter form. The letter might fairly be called a love letter, then; between two men passionately attached and also passionately attached to and by their shared intellectual, ethical and political concerns. The existence of the later version of the desired 'corresponding' reader may allow us to read the essays as a form of open love letter, but the imagined reader is a dilution of the lost, ideal reader, for he is a version of Montaigne. Moreover, there are tensions in Montaigne's thinking about what it means to be read: on the one hand he wants difference, on the other, at times likeness prevails.

We need to translate this tension into its ethical and poetic equivalents, before exploring further the effects of the loss of the ideal reader. This will not resolve the tension between a longing for correspondence and an insistence on difference. Rather, it is precisely this tension that is acknowledged in the ethics and

---

[25] Montaigne was, in fact, a frequent letter-writer: dedicatory letters, letters written in his capacity as Mayor of Bordeaux and personal letters. See Rigolot, *Les Métamorphoses*, ch. 4, and Balsamo's entry on 'Lettres de Montaigne', in Desan, *Dictionnaire* (Paris, 2007), pp. 580–4.

poetics of Montaigne's writing, which together work to sustain interpretative freedom, despite the anxieties it may involve. It is ethics which demonstrates why this tension must be tolerated: without it imaginary relations would persist (relations based on illusory likeness), and difficult differences would be ruled out by such imaginary bonds. Montaigne's writing makes demands on his readers, and requires that they be open to surprise and ambiguity; it rests on their desire to read, without 'profit' – for he does not offer himself as an example (see p. 663). The ethics of writing and reading his text turn around this, that the text is an end in itself rather than a means to an end. In this, the imagined relationship with the reader matches his ideals for conversation, which should be simply: 'l'exercice des ames, sans autre fruit' (the exercise of minds, with no other end) (p. 824), or: 'pour m'assagir... pour m'ebastre: jamais pour le quest' (to become wiser ... for entertainment, but never for gain) (p. 829).

Moreover, as Montaigne insists more than once, the reader must have a freedom to interpret unpredictably, for such is the nature of the written word: meaning is not fixed even for him as reader of his own text: 'en mes escris mesmes je ne retrouve pas tousjours l'air de ma premiere imagination: je ne sçay ce que j'ay voulu dire' (even in my own writing I cannot always recover quite what I first had in mind; I do not know what I meant to say) (p. 566).

For all his claim that 'toute la beauté, toute la grace et pris est nostre' (all the beauty, all the grace and all the value is ours) (p. 400), 'un suffisant lecteur descouvre souvant és escrits d'autruy des perfections autres que celle que l'autheur y a mises et aperceües' (in others' writings a good-enough reader often discovers perfections other than those that the author has included or been aware of) (p. 127). The use of 'perfections' underscores the paradox here: there is still room for something other in the text, although the noun suggests plenitude. Thus the figurative space of the text and its potential meaning is materially impossible: both already full and perfect but still open to 'perfection'.

The relationship between text and reader is akin to the kind of conversation Montaigne favours (and prefers to reading) – not least in terms of the ambivalence that runs through his representation. His preferences seem unambiguously masculine: he seeks 'vigueur masle et obstinée' (obstinate masculine vigour) (p. 8), even roughness, 'ceux qui me gourment' (those who manhandle me) (p. 925). 'J'ayme une société forte et virile, une amitié qui se flatte en l'aspreté et vigueur de son commerce, comme l'amour, és morsures et esgratigneures sanglantes' (I like strong, manly company, friendship which enjoys the sharpness and vigour of its intercourse, like love, with its bites and scratches that draw blood) (p. 924): homoerotic aggressivity combines with the heterosexual eroticism of his relationship with what guides his speaking: 'je festoye et caresse la verité' (I welcome truth with warm caresses) (p. 924). His model is Socrates (see pp. 925, 927 and 932); he is clear, such interlocutors are 'bien rares' (very rare) (p. 932).

At the same time, however, the vocabulary associated with open-mindedness and the free exchange that good conversation should allow pulls against the masculine ethos: 'doux' and 'mollement', gentle or sweet and softly, mildly,

prevail here. That which is 'mou' or 'molle' is, equally, the antithesis of that
which is disputatious or contentious, over-aggressive or perverse disagree-
ment: 'mes meurs molles, ennemies de toute aigreur et aspreté' (my mild ways,
opposed to all bitterness and asperity) (p. 820). Conversation is his most prized
activity: 'j'en trouve l'usage plus doux qu'aucune autre action de nostre vie' (to
me it is sweeter than any other action in our lives) (p. 922). It is open-minded:
'nulles propositions m'estonnent, nulle creance me blesse, quelque contrariété
qu'elle aye à la mienne … nous autres, qui privons nostre jugement du droict
de faire des arrests, regardons mollement les opinions diverses' (Nothing astonishes me, no belief offends me, however much it differs from my own … we
who deny our judgement the right to pass sentence consider other opinions
mildly) (p. 923) – as did the ancient Pyrrhonists. The antithesis is 'un aigreur
tyrannique de ne pouvoir souffrir une forme diverse à la sienne' (a tyrannical
bitterness which cannot bear a way of thinking different from its own) (p. 928),
and with this, we have another trace of the context of war. But now we arrive
at a paradox: defending one's faith and satisfying conversation may both require
masculine 'vigueur', but qualities associated with the feminine and which even
threaten the masculine are also essential.[26] 'Mollesse' and 'douceur' must not
be excluded by 'vigueur'; without them, the danger is 'tyrannical' resistance
to differing views. To use such countercultural terms, without resolving the
tensions between 'masculine' and 'feminine' qualities, involves risk and exemplifies the kind of openness that is desirable.

The quality of Montaigne's openness is also well conveyed by the tensions in
his description of it, for it rests on his internal difference: 'mon imagination se
contredit elle mesme si souvent et condamne, que ce m'est tout un qu'un autre
le face' (my ideas and imaginings so often contradict and condemn themselves
that I don't mind at all if someone else does so) (pp. 924–5). It also reckons
with the contingencies of our thought processes: 'ma volonté et mon discours
se remue tantost d'un air, tantost d'un autre, et y a plusieurs de ses mouvemens
qui se gouvernent sans moy. Ma raison a des impulsions et agitations journallieres et casuelles' (my will and reasoning move now this way, now that, and
many of these movements are independent of me. There are daily changes in
my reason which are contingent and unsettling) (p. 934). What also matters is
lack of narcissism: in 'De la præsumption' he feigns envy of writers who enjoy
their own work: easy pleasure, as they take it in themselves (see p. 636). The
narcissistic writer's fantasized, indeed only, reader, is himself; his enjoyment
rests on the lack of openness to, or interest in, other readers.

The erotics of conversation are masculine but its ethics are less forcefully
gendered; these complexities are sustainable in the company of those rare individuals he considers worthy interlocutors. But where the text's relationship with
readers differs is that readers are countless unvetted strangers, and the cost of

---

[26] For developed discussion of the value of 'mollesse' in Montaigne's ethics, see Quint,
Montaigne and the Quality of Mercy.

the ethics and poetics of this text is vulnerability to misreading – for not all the other, unexpected interpretations will be made by fair, skilled readers. Think of those who figuratively rob him; or think also of the failures due to incompetence of his interpreter in 'Des cannibales'. Twice Montaigne inveighs with horror against misreading, in 'Sur des vers de Virgile' expressing his dread of being mis-taken (see pp. 130–8), and in 'De la vanité': 'je reviendrois volontiers de l'autre monde pour démentir celuy qui me formeroit autre que je n'estois, fut ce pour m'honorer' (I would willingly return from the dead to give the lie to anyone whose version of me was other than I was, even if it honoured me) (p. 983).

This threatened haunting of future readers signals Montaigne's anxiety and the vulnerability of the text, as well as the cost of an ethics and poetics that insists on not possessing the meaning of the text and on there remaining something not yet known. An ethics to which Montaigne holds, despite insisting that he leaves nothing of himself out (see p. 983). Two pages later, temporarily, Montaigne casts the lack of knowledge on the reader: the 'image' of himself in his writing results from his need to read himself, in the absence of the only reader who knew him fully. In this passage, added in 1588 but suppressed thereafter, La Boétie returns:

> je sçay bien que je ne lairray après moy aucun respondant si affectionné bien loing et entendu en mon faict comme j'ay esté au sien. Il n'y a personne à qui je vousisse pleinement compromettre ma peincture: luy seul jouyssoit de ma vraie image, et l'emporta. C'est pourquoy je me deschiffre moy-mesme si curieusement. (p. 983)

> (I well know that I shall not leave behind any one to answer for me who is remotely as affectionate or understanding as I was towards him. There is no one I would want to trust fully with my portrait: he alone enjoyed my true image, and he has taken it with him. This is why I decipher myself so attentively.)

In the light of this, the 'image' of Montaigne in his *Essais*, which he is so concerned is accurate ('ne trahir l'histoire de ma vie … ne desmentir l'image de mes conditions' (to not betray the story of my life … not give the lie to the image of my qualities) (p. 980)), is (only) what remains, once the 'true image' has been taken away. This still casts La Boétie as the only one who 'knows', the Other who 'holds the truth of the subject and the power to make good its loss'.[27] 'Image', which elsewhere in the chapter has the force of 'ghost', now also inclines towards 'what remains' and 'living image', in an incalculable relationship. The image is produced in the gap between 'jouir' and 'emporter', which is the space of not yet known aspects of himself, still to be deciphered. The lost 'truth' of the subject can be gestured towards by re-presenting La Boétie: the ghost in the text is not only the friend, but also Montaigne's version of himself

---

[27] Rose, 'Introduction II', in Mitchell and Rose, *Feminine Sexuality* (London, 1982), pp. 27–57 (p. 32).

as ascribed to being known by him; ghosts and fantasy selves start to merge here.

We need to reunite this added, then excised, comment with what just preceded it in the text:

> je ne laisse rien à desirer et deviner de moy. Si on doibt s'en entretenir, je veus que ce soit veritablement et justement. Je reviendrois volontiers de l'autre monde pour démentir celuy qui me formeroit autre que je n'estois, fut ce pour m'honorer … Et si à toute force je n'eusse maintenu un amy que j'ay perdu, on me l'eust deschiré en mille contraire visages. (p. 983)

> (I leave nothing to be desired or guessed about me. If you must talk about it, I want it to be true and just. I would willingly return from the dead to give the lie to anyone whose version of me was other than I was, even if it honoured me … and had I not protected with all my strength a friend I have lost, they would have torn him into thousands of different appearances.)

The passage is saturated with anxieties and aporia: it begins with an assertion that there is nothing left to say, his self-representation is complete, no deciphering is needed. Where something more, or less, slips in, is in the way the representation is talked about: once it is put into circulation and becomes a complex object of exchange between readers, it might be deformed – and for Montaigne, the desire to enhance (even to honour) is a deformation. So even if perfect representation were possible (which it is not), the desire to interpret and re-present, from which the representation cannot be safeguarded, paradoxically, would still remain. All re-presentation deforms; all speech, all language deforms. From which condition, self-representation presumably is not exempt? The assertive stance of the first sentence needs to be revisited, with caution. For the weight and affective force of the ideas here pull against it and against the existence of the desired reader, who will be on the side of truth and justice, as the violence of the final words underlines. Reading metamorphoses into savage destructiveness, and the imperfections of language and interpretation assume terrible potential. All the more so because, as Montaigne laments in the added and then subtracted passage, he will have no one to protect him as he protected his friend: by not publishing, of course – thereby simultaneously being disloyal to his friend's desire, which is inescapably another form of violence. To save is to betray.

Past and future converge here: the self-representation that is always already something of a ghost – 'image'; the haunting of his text by representations of his friend – for despite being later subtracted, the added text leaves a trace, effects a way of re-presenting loss and absence; the fantasy of his own return from the dead to haunt those who misrepresent him.

However, there is room for further reflections on death and his writing, supplementing his anxieties about his self-representation in the future. The text is a form of future for past others who are other than him, as they live on by their words being constantly written into his 'own' text in the form of quotations, allusions and anecdotes. Here the text is more than a form of commemoration of the dead and the lost ideals they represent. It is a form of *care*, 'soing des morts' (care of the dead) (p. 996); being helpless, he goes on, they need his care all the more. This form of care opens up a different economy:

> le bien-faict est moins richement assigné où il y a retrogradation et reflexion ... Ceux qui ont merité de moy de l'amitié et de la reconnaissance ne l'ont jamais perdue pour n'y estre plus: je les ay mieux payé et plus soigneusement, absens et ignorans. Je parle plus affectueusement de mes amis quand il n'y a plus moyen qu'ils le sçachent. (p. 996)

> (benefit is less richly bestowed when it can be repaid or reciprocated ... Those who have deserved my friendship and recognition have never lost it through being no longer with us; I have repaid them better and more carefully in their absence, without them knowing. I speak more affectionately of my friends when they can no longer know of it.)

To write about them is akin to the experience of giving, free of the taint of exchange, a form of 'pure liberalité ... hospitalité ... franche et gratuite' (pure liberality ... free and open hospitality) (p. 969); an emotional and ethical economy which he has found only in his friendship with La Boétie: 'en la vray amitié ... je me donne à mon amy plus que je ne le tire à moy' (in true friendship ... I give myself more to my friend than I draw him to me) (p. 977). Thus the text becomes a form of recovery of that ideal economy; but now the ethical stakes are more complex and risky, for he must put his gift (to the dead) into the hands of the living, knowing that no reader will ever take the place of the dead friend; on the contrary, he anticipates inhospitability among his readers. This is, then, to write in awareness of the failings of both language and humans, but nonetheless to stake his 'life' on it. The condition of this is that the reader must not look to him for 'truth', and he must allow the reader to 'fail': an ethical stake so high that it can only be represented by that image of his return from the dead ...

This can be interpreted in three coexisting way. Firstly, as a measure of his otherwise unsymbolizable anxiety about his future in his text, for language is insubstantial, and identified with uncertainty and mortality (see p. 982); secondly, it invites the future reader to remember both that he is dead and that his writing is a form of care for the dead, which now include him in their number; thirdly, it is a reminder that it is language that enables him to envisage his own death: 'il touche du doigt qu'il peut manquer à la chaine [sc. signifiante] qu'il est' (he becomes fully aware that he may disappear from the [signifying] chain of what he is).[28] Language is also already a form of death, in that the symbol replaces the thing symbolized, and this substitution is, for Lacan, after Kojève, the (figurative) 'meurtre de la chose' (murder of the thing).[29]

---

[28] Lacan, *Le Séminaire VII*, p. 341.

[29] Lacan, *Écrits* (Paris, 1966), p. 204. 'When the Meaning (Essence) "dog" passes into the *word* "dog" – that is, becomes an *abstract* Concept which is different from the *sensible*

The episode in Freud that prompts Lacan's comment is his infant grandson's play with a cotton reel, representing his mother's absence. As he throws the reel out of his cot, he cries out (*fort*, gone) and pulls it back in again (*da*, there). For Freud this play raised questions relating to the pleasure principle; his answer to them was a form of theory of art, even of tragedy: 'making what is in itself unpleasurable into a subject to be recollected and worked over in the mind' – presumably with (enough) pleasure.[30] Lacan's interest in this play is as an example of the start of symbolization: in absence. 'The child gets its first sense that something could be missing; words stand for objects, because they only have to be spoken when the first object is lost.'[31] The consequence of this origin is clear: 'language speaks – by which I understand: goes on speaking, in spite of us – the loss which lay behind that first moment of symbolization' (Rose, p. 32). So now let us put this back together with questions of the pleasure principle: language is that which, in all its failings, protects us from, or masks, unpleasure, that is, pain; in art, for Lacan (among others) this might be the role of beauty; it might also be the form that is given to the void (of death) by the artist. Or both converge: 'la fonction du beau étant précisément de nous indiquer la place du rapport de l'homme à sa propre mort, et de ne nous l'indiquer que dans un éblouissement' (the function of the beautiful being precisely to reveal to us the place of man's relationship to his own death, and to reveal it to us only in a blinding flash).[32] Lacan, again: 'le premier symbole où nous reconnaissons l'humanité dans ses vestiges, est la sépultre' (the first symbol in which we recognize humanity in its vestiges is the sepulture);[33] Montaigne: 'le plus beau sépulcre, c'est celui *di Santa Rotonda*' (the most beautiful of sepulchres is the Santa Rotonda) (*Journal*, p. 228). We call this perfect circular monument the Pantheon, an extraordinary example – the most beautiful – of the way in which art gives form to nothing, and in so doing, brings it retroactively into being; not filling it but sustaining it as empty.

It helps us to understand how this bears on Montaigne's desire to write about himself, flesh and blood, if we move from the drama of the figurative murder of the object to the following version of the cost of language: 'our subjection to language throws our whole relation to the body off balance; we are "cut off" from our instincts by "castration"'. Therefore: 'the child's desire for the mother does not refer *to* her but *beyond* her, to an object ... whose status is first imaginary (the object presumed to satisfy *her* desire [my italics]) and then symbolic (recognition that desire cannot be satisfied)'.[34] Žižek's version of this Lacanian

reality that it reveals by its Meaning – the Meaning (Essence) *dies*: the word "dog" does not run, drink and eat ... the *conceptual* understanding of empirical reality is equivalent to a *murder*.' Kojève, *Introduction to the Reading of Hegel* (New York, 1969), pp. 372–3.

[30] Freud, 'Beyond the Pleasure Principle', in *Beyond the Pleasure Principle* (London, 1955), pp. 7–64 (p. 17).

[31] Rose, 'Introduction II', in Mitchell and Rose, *Feminine Sexuality*, p. 31.

[32] Lacan, *Le Séminaire VII*, p. 342.

[33] Lacan, *Ecrits*, p. 319.

[34] Rose, 'Introduction II', in Mitchell and Rose, *Feminine Sexuality*, p. 38.

concept emphasizes more clearly the ambiguous compensation for this loss, language: 'this means that sexual enjoyment is never fully achieved or achievable in itself; instead we get "surplus enjoyment" … the renunciation of bodily enjoyment *in favour of* language and the concomitant infection of language *by* enjoyment'.[35]

The future reader who will read Montaigne 'truly and justly' and with the 'care' that his writing gives the dead needs to be recognized as imaginary, and far from the probable reality, which is the irreducible otherness of his future readers. Even if the difference between imaginary reader and real readers plural had not already been acknowledged, the experience of being read by Vatican censors (not all of whom could even read French)[36] and the experience of the fate of La Boétie's essay, only saved from being torn apart in innumerable contradictory readings by not being published, inescapably demonstrates the gap. The poetics and ethics of writing and reading have to recognize the different violences that inhabit the text, all of which relate to death or that which is deadly in the living. Montaigne's resource, as well as finally setting aside the illusions of imaginary identifications – the reader who is just like him – and requiring that the reader read 'against the grain', is to never end the text, the place in which meaning goes on circulating.

This reading does not intend to make a Lacanian of Montaigne. Rather, its aim is to extend our understanding of Montaigne as a thinker and writer who struggled, in his way, with the problematic of how adequately to grasp the relationship between I think, I speak, and I represent myself. His subject can only grasp himself by missing himself, and must allow that an interlocutor or reader will find 'des perfections autres' (other perfections) (p. 127) than he himself had been aware of. The qualifier 'autres' puts 'perfections' in doubt; there is always room for something else. There is also always something missing, a lack of perfect representation, and, moreover, something else that the writer, and in turn the reader, misses.

By never ending and keeping ideas in play: 'tousjours demandant et esmouvant la dispute, jamais l'arrestant, jamais satisfaisant' (always asking questions and keeping the discussion moving, never concluding, never satisfying) (p. 509), Montaigne sends the reader the message: 'je te demande de refuser ce que jc t'offre (parce que ce n'est pas ça)' (I ask you not to accept what I offer you (because that's not it)).[37] The text gives neither writer nor reader fully what is wanted, although it also holds further potential, and as readers we are only ever substitutes. There is in a sense no 'à qui parler' (person to talk to), 'aucun respondant' (no one to answer for one), other than a substitute; we are only ever 'in place of'. Through writing which sustains Montaigne's place as empty, we are called upon to accept that our own demand for knowledge (a transform

---

[35] Kay, *Žižek*, p. 49.

[36] According to Scholar's account, the more senior of the two censors with whom Montaigne met, Sisto Fabri, 'had no French' (*Montaigne*, p. 168).

[37] Lacan, *Le Séminaire XX*, p. 101.

of the questions, do you love me? what I am to you?) will never be satisfied. This would mean that there would be an outside chance that the relationship between text and reader could become a form of *philia*: not the same as Montaigne's friendship with his lost reader, but the possibility of a different staging of its spirit and principle: namely a 'refusal to calculate: a place where interest, in the narrow sense of the pursuit of equivalence in exchanges, is suspended'.[38] This is no utopian dream: as I have tried to bring out, the risks and costs of such a freedom, Montaigne reckoned, were almost intolerably high. But if the text could try to produce a future 'place of the brother', this would be a form of care for, and containment of, that which is death-driven in all of us and our language, and a resource for greater tolerance and openness, however precarious or unsettling.

---

[38] Bourdieu, 'The Family as a Realized Institution/Category', *Theory Culture and Society* 13/3 (1966), pp. 19–26 (p. 20).

BIBLIOGRAPHY

Primary texts

Montaigne

Montaigne, M. de, *Essais de Michel Seigneur de Montaigne*, vol. 5 (The Hague, 1727)

—— *Montaigne: Oeuvres complètes*, ed. A. Thibaudet and M. Rat (Paris, 1962)

—— *Journal de voyage*, ed. F. Garavini (Paris, 1983)

—— *Michel de Montaigne: The Complete Essays*, trans. M. Screech (Harmondsworth, 1987)

—— *Michel de Montaigne: The Complete Works*, trans. D. Frame (London, 2003)

—— *Montaigne Essais II*, ed. A. Tournon (Paris, 2003)

—— *Essais*, ed. P. Villey and V.-L. Saulnier (Paris, 2004)

Other

Aristotle, *The Art of Rhetoric*, trans. J. H. Freese, Loeb Classical Library vol. 22 (Cambridge, Mass. and London, 1926)

—— *Nicomachean Ethics*, trans. H. Rackham, Loeb Classical Library vol. 19 (Cambridge, Mass. and London, 1926)

—— *Eudemian Ethics*, trans. H. Rackham, Loeb Classical Library vol. 23 (Cambridge, Mass. and London, 1935)

Bèze, T. de, *Satyres Chrestiennes de la cuisine papale*, ed. C.-A. Chamay (Geneva, 2005)

Camus, J.-P., *Spectacles d'horreur*, ed. N. Cremona (Rennes, 2010)

Castellio, S., *Contra libellum Calvini* (n.p., 1612)

—— *Conseil à la France désolée, auquel est montré la cause de la guerre présente et le remède qui pourroit estre mis, et principalement est avisé si on doit forcer la conscience*, ed. M. Valkhoff (Geneva, 1967)

Cicero, *Laelius de Amicitia*, trans. W. A. Falconer, Loeb Classical Library vol. 20 (Cambridge, Mass. and London, 1923)

Du Bellay, J., *La Deffence et illustration de la langue françoyse*, ed. H. Chamard (Paris, 1948)

La Boétie, E. de, *De la servitude volontaire ou Contr'un*, ed. N. Gontarbert and A. Prassoloff (Paris, 1993)

—— *Mémoire touchant l'edit de janvier 1562*, in N. Gontarbert and A. Prassoloff (eds), *De la servitude volontaire ou Contr'un* (Paris, 1993), pp. 268–303

Léry, J. de, *Histoire memorable de la ville de Sancerre* (Fribourg, 1975)

—— *Histoire d'un voyage faict en la terre du Bresil*, ed. F. Lestringant (Paris, 1994)

Mainardo, M., *Anatomie de la messe et du missel* (Lyon, 1562)

Marguerite de Navarre, *L'Heptaméron*, ed. M. François (Paris, 1967)

Osorio da Fonseca, J., *Historia de rebus Emmanuelis Lusitanae Regis virtute gestis* (Cologne, 1574), trans. *L'Histoire de Portugal* (Geneva, 1610)

Pasquier, E., *Exhortation aux Princes et Seigneurs du conseil privé du Roy* (n.p., 1561)

—— *Le Cathéchisme des Jésuites* (Paris, 1602)

Plato, *The Symposium*, trans. C. Gill (Harmondsworth, 1999)

Ronsard, P. de, *Les Amours*, ed. C. Weber and H. Weber (Paris, 1963)

Sextus Empiricus, *Against the Logicians*, trans. R. Bury, Loeb Classical Library vol. 2 (Cambridge, Mass. and London, 1935)

—— *Outlines of Pyrrhonism*, trans. R. Bury, Loeb Classical Library vol. 1 (Cambridge, Mass. and London, 1967)

Thevet, A., *Les Singularités de la France antarctique autrement nommée Amérique: et de plusieurs terres et îles découvertes de nostre temps* (Paris, 1982)

Xenophon, *Symposium,* in *Xenophon: The Shorter Socratic Writings*, trans. R. Bartlett (Ithaca and London, 1996), pp. 133–72

Secondary literature

Abraham, N. and Torok, N., 'Introjecter – incorporer: deuil ou mélancholie', *Nouvelle Revue de Psychanalyse* 6 (1972), pp. 111–22

Allen, A., 'La Mélancolie du biographe: le *Roman du Castelain de Couci* et le deuil de la voix', *Neophilologus* 85 (2001), pp. 25–41

Arens, W., *The Man-Eating Myth* (New York, 1979)

Arlette, J., *La Saint-Barthélemy: les mystères d'un crime d'Etat* (Paris, 2007)

Atkinson, G., *Les Nouveaux Horizons de la Renaissance française* (Geneva, 1935)

Aulotte, R., *Montaigne: Apologie de Raimond Sebond* (Paris, 1979)

Baldinger, K., *Dictionnaire étymologique de l'ancien français* (Quebec and Tübingen, 1997–2000)

Balsamo, J., 'Lettres de Montaigne', in P. Desan, *Dictionnaire de Michel de Montaigne* (Paris, 2007), pp. 580–4

Baltrusaitis, J., *Anamorphoses: ou perspectives curieuses* (Paris, 1955)

Barker, F., Hulme, P. and Iversen, M. (eds), *Cannibalism and the Colonial World* (Cambridge, 1998)

Bauschatz, C., 'Montaigne's Conception of Reading in the Context of Renaissance Poetics and Modern Criticism', in S. Suleiman and I. Crossman (eds), *The Reader in the Text* (Princeton, 1980), pp. 264–91

Benedict, P., 'The Saint Bartholomew's Massacres in the Provinces', *The Historical Journal* 21 (1978), pp. 205–25

—— *Rouen During the Wars of Religion* (Cambridge, 1981)

Bersani, L., 'Introduction' to Freud, *Civilization and its Discontents* (Harmondsworth, 2002), pp. vii–xxii, republished as 'Can Sex Make Us Happy?', *Raritan* 21/4 (Spring, 2002), pp. 15–30

—— *Is the Rectum a Grave?* (Chicago, 2010)

Bhabha, H., 'The Other Question', in *The Location of Culture* (London, 1994), pp. 94–120

Bion, W., *Learning from Experience* (London, 1962)

Black, M., *Models and Metaphors* (Ithaca, 1962)

Blakemore, S.-J., Wolpert, W. and Firth, C., 'Why Can't You Tickle Yourself?', *Neuroreport* 11/11 (3 August 2000), pp. 11–16

Blanchard, J., 'Of Cannibalism and Autobiography', *MLN* 93 (1978), pp. 654–76

Blum, C., 'De la *Lettre sur la mort de La Boétie* aux *Essais*: allongeail ou répétition?', *RHLF* 88/5 (1988), pp. 934–48

Blum, C., Deredinger, P. and Toia, A. (eds), *Montaigne: voyage en Alsace et en Suisse* (Paris, 2000)

Bossy, J., 'The Social History of Confession in the Age of the Reformation', *Transactions of the Royal Historical Society*, 5th series, 25 (1975), pp. 21–38

Bourdieu, P., 'The Family as a Realized Institution/Category', *Theory Culture and Society* 13/3 (1966), pp. 19–26

Boutcher, W., 'Le Moyen de voir de Senecque escrit à la main: Montaigne's *Journal de voyage* and the Politics of *Science* and *Faveur*', in J. O'Brien (ed.), *(Ré)interprétations: études sur le seizième siècle*, Michigan Romance Studies 15 (Ann Arbor, 1995), pp. 177–214

Brahami, F., *Le Scepticisme de Montaigne* (Paris, 1997)

Brancher, D., '"Ny plus ne moins que la rubarbe qui pousse hors les mauvaises humeurs": la rhubarbe au purgatoire', in M.-L. Demonet and A. Legros (eds), *L'Ecriture du scepticisme chez Montaigne* (Geneva, 2004)

Briggs, R., 'The Sins of the People: Auricular Confession and the Imposition of Social Norms', in *Communities of Belief: Cultural and Social Tension in Early Modern France* (Oxford, 1989), pp. 277–337

Brush, C., 'The Secretary, Again', *Montaigne Studies* 5/1–2 (1993), pp. 113–38

Burnyeat, M., 'Can the Skeptic live his Skepticism?', in M. Burnyeat (ed.), *The Skeptical Tradition* (Berkeley, 1983), pp. 117–48

Butler, J., *Precarious Life: The Powers of Mourning and Violence* (London, 2004)

—— *Giving an Account of Oneself* (New York, 2005)

Butor, M., *Essais sur les Essais* (Paris, 1968)

Cameron, E., *The European Reformation* (Oxford, 1991)

Campbell, M., *The Witness and the Other World: Exotic European Travel Writing, 400–1600* (Ithaca, 1988)

Carroll, S., *Noble Power during the French Wars of Religion: The Guise Affinity and the Catholic Cause in Normandy* (Cambridge, 1998)

—— *Martyrs and Murderers: The Guise Family and the Making of Europe* (Oxford, 2009)

Cave, T. C., *The Cornucopian Text: Problems of Writing in the French Renaissance* (Oxford, 1979)

—— 'Problems of Reading in the *Essais*', in I. D. McFarlane and I. Maclean (eds), *Montaigne: Essays in Memory of Richard Sayce* (Oxford, 1982), pp. 133–66

—— 'Le Récit montaignien: un voyage sans repentir', in Z. Samaras (ed.), *Montaigne: espace, voyage, écriture* (Paris, 1995), pp. 125–35

—— *Pré-histoires: textes troublés au seuil de la modernité* (Geneva, 1999)

—— *How to Read Montaigne* (London, 2007)

—— 'Imagining Scepticism in the Sixteenth Century', in N. Kenny and W. Williams (eds), *Retrospectives: Essays in Literature, Poetics and Cultural History* (London, 2009), pp. 109–29

Certeau, M. de, *L'Ecriture de l'histoire* (Paris, 1975)

—— 'Montaigne's "Of Cannibals": The Savage "I"', in *Heterologies: Discourse on the Other*, trans. B. Massumi (Minneapolis, 1986), pp. 67–79

Charpentier, F., 'Ecriture et travail du deuil dans les *Essais*, de 1580 au troisième allongeail', *RHLF* 5 (1988), pp. 823–38

—— 'Ecriture de l'errance, errances de l'écriture', in Z. Samaras (ed.), *Montaigne: espace, voyage, écriture* (Paris, 1995), pp. 243–52

Chinard, G., *L'Exotisme américain dans la littérature française au XVIème siècle* (Paris, 1911)

Clark, C., 'Seneca's Letters as a Source of Some of Montaigne's Imagery', *BHR* 30/1 (1968), pp. 249–66

—— *The Web of Metaphor: Studies in the Imagery of Montaigne's Essais*, French Forum 7 (Lexington, Ky., 1978)

Clark, F., *Eucharistic Sacrifice and the Reformation* (Oxford, 1967)

Conley, T., 'The *Essays* and the New World', in U. Langer (ed.), *The Cambridge Companion to Montaigne* (Cambridge, 2005)

Cottrell, R. D., *Sexuality/Textuality: A Study of the Fabric of Montaigne's Essais* (Columbus, 1981)

Crouzet, D., *Les Guerriers de Dieu: la violence au temps des troubles de religion, vers 1525–vers 1610*, 2 vols (Paris, 1990)

—— *La Nuit de la Saint-Barthélemy: un rêve perdu de la Renaissance* (Paris, 1994)

Dandrey, P., *Les Tréteaux de Saturne* (Paris, 2003)

Davis, N. Z., 'The Sacred and the Body Social in Sixteenth-Century Lyon', *Past and Present* 90 (1980), pp. 40–70

Defaux, G., 'Un cannibale en haut de chausses: Montaigne, la différence et la logique de l'identité', *MLN* 97/4 (1982), pp. 919–57

—— 'Montaigne et l'expérience: réflexions sur la naissance d'un philosophe scep-tique – et "impremedité"', in M.-L. Demonet and A. Legros (eds), *Ecriture du scepticisme chez Montaigne* (Geneva, 2004), pp. 289–302

Delumeau, J., *La Peur en Occident (XIVe–XVIIIe siècle)* (Paris, 1978)

—— *L'Aveu et le pardon: les difficultés de la confession, XIIIe–XVIIIe siècle* (Paris, 1990)

Demonet, M.-L., *A Plaisir: sémiotique et scepticisme chez Montaigne* (Orléans, 2002)

Demonet, M.-L. and Legros, A. (eds), *L'Ecriture du scepticisme chez Montaigne* (Geneva, 2004)

Derrida, J., *De la grammatologie* (Paris, 1967)

—— 'La Mythologie blanche', in *Rhétorique et philosophie, Poétique* 5 (Paris, 1971), pp. 1–52

—— *La Vérité en peinture* (Paris, 1978)

—— 'Entretien avec Jacques Derrida', in D. Cahen, *Digraphe* (1987), pp. 11–27

—— *Donner le temps* (Paris, 1991)

—— *Donner la mort*, in *L'Ethique du don* (Paris, 1992)

—— '"Il faut bien manger" ou le calcul du sujet', in *Points de suspension: entre-tiens* (Paris, 1992), pp. 226–302

—— *Politiques de l'amitié* (Paris, 1994)

—— '"Eating Well", or the Calculation of the Subject', trans. P. Connell and A. Ronell, in *Points ... Interviews 1974–1994* (Stanford, 1995), pp. 255–87

—— *Politics of Friendship*, trans. G. Collins (London, 1997)

Desan, P., *Les Commerces de Montaigne: le discours économique des Essais* (Paris, 1992)
—— *Dictionnaire de Michel de Montaigne* (Paris, 2004)
Diefendorf, D., *Beneath the Cross: Catholics and Huguenots in Sixteenth-century Paris* (Oxford, 1991)
Doueihi, M., *A Perverse History of the Human Heart* (Cambridge, Mass., 1997)
Douglas, M., *Purity and Danger: An Analysis of Concepts of Pollution and Taboo* (London, 1966)
Dover, K., *Plato: Symposium* (Cambridge, 1980)
Duval, E., 'Lessons of the New World: Design and Meaning in Montaigne's "Des Cannibales" (I, 31) and "Des Coches" (III, 6)', in *Montaigne: Essays in Reading*, Special Edition, *Yale French Studies* 64 (1983), pp. 95–112
El Kenz, D., *Les Bûchers du Roi: la culture protestante des martyrs: 1523–1572* (Paris, 1997)
Elwood, C., *The Body Broken: The Calvinist Doctrine of the Eucharist and the Symbolization of Power in Sixteenth-Century France* (Oxford, 1999)
Evans, D., *An Introductory Dictionary of Lacanian Psychoanalysis* (London, 1996)
Freud, S., 'The Uncanny', in *An Infantile Neurosis and Other Works*, Standard Edition vol. XVII (London, 1955), pp. 219–52
—— 'Beyond the Pleasure Principle', in *Beyond the Pleasure Principle, Group Psychology and Other Works,* Standard Edition vol. XVIII (London, 1955), pp. 7–64
—— 'On Narcissism', in *A History of the Psycho-Analytic Movement, Papers on Metapsychology and Other Works*, Standard Edition vol. XIV (London, 1957), pp. 73–102
—— 'Mourning and Melancholia', in *A History of the Psycho-Analytic Movement, Papers on Metapsychology and Other Works*, Standard Edition vol. XIV (London, 1957), pp. 243–58
—— *Mass Psychology*, in *Mass Psychology and Other Writings* (London, 2004)
Friedrich, H., *Montaigne*, trans. D. Porter (Berkeley, 1991)
Garavini, F., *Itinerari a Montaigne* (Florence, 1983)
—— *Monstres et chimères: Montaigne, le texte et le fantasme* (Paris, 1994)
Gaunt, S., *Love and Death in Medieval French and Occitan Courtly Literature: Martyrs to Love* (Oxford, 2006)
Ginzburg, C., *Il Filo e le trace*: *vero falso finto* (Milan, 2006)
Giocanti, S., *Penser l'irrésolution: Montaigne, Pascal, La Mothe Le Vayer* (Paris, 2001)
Girard, R., *La Violence et le sacré* (Paris, 1972)
Goyet, F., 'Montaigne and the Notion of Prudence', in U. Langer (ed.), *The Cambridge Companion to Montaigne* (Cambridge, 2005), pp. 118–41
Green, A., 'Cannibalisme: réalité ou fantasme agi?', *Nouvelle Revue de Psychanalyse* 6 (1972), pp. 27–52
Greenblatt, S., *Renaissance Self-fashioning* (Chicago, 1980)
—— *Marvellous Possessions* (Oxford, 1991)
—— '1563: Anti-Dictator', in D. Hollier (ed.), *A New History of French Literature* (Cambridge, Mass., 1994)
—— 'Remnants of the Sacred in Early Modern England', in M. de Grazia, M. Quilligan and P. Stallybrass (eds), *Subject and Object in Renaissance Culture* (Cambridge, 1996), pp. 337–45

Greengrass, M., 'Conclusion: Moderate Voices, Mixed Messages', in L. Racaut and A. Ryrie (eds), *Moderate Voices in the European Reformation* (Aldershot, 2005), pp. 196–211

—— *Governing Passions: Peace and Reform in the French Kingdom 1572–1585* (Oxford, 2007)

Grell, O. P. and Scribner, B. (eds), *Tolerance and Intolerance in the European Reformation* (Cambridge, 1996)

Guerrier, O., 'Fantasmes – Fantasie', in P. Desan, *Dictionnaire de Michel de Montaigne* (Paris, 2007), pp. 387–90

Guggisberg, H. R., *Sebastian Castellio 1515–1563, Humanist and Defender of Religious Toleration in a Confessional Age*, trans. B. Gordon (Aldershot, 2003)

Helgeson, J., *Harmonie divine et subjectivité poétique chez Maurice Scève* (Geneva, 2001)

Henry, P., *Montaigne in Dialogue: Censorship and Defensive Writing* (Stanford, 1987)

Hillman, D., 'Visceral Knowledge: Shakespeare, Skepticism and the Interior of the Early Modern Body', in D. Hillman and C. Mazzio (eds), *The Body in Parts: Fantasies of Corporeality in Early Modern Europe* (London, 1997), pp. 81–106

Hoffmann, G., *Montaigne's Career* (Oxford, 1998)

—— 'Anatomy of the Mass: Montaigne's "Cannibals"', *PMLA* 117/2 (March 2002), pp. 207–21

Huguet, E., *Dictionnaire de la langue française du seizième siècle* (Paris, 1925)

Jameson, F., 'On the Sexual Production of Western Sexuality: or, St Augustine as a Social Democrat', in R. Salecl and S. Zizek (eds), *Gaze and Voice as Love Objects* (Durham, NC and London, 1996), pp. 154–78

Jeanneret, M., *Des Mets et des mots: banquets et propos de table à la Renaissance* (Paris, 1987)

—— *Perpetuum mobile: métamorphoses des corps et des oeuvres, de Vinci à Montaigne* (Paris, 1997)

Jeay, M., 'Consuming Passions: Variations on the Eaten Heart Theme', in A. Roberts (ed.), *Violence Against Women in Medieval Texts* (Gainsville, Fla., 1998), pp. 75–96

Jenny, L., *L'Expérience de la chute: de Montaigne à Michaux* (Paris, 1997)

Kay, S., *Subjectivity in Troubadour Poetry* (Cambridge, 1990)

—— *Žižek: A Critical Introduction* (Cambridge, 2003)

Kilgour, M., *From Communion to Cannibalism: An Anatomy of Metaphors of Incorporation* (Princeton, 1990)

Kingdon, R. M., *Myths about the St. Bartholomew's Day Massacres 1572–76* (Cambridge, Mass., 1988)

Klibansky, R., Panofsky, E. and Saxl, F., *Saturn and Melancholy: Studies in the History of Natural Philosophy, Religion and Art* (London, 1964)

Kojève, A., *Introduction to the Reading of Hegel*, trans. J. H. Nichols (New York, 1969)

Kristeva, J., *Soleil noir: dépression et mélancolie* (Paris, 1987)

—— *Etrangers à nous-mêmes* (Paris, 1988)

Kritzman, L., 'Le Roman de la pierre ou Montaigne et l'archéologie du moi', *BSAM* 13–16 (1988–89), pp. 119–26

—— *The Rhetoric of Sexuality and the Literature of the French Renaissance* (Cambridge, 1991)

—— *The Fabulous Imagination* (New York, 2009)

Lacan, J., *Ecrits* (Paris, 1966)

—— *Le Séminaire livre XI: Les Quatre Concepts fondamentaux de la psychanalyse* (Paris, 1973)

—— *Le Séminaire livre I: Les Ecrits techniques de Freud* (Paris, 1975)

—— *Le Séminaire livre II: Le Moi dans la théorie de Freud et dans la technique de la psychanalyse* (Paris, 1978)

—— *Le Séminaire livre VIII: Le Transfert* (Paris, 1991)

—— *Le Séminaire livre IV: La Relation d'objet* (Paris, 1994)

—— *Le Séminaire livre VII: L'Ethique de la psychanalyse* (Paris, 1994)

—— *Le Séminaire livre XX: Encore* (Paris, 1999)

—— *Le Séminaire livre X: L'Angoisse* (Paris, 2004)

Langer, U., *Perfect Friendship: Studies in Literature and Moral Philosophy from Boccaccio to Corneille* (Geneva, 1994)

—— (ed.), *The Cambridge Companion to Montaigne* (Cambridge, 2005)

Legros, A., 'Montaigne face à ses censeurs romains de 1581 (mise à jour)', *BHR* 71/1 (2009), pp. 7–34

Lestringant, F., 'Catholiques et cannibales. Le thème du cannibalisme dans le discours protestant au temps des Guerres de religion', in J.-C. Margolin and R. Sauzet (eds), *Pratiques et discours alimentaires à la Renaissance* (Paris, 1982), pp. 233–46

—— *Le Cannibale: grandeur et décadence* (Paris, 1994)

—— *Cannibals: The Discovery and Representation of the Cannibal from Columbus to Jules Verne*, trans. R. Morris (Cambridge, 1997)

—— *Une Sainte Horreur ou, Le Voyage en eucharistie: XVIe–XVIIIe siècle* (Paris, 1996)

Lévi-Strauss, C., *Tristes Tropiques* (Paris, 1955)

—— *Anthropologie structurale* (Paris, 1958)

Lyons, J., *Before Imagination: Embodied Thought from Montaigne to Rousseau* (Stanford, 2005)

Maclean, I., *Montaigne philosophe* (Paris, 1996)

MacPhail, E., *The Voyage to Rome in French Renaissance Literature*, Stanford French and Italian Studies 68 (Stanford, 1990)

Macy, G., *The Banquet's Wisdom: A Short History of the Theologies of the Lord's Supper* (Mahwah, NJ, 1992)

Margolin, J.-Cl. and Sauzet, R. (eds), *Pratiques et discours alimentaires à la Renaissance* (Paris, 1982)

Massa, J.-M., 'Le Monde luso-brésilien dans la joyeuse entrée de Rouen', in *Les Fêtes de la Renaissance*, vol. 3 (Paris, 1975), pp. 105–16

Mathieu-Castellani, G., *Montaigne: l'écriture de l'essai* (Paris, 1988)

Mayor, I. S. 'Montaigne's Cure: Stones and Roman Ruins', *MLN* 97 (1982), pp. 958–72

McGowan, M. (ed.), *C'est la deduction du sumptueux ordre plaisantz spectacles et magnifiques theatres dresses*, in *L'Entrée de Henri II à Rouen 1550* (Amsterdam, 1970), n.p.

—— 'Contradictory Impulses in Montaigne's Vision of Rome', *Renaissance Studies* 4/4 (1990), pp. 392–409

McKinley, M., 'Poétique du lieu: Rome, l'enfance et la mort', in *Montaigne e l'Italia*, Gruppo di studio sul Cinquecento francese 2 (Geneva, 1991), pp. 339–50

—— *Les Terrains vagues des 'Essais': itinéraires et intertextes* (Paris, 1996)
Mentzer, R. and Spicer, A. (eds), *Society and Culture in the Huguenot World* (Cambridge, 2002)
Merleau-Ponty, M., 'Lecture de Montaigne', in *Signes* (Paris, 1960)
Michaels, A., *The Winter Vault* (London, Berlin and New York, 2009)
Miller, J.-A., 'On Love: We Love the One who Responds to our Question: "who am I?"', http://www.lacan.com/symptom/?page_id263
Mitchell, J. and Rose, J., *Feminine Sexuality: Jacques Lacan and the École Freudienne* (London, 1982)
Monter, E. W., *Calvin's Geneva* (New York, 1967)
Moriarty, M., *Early Modern French Thought: The Age of Suspicion* (Oxford, 2003)
—— *Fallen Nature, Fallen Selves: Early Modern French Thought II* (Oxford, 2006)
Moureau, F. and Bernoulli, R. (eds), *Autour du 'Journal de voyage' de Montaigne* (Geneva, 1982)
Muir, E., *Ritual in Early Modern Europe* (Cambridge, 2005)
Murray, T., 'Translating Montaigne's Crypts: Melancholic Relations and the Site of Altarbiography', in J. Crewe (ed.), *Reconfiguring the Renaissance: Essays in Critical Materialism* (Lewisburg, 1992), pp. 121–49
Nakam, G., *Montaigne et son temps: les événements et les Essais* (Paris, 1982)
—— *Montaigne: la manière et la matière* (Paris, 1991)
—— *Les Essais de Montaigne, miroir et procès de leur temps: témoignage historique et création littéraire* (Paris, 2001)
Nussbaum, M., 'The Speech of Alcibiades', *Philosophy and Literature* 3 (1979), pp. 131–72
—— *Love's Knowledge: Essays on Philosophy and Literature* (Oxford, 1990)
—— *The Therapy of Desire: Theory and Practice in Hellenistic Ethics* (Princeton, 1994)
O'Brien, J., 'Reasoning with the Senses: The Humanist Imagination', *South Central Review* 10 (1993), pp. 3–19
—— (ed.), *(Ré)interprétations: études sur le seizième siècle*, Michigan Romance Studies 15 (Ann Arbor, 1995)
—— 'Question(s) d'équilibre', in N. Peacock and J. J. Supple (eds), *Lire les 'Essais' de Montaigne: perspectives critiques* (Paris, 1998), pp. 107–22
—— 'Are we Reading what Montaigne Wrote?', *French Studies* LVIII/4 (2004), pp. 527–32
—— 'Montaigne and Antiquity: Fancies and Grotesques', in U. Langer (ed.), *The Cambridge Companion to Montaigne* (Cambridge, 2005), pp. 53–73
Onians, R. B., *The Origins of European Thought* (Cambridge, 1951)
Ortony, A. (ed.), *Metaphor and Thought* (Cambridge, 1979)
Parker, P., *Literary Fat Ladies: Rhetoric, Gender, Property* (London, 1987)
Persels, J., 'Cooking with the Pope: The Language of Food and Protest in Calvinist and Catholic Polemic from the 1560s', *Mediaevalia* 22 (1999), pp. 29–53
Phillips, A., 'On Tickling', in *On Kissing, Tickling and Being Bored* (London, 1993), pp. 1–4
Pineaux, J., 'Poésie de cour et poésie de combat: l'amiral Gaspard de Coligny devant les poètes contemporains', *Bulletin de la Société du Protestantisme Français* (jan.–mars 1972), pp. 32–54
Popkin, R., *The History of Scepticism from Erasmus to Spinoza* (Berkeley, 1979)

Pot, O., *L'Inquiétante Etrangeté. Montaigne: la pierre, le cannibale, la mélancolie* (Paris, 1993)

Quint, D., *Montaigne and the Quality of Mercy: Ethical and Political Themes in Montaigne's Essais* (Princeton, 1998)

Racaut, L. and Ryrie, A., 'Introduction: Between Coercion and Persuasion', in L. Racaut and A. Ryrie (eds), *Moderate Voices in the European Reformation* (Aldershot, 2005), pp. 1–12

Regosin, R. L., *The Matter of my Book. Montaigne's 'Essais' as the Book of the Self* (Berkeley and London, 1977)

Richards, I. A., *The Philosophy of Rhetoric* (Oxford, 1936, 1971)

Ricoeur, P., *La Métaphore vive* (Paris, 1975)

Rigolot, F., *Les Métamorphoses de Montaigne* (Paris, 1988)

—— 'Montaigne et la "servitude volontaire": pour une interprétation platonicienne', in I. Zinguer (ed.), *Le Lecteur, l'auteur et l'écrivain: Montaigne 1492–1592–1992* (Paris, 1993)

—— *L'Erreur de la Renaissance: perspectives littéraires* (Paris, 2002)

Rorty, R., *Contingency, Irony and Solidarity* (Cambridge, 1989)

Rose, J., *Sexuality in the Field of Vision* (London, 1986)

—— *The Last Resistance* (London, 2007)

Rubin, M., *Corpus Christi: The Eucharist in Late Medieval Culture* (Cambridge, 1991)

Safouan, M., *Lacaniana: les séminaires de Jacques Lacan, 1953–63* (Paris, 2001)

Samaras, Z. (ed.), *Montaigne: espace, voyage, écriture* (Paris, 1995)

Sayce, R., *The Essays of Montaigne: A Critical Exploration* (London, 1972)

Scarry, E., *The Body in Pain: The Making and the Unmaking of the World* (Oxford, 1985)

Schäfer, P., *Judeophobia: Attitudes towards the Jews in the Ancient World* (Cambridge, Mass., 1997)

Schiesari, J., *The Gendering of Melancholia: Feminism, Psychoanalysis and the Symbolics of Loss in Renaissance Literature* (Ithaca, 1992)

Schmitt, C. B., *Cicero Scepticus: A Study of the Influence of the Academica in the Renaissance* (The Hague, 1972)

Schmitt, C. B. and Skinner Q. (eds), *The Cambridge History of Renaissance Philosophy* (Cambridge, 1988)

Schneewind, J. B., 'Montaigne on Moral Philosophy and the Good Life', in U. Langer, (ed.), *The Cambridge Companion to Montaigne* (Cambridge, 2005), pp. 207–28

Schneikert, E., *Montaigne dans le labyrinthe: de l'imaginaire du Journal de voyage à l'écriture des Essais* (Paris, 2006)

Scholar, R., *Montaigne and the Art of Free-thinking* (Oxford, 2010)

Screech, M., *Montaigne and Melancholy: The Wisdom of the Essays* (London, 1983)

Sellevold, K., *'J'ayme ces mots –': expressions linguistiques de doute chez Montaigne* (Paris, 2004)

Sheffield, F. C., *Plato's Symposium: The Ethics of Desire* (Oxford, 2006)

Silverman, L., *Tortured Subjects: Pain, Truth and the Body in Early Modern France* (Chicago and London, 2001)

Siraisi, N. G., *Medieval and Early Renaissance Medicine: An Introduction to Knowledge and Practice* (Chicago, 1990)

Skinner, Q., *The Foundations of Modern Political Thought: The Reformation* (Cambridge, 1978)

Smith, M., *Montaigne and Religious Freedom: The Dawn of Pluralism* (Geneva, 1991)

Starobinski, J., *Montaigne en mouvement* (Paris, 1982)

Still, J., *Derrida and Hospitality: Theory and Practice* (Edinburgh, 2010)

Todorov, T., 'L'Etre et l'autre: Montaigne', *Montaigne: Essays in Reading*, Special Edition, *Yale French Studies* 64 (1983) pp. 113–44

Tournon, A., *Montaigne: la glose et l'essai* (Lyon, 1983)

—— *Montaigne en toutes lettres* (Paris, 1989)

—— 'Un langage coupé', in R. La Charité (ed.), *Writing the Renaissance: Essays on Sixteenth Century Literature in Honor of Floyd Gray* (Lexington, Ky., 1992), pp. 219–31

—— 'Syntaxe et scansion: l'énergie du "langage coupé" et la censure éditoriale des *Essais*', in J. O'Brien, M. Quainton and J. Supple (eds), *Montaigne et la rhétorique* (Paris, 1995), pp. 117–33

—— 'La Segmentation du texte: usages et singularités', in C. Blum and A. Tournon (eds), *Éditer les Essais de Montaigne* (Paris, 1997), pp. 173–83

—— 'L'Inquiétante Segmentation des *Essais*', *Le Discours Psychanalytique* 18 (1997), pp. 277–306

—— '"Ny de la ponctuation": sur quelques avatars de la segmentation autographe des *Essais*', *Nouvelle Revue du seizième siècle* 17/1 (1999), pp. 147–59

Turchetti, M., 'Concord and Political Tolerance in Sixteenth- and Seventeenth-Century France', *The Sixteenth Century Journal* 22/1 (1991), pp. 15–25

Viano, C., 'Lo Scetticismo antico et la medicina', in G. Giannantoni (ed.), *Lo Scetticismo antico* (Naples, 1981), pp. 563–658

Vickers, B., *In Defence of Rhetoric* (Oxford, 1988)

Vigarello, G., 'The Upward Training of the Body', in M. Feher (ed.), *Fragments for a History of the Human Body*, vol. 2 (New York, 1989), pp. 148–99

Vlastos, G., 'The Individual as an Object of Love', in G. Vlastos (ed.), *Platonic Studies* (Princeton, 1981), pp. 1–34

Wanegffelen, T., *Ni Rome ni Genève: des fidèles entre deux chaires en France au XVIe siècle* (Paris, 1997)

Weiss, N., 'Un témoin de la Saint-Barthélemy', *Bulletin de la Société de l'Histoire du Protestantisme Français* 50 (1901), pp. 445–8

White, H. V., *Tropics of Discourse: Essays in Cultural Criticism* (Baltimore and London, 1985)

Žižek, S., *Enjoy Your Symptom! Jacques Lacan in Hollywood and Out* (London, 1992)

—— *The Metastases of Enjoyment* (London, 1994)

—— *The Plague of Fantasies* (London, 1997)

—— *The Puppet and the Dwarf* (Cambridge, Mass., 2003)

—— *How to Read Lacan* (London, 2006)

INDEX

Already Published